Amazon Town

....

A Study of Human Life in the Tropics

Anniversary Edition

By Charles Wagley

With a new foreword by Conrad Phillip Kottak
Edited, with a new preface and chapter by
Richard Pace

New York   Oxford
OXFORD UNIVERSITY PRESS

Oxford University Press is a department of the University of Oxford.
It furthers the University's objective of excellence in research, scholarship,
and education by publishing worldwide.

Oxford   New York
Auckland   Cape Town   Dar es Salaam   Hong Kong   Karachi
Kuala Lumpur   Madrid   Melbourne   Mexico City   Nairobi
New Delhi   Shanghai   Taipei   Toronto

With offices in
Argentina   Austria   Brazil   Chile   Czech Republic   France   Greece
Guatemala   Hungary   Italy   Japan   Poland   Portugal   Singapore
South Korea   Switzerland   Thailand   Turkey   Ukraine   Vietnam

For titles covered by Section 112 of the US Higher Education
Opportunity Act, please visit www.oup.com/us/he for the
latest information about pricing and alternate formats.

Published in the United States of America by
Oxford University Press
198 Madison Avenue, New York, NY 10016
http://www.oup.com

Library of Congress Cataloging-in-Publication Data
Wagley, Charles, 1913–
Amazon town: a study of human life in the tropics / by Charles Wagley; with a new foreword by
Conrad Kottak; edited, with a new preface and chapter by Richard Pace.—Annivesary edition.
    pages cm
Includes bibliographical references and index.
ISBN 978-0-19-933525-1
1. Amazonas (Brazil)—Social life and customs. 2. Amazonas (Brazil)—Social conditions.
3. Human ecology—Brazil—Amazonas. I. Title.
F2546.W16 2013
981'.13—dc23
                              2013017152

Printing number: 9 8 7 6 5 4 3 2 1

Printed in the United States of America
on acid-free paper

To Cecilia

CONTENTS

Foreword to Amazon Town, Anniversary Edition
  by Conrad Phillip Kottak ix
Preface to the 2013 Anniversary Edition by Richard Pace xv
Preface to the 1976 Edition xxi
Preface xxvii

CHAPTER ONE   The Problem of Humanity in the Tropics   1

CHAPTER TWO   An Amazon Community   15

CHAPTER THREE   Making a Living in the Tropics   66

CHAPTER FOUR   Social Relations in an Amazon Community   106

CHAPTER FIVE   Family Affairs in an Amazon Community   148

CHAPTER SIX   People Also Play   187

CHAPTER SEVEN   From Magic to Science   217

CHAPTER EIGHT   A Community in an Underdeveloped Area:
The Struggle for Liberation and Sustainable
Development   256

APPENDIX ONE   Pseudonyms and Names of People in Gurupá
Identified through Wagley's Photographs and
Fieldnotes   294

APPENDIX TWO   Gurupá Researchers and Principal Works   295

References   297
Index   306

FOREWORD TO AMAZON TOWN, ANNIVERSARY EDITION

By Conrad Phillip Kottak

I write this during the centennial year of Charles Wagley's birth (in 1913) and the 60th anniversary of the first publication of *Amazon Town* (1953). Oxford University Press, which published the last edition of *Amazon Town* in 1976, would not be offering this anniversary edition were the book not an enduring and still relevant classic. One of the reviewers of the proposal for this anniversary edition praises Wagley's "masterful, ethnographic treatment of his subject matter" and "his engrossing prose." Another rightly calls it a classic ethnography. As much today as in the 1950s, this highly engaging book should be read by anyone with a serious interest in the Amazon. Richard Pace has performed an important service by updating this edition based on his decades of research in Itá/Gurupá since the 1980s. When Wagley wrote *Amazon Town*, he gave it the pseudonym "Itá." Its actual name is Gurupá, which we use in this edition, based, among other things, on the wishes of local people to have their history documented, recognized, and remembered.

As published originally in 1953, *Amazon Town* reflected the context of postwar and postcolonial changes then influencing anthropology and the larger world. Like many other anthropologists at that time, Wagley was grappling with the question of how anthropology might change to fit such a world. Nations and cultures were being reconstructed after a devastating war, and a series of former colonies were moving rapidly toward independence. American anthropologists were becoming more vocal about the potential usefulness of their discipline. *Amazon Town* illustrates this trend, although the community described by Wagley had escaped wartime devastation. Indeed, the War years were rather kind to the Brazilian Amazon, which benefited from a public health and rural sanitation program known as SESP (*Serviço Especial de Saúde Pública*), and from a mini rubber boom that developed as Asian rubber plantations fell into Japanese hands.

Wagley became a leader in SESP, created in 1942 through an agreement between Brazil and the United States, originally as a wartime program. SESP extended its large-scale public health initiative throughout the Amazon region so that by 1949 health posts had been established in thirty Amazon towns. The program also brought water-supply systems to several small communities and built more than 8,000 sanitary privies throughout the Valley. Wagley's de facto career as an applied anthropologist can be traced to his three-and-a-half-year involvement with SESP during World War II.

Wagley believed that knowledge of local culture, of the sort he provided in *Amazon Town*, would be helpful to planners and change agents. Throughout the book he spends considerable time addressing how anthropological knowledge and understanding can help to plan and guide programs of development and technical assistance, in areas including public health, agricultural reform, educational campaigns, and other efforts aimed at improving economic and social conditions. We learn from Richard Pace's inspiring new preface and concluding chapter that many of Wagley's goals were realized. His findings and policy suggestions based on knowledge of local and regional culture have informed sustainable development projects in Gurupá and surrounding municipalities. As Pace writes in the Introductory Notes to Chapter 1, such development efforts have "fulfilled Wagley's desire to help the poor and marginal through anthropological expertise."

Amazon Town also should be seen in the context of a shift in the anthropological focus from tribes toward complex societies, including nation states such as Brazil. Wagley, whose Brazilian research had begun in 1939 with a study of the Tapirapé, a tribal population in interior central Brazil, gradually turned to communities more directly affected by the Brazilian nation. He turned his attention first to acculturating Tenetehara Indians, then to towns in the Amazon basin, next to a series of communities in Bahia state, and finally to Brazilian national culture in his 1963 book *Introduction to Brazil*.

Although Wagley viewed the Amazon town he first visited, and eventually studied, in the 1940s as traditional and backward, he never lost sight of its participation in Brazilian history and national culture. In Chapter 2, he states that "Itá serves admirably as a 'case history'" of the Brazilian Amazon. Within its long history (dating back to the 1600s), "most of the trends of regional history have been reflected." Wagley recognized how Brazilian and world history had affected Gurupá, which had participated in two rubber booms—the major boom whose heyday was between 1880 and 1910 and the World War II mini boom. Wagley traced continuing relations of dependence and patron–client relationships, which he viewed as debilitating, in Gurupá to its history of colonialism, slavery, and enduring patterns of inequality and debt peonage.

Although, interestingly, the word "theory" appears nowhere in *Amazon Town*, Wagley's work can be seen as part of a major paradigm shift in anthropology involving the expansion of the anthropological lens beyond tribal societies to more modern ones. Wagley and his colleagues at Columbia University, along with Robert Redfield and his associates at the University of Chicago, were at the vanguard of this shift. Anthropologists had returned from World War II with a new appreciation of how world events affected the supposedly isolated groups anthropologists traditionally studied—and also realized that peasant cultures in Europe, Asia, and Latin America merited anthropological attention. Wagley's Columbia colleague Julian Steward and Steward's graduate students (including Sidney Mintz and Eric Wolf) planned and conducted coordinated field work in Puerto Rico, demonstrating how anthropology might be done in complex societies by studying a series of communities in different regions and with different economies, histories, and ecological adaptations. Wagley, collaborating with Brazilian colleagues, and bringing in his own Columbia graduate students (Marvin Harris, William Hutchinson, and Ben Zimmerman), would do something similar in Bahia concurrently with Steward's team project in Puerto Rico. Wagley at Columbia, like Redfield at Chicago, also became a leader in the movement for foreign area studies that helped create enduring area studies centers at many universities. Wagley would eventually direct the Institute of Latin American Studies at Columbia.

In Chapter 2 of *Amazon Town* Wagley faults the "impersonal" studies by economists and sociologists that "seem lifeless, to say the least.

They tell us little or nothing of life situations, of the working of widespread patterns and institutions as they are lived by people." Anthropology, he thought, had something unique to offer—ethnography, understanding of local culture, and attention to real people perceived and appreciated as individuals. Anthropologists needed to develop distinctive ways of studying nation-states, where prior research had been dominated by sociologists, political scientists, economists, and historians. One such research strategy was the community study. Anthropologists could extend the personal, face-to-face ethnographic methods they had developed for small groups in tribal societies to towns and neighborhoods in modern nations. It's clear from the justification he offers for studying his "Amazon town" that Wagley was aware of the limitations of the community study approach. Gurupá certainly could not be a sample of all communities and all regions of Brazil. It was not a city, and it lacked the economic institutions, histories, demographics, and particular cultural patterns of other areas of Brazil. But it did partake in Brazilian national patterns, as it does (as we see from Pace's work) even more today.

As *Amazon Town* makes clear, Gurupá developed as part of Brazilian history. Its population includes descendants, often mixed, of the three main groups important in the colonial settlement of Brazil— Indigenous (Native American) Brazilians, Portuguese, and Africans. Although it was a backwater town on the Amazon River, everyone in Gurupá spoke the national language. Its local government followed a structure that exists throughout Brazil. Its in-again, out-again political factions were, and still are, familiar to residents of any rural Brazilian community, as was its pattern of race relations. Local people liked to depend on government to solve problems, rather than getting together and doing it on their own. (As Pace's new chapter makes clear, this shift from passivity to agency by ordinary Brazilians is one of the more striking aspects of change in the community.) Class differences familiar to any Brazilian marked Gurupá. Like Brazilians in general at that time, most people in Gurupá (96 percent) were Roman Catholics. Charles Wagley's mentors at Columbia University included Ruth Benedict and Ralph Linton, both of whom viewed culture as a patterned entity meriting detailed study. Wagley liked to describe himself as a "social" rather than a "cultural" anthropologist, and he shared a view of cultures and societies as patterned and integrated not only with Benedict and Franz Boas, but also with such contemporaneous British social anthropologists as A.R. Radcliffe-Brown. Like Boas, another of his teachers, Wagley regarded successful social change as based on a process of integration of new traits into existing structures. New methods and ideas, he states in Chapter 7, must be integrated into the matrix of the preexisting culture. Innovations may be introduced from outside, but the change is never complete without integration into the conceptual scheme of the people concerned.

Let me focus now on this new edition. The study of change, and its integration into local and regional culture, also has guided the ongoing work of Richard Pace and his students and associates in Gurupá since the mid-1980s. (Pace provides us with a useful list of the many students and scholars, Brazilian, French, and American, who have worked in Gurupá after Wagley.) We are extremely fortunate to have in this anniversary edition Pace's updates (a new preface and concluding chapter, along with footnotes) based on his decades of fieldwork there. Pace's focus has been not only on media, the subject of his recent book *Amazon Town TV* (Pace and Hinote 2013), but also on the total transformation of the town and region. His new concluding chapter here is a masterful synopsis and analysis of the many currents of change, and the reader will be eager to consult Pace's other work on Gurupá, especially *Amazon Town TV*.

One of Pace's contributions here, seemingly minor perhaps, but really important in bringing *Amazon Town* up to date, has been to adjust word usage in the original work to fit contemporary parlance. Wagley's use of "man" and "men" to refer, respectively, to humankind and people is jarring to hear or read today. Removal of this language makes Wagley's case for *Amazon Town* even more persuasive.

Thanks to Pace's hard work, *Amazon Town* is now as up to date as any "classic" can be. The rich new footnotes document specific changes in the parts of the book where particular topics are discussed. The new concluding chapter moves Gurupá through its various ups and downs into the anniversary year of 2013. Fortunately, the community's future may be more promising now than when Wagley wrote the original. With the support of socially conscious priests, activists, and change agents, local people have organized to promote their own interests, including property rights. As of this writing, at least, they have been remarkably successful in achieving their goals, but challenges lie ahead.

Most immediate are the environmental, economic, demographic, and social consequences of the huge Belo Monte dam now under construction in the region. As Pace notes, those likely effects (which he discusses in the concluding chapter) will inevitably test the strength of Gurupá's rural union, political parties, and Church and the continuity of the successes obtained so far. That is a story—hopefully one with a happy ending—that can only be told in a future work.

Pace's careful editing of *Amazon Town,* combined with his new preface, notes, and concluding chapter, have preserved an ethnographic classic while enlarging it to form a very current, compelling, and inspiring study of changing local and regional culture. There are various ways to read this book. One might, for example, first read Pace's new preface and Wagley's original chapters, to get a sense of what the revision is attempting and how things were "then"—leaving the new chapter and footnotes for the end. Or one might follow, as I did, the page order, reading the footnotes as they appear. The preface, new chapter, and notes can almost be seen as an original minibook within a larger work. However one decides to read this book, it's clear writing—and its insightful discussions of domination, resistance, development, and globalization—make *Amazon Town: Anniversary Edition* a useful and attractive case study, not only for people interested in the Amazon or Brazil, but also for students in, and faculty teaching, an array of courses in cultural anthropology and area studies.

On now to the riches of a classic made contemporary.

PREFACE TO THE 2013
ANNIVERSARY EDITION

··

By Richard Pace

Ever since its first publication in 1953, Charles Wagley's *Amazon Town* has been the stalwart of ethnographic classics for traditional (peasant) cultures in the Brazilian Amazon. Clearly written and rich in detail, his depiction of rubber tappers and small-scale subsistence farmers in the rain forest has continued to inform Amazon enthusiasts and budding anthropologists for generations. Along with its companion book, *Santos e Visagens* (Saints and Spirits—1955), researched contemporaneously by Wagley's student and colleague Eduardo Galvão, the work has served as a baseline for scores of successive studies throughout the region. The Portuguese version of the book, *Uma Comunidade Amazônica* (1988), has become an important cultural document for the entire region and is commonly required reading in University courses. Even in Itá—the pseudonym Wagley used for the community of Gurupá—the book is read proudly as a true and faithful description of the lives of grandparents and great-grandparents. With this new Anniversary Edition of *Amazon Town*, marking 60 years since the book's publication as well as commemorating Wagley's centennial birthdate, we hope to ensure that future generations will have the chance to appreciate this wonderfully humanistic description of a way of life in a still little-studied part of the world.

The decision to reissue *Amazon Town*, however, has required some difficult choices. For all of its positive qualities, the book is very much a product of its time. Some of the key ecological, economic, and even political assumptions about Amazonia available to Wagley at the time of his research are now considered antiquated. To remedy this, for most of the Anniversary Edition of *Amazon Town* (e.g., Chapters 2 through 7) the discrepancies between past and present factual knowledge are simply footnoted as they occur in the text. For Chapter 1 (originally titled "The Problem of 'Man' in the Tropics") however, the discrepancies are great enough to require substantial editing, including introductory notes, explicatory inserts, and selective abridgement. Chapter 8 ("A Community in an 'Under-Developed' Area") is even more problematic in terms of its fit with current knowledge. To maintain relevancy for contemporary Amazonian studies, the chapter is replaced by a new chapter on recent developments in the region that comes from my 30 years of research in Gurupá. The new chapter, "A Community in an Underdeveloped Area: The Struggle for Liberation and Sustainable Development," updates the political, economic, and environmental conflicts in the region and community since 1948. It also documents the innovative solutions to problems of underdevelopment and poverty coming from the local population, supported by the Catholic Church and the NGO FASE-Gurupá. In this chapter many of the fundamental questions Wagley raised in his original Chapter 8 are addressed.

For literary purists and staunch admirers of the original work, the idea of making these changes might trigger alarm. The options, however, are clear. Do not make any alterations to the text, do not reissue the book, and let the classic inevitably fade into obscurity and be lost to future generations (each year it is harder to find the book, with some copies already placed into the rare collections at libraries). Or conversely, as we have chosen to do, make the needed updates while leaving the majority of the book in its original form (85 percent to be exact), reissue the book, and make the classic assessible once again.

For the updated sections there is no claim that the prose is comparable to that of the original. Wagley's style is uniquely his, and I have no pretentions to try and imitate it. Rather, my contribution to the Anniversary Edition lies in the knowledge gained during the previously mentioned 30 years of ethnographic study dedicated to the community (1983–2013), which includes 14 different trips for a total of nearly three years in residence. During this time I have interacted with and befriended many of Wagley's original consultants, as well as their children and grandchildren. I wrote my dissertation on the community while at the University of Florida, directed by Wagley as his last graduate student. At my dissertation defense in 1987, he announced my successful passing while issuing the challenge, "Here's to the next Amazon Town" (an incentive he also penned as he autographed a copy of the book as a gift to me). I have heeded the challenge, writing *The Struggle for Amazon Town: Gurupá Revisited* (Pace 1998) and *Amazon Town TV: An Audience Ethnography of Gurupá, Brazil* (Pace and Hinote 2013) along with various articles on the community (see Pace 1990, 1992, 1993, 1995, 1997, 2004, 2006, 2009). None of these publications, however, match Wagley's work in style or literary detail. The driving motivation behind the reissue of the book is a sincere desire to keep this masterpiece in print, modifying only what is outmoded, so that it can continue to inform and fascinate audiences interested in Amazonia and anthropology.

In 2010 the University of Florida Digital Collections began posting online many of Wagley's photographs taken among the Tapirapé, Tenetehara, and in Gurupá (http://ufdc.ufl.edu/dlosawagley). The Gurupá images, combined with a set of color slides Wagley had given me and other Gurupá photographs found in Isabel Wagley Kottak's and Conrad Phillip Kottak's home (Wagley's daughter and son-in-law), provide an excellent opportunity to visually enhance *Amazon Town*. Twenty-one of his photographs appear in this edition—four of which can be found in the University of Florida Digital Collections and the rest never published. Each image has been shown in Gurupá, and with some effort we have been able to identify many of people Wagley mentions in his work (despite the use of pseudonyms). We also were able to retake many of the 1948 town images in 2010–13, providing a before-and-after perspective (three pairs of these images are included in this edition). Ethical concerns over the loss of anonymity of individuals we identify have been addressed by obtaining oral consent from relatives (if they still resided in the town) to use the images. All descendants we found were pleased and proud to have their parents, grandparents, uncles, great-uncles, aunts, and great-aunts included in the book. It seems that the book has become much more than an academic text written decades ago by a foreigner and his Brazilian companions. To the people of the lower Amazon, and particularly to Gurupá, it is an important historical document that is factual and accurate, except for the use of the pseudonyms (see Appendix 1 for the names of people in Wagley's work who we have identified next to the pseudonym used in the book). Also due to the text's historical significance, Chapter 2 has been heavily footnoted to include as much of the recent historical research on the community as possible.

Just as *Amazon Town* was a group project combining the research skills of Charles Wagley and his wife, Cecília Roxo Wagley (see Figure 3.1), and Eduardo Galvão and his wife, Clara Galvão (see Figures 2.5 and 2.6), my continuing research has also relied on the ethnographic skills of my wife Olga Torres Pace and, in recent years, our daughters Cynthia and Ann Pace. In addition, critical to this Anniversary Edition is the work of over 30 researchers who have "followed in the footsteps" of Wagley and Galvão in Gurupá. Darrel Miller, a graduate student of Wagley while at the University of Florida, spent two months in Gurupá in 1974 conducting his master's research, from which he also who wrote an updated chapter in the 1976 edition of *Amazon Town* (see the Preface to the 1976 edition—Miller's chapter, however, is not included in this edition).

From the mid-1970s until the early 1980s, the historical demographer Arlene Kelly (1984)—also a student of Wagley—studied the 17th-through 19th-century historical documents available from the community for her dissertation. Her research has greatly expanded our historical knowledge of Gurupá, as is indicated in many of the footnotes in Chapter 2. Emílio Moran, a prominent student of Wagley, visited Gurupá for a several weeks in the 1970s. Although he did not write directly about his experiences there, the visit provided him with a baseline understanding of traditional riverine culture from which to compare the many changes occurring along the frontier areas of the Transamazon Highway (in a similar manner, Roberto DaMatta visited Gurupá and took away an understanding of the essence of the ribeirinho culture). As the last of the Wagley line, I began ethnographic research in 1983 and have continued until the present (Pace 1987, 1998; Pace and Hinote 2013).

Other researchers have also contributed to a growing body of literature on Gurupá. Paulo H. R. Oliveira (1991) spent a year researching and organizing rural workers as part of his Masters' thesis at the Federal University of São Paulo, Campinas. He later returned to create the NGO FASE-Gurupá, which was active in the creation of sustainable development projects in the community from 1992–2002. Jean-Marie Royer (2003), a French anthropologist, also spent a year in the quilombo (remnant of an African slave refugee) of Maria Ribeira conducting ethnographic research on ethnicity and cultural change for his dissertation at Université Paris III-Sorbonne Nouvelle. Girolamo Treccani (2006), a lawyer from Belém, likewise spent a year studying Gurupá's complex land tenure system from colonial times to the present for his dissertation at the Federal University of Pará-NAEA. Information obtained during his research has been critical in the regularization of land title for small farmers and extractors. Many researchers from the previously mentioned FASE-Gurupá conducted projects on sustainable forestry, agriculture, and fishing techniques in addition to land regularization and titling. Some of this material has been printed in FASE's various publications (bulletins, newsletters, and research reports). Among the researchers are Jean-Pierre Leroy, Carlos Augusto Ramos, Nilza Miranda, Sheyla Leão, Raoni Nascimento, Jorge Pinto, Manoel (Bira) Pantoja, Pedro (Tapuru) Alves, Sérgio Alberto Queiroz, José Pedro Monteiro, Selma Gomes, Renata Teixeira, Adamor Silva, Pâmela Melo, Sandra Costa, Cléo Mota, and Fátima Pinã-Rodrigues.

Pennie Magee and Neila Soares da Silva, both University of Florida graduate students under the direction of Marianne Schmink—a colleague of Wagley's at Florida—spent several months each researching in Gurupá for their Master's degrees. Magee (1986) looked at medicinal plants used in the town, and Soares (2004) examined changes occurring in the quilombo of Jocojó. Mônica Barroso (2006) from the London School of Economics examined the use and impact of shortwave radios on the rural inhabitants of Gurupá. Monte Hendrickson (2006), a graduate student under my direction at Middle Tennessee State University, studied the concept of childhood and the occurrence of child labor in Gurupá. Finally, two graduate students working on advanced degrees in education at the Federal University of Pará, Émina Márcoa Nery dos Santos (2008) and Benedita Alcidema Coelho dos Santos Magalhães (2009), looked at the challenges of Gurupá's rural school system and the success of the innovative *Casa Familiar Rural* school (Rural Family House). For a complete listing of Gurupá's researchers and their principal works, see Appendix 1.

I would like to thank the following reviewers for their suggestions on how to update Wagley's material: Juliet S. Erazo, Florida International University; Emilio F. Moran, Indiana University; Rosana Resende, University of Florida; and Leslie Ellen Straub, Providence College. I also wish to thank Isabel Wagley Kottak and Conrad Phillip Kottak for their support on this project and their kind permission to modify and edit parts of the original text as well as publish the photographs. To the hundreds of *Gurupaenses* (people from Gurupá) and friends of Gurupá that we have come to know and befriend over the years, my deepest gratitude for your assistance, patience, and kindness. The reissue of this book, with its updates, is long awaited by you and we hope you will be pleased. And finally, I wish to acknowledge the tremendous impact Charles Wagley had on me and so many others as a mentor and friend. The Anniversary Edition of *Amazon Town*, reissued 60 years after its first publication, is a true testament to his research skills and cross-cultural insight. His work, supported by the contributions of Eduardo Galvão, Cecília Wagley, and Clara Galvão, has created a truly classic study.

Richard Pace
Gurupá, Pará, Brazil
2013

PREFACE TO THE 1976 EDITION

This is a new edition of a book that appeared first in English in 1953 and was published in Portuguese translation in 1956. But it is in a sense a "new book" because the entire situation of the Brazilian Amazon has changed as I shall indicate in this preface [omitted from this edition is an epilogue written by Charles Wagley in the 1964 edition and a chapter written by Darrel L. Miller, a graduate student who spent two months in Gurupá in 1974]. Brazil has embarked on a gigantic program for the "conquest of the Amazon." This involves the construction of over 13,500 kilometers of roads throughout the Amazon Valley including the East-West Transamazon Highway, the North-South road from Cuiabá to Santarém, and finally the great Perimetral Norte [never completed] that will encircle the Amazon Rain Forest in a broad horseshoe-shaped arc along the borders of the Guianas, Venezuela, Colombia, and Peru. With these roads, the last great world frontier will be open to automobile and truck transportation and will be connected to the main arteries of Brazil. It also must be said that one of the world's most delicate ecological systems, namely, that of the Amazon rain forest, will therefore be threatened. The whole emphasis of life in the Amazon region will be shifted from the great river system to roads. Now the uplands (*terra firme*) of Amazonia will be occupied rather than the river lowlands (várzea). As lands that annually receive silt, the várzea provide the good soils of the Amazon region while the uplands are generally poor. It is through the less fertile *terra firme* that the new highways penetrate.

Brazil has also embarked on a program of colonization of the Amazon region, principally along the new roads. At first, it was planned to bring hundreds of thousands of people to occupy the uninhabited regions opened up by the roads. Now there seems to be some doubt whether this great program is economically feasible, although *agrovilas* (planned villages) and at least one *agropolis* (planned town) and a half-completed *ruropolis* (planned city) already exist along the Transamazonian Highway. There are people not only from Northeastern Brazil, but also from Minas Geraes, Santa Catarina, São Paulo, and from Rio Grande do Sul among the migrants. Not since the migration of the *nordestinos* to the Amazon in the late nineteenth century and the migrations of the *soldados de borracha* (soldiers for rubber) during World War II have so many people arrived. I could not count them, but I have seen them in their new settlements and in old settlements such as Altamira and Itaituba. Not only are there colonists financed by the government, but there are many who came voluntarily at their own expense to find a new life in a new world. Never again will the Amazon be the same; for these Mineiros, Gauchos, Goianos, and even Paulistas are modifying Amazon culture and in turn they are learning from the Amazon people.

Even old river towns, off the highways, such as Gurupá, are feeling the impact of the Brazilian surge to finally "conquer" the Amazon. This can be judged by Darrel L. Miller's [1974] research. I must confess that Gurupá has changed more than I could ever imagine in my lifetime, but not in the way that I had hoped that it would change. It has *movimento*; it has automobiles; it has some roads opening up the backlands of the municipality; it has grown in population; it has more schools; and it has more State and Federal agencies; but it still has a dubious extractive economy. It seems to me that neither the highway system nor the very old river system of transportation will ever be successful until they are connected. The natural river "highways" can transport goods, which then can be transferred to the new highways. If the energy crisis of the end of the twentieth century continues, then it would seem natural to connect the river ports by roads to the main artery of the Transamazon highway.

I have not changed this book except for this new preface and the new chapter written by Darrel L. Miller [omitted in this edition]. I want the description of "traditional" Amazon society and culture to stand as it is. Combined with Eduardo Galvão's [1955] excellent book *Santos e Visagens*, it is a monument to a people at a particular time and place in

Brazilian history and cultural development. Even more, both books are important to an understanding of modern development of the Amazon because they describe the basic culture on which Amazon social and economic development must ultimately depend. A new society is not fabricated out of a vacuum. It must be built on historical antecedents. The new society that Brazil hopes to create in Amazonia will be built from the knowledge the people of that region have accumulated over centuries from aboriginal times to the present. Over these centuries the Indigenous populations and the Luso-Brazilian inhabitants who followed them in time learned to coexist and to exploit the Amazonian environment. They know the soils, the flora and fauna, the rise and fall of the great rivers, the epoch of rains and of relatively dry weather, the dangers of insects and of endemic disease, and many other aspects of their own milieu. And, out of this experience they fashioned their own Amazonian culture with its own social system, cuisine, forms of recreation, and mythology. This is a rich heritage that should never be ignored in the modern conquest of Amazonia.

However, this traditional Amazonian culture and the social and economic system that supported it has also been a barrier to change and to the formation of the new Amazonian society and culture that Brazilians hope to develop. The exploitative economic system that resulted from the extractive system of collecting wild rubber and other products of the forest and the system of debt servitude that tied the rubber collector to the owner of the trading post—the so-called patron–client system or *seringalista-seringueiro* system—which are described in this book, have been definite barriers to development. Under the impact of the modernizing Brazilian economy, both are disappearing in the Amazon valley. But even in the 1970s, these systems have not disappeared entirely; sometimes the old barracão (trading post) of the traditional patron exists side by side with a modern building of the Bank of Brazil. In Gurupá, as we will learn in the last chapter of this book, the recent surge of extraction of hardwoods for export was organized by the extension of credit by large companies to local entrepreneurs who, in turn, extend credit to local extractors in a manner reminiscent of the traditional system of rubber extraction. The traditional system dies slowly, and as yet a more modern commercial and productive system has not taken form.

Furthermore, the new economy of Amazonia trends toward the continuation of extractivism but in a new form. Despite the efforts of the Brazilian government to establish small farmers on the land, huge tracts of land are being granted to large corporations both Brazilian and international. These lands are being devoted to the raising of cattle on enormous ranches on which forest is cleared and pasture grass is planted. Cattle raising requires little labor, so few people are required. Such ranches will not populate the Amazon Valley, but they may increase beef production. Other large land concessions are made for planting rapidly growing trees whose ultimate destiny is paper pulp; again there may be developmental and temporary benefits as these large companies raise some food crops (such as rice and sugarcane) on portions of the land. But the long-term aim is to produce export products, not to occupy the land. In addition, there is a fervor of exploration and development of mining for bauxite, iron ore (one of the largest deposits of iron ore in Brazil, if not of the world, has been discovered at the Serra de Carajás), and other minerals. Again, Brazil runs the danger of developing an essentially extractive economy in Amazonia—a system of exploitation of the gigantic area that will benefit little, or not at all, the people of the region. It will produce raw materials for export to the bulging industrial system of South Brazil or the mass of consumers of Japan, the United States, and Europe.

In this preface I do not want to sound overly pessimistic about the future of the Amazon Valley. Yet, at this time I must admit I am discouraged if not somewhat frightened. Brazil seems to be attempting to change Amazonia more with patriotic spirit than with true scientific planning. Long ago (and in the first edition of this book), I asked for a "tropical science" and a "tropical technology" distinct from that developed for the temperate zones of the world, which has always been copied in the tropical Amazon. It is true that the government of Brazil has restored some Amazonian scientific institutes such as the Museu Paraense Emilio Goeldi, the Institute Evandro Chagas (Belém); and it has supported strongly the National Institute of Amazonian Research in Manaus. The government has supported other educational and research institutions, including the relatively new Federal University of Pará in Belém, which now has a Center for Amazonian Advanced Studies [NAEA]. Even a new scientific center called the Cidade Von Humbolt is planned for the state of Mato Grosso. But these are as yet, to speak frankly, weak scientific institutions compared to those in South Brazil. There is a group of devoted scientists, but they are small in number and weakly supported. If Brazil sincerely wishes to develop Amazonia, then it must invest in scientific manpower and funds equal to those invested in the highways. In fact, I can only quote the eloquent and sincere words of Paulo Almeida Machado, who spent some years as director of the National Institute of Amazonian Research and in doing so came to understand Amazonia and to have a sincere affection for that region of his country. In 1974 he wrote

> The history of the Brazilian Amazon contains a serious warning and an eloquent example of confusing economic prosperity with development. It does not matter how great the volume of circulation of money is, development will take place only when one knows the environment and the natural resources better and when man changes his behavior accordingly. Only education and research can guarantee the perpetuity of the new surge of progress that exists in the Brazilian Amazon. If man in the Amazon can develop and establish a partnership with the environment, the Amazon will take off definitely from its underdeveloped stage (In *Man in the Amazon*. Charles Wagley, ed. Gainesville: University of Florida Press, p. 330).

In this short paragraph, Paulo Almeida Machado caught the spirit and perhaps the essence of the thought in this book, which I wrote many years ago. It is rather sad to say that this message is more up to date today than it was 20 years ago. For this new edition, I have a few people to thank and acknowledge. I want to thank first Darrel L. Miller (and his wife), who went to Gurupá in 1974 and documented changes that had taken place in my little Amazon hometown. My wife, Cecilia Roxo Wagley, and I returned for a two-day visit in 1961 and I wrote a brief note for the second edition of this book [omitted from this edition]. I also want to thank the many students both in the United States and in Brazil who after reading this book in its early editions wrote letters of appreciation and warmth about the people described and the town. In fact, a group of secondary students from the American School in Recife (Brazil) made an excursion to Amazonia; they discovered the real name of the town and they spent a whole day trying to find personages who are described and interviewing them. They wrote a series of reports, which was mimeographed in two volumes that I shall always cherish. Furthermore, I want to thank Mercio Gomes, who has translated this preface, and Darrel L. Miller's contribution for a new Brazilian edition of the book. It should be clear that my book on Gurupá (Amazonas) is not a study in the vein of modern social science, although it uses the framework of social anthropology. As I look back, I know now that I am essentially a humanist; and I realize that this was a humanistic book with a humanistic message.

Charles Wagley
Gainesville, Florida
1975

PREFACE

W hen I went to central Brazil in 1939, it was but one of several possible areas of the world that might have been selected for research among traditional peoples. For almost eighteen months I lived and studied among the Tapirapé, an isolated tribe who still followed, in the main, their aboriginal way of life. They provided an excellent field of research for a social anthropologist, but living among them I learned little of modern Brazil. When I left Brazil in 1940, I knew that I would return. My casual acquaintance with the country during my passage from Rio de Janeiro through São Paulo and Goiás to and from the Tapirapé village convinced me that Brazil was one of the world's most exciting laboratories for research in social anthropology. Since that time I have devoted myself in one way or another to the study of modern Brazil.

In 1941 I returned to do research among the Tenetehara, a tribe that was in close contact with rural Brazilians and that was being gradually incorporated into the nation. Then, in 1942, world events brought me directly into contact with the problems of modern Brazil. That year, as part of their common war effort, the Brazilian and United States governments established the cooperative public health program that came to be known as SESP (Serviço Especial de Saúde Pública). SESP was first conceived as a wartime measure, and one of its principal programs was to provide medical protection to the producers of strategic raw materials—the rubber gatherers in the Amazon Valley, the migrants from the drought-stricken northeast who were moving into the Amazon to collect rubber, and the mica and quartz miners in the mountains of central Brazil. Because so many of these people lived in the backlands, a social anthropologist with experience and knowledge of these Brazilian hinterlands could be useful to the program. During the three-and-a-half years that I was a member of the United States field party of the Institute of Inter-American Affairs connected with SESP, I served in several capacities: as a member of the SESP field staff in the Amazon Valley, as director of its migration program giving medical protection to the thousands of people who left their homes in the arid northeast to work in Amazonas, as assistant superintendent of the SESP, and finally as director of its Educational Division. During these years I learned about Brazil both as an anthropologist and as a practical administrator. My anthropological perspective was of tremendous help in the work of administration and planning, and in return my growing familiarity with practical problems helped to sharpen the focus of my scientific interest in Brazil. In traveling over a large part of the Brazilian hinterland, and by living with rural Brazilians, I became aware of rural problems as viewed both by the people themselves and by the planners and executives from the city.

I first visited the small Amazon town of Gurupá in 1942, on a survey trip preliminary to the planning of SESP's Amazon Valley health service. It was on this slow trip by launch down the Amazon River, with my young Brazilian assistant and companion Cleo Braga, that I first became aware of the richness of Amazon culture and of the need for a study of human life in the Amazon. As we visited the towns and trading posts of the lower Amazon River and as we talked with people of all classes, I came to realize that the exotic grandeur of the tropical scene had drawn attention away from the activities of humans in the Amazon Valley. The classical accounts of H. W. Bates, of Alfred R. Wallace, of Lieutenant William Herndon, of Louis Agassiz, and others who describe the great valley have devoted astonishingly little attention to humans and to human affairs. The little town of Gurupá seemed to be an excellent locality for such studies.

After 1943, when a health post of SESP was established in Gurupá, I was able to follow events in the town from a distance by reading the physicians' reports and to collect considerable data on the community. In 1945 I visited Gurupá again. On that occasion I was accompanied by Edward Cattete Pinheiro, a specialist in health education and a native of the region, and by Dalcídio Jurandir, a well-known Brazilian novelist who was writing the text for educational materials to be used in the Amazon Valley by SESP. In his earlier years, Dalcídio had lived in Gurupá and served as the secretary to the town's mayor. His intimate knowledge of the life of the town and the large circle of friends into which he introduced me made it possible to learn more about Gurupá[1] in a month than I might have learned in more than twice that time without his help. Both Cattete Pinheiro and Dalcídio Jurandir taught me much about the Amazon out of the fabric of their own lives.

This book is mainly based, however, on data collected from June to September, 1948, during the United Nations Educational, Scientific, and Cultural Organization Amazon survey for the International Hylean Amazon Institute. During these months of research and residence in Gurupá, I had the assistance and the collaboration of Eduardo and Clara Galvão and of my wife, Cecilia Roxo Wagley, who had also accompanied me to Gurupá in 1942. Our research group rented a house in Gurupá where we lived and worked. We took our meals in the home of a local merchant. We visited with people in their homes and they returned our visits. We attended parties and dances, gossiped in the streets and in the stores, accompanied friends to their gardens, and traveled by canoe to rural festivals and to the trading posts where rubber collectors brought their products. We participated as much in Gurupá life as it is possible for outsiders to do. There was no linguistic barrier, for three of our research group were Brazilians and I have an adequate command of Portuguese. Each of us had long interviews each day with a number of people from all walks of life, and we wrote down copious daily notes. Case studies of 113 families, which covered details of their diet, expenditures, income, personal possessions, and much other specific economic and social information, were carried out in the community by our research group with the help of two local assistants. In addition, the SESP also made available the results of a household survey in Gurupá that was concerned mainly with diet. In 1950 Iris Myers, who is trained both in anthropology and in psychology, spent several weeks in Gurupá at my suggestion. The results of her psychological tests are unfortunately not available at this time, but her letters and field notes provided me with additional data and many insights

---

[1]Dalcídio Jurandir wrote a series of novels based on his experiences in the region. The last of the series, *Ribanceira*, was based on people in Gurupá (Neto 2013).

into Gurupá society. All of the sources mentioned previously have been at my disposal during the preparation of this book.

The illustrations for the book were drawn by the well-known Brazilian artist João José Rescála. For his "Tour of Brazil," a travel prize awarded annually to a Brazilian artist, he traveled through the Amazon Valley. He saw and visited people similar to those described in this book, and his drawings are based both on his memory and on innumerable sketches made during his travels in the Amazon. [In this Anniversary Edition Rescála's illustrations are replaced by original photographs taken by Charles Wagley.]

I wish to express my great indebtedness to all those mentioned previously. In varying degrees, all of them have participated in the research that led to this book. I particularly want to thank, however, my research companions on the UNESCO mission in 1948, for they have allowed me the use of the wealth of information in their field notebooks. And, above all, I wish to thank our many friends in Gurupá whose hospitality and cooperation, and whose patience with the anthropologist's constant questions about every aspect of their life, made this study possible. Unfortunately, they must remain unnamed; it is the responsibility of the anthropologist to protect, as far as possible, the people who open up their personal lives to him and give information about others. In this book many of our Gurupá friends appear, but their names have all been changed. For the same reason the town itself has been given a fictitious name.

I wish to acknowledge the financial support of UNESCO and of the Council for Research in the Social Sciences of Columbia University for our studies in the Brazilian Amazon. UNESCO has granted permission to make use of the information collected during the Hylean Amazon survey, but the opinions expressed in the book are entirely my own and do not reflect UNESCO policy. Some of the data presented have been published elsewhere in different form. A chapter on "Race Relations in an Amazon Community" appeared in Race and Class in Rural Brazil (UNESCO, Paris, 1952), and a lecture given at the Brazilian Institute at Vanderbilt University; which summarizes some aspects of Gurupá culture, was published under the title "The Brazilian Amazon; the Case for an Under-Developed Area," in Four Papers Presented to the Brazilian Institute (Vanderbilt University Press, Nashville, 1950). The data on Gurupá religion have been elaborated by Eduardo Galvão in his doctoral dissertation *The Religious Life of an Amazon Community*

(Columbia University Library, microfilm, 1952); Chapters 6 and 7 of this book owe much to his study of this aspect of Gurupá culture. Finally, I am grateful to Alfred Metraux, of UNESCO, who has done much to make possible my continued study of Brazil. I wish to thank Carl Withers, Gene Weltfish, and Cecil Scott of The Macmillan Company, all of whom read the manuscript before its final revision and who offered numerous suggestions for correction and improvement.

Charles Wagley
New York, 1953

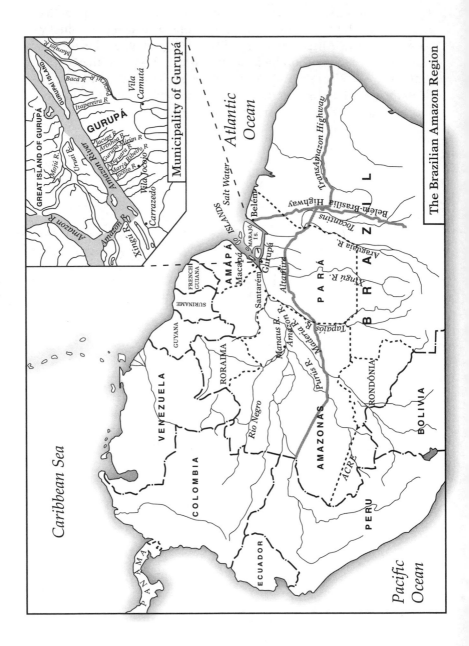

Municipality of Gurupá

The Brazilian Amazon Region

CHAPTER 1

....

The Problem of Humanity in the Tropics

Introductory Notes
by Richard Pace

The Lower Amazon Region of Brazil (see Map), home to the town and municipality of Gurupá, which are the focus of this book, is today a very different place from what Charles Wagley came to know in the 1940s. Absent then were the thousands of kilometers of highways linking scores of cities with hundreds of thousands of inhabitants, huge cattle ranches carved out of the rain forest, massive mining and hydroelectric dam projects, and widespread conflict over land accompanied by much violence and bloodshed. Also absent were vast expanses of legally protected areas to ensure biodiversity preservation and innovative projects for sustainable development to improve rural livelihoods while maintaining the rain forest.

Wagley kept track of many of these occurrences up until his death in 1991 (see the 1976 Preface; also see Wagley 1974). Yet, these events did not inform his work presented here. Rather, what he observed in the Lower Amazon during the 1940s was a seemingly untouched[1] and

---

[1]Archaeological research from the 1990s forward suggests the Amazon region was extensively populated in pre-contact times and much of it was transformed by agricultural pursuits (Heckenberger et al. 2003, 1999). The "pristine" appearance of the forest is the result of massive depopulation of Indigenous peoples after contact with Europeans, leaving much of the region unused by humans for 400 years in some cases (Dobyns 1993).

1

unending mosaic of rain forests, savannas, swamps, and waterways, all sparsely populated. Among the ribeirinho populations[2] he so aptly describes in the following pages, he found a generalized misery brought on by centuries of endemic diseases, high infant mortality, substandard nutrition, little to no access to Western medicine, illiteracy, stagnant economic conditions, and a rigid patron-client system keeping lowly workers in perpetual debt. The Amazon of the 1940s from this perspective was clearly a "backward and underdeveloped" area in desperate need of improvement. Wagley took it to heart to try and use his anthropological insight to find solutions to these problems.

In this chapter, Wagley sets out to explain "The Problem of Man in the Tropics" (his original chapter title) by detailing the region's deficiencies. He discusses some of the theories of poverty and underdevelopment in common use during the first half of the 20th century and how they were applied to the Amazon. He carefully discredits the environmental determinist rationales, which in one way or another blame the tropical climate or scarce natural resources for limiting human cultural development. He unambiguously rejects racist notions for backwardness—such as the mixture of European and Indigenous populations inevitably leading to an inept adaptation and a failed, ersatz population (see Nugent 1993). By contrast, Wagley explains Amazonian underdevelopment as stemming from the lack of Western scientific knowledge and agricultural technology as well as an insufficiency of education (specifically, scientific views) and Western health care for the population.

In a nutshell Wagley is arguing for an early form of modernization theory (see Myrdal 1957; Rostow 1960), which flourished in American social science in the 1960s. Modernization theory has many versions, but common to most is the idea that the improvement of the human condition can be accomplished by the diffusion of modern (meaning Western, industrial, and capitalist) technologies, institutions, and values to the poor and underdeveloped regions of the world. Wagley's work with SESP (*Serviço Especial de Saúde Pública*—Special Public Health Service) during World War II (an early example of applied anthropology) made him a strong believer in the promises of progress through

---

[2]Ribeirinho means "river bank dweller." The population consists of traditional (or peasant) subsistence farmers (with manioc as their staple crop) and extractors of forest products (most famously rubber tapping) living along the region's waterways.

science. Through his involvement with public health education and the creation of health posts in the Lower Amazon Region, he saw positive and measureable improvements in the lives of the people. Yet, despite the successes he witnessed, there have been countless other examples worldwide in which modernization theory fell short and the human condition worsened. These failures have led to methodical rebukes, most falling under two general lines of criticism (see Escobar 1995; Wolf 1982).

First is the problem of a strong undercurrent of ethnocentrism—that is, these theories only considered American or European models for development possibilities while disregarding or disparaging others that varied—particularly indigenous models and socialist ones. All non-Western (and noncapitalist) socioeconomic models were lumped together as traditional systems that needed transformation by the diffusion of modern technology (e.g., industrial farming, industrial manufacturing), modern social structure (e.g., nuclear families, private property, democratic governments), modern values (e.g., faith in science and technology, education, individual initiative), and modern population control.

As evidenced in his writings, Wagley is swayed by the promises of modern science and Western progress. Of course he is not privy to future research that points out multiple flaws in this logic and the all too often devastating consequences of its uncritical application (see Hobart 1993, Escobar 1995, and Venkatesan & Yarrow 2012). Nor does he have access to the innovative research by anthropologists and ecologists that point to effective and sustainable models for rainforest utilization based on Indigenous traditions—the so called "rainforest guardian" models that emerged in the 1980s and 90s (Posey and Balée 1989; Posey 2000; Allegretti 1995, 1990). He also did not have to contend with the polemic and often belligerent theoretical battles waged by postmodernists/poststructuralists to challenge the very nature of science. In some of these views, common from the 1990s until the present, science is seen as simply one narrative of reality that is equal to, but no better than, all others. In other words, it is given no special status among myriad of folk views extant among humans. In other versions, science is seen as a politically biased methodology or tool used in the domination of one group over another. Most commonly this critique cites its use by Europeans to represent, define, and thereby control non-Europeans. In still other versions there is claim of bias favoring males over females (see McGee and Warms 2011).

Despite the reproach that critics of science and modernization theory may heap on the epistemological footings of *Amazon Town*, Wagley's detailed description of ribeirinho lifeways has been effectively utilized by nongovernmental organizations (NGOs) working in the region on sustainable development projects—albeit four decades later. As a testament to the quality of the research, his findings and many policy suggestions have enabled change agents to understand the cultural context of socioeconomic transformations (both limitations and potentials), allowing them to create superior sustainable development projects in Gurupá and surrounding municipalities (see Chapter 8). In this manner they have, in effect, fulfilled Wagley's desire to help the poor and marginal through anthropological expertise.

The second critique of modernization theories focuses on their ahistoricism—namely, ignoring the devastating impact of European colonialism on native and peasant economies, which in many cases led directly to the historic conditions of poverty and underdevelopment and continues to maintain them today (Wolf 1982; Escobar 1995). Wagley is more prudent on this issue. His writings identify forms of external exploitation originating from a global capitalist system that have created long-term patterns of underdevelopment in the Amazon. This point he makes most explicitly in his discussions of the rubber extraction system described in Chapter 3. Yet, with the benefit of more recent scholarship, we can today construct a more precise picture of how articulation with the emergent world economic system has systematically underdeveloped the Amazon Region ever since the first European encounter in the 1500s (see Wolf 1982; Weinstein 1983; Bunker 1985).

In this chapter, as well as throughout the book, certain vocabulary choices common in the 1940s and 1950s that Wagley uses to represent the people of the Amazon are modified. For example, the use of the generic masculine (nouns and pronouns such as *man, mankind,* or *he*) to denote both females and males is changed to reflect contemporary gender neutral representations prevalent in anthropological writings (e.g., *people, humans, humankind,* or *they*). Words such as "backward" or "primitive" are likewise replaced with terms less rooted in historic notions of Western superiority. The most extensive changes, however, are to the sections using outdated or falsified concepts. For example, some sections expressing faith in the pesticide DDT (dichlorodiphenyltrichloroethane) to control malaria-carrying mosquitoes without an awareness of its severe environmental and health impacts are omitted. The notion of very small prehistoric population levels in Amazonia, which lacked sociocultural complexity and did not extensively alter the rainforest ecosystem (the so-called standard model that originated in Julian Steward's *Handbook of South American Indians*—1946 to 1950—and refined by Meggers 1971) is likewise corrected (see Viveiros de Castro 1996). The ideas that slash-and-burn agriculture and extraction of forest resources are inevitably "backward," destructive, or otherwise limiting activities in need of replacement are updated with current research showing the positive contributions these practices can have for sustainable development models, such as in the maintenance of extractive reserves and other protected lands. In each of these cases where outmoded knowledge is supplanted by more current research, the changes are clearly marked in the footnotes.

***

This book is a study of a region and the way of life of its people. The region is the Brazilian Amazon where a distinctive tropical way of life has been formed by the fusion of Native American and Portuguese cultures during the last four centuries. In a larger sense, the book is a study of the adaptation of humans to a tropical environment. It is also a case study of a poor and underdeveloped region.

There is an awakening interest in the economically marginal regions of the world. Vast quarters of the globe, inhabited by nonindustrial undernourished peoples, once seemed of little importance to our own welfare. It has gradually become clear to us that the plight of these people is the world's concern. In 1949 President Truman placed before the public the problem that such areas offer both for the peoples who inhabit them and for the more fortunate inhabitants of the wealthier nations. "More than half of the people of the world," he stated, "are living in conditions approaching misery. Their food is inadequate. They are victims of disease. Their economic life is primitive [sic.] and stagnant. Their poverty is a handicap and a threat both to them and to prosperous areas."[3]

Yet the improvement of the condition of life of these people need not await new scientific advances. Humankind possesses the technical knowledge, the result of an accumulation over many centuries of the

---

[3]Inaugural address of Jan. 20, 1949.

contributions of people of many nations, to improve their lot. The problem is the extension of the knowledge and the technical skills that the world already possesses to the half of the world that has not acquired them. This is one of the crucial problems of our time.[4]

The Amazon Valley, almost as large as the continental United States, is one of [these areas of concern]. It is also, perhaps, the most sparsely inhabited of them all. The drainage system formed by the great Amazon River and its many tributaries reaches into ten South American nations—into Brazil, Bolivia, Colombia, Ecuador, French Guiana, Guyana, Peru, Surinam, and Venezuela. The major portion of the great valley is Brazilian. The total population of the Brazilian Amazon region, about one and a half million people,[5] is lost in an area of three million square kilometers.[6] Present conditions in the Amazon Valley certainly qualify it without any doubt as an underdeveloped area. Approximately 60 percent of the people who inhabit the Brazilian Amazon are illiterate.[7] Although vital statistics for the region are admittedly deficient, it is recorded that in 1941, of 1,000 infants born in Belém, the capital of the Amazonian state of Pará, 189 died before reaching one year of age. In Manaus, the capital of the state of Amazonas situated in the heart of the Valley, the infant mortality rate per thousand in the same year was 303. In eight rural communities in the state of Pará from which statistics were gathered in 1941, infant mortality during the first year reached 304 out of each 1,000 born. It is the opinion of public health authorities, however, that these figures are lower than the true index. Typhoid, which accounted for only 1.3 deaths per 100,000 people in the United States in 1937–1941, had a rate of 28 per 100,000 in Manaus. Tuberculosis caused 242.5 deaths out of 100,000 in Manaus in 1941 as against 45.8 in the United States; and malaria, a so-called tropical disease, had the rate of 334.9 in Manaus in 1941 as compared with only 1.1 in the United States. Yet health

---

[4]Seventeen lines were omitted describing the non-Brazilian tropics and poverty, as well 1940 statistics.
[5]By comparison, the Amazon Region in 2010 is home to 15.9 million people (IBGE 2012).
[6]Six lines were omitted comparing the Amazon to New Guinea.
[7]By 2010 literacy campaigns have reduced the official illiteracy rate to 11 percent for the Amazon (North) region of Brazil (IBGE 2012).

conditions in this Amazonian metropolis were superior to those of most small communities in the Valley in 1941.[8]

In addition, the people of Amazonia do not have enough to eat. A study of the diet of working-class families in Belém carried out a few years ago showed the average diet deficient in calories and even more so in vitamins and minerals (Castro 1946:67). It is the general impression of all observers that dietary deficiency and even semistarvation are general throughout the Valley.[9]

The economic life of the Valley is clearly stagnant. The agricultural techniques used in Amazonia are mainly those inherited from its Indigenous inhabitants' slash-and-burn subsistence agriculture.[10] In 1939 only less than one-half of one percent of the total area of the state of Pará was reported to be under cultivation, and that is probably somewhat high for the Valley as a whole. Transportation is by slow river boats, most of which are fueled by wood. There are only 1,600 miles of automobile roads and 238 miles of railroad in the entire valley.

---

[8]In 2010 the infant mortality rates for the Amazon (North) region of Brazil were 18.1 as compared to 17.1 for Brazil as a whole and 7 for the United States (IBGE 2010; UN Children's Fund 2012). Malaria rates were reported as 28.4/1,000 for the state of Pará, although in the delta region of the Amazon (Marajó region) the rates remain high at 104.8/1,000 (IBGE 2012; Instituto Peabiru 2011).

[9]Two lines were omitted citing outdated nutritional data. Nutritional studies from the 1990s until the present show continuing problems for rural populations in the Amazon (Murrieta et al. 1999), although results vary considerably by area. For example, in a study near Santarém, Adams, Murrieta, and Sanches (2005) found an adequate diet in terms of macronutrition (e.g., protein intake), but lacking in overall caloric intake (72.7 percent of World Health Organization recommendations) and with much seasonal variation. In a study of the delta region of the Lower Amazon, Silva (2009) found much higher rates of undernutrition, some approaching chronic levels. Stunting (low height for age) in all studies of Amazonia remains common.

[10]The scientific consensus when *Amazon Town* was written maintained that the use of slash-and-burn agriculture was an environmentally destructive practice and a principal cause of the underproduction of food. Research from the 1980s until today, by contrast, points out the sustainable nature of the agricultural technique that does not destroy the rainforest when practiced with small population density (Sponsel et al. 1996; Smith and Wishnie 2000; Schwartzman, Nepstad, and Moreira 2000; Posey and Balée 1989; Anderson and Balick 1991). Slash-and-burn agriculture is now understood as an important part of a balanced system of agriculture and extraction that can provide an adequate standard of living for rural populations. It cannot, however, feed large populations.

Industry is technologically unsophisticated and almost nonexistent. The commerce of the region is based on the collection of forest products such as wild rubber, palm oils, pelts, and tropical hardwoods. Public facilities such as waste disposal, electric lights, and water supply are minimal. A few small towns have electric lights, and a few others once maintained electric plants, but they have allowed them to fall into disuse. Until quite recently only Belém and Manaus had public sewerage and water-supply systems, and these systems were clearly antiquated. In Belém, after World War II, the public tramways had ceased to run and the electric-light plant was so rundown that the city was thrown into total darkness several times each night. In view of such conditions it is quite understandable why the Amazon region of Brazil did not increase in population from 1920 to 1940, while Brazil as a nation had an increase in population of 36 percent. Only in the arid region of northeastern Brazil, where living standards are almost as low as those in the Amazon, is the Brazilian population static.

Does this sparse population, these wretched health conditions, the deplorably low standards of living, and the lack of industry mean that the Amazonian environment is an insurmountable obstacle to development? In other words, does a hot and humid tropical environment impose limitations on human development that make it next to impossible to raise living standards in such areas? This is a critical question for all tropical regions. In the specific terms of the Amazon, is it a frontier to be populated and developed for the benefit of the world's hungry or is it doomed to be forever a "green desert"? Opinions regarding the potentiality of the Amazon have been mixed. On the negative side it has been described as a "green hell," and because so many grandiose dreams have centered on the region, it has been called "green opium." In the same vein an agronomist once suggested, in half serious jest, that the only solution for the problems of the Amazon Valley was to fence it off and slowly remove all of the people. Yet, since the time of Alexander von Humboldt and even before, people have dreamed of great cities, rich agricultural lands, and thriving industries in the great Valley. One of these optimists was Alfred Russell Wallace (1853:334–35), the famous English naturalist who visited the Amazon in the nineteenth century. "I fearlessly assert," he wrote enthusiastically, "that here the primeval forest can be converted into rich pasture land, into cultivated fields, gardens and orchards, containing every variety of produce, with half the labor, and, what is more important, in less than half the time that would be required at home." Similar opinions, both pro-Amazon and anti-Amazon, might be cited at length, for writers have taken one side or the other with considerable fervor.[11]

The climate of the Amazon is most certainly hot and humid. On the map the equator seems to bisect the area. Yet there are many misconceptions regarding the Amazonian climate. The heat is not unbearable. The average temperature at Manaus is only 78.1° F, and the record heat in Manaus over a thirty-year period was 97.1° F—about equal to a summer heat wave in New York City and not an unusual high for the North American Midwest. The difference between day and night temperatures is often as much as fifteen degrees in Amazonia. Along with a steady breeze, the lower temperature makes the nights quite comfortable. The humidity, however, is high; at Manaus it averages 78 percent. The humidity and perhaps the lack of seasonal variation in temperature are perhaps the most uncomfortable aspects of the climate. There is only a four-degree difference between the "hottest" month and the "coldest" month. To the Amazon inhabitant seasons are marked by the amount of rainfall rather than by variation of temperature. Although rain is abundant throughout the year, averaging more than eighty inches on the upper rivers and slightly less on the coast, the period of January to June is the "rainy season" and is called the "winter." During these months it rains almost every day, and the streams overflow their banks. The remaining months of the year comprise the "dry season" or "summer." During the summer there are many days without rain, and the waterfall is generally in the form of brief, violent thundershowers. During these months the water level in the river drops and the water drains out of the low flood lands or *várzea*.

The tropical seasons of the Amazon, despite their lack of contrast in temperature, affect the life of humans as do the seasons of the temperate zones. Whereas freezing temperatures of the winter in the temperate zone call for heating of homes and special clothes, the steady rains of the Amazonian winter and the flooded lowlands that cover land trails restrict people to their homes. Fishing is not productive during these months and rubber cannot be collected. The summer,

---

[11]Omitted are 57 lines discussing human adaptation to the topics, including Wagley's dismissal of racist and environmental determinist theories from the 19th and early 20th centuries. For a contemporary discussion of human adaptability in the humid tropics see Moran (1982:259–304).

on the contrary, is a period of activity—of garden making, of rubber production, of fishing, of visiting, and of festivals. In towns the streets are dry, and in the rural districts the overland trails are passable. On the main tributaries of the Amazon River system, sandy beaches are uncovered where turtles deposit their eggs. Clear days make travel more comfortable. The local expressions "summer" and "winter" have connotations analogous to the equivalent terms used in temperate climates; they refer to marked differences in the yearly cycle that break the monotony of life and with which humans associate their various activities. The Amazon climate has its great disadvantages, but in many respects it has advantages over the great extremes of temperature found in many North American areas. Climate is not a barrier impossible to overcome.

A strong case against tropic regions has also been based on the prevalence of disease, especially the so-called tropical diseases, as a primary deterrent to future progress. The fact that hot and moist zones contain not only most of the ailments common to temperate zones but also a series of local diseases is seen as an impossible obstacle to overcome. Leishmaniasis, a tropical ulcer; filariasis, which leads to the monstrous condition known as elephantiasis;[12] onchocerciasis, caused by a larva that burrows into the skin of the scalp; trypanosomiasis, caused by a minute parasite that enters the blood stream and even the tissues;[13] and *fogo selvagem*, a ringworm infection that quickly covers the entire body, are certainly horrible enough. Such exotic diseases, however, have limited distributions; and only rarely, as in the case of trypanosome in Africa, do they have an incidence high enough to form a serious barrier to the health of a total population. The most widespread and deadly of the "tropical diseases" is malaria, although its distribution is not strictly tropical. The ravages of malaria in the past and in the present in the tropical world are well known. Intestinal parasites, including amoebas and the bacilli that cause dysentery and the Ancylostoma (hookworm), thrive in moist and warm climates. It has been estimated that almost 90 percent of the rural population of the Brazilian Amazon is infected with one variety or another of intestinal

[12]This is a chronic condition caused by lymphatic obstruction and characterized by enormous enlargement of the parts affected.
[13]African sleeping sickness is a result of a form of trypanosoma.

parasites.[14] Tuberculosis and syphilis, certainly not limited to tropical environments, are also serious problems in the Amazon. Yaws (frambesia), a contagious disease resembling syphilis, is common, especially in the lower Amazon Basin.[15]

The prevalence of most of these diseases cannot be charged to climate alone; they are more a reflection of the poverty of the region than its cause. Tuberculosis, it is well known, is related to low standards of living and to malnutrition. The prevalence of intestinal parasites is due primarily to the lack of adequate sewerage and water supply. The installation of sanitary privies and of modern water-supply systems by the public health service of the Amazon has already reduced the rate of intestinal infections. Syphilis and yaws are social diseases. Neither is difficult to treat nowadays, and the prevention of both is a question of public education. Malaria, the "tropical disease" with the highest mortality rate in the Amazon, is today giving way to powerful drugs and to new preventive measures.[16] The control of other diseases with high mortality in the Amazon is primarily a question of better living conditions, a better diet, increased education of the population, and full use of the available scientific knowledge and equipment.

But the health of the Amazon population depends as much on improvement in nutrition as on better medical facilities. A better diet for the majority of the Amazon population depends in turn on increasing agricultural production in the region. Here again the tropical environment would seem to set a limit to cultural development.[17] Although it is commonly thought that tropical soils, with their lush and luxuriant

---

[14]In the Santos et al. (2010) study of the rural municipality of Coari, Amazonas, the authors found intestinal parasites in 83 percent of children in their sample population—all associated with poor basic sanitary conditions.

[15]Yaws cede easily to treatment with arsenic lead.

[16]In 2013 there is still no vaccine against malaria, although there is considerable research underway to find one. Destruction of mosquito breeding habitats, selective spraying of insecticides, and careful isolation and treatment of infected individuals can greatly reduce the occurrence of malaria in a population, but it continues to be a major health problem in many parts of the Amazon.

Nineteen lines were omitted that discuss the spraying of the insecticide DDT by SESP in the 1940s as a primary form of mosquito control. This practice predates the understanding of the insecticide's negative environmental effects.

[17]With more recent archaeological research in Amazonia, the idea that the tropical environment limits cultural development is not supported. Large population

covering of vegetation that grows with such rapidity, are exceedingly rich, this does not seem to be true. Tropical soils have been judged by soil scientists to be in general of poor quality. The vegetation grows fast because of the warm and moist climate during the entire year; yet the root systems of even the largest trees are surprisingly shallow. The humus is thin. Rapid decomposition of organic matter in the tropics makes for slow deposition of humus even in the thick forest; and when deforestation takes place for plantations or for settlements, erosion and leaching soon waste the earth. Amazon soils are clearly inferior to those of more favored temperate areas. Yet the poverty of the soil can easily be exaggerated in an effort to correct the popular misconception of the fertility of the tropics. One soil scientist estimated that, despite the mediocre quality of the soils, more than 70 percent of the total area of the Amazon Valley permits agriculture (Castro 1946:106).[18]

Like the floodplain of most great river systems, that of the Amazon River network is wide. Below Manaus, the area annually flooded by the river is 25 to 30 miles on each side. As on the Mississippi, the river towns and villages are situated on bluffs and outcrops of *terra firme*. It is unfortunate that these lowlands are not more extensive, for the extensions of flood lands are notably rich, as is true of most deltas. The scientific exploitation of these alluvial lands, which are seldom used by the Amazonian farmer, would multiply Amazonian food production many times over (Gourou 1948:6). Furthermore, the mediocre soils of *terra firme* can be made to produce more. Gourou points out that one limited area of the Valley, the land along the railroad between Belém and Bragança, which is mainly *terra firme*, supports a population many

---

concentrations with complex social organization existed in the Amazon Region as they did in semitemperate and temperate climates of the Americas. The precontact diet of these populations, as seen from the few bioarchaeological studies of burials, appears to have been superior to current regional diets (Roosevelt 1991, 1994).

In other words, the relatively poor diet of contemporary rural populations is not inherently linked to the tropical environment but to the cataclysmic disruptions in the regional economy initiated during contact and conquest in the 16th and 17th centuries, followed by a colonial and postcolonial political economy favoring export commodities over food production for local consumption (discussed in Chapter 2).

[18]Twenty-one lines were omitted that discuss the soils and geography of the lower Amazon region. For a more up-to-date perspective see Moran (1993).

times as dense as the average for the Valley as a whole without any essential modification of the traditional methods of cultivation. The Amazonian soil is not in any way comparable to such fertile and productive areas as the Midwestern United States, yet it can be made to produce food not only for the present population of the Amazon but for several times as many people.[19]

While the Amazon Valley is not an especially propitious setting [at least for Western industrial societies], it must be concluded that the physical environment is not the most serious obstacle to its eventual development and to higher standards of living for its inhabitants. All peoples have an equal potentiality to improve their social conditions, and their physical environment is only one factor of several that determine their final adjustment to their habitat. As one writer stated, "The land, the climate, the mineral wealth are not determinants of human progress. They are merely determinants of theoretical limits beyond which the native inhabitant cannot go. Science and technology are pushing the limits back but they are finite. To what extent a given nation approaches the finite limit of civilization depends upon human factors" (Meyerhoff 1949:92). This "finite limit" is still a distant horizon for the Amazon Basin, where modern science and technology [as well as the precontact Indigenous knowledge for supporting large population levels] are all but unknown. The "human factors" on which so much depends are part of the culture and the social system of the people. It is their cultural traditions that make available to them the tools, the knowledge, and the technology to cope with the environment. It is the culture that determines the ends toward which the people of a particular area make use of their technology, and it is the social system that determines the organization of work and the distribution of the products of their work.

The main reasons why the Amazon Valley is today a poor and underdeveloped area must be sought in Amazon culture and society, and in the relationship of this region with the centers of economic and political power and with the sources of cultural diffusion. What is the present technical equipment of the inhabitants of the Amazon for exploiting their environment? How did they come to possess their

---

[19]Thirteen lines were omitted that discuss other factors effecting fertility of soil, including cultural perceptions. For a more contemporary view of soils and their use in Amazonian, see Moran (1993).

present technology? What is the "good life" to Amazon people? In other words, what are their systems of values, incentives, and motivations? What is the local form of the fundamental and universal institutions—family, church, and government—by which people everywhere organize their lives? What has been the economic and political relationship of the Amazon with the outside world? The answer to why the region is poor lies in such questions.

This book is, then, the study of a culture, of the way of life that has been created by humans in the Amazon Valley of Brazil. Because cultures are historically developed, and because they are formed from elements of widespread origin by culture borrowing, we must look into the past and beyond the Valley for the sources and events that have influenced the contemporary culture of the Amazon. A knowledge of the way of life of Amazon societies will indicate where changes must be made if living standards are to be improved.[20]

---

[20]Forty-two lines were omitted that discuss technology transfer (modernization theory) and cultural resistance or acceptance as understood in the 1940s and 50s. See Escobar (1993), Hobart (1993), and Venkatesan & Yarrow (2012) for a critique of actual attempts of such technology transfer in Latin America.

CHAPTER 2

An Amazon Community

No one community is ever typical of a region or of a nation. Each has its own traditions, its own history, its own variation of the regional or the national way of life. The culture of a modern region or nation has an organization that is greater than simply the sum total of the local communities that form it. There are institutions and social forces of regional, national, and even international scope that determine the trend of life in each small community. The church, the political institutions, the system of formal education, the commercial system, and many other aspects of a culture are more widespread and more complex in their organization than in any local community manifestation. Nor does any one community ever contain the total range of a regional culture; it may not contain all of the social classes, all occupations, or all of the political parties that are found in the region as a whole. A study of a small agricultural village of the United States, for instance, would probably tell us little of the complexities of American organized labor, of the elaborate commercial and financial system, or of the ostentation of the rich in our big cities. Yet studies of the banking system of a region, of the formal organization and the ideology of its religion, of its imports and exports, or of the dynamics of its population in the impersonal and objective terms of the economists or the sociologists seem lifeless, to say the least.

They tell us little or nothing of life situations, of the working of widespread patterns and institutions as they are lived by people.

Everywhere people live in communities—in bands, in villages, in towns, in rural neighborhoods, and in cities. In communities, face-to-face human relations take place, and each day people are subjected to the dicta of their culture. In their communities the people of a region make a living, educate their children, live as families, form themselves into associations, worship their supernaturals, have superstitious fears and taboos, and are motivated by the values and incentives of their particular culture. In the community economics, religion, politics, and other aspects of a culture appear interrelated and part of a total culture system, as they are in life. All of the communities of an area partake of the cultural heritage of the region, and each is a local manifestation of the possible interpretations of regional patterns and institutions.

Any community in the Brazilian Amazon would serve our purpose as a laboratory for the study of regional culture as it is lived out by one group of Amazon people. This study will focus Gurupá,[1] a small community on the Lower Amazon in which the author and his coworkers lived and studied. It is not an average Amazon town. Monte Alegre, Óbidos, Faro, Abaetetuba, and many others are larger and more prosperous. There are differences in Amazon culture patterns characteristic of the Upper Amazon, the Salgado, or the Islands that do not appear in Gurupá culture. Yet Gurupá serves admirably as a "case history." It has a long history in which most of the trends of regional history have been reflected. The present way of life in Gurupá and in its surrounding rural neighborhoods might seem old-fashioned and rustic to the urbanite of Belém, Manaus, or even Santarém, but it is shared in its broad outlines by the majority of the rural population of the Amazon Basin and by the inhabitants of the working-class districts of the cities, which are filled with recent rural migrants. Because Gurupá is a poor community without any special industry or natural gifts and without any special distinction, a study of Gurupá focuses a spotlight on the basic problems of the region.

---

[1] In the original work, Wagley used the pseudonym Itá—a Tupian term meaning rock—for Gurupá. Pseudonyms are a way of protecting the identity of communities and individuals if case-sensitive or embarrassing information is revealed (sometimes inadvertently). Beginning in the 1980s, however many researchers have used the name Gurupá to identify the community, nullifying the need to protect its identity and the need for the pseudonym.

II

Gurupá is situated in the subregion known as the Lower Amazon, below the juncture of the Negro and Solimões rivers. In addition, it lies close to the Islands of the delta, and thus two ecological subregions of the valley affect the life of the community. It is a small town with about five hundred inhabitants, yet it is the seat of a municipality, a county-like political subdivision of the state, which covers an area of 6,094 square kilometers[2]—almost the size of the State of Rhode Island. The town lies on a low bluff formed by an outcrop of laterite, which rises only three or four meters above the river but affords a view extending for many miles up and down the southern Amazon channel. From the river the sight of the town is a welcome break in the monotonous forest-lined banks of the Amazon. It stands out neat and colorful against the dark green vegetation. The gleaming white church with its orange tile roof is the first building to be distinguished; then the two-story town hall, which has recently been completed; and a row of low houses, washed in bright colors and facing the river, appear. There is a dark red municipal wharf (*trapiche*) set on piles in the river channel and connected to the shore by a long boardwalk. A little downriver is a smaller *trapiche* owned by a local merchant where a sailboat with rust-colored sails is tied up. River steamers that stop at Gurupá always use the municipal wharf, which has a small covered warehouse. From the river the town appears framed by the dark green foliage of the enormous mango trees and the stately palms that line the waterfront. It seems an inviting place.

As one leaves the river boat and crosses the boardwalk, the romantic setting fades into realism. The street facing the river is unpaved, as are all Gurupá thoroughfares. If the time is that of the rainy season, the street oozes with mud. A sidewalk graces the front of some of the houses on the riverfront street, but others open directly on the street. Many of the buildings are in bad repair, and one or two are ready to fall in from neglect. Back from the riverfront, the houses are less colorful and more run-down, and there are numerous palm-thatched dwellings where the poorer inhabitants live. Gurupá offers its best profile to the river, but close inspection shows even the riverfront to be somewhat worn by age.

A map on display in the town hall shows Gurupá to have a gridiron plan. Three main streets (*ruas*) run lengthwise parallel to the river and are intersected by side streets (*travessas*) that wind back from the river.

---

[2] The 2010 census lists the municipal territory as 8,540 square kilometers (IBGE 2012).

FIGURE 2.1 | *Municipal wharf.*
Photograph by C. Wagley 1948.

FIGURE 2.2 | *First Street.*
Photograph by C. Wagley 1948.

FIGURE 2.3 | *Second Street.*
Photograph by C. Wagley 1948.

FIGURE 2.4 | *Town Hall.*
Photograph by C. Wagley 1948.

Three public squares (*praças*) are shown on the map, and there is a riverfront garden. All the squares and thoroughfares have names. Each *rua* has the name of a patriotic hero of the state of Pará; each *travessa* is named after a saint; and two of the *praças* carry the names of famous men. It is soon apparent, however, that such city planning is an idea imposed from outside. The names shown on the map are seldom, if ever, used. Instead, the three *ruas* are referred to as "First Street," "Second Street," and "Third Street" (beginning at the riverfront), and no one can remember any of the names of the side streets at all.[3] Whereas the *ruas* are fairly straight, and the two *praças* are well marked out, the *travessas* wind somewhat dizzily in and around the houses. Some of them are no more than narrow paths. The town hall, which is situated in the middle of the largest *praça*, may be considered the central point of the city. Occupying an entire side of the square is the public health post with its landscaped yard and vegetable garden. The other *praça* is empty except for a small monument to a state hero. The other two important public buildings, the school and the church, are situated beyond the end of the long First Street, somewhat apart from the town. The school, a new building built by the federal government for adult education classes, is an adobe structure with a tile roof. It has one classroom and several rooms intended as living quarters for the teacher and family. The church lies several hundred meters beyond the school house, still farther out of town, which is contrary to the general practice in the Amazon of making the church the central edifice. Between the church and the school is a soccer field where the two rather haphazard teams of Gurupá play on Sunday afternoons during the "summer" months.[4]

The square blocks formed by the intersecting streets and side streets indicated on the town plan are in reality hard to discern. A block here

---

[3]By 2013 Gurupá has expanded southward from the river to include sixteen streets, although the last eight are part of a new extension with relatively few houses. The first five streets are paved with asphalt or octagonal concrete blocks, whereas the remaining ones are dirt. The streets are still called by their number, not by their names. In fact, no one in town could recite the proper street names in 2013, although individuals can often recall their own house and street number for a mailing address.
[4]During the 2000s the first seven blocks of town have filled up, with no vacant lots (see Figures 8.2 and 8.3). Only in the last nine streets is the pattern described by Wagley still seen. Even here, the houses tend to be well-built, using concrete blocks or wood, and none with palm thatching.

FIGURE 2.5 | *SESP health post with Eduardo Galvão in front.*
Photograph by C. Wagley 1948.

and there is solidly occupied, but there are so many vacant lots in others that the form of the plan is lost. Paths cut through empty spaces and get lost in the wilderness of Third Street. Yet with so much space, the better dwellings of Gurupá are built flush on the street and connected with each other, presenting a solid front to the passerby. The backyard (*quintal*), surrounded by walls, is the focus of these long houses, which are larger than they seem from the street. Today only two full blocks of Gurupá are solidly built in the traditional manner. Because of the rapid decline in population after the Amazon rubber boom, many houses tumbled in, and a recent tendency to build homes surrounded by gardens has changed the town's appearance. On First Street is a series of two-family bungalows built as a housing project by the municipal government. They are set back two or three meters from the street with a narrow space between each. These are occupied by the mayor, the police chief, the federal tax collector, the postmistress (who uses her parlor as the post office), and the agent of the Federal Statistical Bureau. Although these new houses have some space for circulation of air, they have miserably low ceilings and small rooms and are exposed on all sides to the sun. Though they are modern, they are hardly designed for the Amazon tropics, and are far inferior in comfort to the traditional houses with their high ceilings and protected veranda facing a shaded backyard.

All but one of the commercial houses of Gurupá are situated on First Street.[5] This exception, behind the town hall on Second Street, is a small shop with little stock. Of the three stores on First Street, the Casa Borralho, which has survived since the days of the rubber boom, has by far the largest stock. It also has a choice location near the boardwalk leading to the municipal wharf. The other two stores are farther down the street and are more recently established. All of these stores are also dwellings. A large front room opening onto the street is the shop. This contains the *balcão* (counter) and the current stock. Behind the shop is a large storeroom where the rubber and other products that the shopkeeper accepts in exchange for goods, as well as bulky stock such as sacks of salt, are kept. Customers lounge about in the shop, and *cachaça* (sugar-cane rum) is served over the counter. The living quarters of the shopkeepers and their families take up one side of the house, and the shopkeepers withdraw frequently during the day for a bit of conversation with their families. Important customers are invited into the parlor, or, if they are intimates of the family, into the dining room for the inevitable *cafèzinho* (demitasse of black coffee).

All of the buildings on First Street are built of *taipa*[6] or of wood, all have wooden or cement floors, all have ceramic tile roofs, and all are painted either with a white or with a bright-colored wash. This type of dwelling is classified in Gurupá as a *casa* (house) to distinguish it from the less permanent palm-thatched structures of the town, which are called

---

[5]In 2013 by far most businesses are located on Second Street. Many are by the municipal wharf (*trapiche*), a former swampy area that has been built up and now experiences heavy pedestrian, motorcycle, and automobile traffic.

[6]A type of wall construction traditional of Brazil. It is wattle work filled with clay and with a sand and lime plaster finish.

FIGURE 2.6 | *Casa Barralho in background with Clara Galvão (left) and Dona Inacinha (right).*
Photograph by C. Wagley 1948.

barracas (huts). All the dwellings on Third Street, except two, are huts. They are two- or three-room structures, with woven palm walls and roof, set on stilts above the damp earth. The floors, which are generally made of narrow slats from the trunk of the paxiuba palm, provide an uncertain footing, but a few huts have floors of wooden planks. The homes on Second Street are a mixture of the two types. There are buildings that are classified by local people as "houses" but are in exceedingly bad condition, and there are "houses" of whitewashed taipa walls that have palm-thatched roofs. A few dwellings on Second Street are clearly huts. One "house" on Second Street is also a bakery where a husband and wife make wheat bread whenever wheat flour is available. The electric powerhouse where the machinery of the defunct wood-burning generator is kept is also on Second Street, which in addition boasts two barbers, one of whom has one room of his dwelling arranged as a shop. In 1948 a shoemaker who had recently arrived and who was not expected to stay for long was established in a hut on Second Street. Thus in Gurupá the more permanent and better dwellings are near the riverfront, whereas the poorer huts lie back from the river and are hidden from view. On Second Street is found the confusion of the middle ground. The equivalent of the "wrong side of the tracks" in Gurupá is "back from the river."

First Street and even Second Street are generally relatively clean and free of weeds, for the municipal government pays day workers during the dry season to weed the thoroughfares. Especially before a holiday or the visit of a politician from Belém, street cleaning becomes energetic. Third Street, however, is overgrown with vegetation, which is much too high to be called weeds. Only here and there on Third Street has some neat householder cleared the area in front of his house. Most of Third Street and the side streets that lead into it have the appearance of winding paths. Because those who live there complain of the unfair neglect of their street, the mayor from time to time arranges to have Third Street cleared. The most imposing buildings in Gurupá are, as we have seen, the church, the town hall, and the Health Post. The church, a tall simple structure, has recently been renovated, completely re-roofed, and whitewashed both inside and out by a German missionary priest aided by local labor. As a result it is somewhat austere and entirely lacking in the elaborately decorated interior of the average small-town church in Brazil. The Health Post is a low building designed by a Swiss-American architect and built by North American engineers who worked with the Amazon health service during the war. It has a long veranda porch, large screened windows, long narrow windows near the roof for ventilation, and other features designed for the climate. It stands apart in Gurupá as a modern building that is not merely a copy of temperate zone construction and at least attempts to conform to its setting. The two-story town hall, however, is the most famous building along the lower Amazon. It would do credit to a North American or European town several times larger than Gurupá. Its architecture would be more fitting to the temperate zone. A portion of the upper floor houses all the public offices, leaving the entire lower floor empty. Standing in the middle of one of the public squares, it is exposed on all sides to the sun, and it has poor ventilation. The second-floor offices boil during the afternoon. The town hall, as we shall see, figures in Gurupá history as a "white elephant," and the cost of constructing it has drained the public coffers several times.

III

The county-like municipality of which Gurupá is the seat extends south of the Amazon and downstream, taking in numerous islands of the delta region. The area is so large that most of the approximately eight thousand people who live within the municipality seldom, if ever, visit the town.[7] Deputy tax collectors, who are generally also rural merchants or traders, are stationed at several points over the area. From time to time, the mayor, the state tax collector, the federal tax collector, and even the police chief make inspection trips of two to three weeks' duration. Trading posts (*barracões*) are situated at intervals along the waterways of the municipality. Most of them renew their stock and send away the products they buy via regular river steamers owned by Belém commercial houses. Each trading post is the regular customer of a particular firm whose boat visits them each month or so. Because the exports and imports of most of the trading posts do not pass through Gurupá, the town is not the commercial center of the political unit it controls. Nor is it the social center for the municipality.[8] People from distant localities in the municipality do sometimes visit Gurupá for the annual festival of St. Benedict, but this event draws people from the entire lower Amazon, and the distant inhabitants come as visitors just as do people from outside. The municipality of Gurupá is not a social or even a geographical unit easily controlled from the municipal seat. In a few Amazon municipalities, such as Altamira on the Xingú River, the seat is strategically located where political control may be exerted over its territory and its inhabitants, but in the municipality of Gurupá even political unity is weak.

---

[7] In the 2010 census the municipal population of Gurupá is listed as 29,060, whereas the town population is 9,580 (IBGE 2012).

[8] By the 2000s, with ready access to motorized boats as well as trucks, cars, motorcycles, and bicycles for the municipality's 30 or so kilometers of dirt roads, Gurupá has become the economic, political, and social center for the municipality. Only in the farthest-most reaches to the Northeast, which are much closer geographically to Macapá, are the town's ties still weak.

FIGURE 2.7 | *Trading Post of Paraíso owned by Manuel Pere Serra (second from left).*

Photograph by C. Wagley 1948.

A more restricted area, immediately surrounding the town and comprising about one-fifth of the total territory of the municipality, looks to the town as the center both of its economic and of its social life. Most of this area, which we will call the "community of Gurupá," lies, as does the town, on the south bank of the Amazon; but it includes also a few small islands in the channel immediately in front of the town.[9] This community area includes approximately two thousand people, of whom only about five hundred live in the town. In front of Gurupá

---

[9]Wagley states that the name Gurupá (Itá in his version) will be used henceforth to refer to the community—the town and its immediate rural area—and not to the larger political unit of that name. He made this statement not only because it conformed to the reality of the 1940s but also because it was methodologically important to his community study approach to delineate the boundaries of the unit he wished to describe (see Arensberg 1954). In 2013, due to the available motorized water and

FIGURE 2.8 | *Palm-thatched hut in the interior of Gurupá.*
Photograph by C. Wagley 1948.

town the Amazon channel is more than five kilometers wide, and to cross it in canoes and small sailboats is often dangerous. For that reason, although many people from the south bank regularly work at rubber collecting on the Great Island, as the north bank is called, social relations with its inhabitants are normally infrequent. The land south of the river is for the most part terra firme. The area included in the community of Gurupá extends upriver as far as the Rio Jocojó and downstream as far as the Rio Pucuruí, both of which are small tributaries (igarapés) of the Amazon. Between these two tributaries are ten others, and the rural inhabitants of the community live in isolated homesteads scattered along the banks of these small streams. In fact, throughout the Amazon the main pattern of settlement is one of scattered households, situated close to the waterways, the principal transportation routes. There are two overland footpaths, however, which

---

land transportation and access to cell phones, this delineation is no longer valid. The "community" of Gurupá is very close to its geographic boundaries. Regardless of this change, with current theoretical concerns in anthropology focused on the process of globalization and movement of materials, ideas, and people around the planet, the focus on boundaries has been replaced by a focus on connections, networks, and exchanges across space.

run east and west from the town, providing communication with the rural zones by land during the summer. Even in the dry season, however, heavy cargoes and burdens can best be transported by canoe.

The people who live on the tributaries nearest to the town, such as Itapereira and Jacupí, visit town each day or two to buy food, to loaf in the shops, or even to work for the municipal government. The people who live on the more distant tributaries such as Bacá and Jocojó come to town only once each ten days for their *quinzena*,[10] the day selected for trading. They may also appear now and again on Sunday for Church services and on almost any other day to visit friends and relatives. In the summer months there are numerous saints' festivals in the rural zone, and people from the different small tributaries travel about to attend them and to visit. Within the community area all families bury their dead in the town cemetery; those who live outside have their own cemeteries. Within the community there is an in-group feeling of belonging, and the public ceremonies on Independence Day and the festivals of St. Benedict and St. Anthony celebrated in town are spoken of as "our festivals." People living outside the community area are strangers. A brass band of the community, which often plays for local dances, refused, for example, to play at a saint's festival being held on a stream near their homes but outside the community area. The people were *bravo* (rude or tough) and their festivals were hardly more than *farras* (wild parties) was the explanation of the bandleader. He did not feel at home among these strangers. People on a tributary that flows into the Amazon channel across from the town, and therefore outside the special limits of the community, told us, "We sometimes attend their festivals," or, "We haven't been to Gurupá for over two years."

The people living along the banks of each small stream form a "neighborhood," or a subunit, as it were, of the larger social unit that is the community. Along the banks of a typical tributary, some fifteen to twenty houses are situated at intervals of two to three hundred or even five hundred meters apart. There are sometimes clusters of houses inhabited by different members of the same family. In one place three houses, only about one hundred meters apart, held the families of a man and his two married sons; in another, six houses stretched over more than three kilometers of one tributary were inhabited by cousins.

---

[10]Literally "fifteenth"; traditionally, on the Lower Amazon, the trading day was set at fifteen-day intervals.

The homes of a patriarch and his sons-in-law and of a widow and her three daughters and their husbands formed two other neighborhood clusters. Although kinship ties are often important in determining the residence of people within a neighborhood, and in assuring mutual assistance among the inhabitants, such neighborhoods are not kinship units, nor are they clan-like social groups. Common residence, friendship, and the ceremonial tie of the godparent relationships are as strong as family ties between these neighbors.

Devotion to a particular saint forms another bond between the people of a particular neighborhood. On each tributary there is a religious brotherhood (*irmandade*) dedicated to a saint—to Our Lady of Nazareth, to St. Peter, or to St. John. Each year the saint's day is celebrated in the locality, and the organization of the festival is an important function of the brotherhood. It is within the neighborhood that people exchange labor with each other and form cooperative work parties for agriculture. Beyond the immediate family group the neighborhood is the setting for daily life in the rural zone of Gurupá. In fact, for the rural inhabitant neighborhood ties overshadow those of the community; yet the neighborhoods are integral subdivisions of the community. Events taking place in any of the rural neighborhoods are soon known on the streets of the town.

Two neighborhoods in the Gurupá community differ from the dispersed type described previously. The people who live on the Jocojó and Maria Ribeiro tributaries form small villages. The *vila* of Jocojó contains nineteen houses built along one fairly straight street. It is a small village with a white wooden chapel (see Figure 6.2) and a *ramada*, a large open structure used for dancing during festivals. An overly large hut without walls is used as a school; and in 1948 it functioned with about the same regularity and efficiency as the one in Gurupá. Jocojó parents were exceedingly anxious that their children take advantage of the school, for it was the only rural neighborhood that boasted one. The village on the Maria Ribeiro Tributary consisted of a small cluster of houses without a chapel for its saint and without a school, but both these village neighborhoods were characterized by unity of organization and the progressivism of their inhabitants. As long as the populations of rural Amazonas live scattered and distant from one another, it will be difficult to provide accessible educational facilities and adequate health protection for them. Concentrated villages such as these two atypical neighborhood groups of Gurupá would make it possible for the government to provide schools. A concentrated population allows the physician from Gurupá to give mass treatment. The health service would be able to provide controls for group protection, which would be impossible for the scattered households. Such villages, therefore, provide a possible solution for the problems of the countryside of the Amazon.[11]

IV

··

The people of the community of Gurupá are Brazilians. They participate within the limits of their available knowledge and potentialities in regional and national life. The *ribeirinhos* or *caboclos*,[12] as city people in the Amazon refer to the inhabitants of small towns and to the rural population, speak Portuguese. They discuss state and national politics, and if they are at least semiliterate they vote. In Gurupá and in other similar Amazon communities, September 7th (Brazil's Independence Day) is celebrated. The ribeirinho plays soccer, Brazil's national sport, and may gamble at *jôgo do bicho*, a popular and widespread drawing, similar to a "numbers" game, to which Brazilians are especially addicted. In 1945 festivals in out-of-the-way trading posts in the municipality of Gurupá celebrated VE Day. The farmers and rubber gatherers who attended were not, of course, aware of the full significance of

---

[11]In 2013 another alternative in place is the use of motor boats to bring people to schools, health posts, or to the town's hospital. The municipality of Gurupá has a speed boat ambulance and a small fleet of school boats and regularly rents private motor boats for a wide range of activities. The principal drawback is the high price of fuel, which can at times limit the use of these forms of transportation.

[12]Although commonly used in the Amazon Region, the term caboclo is derogatory— as Wagley acknowledges (also see Pace 2006; Lima 1999, 1992). In 1999 and 2009 we surveyed a sample of Gurupaenses (residents of Gurupá) and asked if they considered it offensive to be labeled a caboclo. Thirty-five percent of the sample population answered that it was offensive in one way or another. The other 65 percent of the sample population responded that it was not offensive to be labeled as such, even though they acknowledged the term was derogatory. All agreed in this group that the label was appropriate because they considered themselves to be uneducated, poor, backward, and generally inferior to others, particularly urban folk. This type of negative self-image is a response to centuries of exploitation and repression experienced by the population (see Lima 1999).

In this Anniversary Edition the terms ribeirinho and agroextractivist are substituted for caboclo—except where the discussion focuses on ethnicity, social race, and racism. Both of these terms are increasingly used by the population and by social scientists sensitive to ethical concerns of representation and labels. Agroextractivist is the term chosen by the leadership of the rural workers union in Gurupá for self-identification.

World War II, but they knew that their country was making war on the Allied side. The legal and political institutions, the educational system, the formal religion, and many other aspects of Gurupá society are those of the nation of which Gurupá is but a small and insignificant part.

Three cultural traditions have fused to form contemporary Brazilian culture. The traditions, the speech, and the governmental and religious institutions of Europe brought to the New World by the Portuguese are the dominant culture patterns throughout the country. Gurupá, like most Brazilian communities, derives most of its culture from Portugal. In addition, however, Brazilian national culture has been influenced strongly by the traditions both of Africa and by those of the native populations who inhabited the area before the Portuguese arrived. At least 3,000,000 African slaves were imported into the country during the colonial period, and it is probable that the total number was much greater.[13] Numerous customs and traditions of African origin have been incorporated into Brazilian life. Brazilian popular music (the samba), Brazilian cuisine, Brazilian folklore, and other aspects of modern life clearly show African influence. Yet Native American culture patterns persist throughout the country. Slash-and-burn agriculture and the major food crops (manioc, maize, beans, etc.) are of Indigenous origin. Most of the names of flora and fauna, and numerous place names in modern Brazilian Portuguese, derive from Tupí, a widespread Indigenous language.[14] Both the European newcomer and the African slave learned to live in the New World from the aboriginal peoples.

These three cultural heritages are not, however, felt with the same force throughout Brazil. Brazil is a nation of striking regional differences produced by very different environmental circumstances and by poor communications. Along the northeastern coast of Brazil, where the majority of the African slaves were on sugar plantations, African influences

---

[13]In research since *Amazon Town* was published, Funes (1995:53–54) estimates that by the late eighteenth century the population of African slaves in Grand Pará (which includes the contemporary states of Pará and Amazônas) reached nearly 24 percent of the total population—19,000 out of a total of 80,000 inhabitants. Altogether, the slave trade brought at least 53,000 Africans slaves to the Amazon (Vergolino-Henry and Figueredo 1990).

[14]The name Gurupá is likely of Tupí origin. Historically the name was written in two ways: Curupá (especially in the 17th century) and Gurupá. Both variations are likely Portuguese corruptions of Indigenous terms that might have referred to one of the following: a green woodpecker, a canoe port, a rock deposit, or a broken rock (Royer 2003:122).

were important in forming the present regional culture. In the extreme south of Brazil, European traditions have taken hold almost to the exclusion of Indigenous and African traditions. In the Amazon Valley, with its distinctive rainforest environment and its magnificent interlaced system of waterways, the Indigenous heritage of Brazil persisted with greater force than elsewhere. In Gurupá, as in other Amazon communities, Indigenous influences are readily apparent in the way people make a living, in their foods, in their folk beliefs, and in their religion. Furthermore, a large portion of the people of Gurupá has Indigenous ancestors. The high cheekbones, the straight black hair, the bronze skin, and the almond-shaped eyes (caused by the epicanthic fold so characteristic of Indigenous populations) of many of the inhabitants of the community indicate the strength of Native American genetic strain.[15]

---

[15]Even in Gurupá where only initial archaeological surveys have occurred, kilometer upon kilometer of thick anthropogenic soils (*terra preto do Índio* or black earth of the Indian) are easily observed and indicate a very large and persistent occupation. Assuming that the area followed similar patterns of human habitation described in nearby locations (see Roosevelt 1994, 1991; Schaan 2010; Martins et al. 2010), it is likely that small bands of foragers began traversing the site sometime after 10,000 years ago. These bands may have stopped for weeks at a time to collect wild plants and hunt animals. By 8,000 to 6,000 years ago, populations throughout the Amazon began specializing in fishing, collecting shellfish, gathering fruit, and growing some manioc. These groups likely began to establish semipermanent villages containing hundreds of people. Gurupá was possibly the site of such a village (see Martins et al. 2010:135).

Between 4,500 and 2,000 years ago the Indigenous population shifted to greater dependence on agriculture, growing crops such as manioc, corn, beans, sweet potatoes, peanuts, fruits, cotton, and tobacco. Sometime before 2,000 years ago the native population apparently grew rapidly, as indicated by the number and size of sites with terra preta anthrosols. Manioc and maize were the staple crops in this period, supplemented by other native crops, fruit gathering, as well as turtles and fish. Complex political organizations known as chiefdoms developed, consisting of settlements containing thousands of people. According to Schaan (2010:189–93), excavations on Marajó Island (a chiefdom complex lasting from 400-1300 AD) reveal "regional aggregation of mound sites, site size hierarchy, elaborate ceremonial ceramics, ancestor worship, differential treatment of the dead, and the presence of long distance exchange items"—all of which indicate sociopolitical complexity—including institutionalized social hierarchy and inequality.

Gurupá was possibly the site of a chiefdom in late prehistory based on its strategic location near the mouth of the Xingú River, the ceramic surface finds, and the extensive areas of anthropogenic soils. According to Martins et al. (2010:136) the ceramic style found at Gurupá is unique and definitely not Marajoara in origin (from the Island of Marajó).

The strength of the Indigenous tradition in rural Amazon society and culture is not due, however, to the numerical strength of the Indigenous population that survived conquest and colonization.[16] The lack of linguistic and sociopolitical unity among the Indigenous groups of Amazonia made the process of conquest difficult for the Europeans and disastrous for the Indigenous populations themselves. Both Portuguese civil officials and religious missionaries established early treaties with the Indigenous chiefs to ensure peaceful relations, but they soon found that such treaties were not recognized by the people of other villages. Unlike the conquest of Mexico and Peru by a handful of Spaniards, where the capture or the capitulation of a handful of leaders led to the subjugation of large populations, the conquest of the Amazon native peoples was necessarily a piecemeal affair. Each "tribe," almost each village, had to be won or attracted peacefully into the orbit of Portuguese colonial life. The result of such piecemeal conquest was a rapid disintegration of native "tribes," especially along the main streams of the Amazon River system, within about a century after the arrival of the Portuguese in the early seventeenth century.[17]

----

[16]Twenty-one lines were omitted in which the "standard model" (precontact low population density/low social complexity thesis) is used to describe the region. To the contrary, as indicated previously, Indigenous populations in the Amazon were likely in the millions (Denevan [2003] estimated between five and six million). The information available to Wagley during the 1940s and 50s also greatly underestimated the level of depopulation that occurred following Old World contact. In addition to the deaths caused by conquest and slavery, many more deaths occurred from the Old World diseases (smallpox, measles, malaria, tuberculosis, influenza, and even the common cold), which quickly spread through the region, devastating populations that had no immunities. Estimates of depopulation rates range well above 90 percent for the Amazon—in other words millions upon millions of souls lost (Dobyns 1993; Hemming 1978).

[17]Today [1950s] a few tribal Indigenous groups still live in out-of-the-way localities of the Amazon Valley, mainly in the headwaters of the nonnavigable tributaries. In numbers these tribal populations are an insignificant percentage of the total population of the Valley. They certainly do not exceed 50,000 people at most, less than one-half of one percent of the total population of the Brazilian Amazon. [The 2010 census records 433,363 Indigenous people in the North Region, or about 2.7 percent of the Amazon population total. For all of Brazil, the Indigenous population is only 0.47 percent of the total (IGBE 2012).] A few tribes, such as the Urubú Indians, inhabiting the forest between the Gurupí and Pindaré rivers, less than 200 miles from Belém at the mouth of the Amazon, and the Hawks (Gaviões) on the lower Tocantins River, are just now feeling the influence of Luso-Brazilian society. [By 2013 that

As in Mexico and in Peru, the Portuguese did not come to the New World to work: they came seeking a fortune. But in Amazonia they found neither the riches of the Potosi silver mines nor, as in Mexico and Peru, millions of natives to provide labor for them. Nor was the Amazon soil as suitable for sugar cane as the rich northeastern coast of Brazil, where a wealthy plantation society was formed in colonial times. The best the Portuguese were able to do in the Amazon was to extract the native products of the tropical forest, such as hardwoods, cacao, and cinnamon, for sale on the European market. It was not very lucrative in comparison with the trade carried on by the Portuguese with Asia. The few colonists attracted to the Amazon region could not afford to purchase slaves from Africa, and few were imported into the region. Instead, the colonist sought the Indigenous populations as household servants, as collectors of forest products, and as agricultural workers to provide food for their settlements. In colonial times, the native Amazonians were the people "who paddled the canoes, who hunted and fished, who worked in the domestic and public services, who raised cattle, who served in the armed forces, who labored in the shipyards," according to Artur Cezar Ferreira Reis (1942:48), the leading student of Amazon colonial history. And the observations of a Portuguese writer in the sixteenth century apply aptly to the Amazon in the seventeenth century. "As soon as persons who intend to live in Brazil," wrote Pedro de Magalhães (1922:41), "become inhabitants of the country, however poor they may be, if one obtains two pair or a half dozen slaves, which might cost somewhere in the neighborhood of ten cruzados, he then has the means of sustenance and crops; so little by little, men become rich and live honorably in the land with more ease than in the Kingdom [Portugal] because these same Indian slaves hunt food for themselves and in this way the men have no expense for the maintenance of their slaves, nor of their own persons." Numerous slave raids called *resgates* were organized in Amazonia, penetrating deep into the

---

frontier is in the farthest reaches of the Brazilian Amazon—on the borders with Peru and Venezuela in particular.] The process of detribalization and of incorporation into Amazon regional society, which began in the early seventeenth century, continues into the present. History in the Amazon is in many respects not a question of an absolute time sequence but one of space. Processes that were completed long ago in the main arteries of the Amazon River system are now occurring in their principal outlines off the beaten track in the Valley.

interior and returning with captured native slaves and leaving behind them men, women, and children massacred in the process. Entire tribes were soon exterminated, and thousands of Indigenous people were brought into the orbit of Luso-Brazilian colonial life.[18]

The appetite of the colonists for slaves soon clashed, however, with the interests of the religious missionaries who came to the Amazon with the first military expeditions. The missionaries, especially the Jesuits, soon established *aldeamentos* (mission villages) at strategic points along the Amazon River and its main tributaries into which they attracted natives from various tribes. Under the close paternalistic régime of the Jesuits, the mission natives were taught catechism and Catholic ritual, new handicrafts, and Old World custom. In a relatively short time thousands of tribal natives were transformed into "Jesuit Indians" living by rules laid down by the Jesuit priests rather than by their aboriginal culture patterns. Christian dogma and Catholic ceremonials were quickly substituted for their native religion, although Indigenous concepts and practices survived alongside the new religion. Even their marriages were supervised by the padres so as not to run counter to Catholic rules of incest and propriety. For a time the missions served to protect numerous Indigenous groups from slave raids. The Portuguese Crown issued numerous edicts prohibiting Indigenous slavery and granting the missionaries full powers over the Indigenous population.

But the scene of battle was far from Europe, and slave-hunting parties even attacked Jesuit missions, carrying off the newly converted Christians as slaves. The colonists found numerous legal loopholes to allow them to enslave natives. They prevailed on the Crown to allow them to make slaves of "prisoners of just wars" and of those who were "ransomed from the cord" (i.e., those who were snatched from the hands of cannibalistic tribes). Just wars and "cannibalism" increased rapidly as soon as these rights were granted. Faced with the necessity of

---

[18]Historian John Hemming (1978:217–37) has called this period in history "anarchy on the Amazon," while the sociologist Pasquale Di Paolo (1990:82) declared that "the Portuguese repression was without precedent, having all the characteristics of genocide" [translation by Pace]. Wagley notes that one Portuguese captain, the infamous Bento Maciel Parente, was accused of killing 500,000 natives during his various expeditions. This he considers an exaggeration, but that he and his men massacred many natives and made many slaves is not to be doubted (see Leite 1938:IV,137).

producing foodstuffs for soldiers and for European colonists, who were not inclined toward manual labor themselves, the Portuguese colonial officials condoned or ignored evasions of the law, and resorted time and time again to forced labor, sending soldiers to bring back Indigenous males for work in Portuguese settlements. Padre Antonio Vieira, whose letters and sermons are classics of Brazilian literature, complained bitterly in letters to the Crown that when missionaries visited native villages, they often found them inhabited by a few half-starved women, children, and old people. The men had been taken off for forced labor during the very months when they should have been planting their own gardens. The men were often away, he wrote, "eight to nine months of the year—without the Mass, without celebrating even a Saint's Day, without [keeping] Lent, without [receiving] the Sacraments, and without being able to make their own gardens" (Leite 1938:IV,52). The Jesuits worked hard to protect the Indigenous populations but, as Roy Nash (1926:106) puts it, "the pocket book emotions of the colonists had been touched deeply." It was a battle "between the Brazilian slave hunters who wanted the Indian's body and the Jesuits (and other missionaries) who wanted his soul in which the aboriginal American was destined to lose both."

The battle was decided, however, in the middle of the eighteenth century when the Marquis of Pombal, who governed with almost absolute powers in Portugal for more than twenty-five years, stripped the missionaries of all temporal power over the Indigenous populations and ordered the Jesuits expelled from Brazil. Pombal issued a series of laws aimed at incorporation of the Indigenous populations, those still living in tribal groups and those of the missions, into colonial life. He ordered that mission stations be transformed into towns and villages. Many important Amazon towns, such as Óbidos, Faro, and Macapá, became civil settlements at this time. Pombal issued decrees that the Portuguese language should be taught instead of the *língua geral*, a modified form of the Indigenous Tupí language, which the missionaries had used in teaching their native converts. There was a conscious policy of stimulating miscegenation between the European and the native. Portuguese male colonists were offered special inducements in the form of land grants, free tools, tax exemptions, and even political posts to marry Indigenous women.

Pombal's reforms were aimed at the assimilation of the Indigenous populations into colonial society and at least theoretically at granting the assimilated native equal rights with the colonials. But freedom for the Indigenous populations was impossible without modification of the Amazonian economic and social system. Someone had to do the work, and the European colonist looked down on manual labor as the work of a slave. Thus the extractive industries and the agriculture that provided food for the colony depended on Indigenous servitude in one form or another. It was necessary to continue compulsory labor during the Pombal regime. It was decreed that all able-bodied native males between the ages of thirteen and sixty were required to register with the government-appointed director of the settlement in which they lived; one-half of the men in each settlement were subjected for some part of the year to forced labor for the Europeans and creoles. The other half were allowed to remain at home to make gardens for themselves. This controlled system soon disintegrated into a form of peonage and debt servitude, and outright slavery persisted in the Amazon region despite laws to the contrary until late in the nineteenth century (Nash 1926:120).

Whereas the protection of the missions had in a sense restrained the process, Pombal's reforms and the continued demands on the Amazon native for labor had the result of stimulating the rate of assimilation of the native into colonial life. By 1821, when Brazil achieved its independence from Portugal, the population of the Amazon Valley was mainly mestizo, and the way of life of the majority of the population was essentially Portuguese, although strongly influenced by the unique Amazonian environment and by the Indigenous cultures that had existed there. A regional culture basically European in its main institutions but strongly influenced by the unique Amazonian environment and by the native cultures of the region had been formed.

The accounts written by nineteenth-century travelers give a picture of the degree to which this process of assimilation and acculturation of the Amazon native had progressed. It is estimated that in 1852 as many as 57 percent of the inhabitants of the Valley were Indigenous and that 26 percent more were mamelucos or Indigenous-European mixtures; the rest were Europeans and Africans. It is evident, however, that these "Indians" and mamelucos were not Indigenous in a social and cultural sense. Their way of life was more Iberian than native. Although the nineteenth-century visitors speak of "Indian custom" and "native life," they actually describe Portuguese customs. Mrs. Agassiz, the wife of the famous Swiss naturalist Louis Agassiz, who led an expedition into the Amazon, speaks of "a hideous old Indian woman who performed the strange rites of crossing herself and throwing kisses into a trunk which contained a print of 'Our Lady of Nazareth'"(Agassiz 1896:181). H. W. Bates, the English naturalist whose account of the Amazon has become a classic, describes the festivals for the patron saint, St. Thereza of Egá, the small village in which he resided for many months. He tells us of the enactment of a folk drama on St. John's eve in which Caypor, a kind of sylvan deity, appeared together with Christian figures—a custom obviously introduced by missionaries to replace aboriginal ceremonies (Bates 1930:284ff.). Herbert Smith's (1879:371–97) short but excellent description of the "semi-civilized Amazonian Indians" near Monte Alegre in the lower Amazon also indicates the strength of Iberian custom. He describes adobe houses rather than the palm-thatched long house of aboriginal times. The music, dancing, and feasting on a saint's day that he mentions is the same as in Gurupá today. The Amazonians gave a "blessing" in good European style, offering their hand and saying, "God bless you my child" (Deus te abençoe). Phenotypically they were "Indigenous," but they were by cultureBrazilians with more in common with the Luso-Brazilian world than with the autochthonous natives still living in the isolated forests of the Amazon. Since the nineteenth century, the descendants of the Amazon Indigenous populations have increasingly been brought into closer touch with regional and national life. They are today citizens of a national state, and their way of life is but a regional variety of a national culture.

The regional culture of Gurupá and of other Amazon communities, as stated earlier, retains many patterns from native heritage. Despite the efforts of the missionaries to make Catholics out of them, many rural Brazilians of the Amazon retain folk beliefs of aboriginal origin. Nowadays in rural neighborhoods, and even in lower-class districts in Amazon cities, shamans (pajés) cure by old native methods. A large number of Tupí terms have been integrated into the Portuguese language as it is spoken in the Brazilian Amazon. The techniques and skills used in hunting and fishing and the folk belief that centers on these pursuits are of Indigenous origin. Indigenous traditions are felt in these and in other spheres of contemporary Amazonian life.

The Indigenous traits that survive as a part of Amazon regional culture are mainly derived from Tupí-speaking tribes. These peoples, who inhabited practically the entire coast of Brazil, and who seemed to be moving inland up the Amazon mainstream at the time of the arrival of the Europeans, were the first tribes with whom the Portuguese had any prolonged contact. It was mainly with Tupí-speaking natives that the Portuguese traded for brazilwood, against whom they made war, and whom they enslaved during the first century of the colonial period. The Tupíans taught the newcomers how to plant "new" crops, and they taught them the names and the utility of the New World flora and fauna. Furthermore, as Gilberto Freyre (1946:15) so picturesquely put it, "No sooner had the European leaped ashore than he found his feet slipping among native women." Portuguese men took native wives and concubines who must have been women from Tupían tribes. The off-spring from these unions, the first Brazilians, raised by their mothers and dominated by their fathers, were carriers of a mixed culture—Tupí and Portuguese—and they were often bilingual. The mamelucos had an important role in the extension of Portuguese control over the Amazon region; and they carried with them customs, knowledge, and beliefs learned from their Indigenous mothers.

Furthermore, during the first century after the arrival of the Europeans in Brazil, Tupí-speaking people were the primary concern of the Catholic missionaries. Most of the earlier descriptions of Brazilian natives were written by missionaries, and they describe the Tupínambá, as the Tupí-speaking coastal tribes were called. Because the missionaries were first faced with Tupí languages, and Tupí speakers must have seemed more numerous to them than the so-called Tapuya (generally Ge-speaking tribes of the interior), the missionaries adopted Tupí as an intermediary language for teaching Christian doctrine, just as Quechua was adopted in Peru and Nahuatl in Mexico. The missionaries learned to speak a Tupí language, and it was reduced to a European script. A generalized and modified form of this language came to be known as *nheengatu* or the língua geral (the general language) and was used for teaching and for preaching Christianity throughout Brazil. Native peoples of other tongues were taught língua geral, and it became the language of the Indigenous-European mestizos and of the natives living in mission stations and in European settlements.

As late as the mid-nineteenth century, perhaps more people spoke língua geral than Portuguese in the Amazon. Bates (1930:282) writes that "Tupí is spoken with little corruption along the main Amazon for a distance of 2,500 miles." Alfred Russel Wallace (1853:169) remarks that in a small settlement near Manaus, "only one of them here could speak Portuguese, all the rest using the Indian language" (i.e., língua geral). Wallace states that near the larger towns and cities, língua geral was "used indiscriminately with Portuguese," and that in the Lower Amazon most people were bilingual, but that above Santarém on the Upper Amazon it was the only language known. It was used by tribal groups who also retained their own language as a means of communicating with traders and with tribes speaking distinct native languages. Not until the late nineteenth century did Portuguese replace língua geral as the language of Amazonia, and even today it is spoken in some isolated areas by partially assimilated natives and mestizos.

With this language, many traditions of Tupí origin spread throughout Amazonia even in areas not inhabited in aboriginal times by Tupían peoples. European concepts transmitted through língua geral were subjected to modification and accretion of aboriginal details in the process. The Christian God and the Devil were given the names (in língua geral) of Tupan and Jurupari. Both took on characteristics of the aboriginal supernaturals of these same names. Witches and werewolves of European medieval belief were easily identified with Tupí forest demons and were also given aboriginal names. Thus, along with the Iberian patterns imposed on and taught to the Amazonian peasant population by their European conquerors, a body of Indigenous culture patterns has persisted in rural culture throughout the Brazilian Amazon. These aboriginal patterns have fused within the fabric of the predominantly Iberian culture to form a way of life, a culture distinctive of the region and well adapted to the particular Amazon environment.

V

Although Gurupá is not an important Amazon town, it has a not unimposing history that reflects practically every major trend in the history of the Amazon Valley. Gurupá is almost as old as Jamestown, Virginia. As early as 1609, a fort was established on the present site of the town by the Dutch.[19] Although the area of the New World in which Gurupá is situated was granted them by the Treaty of Tordesillas in 1494, the Portuguese did not in the sixteenth century have a very firm hold on their New World possessions. Portugal, with a population of a mere

---

[19]According to Kelly (1984:25), Lorimer (1989:52–53), and Borromeu (1946:97), Dutch mariners and traders established a series of three small wooden fortifications along the lower Amazon and Xingú Rivers. On the Xingú River in 1604 they built Orange (also known as Gomoarou and Itacuruçá) located near the current town of Veiros,

one million people in the sixteenth century, had a vast empire and a lucrative trade with Asia. Brazil was necessarily neglected; it had a sparse Indigenous population [following Old World contact and massive depopulation] and its native products, with the exception of brazilwood and a few spices, were not much sought after in Europe. Furthermore, from 1580 to 1640, during the period of "Captivity" when the Portuguese crown passed to the Spanish royal family, Portugal was for all purposes a part of Spain. For these reasons Brazil became fair game for the enemies of Spain. Because the Portuguese lacked the human power and because Spain was occupied on more lucrative fronts, the English, the French, and the Dutch encroached on Brazil. Not only did these countries establish forts and colonies in South Brazil, but by the end of the sixteenth century the Dutch and the English[20] had set up trading posts and forts near the delta on the Amazon River and the French were entrenched at São Luis just south of the mouth of the great river system.

In the late sixteenth century, however, Portugal took a new interest in its New World possessions, especially because sugar cane planted in the rich red earth of the northeastern coast of Brazil began to produce wealth equal to that obtained from Asia. The Portuguese dispatched an armed force to "drive out the foreigners." In 1616 the French were expelled from São Luis and the Portuguese established a fort at Belém in the mouth of the Amazon delta. In the next few years they drove out the English intruders established on the north shores of the great river near its mouth; and in 1623 they captured the Dutch fort at Gurupá, making it a Portuguese stronghold for the control of the lower Amazon. The Dutch attempted to recapture Gurupá in 1639

---

followed by Nassau (known as Materú or Maturú) near the present-day town of Porto de Moz. The third fort, built in 1609, was in Gurupá, or Mariocai (Marú-cai), as the Dutch called the site after the population living there. The Dutch traded for manatee and turtle meat, hides, urucú, timber, cacao, oleaginous seeds, and mother of pearl. They were also interested in the cultivation of sugar cane and tobacco along the Xingú River. The Dutch brought African slaves from Angola with them to do manual labor (Oliveira 1983; Lorimer 1989; Reis 1993). As such, the African presence in the Amazon and likely in Gurupá began nearly as early as the European presence.

[20]According to Lorimer (1989:39–46) the Englishman Sir Thomas Roe explored the area of Gurupá in 1610, searching for the famed city of gold—El Dorado. Between 1611 and 1620 Roe and his associates Matthew Morton and Thomas King, along with an Irishman Phillip Purcell and later Bernard O'Brien, set up a number of English and Irish tobacco plantations just west of Pará Island near Mazagão, Amapá—just to the north of the Great Island of Gurupá.

but failed, and by 1640 the Portuguese had reestablished full control over the lower Amazon region.[21]

---

[21]Kelly (1984) and Lorimer (1989) provide greater detail on these series of events. In 1623 Luís Aranha de Vasconcellos led a force of 74 soldiers and 400 native warriors to expel the Northern European colonists from the general vicinity of Gurupá (Kelly 1984:26). After capturing the Dutch forts of Orange and Nassau along the Xingú River he attacked Mariocai—Gurupá (Moraes Rego 1977:113–17; Kelly 1984:27). The Dutch defended the fort, but were defeated. They fled to the Island of Tucujus (probably the Great Island of Gurupá). Soon after, a Dutch ship with an English captain arrived in Gurupá and the Portuguese attacked and sank it, killing all aboard save one 18-year-old boy (Kelly 1984:27). Vasconcellos returned to Belém, leaving Bento Maciel Parente (the Captain-major of Belém) in control of the area. Parente continued the campaign, attacking the English living on the various islands around the northern boundary with Amapá. The English fled to the nearby Irish settlements where they joined with other Dutch colonists. Vasconcellos returned from Belém and joined Parente to battle the Northern Europeans at a settlement called Okiari. Although inflicting great damage and sinking a ship, the Portuguese were unsuccessful in expelling the Northern Europeans. After the battle, Vasconcellos returned to Portugal while Parente came back to Mariocai (Gurupá). Parente's men build the fort of Saint Anthony. He then left Captain Jerônimo de Albuquerque in command with 50 soldiers and unspecified number of Indigenous troops.
The remaining English, Irish, and Dutch regrouped and under the command of Pieter Jansz, attacked and defeated the Portuguese garrison—eliminating the only Portuguese presence in the region outside of Belém (Lorimer 1989:78–89). They then left Mariocai to build a fort in Mandiutuba, near the Foz of the Xingú River and the Maxipana River (Lorimer 1989:78–89; Kelly 1984:27; Oliveira 1983:172). Under the leadership of Dutch Captain Nicolas Hosdam and the Irish Captain Philip Purcell, the settlement had a fighting force of 200 men (Kelly 1984:28).
In May of 1625 the Portuguese launched a second assault led by Pedro Teixeira with a force of 50 soldiers and 300 Natives. At Mandiutuba they battled for a day and a night, killing between 100 and 114 settlers (Kelly 1984:29). The surviving Dutch and Irish fled by boat and warned the English and Irish spread out on the Great Island of Gurupá about the Portuguese forces. Teixeira pursued them and engaged in a bloody battle at Okiari where his forces killed 60 Northern Europeans, including the leaders Nicolas Hosdam and Phillip Purcell. Teixeira continued on and forced the surrender of another Dutch settlement called Tauregue. Once under the custody of the Portuguese, 45 prisoners were mercilessly massacred. The remaining Dutch fled north to the Guianas, where hostile Caribs killed most of them. The English and Irish survivors, however, evaded the attacks and slipped quietly into the interior where they remained with their Indigenous allies without doubt producing descendants (Lorimer 1989:83–84).
The last attack on Gurupá occurred in 1629 when the English Captain Roger North failed to take the fort and was repelled by Teixeira (Borromeu 1946:89). Two more military engagements involving the garrison occurred, the first in 1639 when soldiers surprised and captured a Dutch war ship near the town of Gurupá and the second in 1697 when the garrison helped stop a French invasion at Macapá (Kelly 1984:29, 69; Hemming 1978:583–85).

The population grew in the shadow of the Portuguese fort at Gurupá, and by 1639 the settlement was given the status of a "town" or *vila*.[22] Numerous Indigenous groups were attracted to the growing settlement, and the Portuguese soldiers at the fort took Indigenous wives. These Portuguese-Indigenous families were the basis of the new town's population.[23] It is reported that Carmelite missionaries were established there by 1654. In the next year the Jesuits arrived. Both of these missionary groups brought Indigenous groups to the settlement, and the Jesuits soon formed "mission villages" in the near vicinity. They also used the town as a base of operation for the founding of other mission villages upriver.[24] The small town continued to grow by attracting Indigenous

---

[22]At this point in time Gurupá was one of only five captaincies (a geopolitical division created to oversee settlement and development) in the entire Amazon (Kelly 1984:72). A permanent fort was constructed and according to Borromeu (1946:89–90), the Carmelites built their convent in 1646.

[23]The Indigenous groups living in the vicinity of Gurupá at the time of contact, such as the Mariocai and the Tapuyusus and Icares of the islands and terra firme to the north, did not survive. Although the reports are sketchy, we know that the English and Irish aided their Indigenous allies in attacks on their native rivals—resulting in many deaths. We also have reports of Indigenous groups allied to the Dutch, English, and Irish fighting against the Portuguese and being devastated (Lorimer 1989:245). In other words the groups in and around Gurupá were very much involved in the European wars of conquest and suffered the consequences. It is also certain that Old World diseases created overwhelming death. Together with slavery, these catastrophes eliminated the rich cultures these groups possessed and left few, if any survivors, except for the offspring of Indigenous-European unions who had a better chance of surviving disease.

[24]Historic research postdating Wagley's study offers additional details about Gurupá. In 1652 the Portuguese Crown permitted the Jesuits to establish a religious mission in Gurupá after Padre Antônio Vieira visited the community (Kelly 1984:38; Kiemen 1954:80). Borromeu records two versions of what happened next. In one version, the Carmelites built a convent and constructed the first church in 1654. In the second version the Jesuits were first to come to Gurupá in 1655. In this version, Padre Vieira sent two Jesuit missionaries, Padre Salvador do Vale and Padre Paulo Luiz, to Gurupá with 100 natives freed from slavery (Borromeu 1946:90; Kelly 1984:40). The priests built the church of Our Lady of Exile and the *aldeia* (village) of Tapará for the natives, all close to the fort (Borromeu 1946:90). Conflict over control of native slaves followed and the colonists expelled the two priests. The colonial governor arrested the perpetrators of the incident, sending two to Portugal for trial and exiling two others to the southern colony in Brazil. After the incident one of the missionaries returned and resumed work in the general area.

By 1656 the Jesuits established a mission named Saint Peter close to the fort in Gurupá. They populated the mission through pacification efforts and slave raids.

For the former they offered European trade goods to natives in exchange for relocation. For the latter, missionaries accompanied slavers on their raids to claim a share of the captives. One example took place in 1658. Gurupá's Captain-major, accompanied by a missionary, led an expedition of 45 Portuguese soldiers and 450 Native Americans to the Tocantins River. They attacked and enslaved members of the Inheyguaras as punishment for unspecified past deeds. Such punitive raids on Indigenous populations originating from Gurupá continued until the beginning of the nineteenth century (Kiemen 1954:103; Kelly 1984:40–41).

Jesuit control over the economy created constant tension with the colonists. In 1661 the colonists revolted in a regional uprising and Gurupá's priest, a German named John Felipe Betendorf, went into hiding to escape the colonists (Hemming 1978:342). When he returned to Gurupá several settlers attempted to arrest the priest. The Captain-major of the fort, however, protected him and arrested and hung the principal anti-Jesuit agitators after they confessed to Betendorf (Betendorf 1909: 275–76; Kelly 1984:46; Hemming 1978:342). In the following year Belém's town council sent a large task force to arrest Betendorf and two other Jesuits who had taken refuge at Gurupá. The Captain-major was unable to intervene, although some colonists tried and failed to defend the Jesuits (Kelly 1984:67). One colonist died in the confrontation, a Gurupí native named Saraiva. An African slave belonging to Antônio da França also tried to defend the Jesuits. The slave was credited with saving the lives of many colonists on that day (Salles 1988:17). With the arrest of Gurupá's missionaries, all Jesuit missionaries in the Amazon Valley were in custody of the colonists.

The Crown rescinded Jesuit control over Native Americans in 1663. The colonial government gave the mission of Saint Peter to the colonists. The Jesuits of Gurupá eventually established another mission farther into the interior sometime around 1670 to minimize the colonists' interference (Kelly 1984:47). In 1667 when Padre Gaspar Misch visited Gurupá to retrieve a bell that the Captain-major Antônio Pacheco had taken, he found the aldeia of Tapará in decay (Borromeu 1946:91). At that point a rivalry spanning two decades developed between the religious order and the Captain-major of the fort, Manuel Guedes Aranha. The Jesuits refused to send priests to minister to the local garrison, residents of Gurupá, or to the mission of Saint Peter (Kiemen 1954:174). Later in 1687 or 1688, Aranha raided a Jesuit mission in an adjoining captaincy and apparently confiscated the Indigenous workers (Kelly 1984:67). In 1692 Aranha disrupted the missionary work of Padre John Mary Gorsony and told the Indigenous groups united in Gurupá to leave the parish (Borromeu 1946:92).

In 1693 the Jesuits where forced to give up the mission at Gurupá to the Franciscans of Piety (Moreira Neto 1992:92–93; Kelly 1984:53). The Mother Church (*igreja matriz*) of St. Anthony of Gurupá was established, becoming the second parish in the state of Pará (Borromeu 1946:92). Over the next 60 years the mission system of Gurupá deteriorated greatly. By 1743 the French naturalist Charles de la Condamine passed through Gurupá and commented that the only Native Americans there were the slaves of the colonists. Six years later Gonçalves da Fonseca reported that successive epidemics of smallpox and measles had eliminated the Indigenous population at Saint Peter (Hemming 1978:445). Other correspondence from this time reported that a second mission established upstream from Gurupá, Saint Joseph of Arapijo (located at Carrazedo), received little attention (Kelly 1984:101).

groups from the nearby missions into its orbit, but not always by peaceful means.[25] In 1667 the capitão-mor at Gurupá is said to have treated a group of Taconhapé, who had been "persuaded" to travel downriver to Belém to work on the construction of the Santa Casa de Misericórdia (a hospital), so brutally that they fled into the forest never to reappear. On another occasion the capitão-mor at Gurupá ordered the missionized natives in the vicinity dispersed by force, a reflection of the battle between the Jesuits and the colonists who were backed by the government. As early as 1692 the Jesuits were forced out of Gurupá, and the religious life of the town was handed over to the monks of Piedade, a less aggressive and less powerful religious order.

The situation of Gurupá on a bluff commanding a wide view of the Amazon main channel gave it considerable strategic importance. Boats moving up and down the river were required to stop at Gurupá to pay taxes, and the little fort was an effective point of control against the possible encroachments of foreigners.[26] Because Gurupá was a control station, most travelers on the Amazon had to stop there, and many writers mention the town briefly. The French scientist Charles de la Condamine visited Gurupá for three days in 1743 and was given the

---

[25]Gurupá played an infamous role in Amazon slavery as it served as a major staging ground for raids conducted upriver and downriver (Kelly 1984:66). The slavers brought many of those captured to the community and forced them into extractive activities and food production. Around 1650 it is believed that most people living in Gurupá were involved in the slave trade (Moreira Neto 1992:78–79). Gurupá was frequently visited by *bandeirantes* (literally flag bearers—in Brazil they are seen as pioneers opening up the frontier) traveling up from São Paulo in the search for gold and slaves. One famous bandeirante to visit Gurupá was António Rapôso Tavares, who passed through the town in 1651 at the end of his famous 11,000 kilometer trek to the Andes and back.

The government established a regional prison at Gurupá because the settlement was sufficiently isolated (Kelly 1984:69–70). Among those imprisoned were Captain João de Souto (who tortured a leader of a mission village) and Captain-major Sebastião de Lucena de Azevedo (who enslaved Indigenous populations illegally and wrote openly about the fact in Portugal). Also imprisoned in Gurupá was the Indigenous leader Lope de Sousa Guaguaíba, who angered Father Vieira in Belém by marrying his own sister-in-law (Kelly 1984:70; Kiemen 1954:67–68; Hemming1978:340–41).

[26]Because individuals from the military garrison, prison, and checkpoint/tax station for the river had enough financial resources to buy African slaves, Gurupá's African population grew to represent 31 percent of the town's population at the time of the first population census in 1783 (Kelly 1984:143, 157). The African slaves worked as household servants and in agriculture.

hospitality due an honored guest by the commander of the fort and other local authorities. In 1758 Governor Francisco Xavier de Mendoça visited the town. He reported that Gurupá was a center of Portuguese influence in the lower Amazon. Many former mission natives had been attracted to Gurupá.[27] At the beginning of the nineteenth century, the town of Gurupá contained "86 fires (individual families) or 564 souls. According to the famous German scientist Karl von Martius, who visited Gurupá in 1819, these people were either a mixture of the "Indigenous race" with Portuguese or "pure Indians." Their houses were for the most part palm-thatched structures. The place seemed isolated and abandoned. One of the townspeople remarked to von Martius that things had been better in the time of Pai-Tucura (Father Grasshopper), as the Indigenous groups called the Capuchin monk who had lived there. The garrison had been reduced and the activities of the religious orders had been curtailed by the laws issued by Pombal. Although there is mention of plantations of cacao and coffee near Gurupá, the people seemed to devote themselves mainly to the collection of sarsaparilla and native cacao, which was found in abundance in the delta islands near the town.[28]

---

[27]During the period, known as the Directorate (1754-1799) when the Jesuits were expelled from Brazil and the mission system secularized, Gurupá served as an administrative center, a checkpoint for river trade, and maintained its prison and fort. The 1783 census classified Gurupá as one of 21 *branco* towns in the colony of Grão Pará (meaning the settlement consisted of people of European descent and mixed descent, but lacked many Native Americans and made no reference to African slaves). The population figures for the missions of Saint Peter and Saint Joseph of Arapijo, renamed Saint Joseph of Carrazedo, were listed separately. The census classified both missions as Native American places without Europeans/brancos, two of nineteen in the colony. The 1784 census described the mission of Carrazedo as possessing a church that was about to fall down, although the residents' homes were in good condition (Kelly 1984:146).

In the early 1760s, a Padre Queiros spent Holy Week in Gurupá and noted that all construction work on the fort of Saint Anthony had stopped due to a lack of manioc flour (Kelly 1984:130). The missions of Saint Peter and Carrazedo also suffered due to epidemics of small pox and measles as well as high rates of defection from the mission (Kelly 1984:115). The soldiers stationed at Gurupá (100 Luso-Brazilian soldiers and 150 racially mixed soldiers) were active in these seek-and-destroy missions to recapture runaway native and African slaves (Kelly 1984:162, 164). It is likely they were attacking the first quilombos established in the region.
[28]Wagley does not mention the Cabanagem Revolt that took place between 1822 and 1836 in the Amazon. The revolt grew out of long-term political and racial tensions that turned violent many times after independence from Portugal (1821) and gradually

In 1842 Gurupá had but two streets with two squares.[29] As in other Amazon settlements, one section of the town was inhabited by the Indigenous groups and their descendants and was known as the "village" (aldeia). The other section was called the "city" (cidade), and there the Europeans and mestizos, who were merchants, government officials, landowners, and artisans, lived.[30] The city evidently grew at the expense

---

faded away without a last decisive battle (Cleary 1998; Harris 2010). The struggle was probably the bloodiest uprising in all of Brazilian history (claiming the lives of 20,000 to 30,000 people—15 to 25 percent of the total population) and the longest lasting rebellion against the Imperial government. It was the only revolt where the rebels completely took over the government and even negotiated with foreign powers (Cleary 1998; Harris 2010). The protagonists of the revolt were *cabanos,* a political and ethnic cover term for mestizos and detribalized natives (often called *tapuias*), as well as freed and enslaved African Brazilians, all of whom were forming a new peasantry (Moreira Neto 1992:271; Pinheiro 2001:81). Many of the cabanos, especially the tapuias, were the grandchildren of people who had left the aldeias during the Directorate. Many spoke lingual geral, despite it being outlawed, as well as Portuguese.

Because Gurupá had a fort and military garrison, cabano forces did not take the town until 1836 (Hurley 1936; Harris 2010:248). However, after the revolt, Gurupá served one of nine military commands for brutal seek-and-destroy missions to eliminate all remnants of the uprising (Di Paolo 1990:335). Some historians have labeled the postrevolt Imperial repression a virtual war of extermination with undeniable racist intentions (Cleary 1998:128).

[29]Post-Cabanagem Gurupá was a miserable place. For example, in 1839 a draft labor program called the *Corpo de Trabalhadores* (the Workers' Corp) required "idle" men (landless or unemployed) to work in state-sponsored public works projects or private enterprises (Kelly 1984:252–53; Weinstein 1983:42). Gurupá was one site (of a total of nine) for this forced labor system and conscripted 608 men by 1848 (Kelly 1984:276). The program quickly degraded into pseudo slavery, with the military commanders obtaining a near monopoly on recruits who were forced into rowing, building canoes, and extracting forest products (Kelly 1984: 176). In another example, in 1842 a Portuguese Lieutenant-Colonel Antônio Ladislau Monteiro Beana reported the poor state of repair of the church that was made of mud and plaster with a tile roof and lacking a belfry, the shortage of manioc that had to be imported, the degenerate state of the military in which 436 men out of 574 had no uniforms or arms, and the misery people lived in despite the abundance their surroundings offered (Kelly 1984:262–65). Beana continued that the town consisted of only two streets running parallel to the river with two grassy cross streets. The mission was in ruins. Most of the houses in town were roofed with palm thatch except for four with tile roofs. In 1846 the French naturalist Francis de Castelnau described Gurupá's houses as poorly constructed, the church as very old, and the fort possessing some obsolete cannons. Castelnau lamented that local inhabitants followed his group around begging for food (Kelly 1984:272).

[30]"Nearly every Amazonian town is divided into cidade and aldeia, the 'city' and the 'village'; the former the modern town; the latter, the original native settlement from which it sprang" (Smith1879:118).

of the village, for as people took on Iberian language and custom they lost their identity as Indigenous peoples and as "slaves." A visitor to Gurupá in 1850 estimated its population as 715 people, of which 482 were classified as "white or mestizo," and only 233 as "slaves" (i.e., Indigenous people).[31] The travelers who paused at Gurupá during the last decades of the nineteenth century mention it only in passing; the town had evidently lost its importance as a customs post, and it is said that the fort was entirely abandoned.

But at the end of the century, with the advent of wild rubber as an important export product, Gurupá seems to have regained some of its past prominence. From 1900 to 1912, the Amazon Valley held a virtual monopoly on rubber production. During this period the Valley was fabulously prosperous. There was a dramatic headlong rush for the "liquid gold"; there was a stampede to purchase rubber forests. A large number of people from northeastern Brazil, where droughts occurring every ten to twelve years caused thousands of people to die of thirst, starvation, or pestilence or to migrate, were attracted to the Amazon as rubber gatherers. The influx into the Amazon was so great in the last part of the nineteenth century that the population of Manaus, which was 5,000 in 1879, was 50,000 in 1890; and Belém, which was only 15,000 in 1848, was over 100,000 in 1890 (Denis 1914:358). The population of the Valley is thought to have doubled from 1850 to 1900. Money was plentiful. A splendid opera house was built in Manaus, halfway up the Amazon River, and opera companies from Europe braved the dangers of yellow fever and malaria to play there. Imitations of European town houses and villas, totally unsuited to the tropical climate, were built in Belém and Manaus with rubber wealth. People imported their clothes from abroad, and many persons are said to have sent their fancy dresses and dress shirts to Lisbon to have them laundered. There was gambling, exploitation of newcomers, prostitution, and lawlessness of all kinds.

The delta islands in front of Gurupá contained rich stands of rubber trees second in their yield only to the headwaters of the Amazon tributaries and the territory of Acre. Gurupá therefore became the center of an active commerce stimulated by the high prices of rubber.[32]

---

[31] According to Kelly's (1984) research, the slaves cited in 1850 were likely of African descent.

[32] In the early years of the boom, Gurupá was one of four municipalities that produced most of rubber for the entire Amazon region (Weinstein 1983:52). Gurupá's share of

The population grew to more than two thousand. Twenty general stores were opened. At the height of the boom, from 1909 to 1910, a weekly newspaper was printed and published. Advertisements in the *Correio de Gurupá*, as it was called, indicate the prosperity, the active social life, and the preoccupation of the townspeople with the outside world during this period. Such stores as the Bola de Oiro (the Golden Ball), the Bazaar, and the Casa Borralho advertised merchandise recently arrived from Belém and abroad. A barber shop called the "15th of November" announced "hair tonics of the finest quality" and advised its clients that no calls for services outside the shop were accepted but that "subscriptions might be paid monthly in advance" for shaves and haircuts. Each week Professor Antenor Madeira offered in a sedate announcement private lessons in Portuguese, French, Latin, arithmetic, algebra, geography, and history. There were editorials on the dangers of the growing independence of women in the United States and on the position of Brazil in the international scene. A local poet writing under the name of Tula published a piece each week or so. It is evident from the news stories that Gurupá people were intensely interested in local and state politics. One editorial accused the women of a local religious brotherhood of praying to the saints to punish the leaders of the political opposition. The editorial asked that the saints be kept out of politics and demanded also that the local priest refrain from political topics in his sermons.

The social notices in the *Correio de Gurupá* tell of birthday parties, the coming and going of important men and their families, and of receptions for important visitors. In December of 1909, for example, the

---

regional rubber production declined as new rubber fields opened farther west in the Xingú and Tapajós River Valleys. Between 1865 and 1900, Gurupá's rubber export increased nearly twenty-fourfold—from 23,140 kilograms to 408,124 kilograms (Kelly 1984:342; Weinstein 1983:190). During the same time Gurupá exported animal pelts, tanned hides, cacao, nuts, capaibla oil, sarsaparilla, and tobacco (Kelly 1984:3342), although these commodities took on increasingly minor roles in the economy as the rubber boom progressed. In 1862 there were also twelve cattle ranches with a total of 6,548 head of cattle and horses. The ranches employed thirty-nine free workers and seven slaves (Kelly 1984:326).

During the "golden years" (1880–1910) of the rubber boom, immigrants from the drought-stricken northeastern Brazil swelled Gurupá's population, replacing many of the rubber tappers from Gurupá who had moved to the middle and upper Amazon in search of better quality rubber trees. Northeasterners' immigration increased the total Amazonian population by 400 percent (from 323,000 to 1,217,000) between 1870 and 1910. This increase effectively occupied vast areas of the region (Santos 1980:109, 115).

intendente (equivalent to the mayor) offered a banquet of fifty places at which two wines and champagne were served in honor of the birthday of Senator Antonio Lemos, the most prominent politician of the state of Pará. In January of 1910, the owner of the Casa Borralho, Coronel Filomeno Cesar de Andrade, offered a birthday party for his two daughters at which there were "dances and games for prizes until late into the night." Old people who remember these days in Gurupá tell of balls held in the two-story *palacetes* of the local rubber barons of the day. At these balls an orchestra played in a large entrance hall for two rooms of dancers, one containing the "first-class" invitees and the other the "second class" or the "people." In the first-class room champagne, wines, beer, imported liquors, fine cakes, and many varieties of Brazilian sweets were served. In the other room *cachaça* (strong sugar rum) and occasionally beer were the drinks, and *beijús* (manioc cakes) and *brôa de polvilho* (muffins of tapioca flour) were served instead of cakes. Often, however, *beijú chica* (a fine manioc cake), a soft drink of *guaraná*, and other regional dishes were served to all, transgressing class difference. Despite the desire to be cosmopolitan, the upper class of Gurupá was regional in formation.

Old people also tell of a demimonde in Gurupá during this epoch. There were several gambling houses where the *seringueiros* (the rubber collectors) from the Islands might spend their pay. And, in common with most Amazon towns during the rubber boom, Gurupá boasted at least one house of prostitution. Old men today speak of a lively night life when they were young. There were long evenings of conversation and drinking in the common room of the bawdy house—for Brazilian houses of prostitution have always been a place for social gathering of young men. They tell of serenades that lasted far into the morning hours. Everyone agrees that the difference between the tempo of social life in Gurupá in those days and now is that between night and day. Today people enjoy the simple occasions of festivals and dances, but they complain that the town is dead and that all the lively young men have moved away to Belém.

Among the varied foreign groups who came to the Amazon in the early part of this century, attracted by the rubber commerce, were a number of Jews from North Africa.[33] Just how many came to the

---

[33]According to Kelly (1984:378) and Barham and Coomes (1994b:49), in the late 1800s most of these merchants were of Portuguese descent, whereas at the turn of the century a large population of Moroccan and Spanish Jews came to dominate much of Gurupá's commerce.

Amazon is not known, but a synagogue was formed in Belém and they opened commercial houses in many Amazon towns. Gurupá became a well-known center for these Jewish immigrants. The *Almanac do Pará*, an official publication, states that as early as 1889, six of the fourteen commercial houses in Gurupá were owned by Hebrews. Such names as Aben Athar,[34] Levi, Bensabeth, and Azulay were important in community affairs in the early days of this century. The Jews had an important role in Gurupá life. They were "strong" commercial families, and two *Hebraicos* were mayor of the town. Today one of Gurupá's most successful native sons, of whom all are proud, is a descendant of one of the Jewish families. Yet the remaining Jewish family in Gurupá tells of occasional hostility against the Jews in former times. It was a sport of youthful drinking companions "to give the Hebrews a beating," and one elderly man recounted with some gaiety the story of the sacking of the Jewish-owned Bazaar by a group of young drunks. Such hostility, however, seems to have been related to the intense political feelings of the times, for our storyteller also remembered that the young men were instigated by a politician whom the Jewish store owner had opposed in an election. Today the Jewish cemetery, which is well kept and clear of weeds, attests to the strong Jewish families who once lived there.[35] Dona Deborah, the widow of the last Jewish merchant, sees to it that it is cared for. She is the only orthodox Hebrew in town; her sons and daughters have all married into the Catholic faith.

It was during the last years of the rubber boom that the fabulous Gurupá town hall was initiated. It was planned as the largest building on the lower Amazon. An Italian engineer arrived to draw the plans for the building and to supervise its construction. It was to be two stories high and there was to be a majestic staircase from the second story to the public square that faced the Amazon. By 1912 the basic framework of the structure was completed. According to local legend, the building was not finished then because the mayor expropriated for the town hall

---

[34]Gurupá's municipal hospital is named Jamie Aben Athar. The descendants of the Aben Athar family have changed their names to Benathar, but remain proud of their Hebrew background.

[35]In 2013 the Jewish cemetery is still maintained, although many of the graves are in poor condition. The cemetery contains some 23 graves, most inscribed in Hebrew, which date between 1905 and 1915.

the stone building materials that had been accumulated to build a church for St. Benedict, the saint to whom the people of Gurupá had become intensely devoted. "The saint put a *maldição* [curse] on the building," the town's people still say. Quite obviously, the saint was aided by the rubber crash in 1912, which put an end to such public extravagance and caused the demise of most of the local commercial establishments.

VI

The collapse of the Amazon rubber industry came as a shock to the people of the Amazon Valley. During the boom years, people were optimistic. The Almighty, it seemed to everyone, had especially blessed the region with "black gold." Even the tropical climate was described as one especially favorable to humans and superior to the cold Temperate Zone. As late as 1909, people in the Amazon were able to say:

> We need not concern ourselves about the Indian-rubber plantations which have sprung up in Asia. The special climatic conditions of the Amazon Valley, the new system of treating our product, now being applied with such success to our crops of hevea, the vast expanse of our Indian-rubber districts, some of which have not yet been exploited, and finally the manifold needs of modern industry, enable us to pay little heed to what others are doing in the same line of business. Indeed, were it not our duty to keep our eyes on the scientific discoveries relating to Indian rubber, we could well afford to disregard foreign plantations altogether. (Album do Estado do Pará 1910:182)

In 1912, as the world knows, the bubble broke. Some years earlier, Henry Wickham Steed had taken rubber seeds out of Brazil to Kew Gardens in London. From these tender plants, the rubber plantations of Ceylon and Malaya were formed. At first the Asian plantations were not too successful; there were difficulties in adapting the Brazilian seedlings to the Asiatic environment. But by 1910 the Asian rubber plantations began to be rewarding. Under plantation conditions a variety of rubber tree was developed that produces more latex than the native *Hevea brasiliensis*. Labor is cheaper and more plentiful in Asia. In 1910 Asia produced only 9 percent of the world's supply of rubber; by 1913 its production equaled that of the Amazon Valley. In the years that followed, the Asian plantations gradually surpassed the Amazon both in production and in price.[36]

After 1912 the Amazon economic structure fell apart, and the optimism and ostentation of the boom years disappeared. Most of the commercial houses of Belém and Manaus collapsed in the 1912 crash, and a chain reaction of economic disaster extended down to the rural traders and to their collectors. The entire commercial system, which was overextended and depended on credit advances from top to bottom, was highly vulnerable. Trading posts were abandoned or continued to do business on a small scale with little stock. Collectors were allowed to leave the rubber fields. Many returned to Ceará; others settled on the traders' land as subsistence farmers; and a few eked out an existence by continuing to collect rubber or other products, such as Brazil nuts, which brought a higher price. Communications with Europe, North America, and southern Brazil became less frequent. The opera house at Manaus was closed, and the public facilities of both Belém and Manaus slowly deteriorated. The population of many small towns suddenly dwindled, for people left to look for work elsewhere or returned to the northeast. In many small towns houses were emptied and abandoned. Soon their streets were dotted with structures caving in from neglect, and the rural population outside the cities and towns lived again in isolation.

---

[36]Weinstein (1983) and Barham and Coomes (1994a, 1994b) propose that merchants and landowners of the Amazon opposed plantation rubber for four main reasons. First, the Amazon's monopoly on world rubber production and the immense stretches of untapped rubber trees did little to impart a sense of urgency to change to a plantation system. Second, merchants/landowners and even international firms had a difficult time inducing workers to cultivate trees. Extraction paid better and rubber tappers retained enough independence in the geographically dispersed and decentralized rubber economy to avoid plantation work (Barham and Coomes 1994a:100). Third, the opportunity costs of capital investment in plantations were prohibitively high and would require a long period to develop. Merchants reasoned, why invest in such a venture when much higher returns on investments were available from wild rubber extraction (Coomes and Barham 1994b:254)? Fourth, the huge profits gained through rubber production enabled the merchants, not the landowning class, to control the regional political economy (Weinstein 1983:34). Simultaneous to this change, the significance of landownership as a source of wealth ebbed as control of exchange relations became the key to the system (Weinstein 1983:49; Bunker 1985:67–68). With such an extraordinary ascendency to power it is little wonder why the merchant class did not embrace rubber plantations and the likelihood of loss of their privileged position (Weinstein 1983:224).

The Amazon Valley, so prosperous and seemingly with such a brilliant future during the first decade of this century [twentieth century], became in a short time isolated and poor. A profound pessimism settled over the region, which was reflected in the attitudes of the inhabitants. Their pessimism influenced in turn the opinions of outsiders who visited the Valley. "The Amazon," wrote one highly gifted local essayist, "has been until now the main victim of its own greatness" (Ladislau 1933:29). Backwardness was explained as "not the fault of man but the fault of the [physical] environment" (Moog 1936:81). Health conditions, which of course became worse owing to lack of medical supplies in the interior, seemed to everyone an insoluble problem. Economic abandon and isolation were charged to the many difficulties that God had created as part of the Amazon environment.

The years 1912 to 1942 were bitter ones for Gurupá, as for most of the Amazon Valley.[37] The political administration that took over just after the rubber crash sold the building materials that had been accumulated to finish the town hall. Even parts of the unfinished structure were demolished to be sold for cash. Numerous families moved away shortly after 1912. Merchants closed their stores and left town either bankrupt or discouraged. The rural population of the community turned

---

[37]In Gurupá, as other parts of the Amazon, access to land after the bust cushioned the decline of rubber tappers. Widespread starvation, epidemics, or insurrections did not happen in the region (Santos 1980:278). Rather, extractors' standard of living fell incrementally. Agroextractivists spent more time in subsistence production but also continued extracting forest goods for sale because they needed income to pay for industrial goods that had become necessities (firearms, cloth, housewares, medicines) and for supplementary food (Weinstein 1983:246).

The economic decline affected landowners and trading posts owners more gravely. Their economic circumstances fell to conditions close to poverty, at times indistinguishable from the extractors. Many landowners sold their land for little to no profit and moved away. Many trading posts closed as they lost access to goods and credit from their suppliers that were greatly weakened or that closed down as well. For the trading posts that managed to stay in business, the ability to generate credit for *freguesia* (customer group) seriously declined. Without credit, landowners and merchants could not maintain debt relations and their ability to control workers. As a result, labor mobility increased. Most landowner/merchants lost most of their freguesia and had to rely on strengthened paternalistic relationships to secure the labor of those workers who remained (Weinstein 1983:245). By the 1930s system stabilized, although in a much weaker form, and the system continued to struggle along.

from rubber collection back to subsistence agriculture. The population of the town declined abruptly, and by 1920 there were only three hundred people living there. The ox-cart road leading from the town to the headwaters of the nearby streams was abandoned and soon became overrun with weeds. The gas (carbide) lighting system that had illuminated the streets during the good years fell into disrepair. Homes and public buildings were empty and soon began to tumble in from lack of protection against the steady work of termites.

In 1929, when two journalists from Belém visited Gurupá, the town had reached the depths of decadence and abandon. At that time it almost might have been described as a ghost town. The writers' stories that were published in the *Folha do Norte*, the foremost newspaper of Belém, mention the dangers of traversing the boardwalk leading to the municipal dock. A few planks were missing, others were rotten, and the whole structure wobbled dangerously. One of these observers, a well-known writer who signed himself "João da Selva" (John of the Forest), called Gurupá an "ex-city on whose streets are grouped the ruins of houses and a few others which are gradually crumbling." He mentions the unfinished town hall and writes that the building serving as a "town hall" at the time "is not worth even classification as a 'decaying house,' for it is literally falling to pieces." The other journalist objects; he found the same building no better than a "stable for goats." The building that once held the gas plant, wrote João da Selva, was but "four walls which the wind has no wish to uncover so that the sky might be testimony to what has happened inside."

In the salon of the ruins of a once fine residence, João da Selva noticed a harp with a few strings and the remains of a grand piano, now half destroyed by termites; the room containing these "memories of civilization" was being used at the time as a stable for a cow. He describes his walk ("Whatever else was there to do?") along a tortuous path to "what they called the Third Street." There he was shown the decaying remains of a hearse, "a first-class hearse as good as those of the Santa Casa in Belém which some mayor purchased out of pity for the poor corpses carried to the cemetery in a hand-barrow or in a hammock." Evidently the hearse had been too wide to pass along the trail leading to the cemetery; and after the rubber crash, the trail was not widened. Again a hammock strung between two poles served to carry the people of Gurupá to their graves. João da Selva was anxious to leave Gurupá, but it was not so easy to escape. In the old days all river steamers paid a call at Gurupá, but now the *Moacyr*, the riverboat on which he had intended to leave, passed majestically down the center of the Amazon without bothering to stop.

Not all Amazon towns reached so low an ebb, but most communities of the region felt the effects of the economic abandonment of the Valley in one form or another. Almost all towns declined in population. The system of transportation, which was mainly by riverboat, slowly began to suffer from the lack of replacement of equipment, and communication between the various centers was less frequent. Steamships from Europe and from southern Brazil to Belém and to Manaus became more and more infrequent, and contact with the outside world diminished. The municipal and state coffers were empty, for the principal source of income had been rubber. The municipal facilities of many towns fell into disrepair. Rural schools often closed for lack of teachers. Even the cities of Belém and Manaus deteriorated during this period. When World War II brought travelers from all the world through Belém, the British-owned electric-light system of the city was in such bad condition that there was insufficient energy to drive the streetcars; and electric power was lacking for hours almost every evening. The streets of Belém were full of holes, and a sewer system that had never been completed was more effective as a breeding place for mosquitoes than as a mechanism for waste disposal. Belém was still using an antiquated telephone system with the old farm-type crank signal system. In the Brazilian Amazon there were short intervals of temporary relief during the period from 1912 to 1942 because of the occasional activities of an energetic politician, a bit of federal aid, or a slight rise in the prices of forest products; but as a whole it was a time of isolation, of slow disintegration, and of increasing poverty.

World War II brought a new epoch to the Amazon Valley. When the rubber plantations of Asia fell into Japanese hands, the Allies turned frantically to the Amazon region for natural rubber. Large sums of money and tremendous efforts were expended in a campaign to increase the production of rubber. The Rubber Development Corporation, a wartime agency of the United States Government, cooperated with the Brazilian Government in improving communications and transportation, in importing trade materials necessary for rubber gathering, in extending credit to producers, and in other enterprises designed to increase production. Taking advantage of a drought in the arid northeast, a large number of refugees were transported into the

Amazon Valley to provide labor for rubber production. Wild rubber was shipped by air from Manaus to the United States. Technicians, many of whom had considerable experience in Asia, flooded into Belém and Manaus and spread out over the Valley. This wartime rubber campaign, however, was not a success. The rubber production of the Brazilian Amazon, which was about 19,000 tons in 1940, increased to only some 25,000 tons in 1944.

The failure of the rubber-development program was due to several causes. First, the very nature of the wild-rubber industry makes for limitations in its development. The trees are spaced wide apart in the forest and the collection of the latex is therefore an arduous and time-consuming occupation. Second, the opening of new (or the reopening of old) rubber trails in the Amazon calls for an intimate knowledge of the terrain and of the process of wild-rubber collection. The inexperienced laborers brought in from the Brazilian northeast and from elsewhere in the country lacked the experience of the Amazon ribeirinho and they were unable to clear trails that were productive. The time was too short and the experienced rubber collectors too few to seriously increase total production. Finally, the campaign was unsuccessful because the experts and administrators from southern Brazil and from abroad did not understand Amazon society. They were unaware of the incentives that would have stimulated the Amazon rural population to greater efforts, and they misunderstood the traditional force of the Amazon commercial system, which they saw as too inefficient and exploitative, and thus as a barrier to a greater rubber output.

But the rubber campaign brought numerous benefits to the Brazilian Amazon. Rubber prices were relatively high, and people were able to buy a few manufactured items that were imported into the region. The Brazilian Government took a new interest in the Valley. As early as 1940, President Getúlio Vargas had promised a renewed national interest in the area in a speech given at Manaus; and beginning with the war, serious steps were taken to implement his promises. In 1942 the SESP (Serviço Especial de Saúde Pública - Special Public Health Service) was formed by international agreement between Brazil and the United States as part of their joint war effort. One of the major programs of the SESP was a gigantic public health program in the Amazon states of Brazil. By 1949 the SESP had established health posts in thirty Amazon towns and hospitals in Breves and Santarém, two important centers of the Lower Amazon. In addition to giving medical assistance to a large portion of the Amazon population, the SESP had installed water-supply systems in several small Amazon communities, constructed over 8,000 sanitary privies throughout the Valley, and built a system of dikes and drainage canals in and near Belém that both reclaimed land and protected the city against malaria. The SESP set up a system of regular spraying of domiciles with DDT,[38] which as early as 1948 protected some 40,000 homes and public buildings in 146 communities.[39]

Gurupá felt the effects of reawakening federal and worldwide interest in the Amazon Valley as early as 1943. Although not an important population center, Gurupá's strategic location on the Amazon mainstream again served it well. Because it was an excellent center from which a large rural population might be reached along the Lower Amazon and in the delta, the SESP established a health post at Gurupá in late 1943. A laboratory technician was first stationed there to collect mosquitoes and to distribute Atabrine, the most efficient antimalaria drug known at the time. Shortly, a physician, a male nurse, and a public health inspector arrived, and a post was established in one of the few houses of sufficient size that still remained standing. In 1944 a modern building was constructed to house the health post, and a diesel launch was stationed at Gurupá for the use of the physician in visiting nearby towns and villages. The selection of Gurupá as a site for a health post increased its importance as a town, and its population began slowly to grow.

The SESP brought important innovations. It constructed hygienic privies for more than 90 percent of the dwellings of the town. A sanitary inspector has stimulated the townspeople to clean up their backyards and to clear out the weeds. Every three months the SESP sends a team of men to spray all homes and public buildings with DDT, and the major foci of mosquito breeding near the town have been eradicated.

---

[38]Studies since the 1940s have shown the high risks of DDT (Dichlorodiphenyltrichloroethane) use, ranging from its toxic effects, environmental persistence, and concentration in the food supply (see Eskenazi et al. 2009). The pesticide has been banned in the United States since 1972 and banned for agricultural use worldwide since 2001 under the Stockholm Convention on Persistent Organic Pollutants (POPs). It is still in limited use for disease vector control, particularly against malaria-carrying mosquitoes.

[39]Fourteen lines were omitted describing the staffing details of SESP.

New cases of malaria are now rare among the townspeople.[40] Whereas 16 percent of 354 individuals examined in Gurupá in 1942 showed positive blood smears for malaria, by June of 1944 less than 1 percent of 337 examined were positive. Gurupá, which was once famous along the Amazon for its serious and almost annual epidemics, is now relatively free of malaria.

In a two-year period (1944–1945), 6,329 people were attended to in the Gurupá health clinic of SESP; it administered 1,069 antismallpox vaccinations (100 percent of the townspeople and many in the rural districts and in nearby towns) and 469 antityphoid immunizations. A health club was formed among the school children to stimulate interest in modern health habits. Pamphlets, posters, talks by the physician, slide projections, and home visits by the *visitadora* (a young nurse's aide trained by the SESP) are being used to educate the people of Gurupá in better health habits and in the advantages of the public health program. The *curiosas* (midwives) were invited to the health post for instruction in the simple hygienic principles to be followed while attending a childbirth. These midwives have been provided with sterile gauze, sterilized instruments, and simple equipment to make their services safer to their patients. Most people of Gurupá still get their water, both for drinking and for general household uses, from the river or from a few wells, all of which the health service has classified as dangerous; but the people of Gurupá hope to be able to construct a water-supply system in the near future, as other Amazon towns have already done, through a cooperative plan with SESP. By 1948, the SESP was an integral part of community life. It had already become a necessity for the Gurupá people. Rumors that the federal government might bring the service to an end because the United States Government might not renew its contract with Brazil to continue the joint health service caused considerable stir. The people of Gurupá were indignant that they might lose their physician and the benefits of the health post.

---

[40]In 2010 Gurupá reported 61 cases of malaria for a population of 29,062, a rate of 0.20 percent. By comparison, in the same year, the neighboring municipality of Breves had a rate of 7.12 percent; Curralinho had 27.58 percent, and Anajás had an alarming rate of 91.52 percent (Instituto Peabiru 2011). Malaria is all but absent from Gurupá due to the continuation of aggressive public health measures initiated during the 1940s. Dengue Fever, also spread by mosquitoes, however, is on the rise in Gurupá as it is throughout Brazil.

They criticized both their own federal government and the policy of the United States, which was only that, they claimed, of "a wartime friend."[41]

Higher prices for rubber and concomitant high prices for other products during World War II also stimulated Gurupá on fronts other than public health. Taxes levied on rubber and palm-nut exports raised the municipal income. As a consequence, the construction of the town hall was finally completed in 1947, except for the installation of the tile floors. After thirty years of delay, the town of Gurupá repeated its ostentatious folly. The cost of finishing the town hall left the municipality so heavily in debt that the municipal income from taxes was mortgaged for years. Still, the municipal government had somehow been able to find funds to repair the public dock, to build the two-family bungalows mentioned earlier, and to pay workers to weed the streets from time to time. The federal government had built a new schoolhouse, which was designed for use as a night school for adults but that was being used as a primary school. With gifts accumulated by the devotees of St. Benedict, the church had been repaired. There were high hopes of converting to diesel fuel the wood-burning electric generator that had been installed many years ago and no longer functioned. Better conditions had by 1948 attracted a few people back to the town; from a low of less than 300 people in the 1930s, Gurupá had almost 500 people in 1948 and more than 600 in 1950.

Despite a few improvements, however, Gurupá is still a poor, decadent, and isolated community. There was no telegraph or wireless station in 1948; the Amazon Cable Company, which once maintained a station there, had ceased to function. A PBY seaplane of the Panair do Brasil (a Pan-American World Airways affiliate) stopped once a week going upriver from Belém and once a week on its downriver run from

---

[41]After the war the United States did stop funds for the program. The Brazilian government, however, continued and expanded the program. In 2013 the Municipal Hospital of Jaime Aben Athar—a 26-bed facility with a laboratory for blood work—provides basic health services along with some minor surgery. It is staffed by two doctors, a dentist, several nurses, several biochemists, and 20 or so public health assistants/technicians. The hospital also has 26 associated health posts—twenty-four of which are located in the rural interior. Despite the improvements, the community ranks low in global standards in terms of doctors per capita (0.22 for Gurupá vs. 1.8 for Brazil and 2.4 for the United States) and hospital beds (.09 for Gurupá vs. 2.4 for Brazil and 3.0 for the United States—Instituto Peabiru 2011; WHO 2012).

Manaus to bring mail and a rare passenger. Most of the boats of SNAPP, a riverboat company owned by the federal government, stopped at Gurupá, and occasionally a privately owned river steamer made a call. During a three-month period, twelve river steamers stopped at Gurupá to leave and to pick up mail, to deliver merchandise, and to load rubber and a few other exports.[42] Considering its meager commerce and the trickle of mail that flows in and out of Gurupá, these communication facilities would seem to be more than adequate. During a normal month, only about forty letters are received in the post office, and about the same number are dispatched. The bulk of any incoming mail is directed to the various government officials or to commercial houses, and most of the outgoing mail consists of government reports. There is little movement of merchandise in and out of the town itself because most of the exports from the municipality are shipped from downriver trading posts directly to Belém.

A mirror of the underdevelopment of Gurupá is the size of its reading public and its facilities for formal education. In 1948 only two people in town regularly received newspapers or magazines, although this reading matter was borrowed by about ten others. More than 40 percent of the townspeople and almost 80 percent of the rural population of the community were completely illiterate: those who read with ease were a small handful.[43] There was little knowledge of the outside world and little interest; the mayor had a battery-run radio, and each evening five or six people gathered outside his house to hear the news broadcast from Rio de Janeiro.[44] Furthermore, the school system offered little hope for a more enlightened and literate public. In the entire municipality of over seven thousand inhabitants, there were seven

---

[42]By 2013 much has changed. Cell phone service has been available since 2009, through which people can access the Internet (Facebook in particular). On a daily basis commercial passenger boats (large and small) stop at the municipal wharf. There is an airstrip behind town for single- and twine-engine planes, but no regular service is provided.

[43]In the 2010 census the illiteracy rate for Gurupá was 24.8 percent. The ranges by age groups included a high of 62.3 percent for adults over the age of 60 to a low of 9 percent for people 15 to 24 years of age (IBGE 2012).

[44]In 2013 reading materials are more abundant in the town, but it is the near-ubiquitous access to television and growing access to the Internet that have greatly increased local knowledge of the wider world (see Pace and Hinote 2013).

one-room primary schools, each with one teacher. Two of these schools were in the Gurupá community—one in the town and another in the small settlement of Jocojó.[45] The teachers, who were women, were not graduates of the state normal school; both had as their major qualification for teaching the ability to read and write. These two primary schools in the Gurupá community, like all primary schools in Brazil, are coeducational. In Brazil primary schools have five grades, but the Gurupá schools offer only the first three years. The two teachers are not equipped to teach the fourth and fifth year.[46] The town school is held five days a week from about 8:00 a.m. until noon; the hours are a little vague because the teacher's clock often stops and it is seldom synchronized with the other clocks of Gurupá. There is a mid-year vacation in July and the long vacations last from December until mid-February.

The town school was almost totally without teaching materials in June of 1948, but in August a long awaited shipment of supplies, sent by the Department of Education, arrived from Belém. It contained 26 ABC books, 27 multiplication tables, 12 pencils, 11 penholders, 20 pen points, 7 envelopes, 1 eraser, 1 blotter, 1 package of chalk, 1 small bottle of red ink, 60 short educational pamphlets, 72 sheets of writing paper, and an attendance book for the teacher. This was to supply more than sixty students for the entire year, and it had to be divided with the Jocojó school. Furthermore, in 1948 neither teacher had received her pay for five months and the town teacher threatened continually to leave. Theoretically, reading, writing, arithmetic, Portuguese grammar, and "general notions of geography" are taught; but because the town teacher was in 1948 also the town *beata* (religious devotee) who cared for the church, stories of saints and prayers were taught whenever possible.

This situation is more or less representative of the entire Brazilian Amazon. Unless educational facilities are made available to Gurupá and to other Amazon communities, it must be expected that the region will continue to be poor. Permanent success cannot be expected for a public health program such as that being carried forward by the SESP,

---

[45]No schooling whatsoever was provided for the rural families of the community except for Jocojó. More than half of the two thousand people in the community lacked educational facilities entirely.

[46]Eighteen lines were omitted that detail school/class size, lack of teacher regulation, and regional graduation rates for the 1940s.

or for any other development program, unless the educational level of the people of the Valley is raised.[47]

Gurupá is limited in other ways. The traditional predatory economic pattern of the Amazon Valley continues in Gurupá as it does in most rural zones throughout the Valley. People still live by collecting rubber and other natural products of the forest or by the old traditional slash-and-burn methods of agriculture. In fact, agriculture in the community is so weakly developed that most of the basic foodstuffs must be imported. Gurupá not only imports beans, rice, sugar, coffee, and canned goods but also large quantities of manioc flour, which is the staple of the people's diet.[48] When the price paid for rubber or another extractive product is high, agriculture is often almost totally neglected. The collectors live on canned goods and dried foods such as dried fish, meat, beans, and rice imported at tremendous cost from southern Brazil. Practically all manufactured articles, from matches and needles to machinery of any kind, come from southern Brazil or from abroad. Transportation is slow, inefficient, and costly. It takes a month to six weeks for a shipment to reach Belém at the mouth of the Amazon River from Rio de Janeiro or Santos, and much longer to reach Gurupá. Manufactured articles and imported foods are thus exceedingly expensive when they arrive. The exaggerated idea of a "normal profit" held by local merchants and the relatively low prices paid for products of the

---

[47]By 2010 educational conditions have improved in that Gurupá has 104 schools, 8 in town and 96 in the rural interior (IBGE 2012). Many teachers are receiving college degrees through a university extension program allowing part-time work toward a BA. By other measurements, however, problems persist. For example, the Instituto Peabiru (2011) reported that in Gurupá the percentage of children of the appropriate age for their grade level was only 58.7 percent for the 4th grade (serié) and 62.7 percent for the 8th. The IDEB (*Indicé de Desenvolvimento da Educação Básica* or the Indices of Basic Education Development) national ranking measures national test scores combined with school performance. The national average is 4, with Gurupá scoring 3 (4th grade) and 3.5 (8th grade). These scores place the municipality in the bottom 9.1 percentile nationwide for 4th graders and the bottom 39 percentile for the 8th (Instituto Peabiru 2011). As with national statistics in many countries around the world, standardized tests fail to consider regional cultural and dialect variations—which generally lowers test scores.

[48]Not until the 2000s did this problem improve. With better transportation to the terra firme interior (primarily Bacá) and the creation of local "farmer's markets" in town, Gurupá has begun to be self-sufficient in manioc production. Other food goods, however, are still imported, particularly in the várzea areas.

forest make such prices even higher to the collector or farmer of Gurupá. The economic structure of Gurupá, and of most of the Amazon Valley, is still as oriented toward export for the foreign market as it was in the past. As in most colonial areas of the world, such orientation actually deprives people of the basic necessities of life by directing their efforts toward the production of raw materials for export rather than toward production for their own consumption. The result, especially during periods of low prices for these exported raw materials, is a low standard of living—even poverty.[49]

Out of the historical background of Gurupá and of the entire region emerge the basic reasons for its relative poverty. A culture is above all a product of history—of the human-made sequence of events and influences that combine through time to create the present way of life in any area. The aboriginal cultures of the Amazon forest were well adapted to the tropical environment.[50] In the first two centuries of the colonial rule, during which a new way of life took form in the Amazon Valley, the European contributed little in the way of new technical equipment or practices that added to a human's ability to wrestle a living from the Amazon environment. From the beginning the Valley offered little to lure the European, who came looking for quick wealth, as did the Spanish conquistadors. The few Portuguese attracted to the region soon established a slave system using the Indigenous people to collect the native products of the forest for export. Neither the most efficient European technology nor the most advanced Western social organization and ideology was brought to the Amazon.[51]

Both the slave system and the extractive economy established early by the European colonists have left an indelible mark on Amazon society. The slave system has resulted in a highly crystallized class system. There is an attitude of dispraisal of all physical labor on the part of those who are not descendants of slaves and an attitude of contentment

---

[49]Here Wagley acknowledges the connection between colonialism and underdevelopment largely ignored by modernization theorists. For more detail on this approach to understanding poverty and underdevelopment for the region, see Bunker (1985), Weinstein (1983), Pace (1998), and Schmink and Wood (1992).

[50]Three lines were omitted referencing the "standard model" of low social complexity for precontact Indigenous populations.

[51]Four lines were omitted that reference the "standard model" and marginality from the world economic system.

with cheap human labor rather than a desire to adopt labor-saving devices. The dominant class has been content, too, with the continuation of the native system of agriculture, which allows the people of the Valley to eke out an existence from the land. Instead of improving the techniques and methods of agriculture, their efforts have been directed toward the increase of the production of extractive products. One cannot change what has gone before; but out of a study of the past it becomes clear that the most serious barrier to a better standard of living for the inhabitants of the Amazon Valley is humanity's inability to direct efforts for its own benefit. With different technological equipment[52] and with a different orientation of Amazon society, a different social and cultural adjustment might have been created.

If the present reasons for the poverty of the Amazon Valley are mainly social and cultural in nature, and are thus human made, then there are no immutable barriers to humanity's ability to plan and to control the direction of its future development. Obviously, there are numerous limitations imposed by the physical environment and climate; and, what is equally obvious, economic and social problems cannot be solved locally because the Amazon region is intimately tied to Brazil as a nation and to the world beyond. Still, social change, whether it comes as a reflection of changes in the nation and the international scene, or as the result of purely local developments, ultimately involves changes in the society and the culture of the local community. It is on this level, within the framework of the small community, that the social anthropologist is best equipped to offer help to the social planner and to the administrator charged with health programs, agricultural reform, educational campaigns, and other efforts toward improving economic and social conditions.

---

[52]In 2013 this scenario would include preservation of Indigenous agriculture and resource utilization that sustained much larger populations than "modern technology" has been able to achieve.

CHAPTER 3

....

Making a Living in the Tropics

The majority of the people of the Brazilian Amazon region earn their living by subsistence level food-production methods and techniques that have long been replaced in other parts of Brazil and in most parts of the Western World. The contemporary resident of rural Amazonia purchases manufactured articles from modern factories, travels on steam- or diesel-driven river steamers, sees modern oceangoing transports and airplanes, and depends on the vagaries of distant markets and of government policies; yet most of these people make a living by traditional hand agriculture (technically, it is horticulture), by hunting and fishing, by collecting the natural products of the forest, or by some combination of these activities. Although people have iron tools, a few new crops, and numerous imported foods and articles, the basic crops and methods of agriculture have been little changed since aboriginal times. The actual products collected from the forest are nowadays dictated by distant markets, but they are still mainly those known to the Indigenous populations.

As it was for the aboriginal people before them, the staple in the diet of the people of the Brazilian Amazon is manioc, or cassava, as it is sometimes called. This root crop, which is by now diffused throughout the tropical world into Africa and Asia, is native to America. Manioc is a hearty plant, well adapted to the tropics and to the leached tropical soils. It grows in a variety of soils. It resists insects, especially the saúva ant, better than most crops. It prospers either in heavy or in light rainfall. In the Amazon, *terra firme* is considered the best land for manioc plantations. A site cleared out of virgin forest is, of course, to be preferred, but in the vicinity of most Amazon towns and villages most of the original forest on *terra firme* has at one time or another been cleared away. *Capoeira alta* (high second growth) is generally the best available land for manioc gardens. People living near the towns are forced to plant on *capoeira baixa* (low second growth). In the flood lands, some maize, rice, and beans, which are quick-growing crops, are raised between the annual rise and fall of the river. Sometimes squash, beans, yams, peppers, peanuts, pineapples, and bananas are planted on the same plot with manioc on *terra firme*. In general, however, the Amazon farmer is a producer of manioc.

It is commonly said in Gurupá that every particle of the manioc tuber is used. Even the peelings are fed to the chickens. From the poisonous juice of the bitter variety of manioc, a famous Amazon sauce called *tucupí* is prepared by exposing it to the sun in a bottle for fifteen to twenty days. From the fine powder, rich in sugar, which is sifted out in making manioc flour, the people of Gurupá prepare *mingau de tapioca* (a sweet pudding). From this same powder and from a heavy dough prepared from the tuber, *beiju*, a sort of biscuit, is made. By far the most common form of preparing manioc is as *farinha* or manioc flour. This flour, with a consistency like that of coarse corn meal, is present at all Gurupá meals. It is eaten dry, mixed with gravy or grease as *farofa*, or simply mixed with a little water as *chibé*. A family of five people normally consumes two kilos or more of *farinha* each day.

The preparation of manioc flour is a time-consuming task. In Gurupá both varieties of manioc, the sweet or nonvenomous variety and the larger tubers of bitter variety (*mandioca brada*), which contain a high percentage of prussic acid, are used in making flour. Because bitter manioc is larger and more productive, however, most of the flour is of that variety. Essentially, the methods of making manioc flour are those used by the tribal Amazonians. The main task is that of removing the poisonous liquid. Two methods are used. First, after the tuber has been peeled, it is grated either on a toothed grater by hand or with a *caitetu*, a cylindrical grater revolved by a set of bicycle-type gears turned by hand. Then the venomous juice is squeezed out of the grated pulp. A tubular basket, called a *tipití*, is used for this purpose as it was in aboriginal times. The pulp is stuffed into this long, flexible tube, and as the *tipití* is stretched, the liquid is squeezed out. Or the juice is removed with a box-like press, the top of which is forced downward with a cantilever device. Once the juice has been removed, the dough is forced through a sieve to take out the fiber and coarse grains. Finally, it is toasted on a large copper griddle. A second way of making manioc flour differs in the method used for preparing the tuber. Instead of being grated, the tuber is placed in a stream or in a trough of water for about four days until it is *puba*, that is, softened to the point of semi-decay. The skin can then be easily removed, the juice squeezed out, the soft dough passed through a sieve, and then toasted. In Gurupá the best *farinha* is made by a combination of the two methods. Half of the tubers are grated and half are allowed to soften in the water. The dough of both is mixed before toasting. It takes a husband and wife a full day's work to prepare one alqueire (30 kilos, or about 66 pounds) of *farinha* after the tuber has been harvested.

Each year in the summer, from June through August, Gurupá farmers work at clearing sites for manioc gardens. Their first job is to clear away the underbrush with a bush knife; then the large trees are felled with an ax. For a month or six weeks the brush and fallen trees are allowed to dry, and in September or October, depending on when the clearing was done, the site is burned off. The farmer then begins the dirty job called *coivara*, which consists of gathering together the partially burned trunks into piles and digging out the worst of the unburned root systems. The more thoroughly the site is burned off, the less difficult is the job of *coivara*. The garden is now ready for planting, although to the unpracticed eye it seems to be but a tangled half-cleared area burned out of the forest. Planting takes place from late October through December, during the early rains of the winter months. "Shoots" or "cuts" taken from the stalk of the bush are planted in the earth, where they soon take root. Sometimes secondary crops such as *jerimú* (a squash), maize, watermelon, and peppers are planted in the same area; they are fast-growing plants and may be harvested before the bush-like vegetation of the manioc takes over.

Manioc is a slow-growing plant. It is usually mature only after one full year of growth; but it may be harvested after six months, while it is green, before the tubers have reached full size. Even after it is ripe, however, harvesting may be done at intervals, as the tubers are needed for a period of almost a year. In harvesting, the manioc bush is cut away and the tubers are dug from the ground with a hoe. Most Gurupá farmers immediately replant manioc on the same spot, and as they harvest they progressively replant the same garden site. Because the second planting is about half as productive as the first, a garden site is generally replanted only once. After the second harvest the site is allowed to return to bush. This in general is the agricultural cycle of Gurupá manioc cultivation.

The farm work involved in manioc cultivation, however, varies in accordance with the type of land selected. Virgin forest and high second growth are more difficult to clear than low brush, but the fresh soils guarantee a higher production. The clearing of low second growth or brush is an easier task and the job of *coivara* is generally not necessary, but weeds grow fast in such an area and the harvest is less productive. Gurupá farmers estimate that one individual working alone in a garden site of one *tarefa*[1] of high second-growth forest would spend five days clearing the underbrush, five days felling the large trees, one day burning off the area, five days piling up the brush and digging up the roots (*coivara*), and twenty days planting the garden. While the manioc was growing, the individual would spend an additional sixteen days clearing away the worst of the weeds. Thus the Gurupá farmer has invested some forty-two work days for one tarefa of manioc. The time involved on one tarefa of virgin forest would be somewhat more, and on a tarefa of low brush considerably less. The work on a garden, however, is never carried out by one person alone, nor is it done as systematically as this estimate might make it appear. First, a work day for Amazon farmers is rarely from dawn to dusk. Generally, farmers leave their house early in the morning after taking a small demitasse of black coffee and a handful of manioc flour. They work until midday, or slightly after, returning to their houses for a heavy midday meal. After the meal they rest and spend the afternoon at other tasks.

A full day is spent in the field only when the farmers are participants or the hosts of a *puxirão* or *convite*, as the cooperative work parties are called. These work parties may be organized for any of the various tasks of manioc cultivation, but they are most commonly held for the heavy work of clearing the garden site. The hosts on such an occasion issue invitations to several close relatives, to *compadres*,[2] or to

---

[1] A tarefa is 25 braças by 25 braças; in Gurupá, a braça is 2.5 meters, and a tarefa is thus 3,906.25 square meters.
[2] See p. 153.

friends. Sometimes neighbors, knowing that a work party is planned, will appear without special invitation. The size of such work parties varies considerably. Nhenjuca, a farmer who lives in Gurupá and plants just outside of town (see Figure 3.2), always invites only four or five old friends, individuals with whom he has worked for many years. In Jocojó a cooperative work party will generally be attended by the fifteen or twenty people living in the neighborhood. On such occasions hosts take care of all expenses. They serve coffee at their house before leaving for the field; they buy cigarettes or tobacco for the participants; and they supply *cachaça* (a crude sugarcane rum) for an occasional nip during the work and for a *mata-bicho* (literally "kill the animal") before the midday meal. The women of the work party prepare a large meal. A pig or several chickens are killed for a large work party. The hosts remember who has participated in the work party when an occasion arises, for the workers are never paid in money and it may be several seasons before the hosts have a chance to repay the guests with a similar amount of work. "We work twice as fast when we work together," explained one farmer, and people prefer to do the heavy agricultural work in cooperative work parties.

In addition, families work together in some of the tasks in the field. The clearing of the field, the burning, and the *coivara* are male endeavors; but women work alongside their husbands at planting and during the infrequent weedings of the garden, as well as in harvesting the tubers and in manufacturing flour. Thus a man and women will be able to plant a tarefa in ten days, which if an individual worked alone would require twenty days' labor. Together a woman and a man can weed a field in eight days' time as well as one person could do it alone in sixteen days. Together they should be able to prepare one alqueire of *farinha* in one day.

Gurupá farmers estimated that a family must have at least four tarefas (15,625 square meters) of garden with ripe manioc to be able to supply the needs of a family of five and to have a surplus for sale if they wish to live from farming alone. To do so, farmers must plant a new site of four tarefas each year. Thus, in September of 1948, farmers should have, for example, four tarefas of manioc that was first planted in 1946 and replanted during 1947 from which they can still harvest a few tubers. They should also have four tarefas of manioc planted in 1947 that is just fully mature. And during the previous months they should have cleared four tarefas to be planted in October or November.

They therefore would be using twelve tarefas of land, or approximately 46,875 square meters at one time. This estimate is based on their own needs, the prices paid for their surplus product, and the average productivity of the land. It will be seen, however, that it is about the maximum amount of land that a family might be able to work without extra help.

One tarefa of relatively good land (i.e., forest or high second growth) will produce enough tubers to make approximately 900 kilos of manioc flour, and the same plot when replanted progressively as the first crop is harvested will produce about half that amount. Farmers who plant four tarefas of land each year should be able to manufacture some 5,400 kilos of *farinha*—3,600 from their new gardens and 1,800 from replanted gardens—during the year. Their families, a spouse and three children, will consume about 720 kilos of manioc flour in a year, leaving them 4,680 kilos, or in local terms some 156 alqueires (30 kilos to the alqueire) for sale. At the prices paid in 1948, this would bring them the sum of about $351 US dollars (in cruzeiros, cr. $7,020),[3] which is an income higher than the average income either of the low-class townsfolk or of the farmers. It is not a good income, however, in view of the cost of medicines, of clothes, of household equipment, of patronizing a festival, and of other necessary expenditures for the family. Under the best circumstances manioc farming with the tools and methods now employed in Gurupá provides only a bare subsistence. Furthermore, if Gurupá farmers were to carry out the ideal program, as described previously, they would have little time for anything else—for fishing, for repairing their houses, for building or repairing a canoe.

Theoretically, the agricultural work for four tarefas each year would add up to 168 days of work, and theoretically it would take another 360 days for a farmer alone to prepare 5,400 kilos of manioc flour. If a spouse aided in planting, in weeding, and in manufacturing flour, the time would still amount to 330 work days, certainly a full-time employment. Actually, of course, few Gurupá farmers have four tarefas of manioc garden in production, and the few who did in 1948 had growing children or other dependent relatives to help them. According to estimates that 39 town dwellers made of their gardens,

---

[3]The rate of exchange is calculated at 20 Brazilian cruzeiros to the dollar, the approximate official rate in 1948. The "open market" rate of exchange, at the time, was about 25 cruzeiros to the dollar.

planted the year before, they had on the average only 2.7 tarefas in manioc. The estimates given by 29 rural farmers averaged only 2.9 tarefas per person. Only 11 town dwellers and only 10 rural farmers of a total of 68 farmers who gave us estimates had as much as four tarefas of mature manioc.[4]

Very few people, therefore, earn a living from agriculture alone. Almost without exception, Gurupá farmers must augment their incomes from other activities, and many people plant only for their own consumption. Townspeople work as day laborers, for which they are paid 15 cruzeiros (about $0.75) per day, and the farmers who live in the rural neighborhoods work at extractive industries—collecting palm nuts, timbó vine, and rubber or cutting firewood for the river steamers. Each year the younger men of the small village of Jocojó leave after the festivals of St. John and St. Apollonio in July to work in the rubber trails in the Island region. They return only in October in time to finish clearing garden sites and to plant their gardens before the heavy winter rains begin. Even those farmers, such as Jorge Palheta, who own land and who are among the few "full-time" farmers, must work rubber trails or spend some time during the year working at another activity that brings in cash. Gurupá is a farming community where it is very difficult to derive even a minimum living from farming alone.[5]

The community of Gurupá, and in fact the whole Amazon Valley, does not produce enough basic foodstuffs to feed even its present sparse population. According to the records kept by the local statistical agent in Gurupá, more than 350,000 kilos of manioc flour, 5,000 kilos of beans, 47,000 kilos of sugar, and 34,000 kilos of coffee—all of which might have been grown locally—were imported into the municipality.[6] The land that is exploited in Gurupá, the terra firme, is mediocre compared to the low-lying islands and lowland banks of the Amazon, the floodlands. These low areas of the municipality offer a great potentiality for the cultivation of wet rice, sugar cane, Indian jute, and of such

---

[4]In 1948 we were able to measure the gardens that twenty Gurupá farmers had prepared for planting in manioc. These gardens, which would be harvested in 1949, averaged only 2.6 tarefas; only five men had four tarefas.

[5]In 2013 these patterns described by Wagley are largely the same for farmers on the terra firme, although they are most likely to supplement their earnings through the extraction of açaí and timber.

[6]Three lines were omitted referencing the idea that slash-and-burn agriculture is inefficient and unproductive.

quick-growing food crops as beans and maize, which may be planted and harvested during the summer when the river is low (Gourou 1949). Even a minimal use of modern agricultural knowledge and techniques would increase the production in the region several times over. Better transportation and a few innovations, such as centralized flour factories, simple machinery, and traction animals, might increase agricultural production in Gurupá as they have in the Belém-Bragança region near the mouth of the Amazon. But as long as the present predatory agricultural methods persist, food will remain a basic problem.

II

The tropical forest Native Americans who inhabited the Amazon region before the arrival of the European depended, in addition to their gardens, on hunting and fishing for their sustenance. In the early days of the European era, hunting and fishing were of great importance in feeding the colonists and their slaves. It was the Indigenous population who taught the European newcomer to live in the strange Amazon environment. The Native was the hunter and fisher, and the methods of hunting and fishing of contemporary Amazon regional culture are therefore mainly of aboriginal origin. Although the modern inhabitants of the Valley hunt with a shotgun or a .44 caliber rifle or fish with a metal fishhook or a European-type net, they do so with knowledge of the local fauna derived from their Indigenous cultural heritage. In addition, numerous aboriginal techniques are still used, and many folk beliefs of Indigenous origin persist in regard to hunting and fishing. Nowadays, however, neither hunting nor fishing is important in the regional economy. Along the main arteries of the Amazon River system, hunting is no longer a lucrative occupation. After centuries of human occupation, the country has been hunted out.[7]

In such Amazon communities as Gurupá, hunting has become almost a pastime; no one would depend on the results of the hunt for food. Fishing is still relatively important, however, as a subsistence activity. Although fish are less numerous than formerly in the main rivers, most Amazon families fish for their own consumption and a few

---

[7]Excellent hunting areas are still found [1950s], however, in the headwaters of the Amazon tributaries—in the state of Mato Grosso to the south and along the Guiana frontier to the north.

often have a surplus for sale. In some localities, such as in Santarém at the mouth of the Tapajós River, there are professional fishers. In the backwater lakes and swamps, or *igapós*, of the upper Amazon, the giant *pirarucu*, a fish which sometimes weighs four hundred pounds, is harpooned to be dried and salted and sold up and down the river as "Brazilian codfish."

The most favorable months for fishing in the vicinity of Gurupá are those of the summer, from June to December. During these months the small streams, swollen during the rainy season, return to their banks or dry up, and the fish return to the main streams. In August and September several species of fish start their annual migration up the Amazon to the headwaters to deposit their eggs. In June and July freshwater shrimp move up river. During the summer months fish are plentiful in Gurupá and are a major item in the diet of most families. During the winter months (the rainy season), on the contrary, there are times when the only fish to be had is dried *pirarucu*, imported codfish, or tinned sardines and tuna. From January to May the Amazon and its tributaries are swollen; the tributary streams overflow into the forest, and, as people say, "the fish go to the forest." During these months fishing by hook and line, by trap, by net, and other methods used during the summer is impossible, and only a few fish may be speared in the flooded lowlands.

Several methods of fishing are used during the summer months. The most common, of course, is by hook and line. Every evening in Gurupá people may be seen moving out into the river in their canoes for a few hours' fishing, and some men fish late into the night with fish lines. The most productive methods, however, are the use of poison, traps, or nets.[8] In Gurupá only one type of net, the tarrafa, a circular net, thrown by one person, is used. Traps are of several varieties.

---

[8]In 2013 subsistence fishers still paddle their canoes out on the river for a couple of hours to catch their meals, using lines and hooks. More common, though, is the use of gill nets of varying lengths strung out at strategic points along the river. *Timbó* fishing is today illegal, although a few families in the interior may still use the technique. A dozen or so *cacurís* (fish weirs) can still be seen along the riverfront near the town in varying states of repair and use. Shrimping is a common activity today, with catches for family consumption or sale (see Chapter 8). The biggest change is commercial fishing, which has generally reduced fish stocks all along the Amazon River, but especially near urban centers. For the struggles with commercial fishers, see Chapter 8.

The largest is a permanent fish trap, the *cacurí*, which projects out into the river some thirty to fifty meters. In 1948 there were five traps in Gurupá. They were owned by Abilio Costa, a storekeeper; by Dona Diná Borralho; by Benedito Pará and his brother; and by Nhenjuca in partnership with the barber, Ernesto Morais. The trap owned by Dona Diná was first built by her husband some twenty years ago, and it has been repaired or rebuilt each year since. Its location is considered especially good, and each year her catch in fish is superior to the others. The trap owned by Nhenjuca and the barber is new, having been built in 1948 at the cost of almost $50 (cr. $1,000). It is estimated that it must be rebuilt again after two years at almost the same cost; thus few people can afford this type of permanent fish trap.

The trap takes the form of a wall of stakes made of the trunk of the açaí palm, which protrudes out into the river and forms a barrier to the fish moving upstream or being carried downstream by the current. At the end of the barrier there is a circular trap into which the fish move, and beyond this trap is a smaller inner chamber that may be closed when the fish are to be removed. During the early part of the summer, trap owners expect to catch only a few kilos of fish each day; but as the fish migrate upriver later in the season, they sometimes remove a hundred kilos daily, selling most of the catch to the townspeople. In 1946, considered an excellent year for fish, Dona Diná Borralho took some 2,000 kilos of fish from her trap. She sold about 300 kilos locally at 4 cruzeiros (20 cents) a kilo, and exported the rest salted to Belém. In 1948, though Nhenjuca and his partner expected to catch less than half that amount of fish, they nevertheless hoped to catch enough to supply their families and to be able to sell the rest on the local market to pay for their trap.

People without the money and the time to build a trap, and especially those who live along the banks of the small streams, often fish by blocking off the stream with tapagens (barrier traps). Gurupá is far enough downstream on the Amazon to feel some effect of the ocean tides. A very small difference in the water level in the main channels causes many small tributaries to fill up and to drain empty twice each day during the dry season. The Amazon fisher builds a barrier across such small streams, with a gate that can be opened to allow fish to enter upstream with the incoming tide and that can be closed to trap them as the tide flows out. For several months each year, such traps provide a welcome addition to the tables of many rural families. In addition, in shallow pools or in small streams, many people fish with timbó roots or the *tingui* vine. The shredded root or the crushed vine produces a poison that when placed in a half-dry pool or shallow stream, stupefies the fish so that they rise to the surface and are easily caught. Fish are also speared or shot with the bow and arrow; in many rural homes one still sees the *espeque*, a multipointed lance or a bow and arrow of the type once used by the Amazon natives.

Though hunting is not an important activity in Gurupá, there are an interest and preoccupation with it that are inconsistent with its contribution to people's livelihood.[9] Many rubber gatherers carry a shotgun with them on their daily round on the rubber trail; sometimes an agouti, a paca, a wild forest fowl such as the jacu, or even a wild pig crosses their path, and they may make a kill. A few rural fanners who own rifles or shotguns spend a day or so now and again hunting. Sometimes they set a *tocaia*, a trap formed by arming a gun so that it will go off when an animal attempts to make off with the bait or when the animal breaks a string stretched across the trail. With a *tocaia* farmers may sometimes kill a small forest deer or a paca that comes to graze in their garden. Hunting, therefore, sometimes provides a welcome addition to the relatively meatless diet of the rural population.

Yet the intense interest in hunting in Gurupá and the numerous folk beliefs that cluster around sport are a reminder of a time when hunting had a basic importance in the town's economy. In the rural neighborhoods of Gurupá, several men are famed as hunters. Such men are Elíos Veiga (see Figure 3.3) and Domingos Alves. Both earn their living from other pursuits—agriculture or rubber collecting. Domingos is a farmer living near his gardens only two or three kilometers from the town. He hunts two or three nights a week. He owns two dogs trained for hunting the paca, and he owns both a rifle and a muzzle-loading shotgun. Domingos almost died in 1947 from a broken leg resulting from a fall when running through the thick underbrush after a tapir he had wounded. There is generally game (*embiara*) in his house.

---

[9]By 2013 hunting near the city of Gurupá was no longer possible. Only in the isolated interior can families still expect to eat wild game on occasion. Some interior communities have been experimenting with game preserves, which might increase the availability of game. For example, Camutá of Pucuruí River created a 3,837 hectare biodiversity reserve to sustain local fauna for future hunting (FASE 2002:11). To date no measurements on their success are available.

The almost inevitable subject of conversation either with Domingos or with old Veiga is hunting. Like most devotees, they tell graphically of successful hunts—of the time they killed a jaguar or of the night they killed two deer. They discuss the habits of animals and the techniques of stalking particular game.

In telling of their hunting experiences, Domingos and other local hunters do not distinguish between the tangible natural world and the supernatural.[10] A class of plants, called by the generic term of *tajá*, of which there are several species, is thought to be of tremendous help to the hunter. There is the *tajá de veado* (for deer), the *tajá de anta* (for tapir), and many others. Hunters plant them near their homes. Each type "calls" or attracts the animal after which it is named, if used correctly by the hunters. Blood from three deer that have been killed by the hunters, for example, must be poured over the leaf of the deer *tajá*; the leaf should then be crushed in the palm of the hand and rubbed over the hunters' forehead, back, and arms. If this is repeated several times, they will have the power to attract deer as they wander in the forest. Hunters also tell of the dangers, both supernatural and natural (but equally real to them), of hunting. The giant constrictor, the Giboia, sometimes attacks hunters. Hunters may pass by the Giboia in the forest without seeing it, but the snake has a mysterious force that causes the hunters to wander in circles, always drawing nearer until the Giboia is able to attack them. One should not kill or eat the tree sloth during the month of August, hunters say, because they are with fever and will transmit it to people. In June the large lizards called *jacuruaru* should not be eaten, for they are believed to fight during this time with venomous snakes and thus to be filled with poison.

Other dangers to the hunter are *Anhangá*, a dangerous spirit that takes the form of an animal, and *Curupira*, a small supernatural who lives in the forest and who calls to the hunters, attracting them deeper and deeper into the forest until they are lost.[11] Furthermore, if hunters

---

[10]The telling of hunting stories in 2013 is becoming rare in the town of Gurupá, as the old hunters have died off and the new generations have little opportunity to find game. Occasionally one will run across someone who can remember the old stories and old ways of hunting, usually a retired elder living in town. Rarer still is someone younger, living deep enough in the interior that finding game is a possibility, who can tell the tales of the natural and supernatural dangers.

[11]The belief in these two supernaturals is discussed in more detail in Chapter 7. Both are of Indigenous origin.

"persecute" a particular species, that is, if they kill too many of the same animal, the animals may steal or rot their shadows, causing them to become insane, to "talk nonsense," to have body aches, and to fall ill with fevers. To protect themselves, hunters like Domingos and Veiga take care not to offend the animals. After killing two or three pacas in a short period, they hunt other game, "a tapir, a deer, and another animal, before again killing a paca." A hunter may wear a cross made of *cera benta* (holy wax from the candles in the church) as protection against *assombração de bicho*, as the spell of the animal is called. Once when Veiga was hunting, a large howler monkey began to advance on him. He remembered that he had killed several recently. Veiga turned and ran. The next evening he had fever and headache. Because he knew that the howler monkey had tried to steal his shadow, he resorted at once to a cure. As Veiga related it, he fumigated his body with smoke produced by burning a mixture of a nest of *cunauaru* frog,[12] a bit of holy wax, one dried pepper, and the shavings of a deer horn. This mixture is burned in a ceramic vessel or in a gourd container. It should be passed three times under a hammock in which the patient is stretched so that the smoke will cover one's body. Sometimes the spell of the animal is so strong that a shaman, or pajé, must be called to bring back the hunter to health.

The difficulty that plagues hunters and fishers most often, however, is *panema*. Hunters or fishers who have had repeated failures that cannot be explained by natural causes attribute them to panema, a negative power that infects people, their guns, their fish lines, or traps. The term has become widely used in rural Amazonia and in the city in the sense of "bad luck." For example, a gambler catches panema and loses steadily. In Gurupá, however, panema means an "impotence in hunting or fishing" resulting from a supernatural cause. It can be transmitted from one person to another, almost like an infectious disease. By eating game or fish, a pregnant woman is believed to be able to transmit panema to the hunter or fisher who killed or caught it. Individuals may catch panema from their friends who have ill feelings toward then caused by a disagreement over food. If a hunter's spouse carelessly throws the bones of the game into the yard, and a dog or pig

---

[12]The *cunauaru* is a small frog that nests in hollow trunks. The nest has the consistency of a rosin, which produces an aromatic smoke when burned. Throughout the Amazon Valley the nest is burned for medicinal purposes.

eats them, the hunter may suffer from panema. Evil magic made by one's enemies can also cause the condition.

Elíos Veiga related a typical case of a hunter suffering from panema. Many years ago, when he was an active hunter, Veiga killed many deer. During a two-month period, however, he did not see a deer in the forest, although he hunted almost every day. One day a friend mentioned that his wife was several months pregnant. Veiga remembered that he had given his friend portions of deer that he had killed. Veiga knew, then, that the woman was "poisonous" and that she had communicated panema to him. "Not all women are poisonous and cause panema, but Verissima was," he said. "When she was pregnant a flower that she picked would wilt at once." Veiga went at once to inform his friend of his predicament; it is considered dangerous for the hunter to seek a cure for panema transmitted by a pregnant woman, for the treatment might well cause her to abort. But Verissima knew a way to cure Veiga without bringing on an abortion or stillbirth.[13]

Panema from other sources—from the ill feeling (*desconfiança*) of one's friends, from evil magic, or from dogs or pigs eating the bones of game or fish—is more difficult to diagnose. Hunters or fishers have no way of knowing of such events; but through their suspicions or through the reconstruction of past events, they are generally able to lay their fingers on the cause. Raimundo Profeta, after he was panema, remembered that he had refused a neighbor a piece of venison and attributed his panema to *desconfiança*. Elíos Veiga believes that he once got panema because two children left his house crying when they were refused a piece of tapir meat. In another case, when envious neighbors collected the fish bones from a fisher's yard and gave them to the pigs to eat, his fish lines and his net became panema, and his catches were negligible during the best months of the fishing season. An enemy may also, by throwing the bones of the animal or fish into a privy, cause the hunter or fisher to suffer from panema. So great is the danger of catching panema that many hunters and fishers hesitate to sell meat or fish. They will make presents only to relatives or close friends in whom they have confidence and whose womenfolk they know not to be pregnant.[14]

---

[13]See Chapter 5 for other cases where treatment of panema by hunters brings on abortion and stillbirths in women.

[14]Domingos Alves avoids this danger by giving or selling only the meat removed from the bone.

This is especially true when a fisher has a new fish line. Under no circumstances should the fish be eaten by anyone other than the immediate family, for the line and the fisher are especially vulnerable to panema. Gustavo Veiga, the son of Elíos, threw the bones from fish caught with his new lines high on the roof of his house, so that they could not be reached by dogs or pigs or picked up by a stranger.

There are numerous prescriptions for curing panema. Most of them are concoctions in which garlic and pepper are the main ingredients, and they are used in the form of baths or fumigations. The composition, the dosage, and the number of treatments vary widely with the individual's preference and with the seriousness of the case. Old Veiga, as a famous hunter, also knows many cures for panema. People come from the rural districts of Gurupá asking him to treat them, and he gladly dispenses his knowledge without charge. One of Veiga's strongest prescriptions for a hunter suffering from panema is this: Mash into a gourd of water a bit of the nest of the *cauré* hawk, a bit of the nest of the *cunauaru* frog, a bit of the leaves of the vanilla plant, a few leaves of the *aninga* (a water plant), two red peppers, and a bit of garlic. Allow the mixture to soak in the sun and in the "dew of the night" for several days. It should be applied lightly in a bath on three successive Fridays beginning on a Friday of a new moon so that the treatment ends before the full moon. A full moon, he explained, would void the treatment. Another prescription recommended by Veiga is applied as a fumigation and is somewhat less complex. A bit of the nest of the cauré hawk, a few peppers, a spider web (specifically, the web of the *aranha rica*), and a bit of garlic are placed in an open ceramic bowl over a few burning coals from the fire. Hunters allow the smoke to pour over their arms, their legs, and over their backs. Veiga recommends that hunters end the treatment by holding the ceramic bowl close under their chins, allowing the smoke to curl up over their faces; they should keep their mouths open, allowing saliva to drop into the bowl until the burning coals are extinguished.

A hunting dog with panema may be treated either with baths or by fumigations in the same way with the same concoctions. A contaminated rifle should be treated by blowing smoke from a fumigation up the barrel. A fish line is washed in a bath prepared according to the fisher's favorite prescription or it may be fumigated with a mixture, preferably in the street or where two paths cross "where many people pass." It is the practice of Domingos Alves and several others, during the fishing season, to cure themselves with a fumigation each week, as a preventive.

The Amazon folk beliefs that cluster around hunting and fishing are for the most part aboriginal in origin. Anhangá was considered to be a ghost or a spirit by the Tupí-speaking peoples of Brazil, and they also believed that it took the form of animals and birds. Curupira for these Tupían peoples was also a forest demon much feared by the

FIGURE 3.1 | *Cecilia and Charles Wagley at door of their residence in Gurupá. 1948.*

Source unknown.

FIGURE 3.2 | *Nhenjuca da Conceição.*
Photograph by C. Wagley 1948.

FIGURE 3.3 | *Elíos Veiga.*
Photograph by C. Wagley 1948.

FIGURE 3.4 | *Dona Diná Borralho.*
Photograph by C. Wagley 1948.

hunter. Fevers and temporary insanity, which in Gurupá are thought to result from the theft of the soul by animals, is similar to the punishments meted out to the Tenetehara hunters by the supernatural "Owners of the Forest." Panema, as a loss of power in hunting and fishing, is a belief also shared by these tropical forest Indigenous populations in a form almost identical with that of Gurupá (Wagley and Galvão 1949: 58ff., 102ff.). The strength of the Indigenous tradition in Gurupá culture seems to concentrate on those aspects of life having to do with humanity's adaptation to the Amazon environment. The Portuguese and the Africans had to learn how to fish and to hunt the paca, the tapir, and the other New World animals from the Native Americans. As they learned, they also acquired their supernatural beliefs.

These folk beliefs explained, as adequately to the European new-comer lacking modern science as to the Indigenous peoples themselves, the unpredictability of hunting and fishing. Why is it that hunters, famed for their knowledge of the habits of deer, skilled at stalking, en-tirely at home in the forest and generally very successful, will suddenly be unable to find a single deer—or if they do, miss their shots? In Amazon agriculture, however, which also follows native methods, su-pernaturalism does not seem to play much of a part. If a garden grows poorly, people explain that the ants attacked it or that the land selected was not appropriate. They do not charge the lack of a good harvest to the spirits of the forest or even to evil magic. The reason for this differ-ence between hunting and fishing and agriculture, in regard to super-natural explanations, lies in the nature of the agricultural pursuit. In the Amazon, agriculture centers on manioc, a plant that is exceedingly hardy. A failure of a manioc crop is almost unheard of. Unlike the situ-ation in semiarid regions, rainfall is not a variable factor. Although Amazonian agriculture is on the subsistence level, it is not uncertain and unpredictable; for this reason supernatural explanations are less called on.[15]

III

From the beginning, one of the products that Europeans sought in the Amazon Valley was rubber from the tree *Hevea brasiliensis*; but for over two centuries, rubber was only one of many useful products to be gathered in the Amazon forest. It was exported in small quantities to be used for shoes, for rubber balls, for bottles, for waterproofing fab-rics, and other similar purposes. Not until the process of vulcanization was developed in the middle of the last century was Amazon rubber sought after in any great quantity. Since then the collection of latex from the wild rubber tree has been one of the major economic activities of the Valley, and it continues to be so, despite the competition of Asian plantation rubber.[16]

---

[15]In 2013 people in the town do not make much reference to panema and it is no longer a common explanation for misfortune or underperformance. In the countryside, however, it is still in use for people and objects and is still cured by folk remedies.
[16]By the mid-1990s the price of natural rubber had fallen so low that it was no longer economically feasible to collect and rubber tapping was abandoned in Gurupá.

Within the municipality of Gurupá, the low islands and the lowland margins of the rivers and tributaries contain rubber forests that produce a latex known as "delta type," which is second in quality only to the *Acre fino* produced in the upper tributaries of the Amazon Valley. Rubber still represents over 50 percent of the total value of the municipal exports. In 1946, 58,479 kilos of "fine rubber" were sent downriver to Belém, and 30,881 kilos were exported in 1947. Most of this rubber comes from the distant areas of the municipality, but some rubber is collected near the town and rubber collection is an important aspect of Gurupá's economic life. Most Gurupá men and some women have at one time or another worked as rubber collectors. Many go each year to work for a few months in the nearby islands of the delta, and a few have signed up to work in the rich rubber forests of the upper Xingú River or upper Tapajós River. In years when rubber prices are high, Gurupá families move across the Amazon mainstream to the island lowlands, abandoning their farms to collect rubber. When rubber prices drop, there is a steady migration to terra firme and to farming. But even with low prices, there are always many families who continue to work at collecting rubber, as they have all their lives, and many others who work at rubber collecting during part of the year to supplement their incomes. Wild rubber is the principal "money crop" of Gurupá.

The methods of exploiting the native rubber forest determine, to a great extent, the settlement patterns and the spatial distribution of population in rubber-collecting areas, and these methods are approximately the same throughout the Valley. Thus, a knowledge of the traditional system of rubber collection is important for the understanding of rural Amazon society. Rubber-producing Hevea trees are not found in homogeneous groves; in general rubber trees are spaced through the forest fifty to one hundred meters apart. Collectors must clear paths from one tree to another. Such paths, connecting approximately 100 trees (or 150 to 200 in the upper tributaries where trees are closer together), form an *estrada* (road). These roads generally begin near the dwelling of the seringueiros and form a large circle ending somewhere near its start. In the Island Region of the Amazon delta, rubber roads average four to seven kilometers in length, depending on the spacing of

---

People in their 20s and 30s no longer possess the knowledge to tap and process rubber. Wagley's description is an important historical reminder of this critically important activity that dominated Gurupá and the region for over 100 years.

the trees in the forest. It is customary for seringueiros to work two roads; they collect from only one road each day, allowing the trees on the other to rest. To take latex from a tree in successive days is said to tire the tree, lowering its production of latex. The huts of the rubber gatherers are, therefore, generally situated at a considerable distance apart; they are found about one to two kilometers from each other along the bank of the main stream or of a small tributary. The rubber roads run inland and back from their houses, and the river is always their means of communication with the trading post or with the town.

The working day of the rubber collectors begins before sunup, as early as three or four o'clock in the morning in the high tributaries, and somewhat later in the island region. An early start is thought to be necessary because the tree is said to produce more *leite* (milk) when it is cool and before the morning winds rise. The collectors' first job is the cutting (*corte*) of the bark, or the bleeding (*sangra*) to allow the latex to flow. Among collectors and among the *seringalistas* (the owners of rubber forests) there is much discussion as to the best method of cutting the tree. Most agree nowadays that the type of *corte* called the *bandeira* (flag) causes less harm to the tree. The type of cut called the *espinha* (fish bone) produces more latex but slowly kills the tree. The *espinha* is formed by cutting one deep vertical incision in the bark and additional incisions each day at an angle to this central cut so that they will drain into it.[17] The bandeira is a spiral circular incision around the trunk; at each visit to a tree seringueiros cut a new spiral directly under that made two days before. Each season the *bandeira* incision begins high on the trunk and is worked downward as the season wears on. Such incisions should not be deep enough to scar the tree permanently; for that reason most owners of rubber forests oblige collectors to use a special knife rather than the small hatchet (*machadinho*) used during the early days of rubber collecting. Under each incision, at the end of the circular spiral cut of the *bandeira*, collectors insert a small tin cup (*tijela*), about two inches deep, which catches the milky white latex as it slowly oozes forth.

It takes rubber collectors about three to four hours to make the trip over a road, cutting each tree and placing the cups to catch the latex. If they begin at 5:00 a.m., they will be back at their huts by 8:00 or 9:00 a.m. In the upper tributaries of the Amazon Valley, many rubber workers,

---

[17] The *espinha* thus forms a pattern like the vertebra and ribs of a fish.

leaving home earlier and in the dark, wear a head lamp. Much has been written about the great dangers to which the collectors are subjected, especially on their early morning rounds—of poisonous snakes that drop out of the trees, of "savage Indians" who waylay them, and of the narrow log bridges over which they must pass in swamps. In a few out-of-the-way areas of the Amazon, Indigenous groups still attack collectors—generally in reprisal for attacks on their own villages—and poisonous snakes are known throughout the Valley; but none of the many rubber collectors of Gurupá with whom we talked had experienced such exotic dangers, even when they worked in the Upper Amazon. Their stories were more concerned with the length of the road and with malaria than with "savage Indians" or snakes.

Most Gurupá collectors take only a small demitasse of black coffee, or no nourishment at all, before setting out on their initial round of the rubber trail; but when they return from bleeding the tree they generally have their *almôço* (midday lunch), the major meal of the day. Often, however, the collectors must find their lunch before they eat. They must take time out after their first trip around the rubber road to fish, unless they have been lucky enough to kill a forest fowl, an agouti, a paca, or even a wild peccary, which they have encountered on the rubber trail. After the meal the collectors must make a second round of the trail. This time they collect the liquid from the cups, depositing the latex in a gourd container. In the vicinity of Gurupá, a rubber road produces only about two or three kilos of liquid latex a day in June and July, the early part of the season. As the season wears on, however, and as the incisions are made lower and on the thicker portions of the trunk, a day's production may rise to four to six kilos. This is still less than the production of the roads in the Upper Amazon tributaries, which give as much as ten kilos per day.

The collectors' day is not over, however, when they return with the day's collection of latex. After having walked some eight to twelve kilometers, they still must *defumar* (coagulate the latex with smoke). After a short rest in a hammock, this job occupies most of the afternoon. It is done in a small palm-thatched hut over a clay fireplace (*buião*). The fireplace is built so that smoke is channeled out through a narrow opening. The best fire for the purpose is kindled with *urucuri* palm nuts, which have a high oil content and provide a great deal of smoke. Green wood placed on a hot fire may also be used. Gurupá collectors estimate that it takes about an hour to smoke four kilos of liquid latex.

The latex is poured gradually over a paddle-like instrument that is slowly turned in the smoke that streams out of the mouth of the fireplace. As the rubber hardens on the paddle, more liquid latex is poured over it until an oval ball is formed of coagulated rubber. Generally, after a layer about a half inch thick has been formed on the paddle, the hardened rubber is removed and wrapped around a pole forming the core for a larger *bolão* (ball). This is added to day by day until it sometimes weighs 75 to 100 kilos. The job of smoking is considered a distasteful one. The fire toasts the legs of the worker and smoke fills the air in the low hut. It is hot inside, and the collector chokes and perspires. Many rubber collectors impute the frequency of pneumonia, and even tuberculosis, to the many hours they spend in smoke huts preparing rubber for the market.

FIGURE 3.5 | *Gurupá rubber tapper with the beginning of a rubber ball.*
Photograph by C. Wagley 1942.

In the Gurupá region rubber collectors are able to work at their occupation only about five months out of the year, although the collecting season is not much longer in the Upper Amazon. During the winter, from December through May, rain drips into the cups that are attached to the trees to catch the liquid latex. The water mixes with the latex, causing the cup to overflow on to the ground. Furthermore, the trees in the Lower Amazon do not produce well in the winter, and the flooded rivers and constant rain make the rubber roads all but impassable. The rubber-collecting season is therefore limited generally to the summer, from June to early December. Yet even in the summer there are a few rainy days, and many days are otherwise lost for work. Because most of the low islands are especially swampy, the collectors must build footpaths of logs above the water level to traverse portions of their rubber trails. During the month of August, the peak of the dry season, the rubber tree flowers. Few people work their rubber roads during this period because the blossoms from the trees fall into the collecting cups, causing the latex to coagulate. Furthermore, it's believed that cutting during this period harms the tree and permanently lowers its production.

The collecting season is relatively short, but if collectors work at least five days a week throughout the full season they may produce as much as 500 kilos of coagulated rubber—at the rate of about 50 to 60 kilos each 15-day period. It is customary in the Amazon to deduct 20 to 30 percent of the weight of the rubber at the trading station to account for the loss through dehydration between the time the collectors deliver it and the riverboat collects it from the trader. After this deduction, known throughout the Valley as the *tara*, the collectors will be paid for only 300 to 400 kilos of their season's work, depending on how dry the rubber balls are when they present them at the trading post. In 1948 traders paid approximately 50 cents per kilo (cr. $10) for rubber. Collectors thus might expect to earn $150 to $200 (cr. $1,500 to cr. $4,000) during a season.

The minimum expenditures for foods and other necessities for collectors and their spouses were estimated at approximately $10 (cr. $200) per month; yet the average expenditures of the collector families included in our household studies showed an average monthly expenditure of $24.25 (cr. $485.20). In any case, collectors who are fortunate enough not to have to purchase cups, knives, a gun, and other instruments for their work might well finish a season with a small profit. In 1948 some collectors in the Gurupá region earned only from $50 to $150 (cr. $1,000 to $3,000) above their basic expenses. The cost of tools for rubber collecting, enforced idleness, sickness, together with the high prices that the collectors pay the trader for their basic supplies, usually eat up most of these meager profits. In most cases collectors must replace cups, knives, and other tools; they must buy fishhooks, a gun, or other necessities; and they often pay the owner of the rubber forests 10 to 20 percent of their production for the right to collect on the land.

Under the present circumstances, and with the techniques of exploiting wild rubber that are widespread throughout the Amazon Valley, rubber collecting does not furnish a minimum living wage. Like agriculture, it must be combined with other economic activities if a person is to eke out a living for one's self and family. Often several members of a family must work at collecting to secure their basic necessities. In one case, a man and his twenty-year-old son worked four rubber trails while the wife and their eighteen-year-old daughter took over the job of smoking the latex. The help of the women allowed the men time to plant a small garden and to fish. In spite of their activities, however, the family was in debt.

Many collectors in the Gurupá region work at other extractive industries during the season of the year when they are unable to collect rubber, for several other native products of the tropical forest, which have a market value, may be collected during the off season. In January and February the nut of the *ucuuba* tree, which grows along the small tributaries, falls into the flooded streams. People in the lowland areas collect them from canoes to sell at the trading posts. They are used for oil. Over a hundred tons of these nuts were exported downriver by Gurupá merchants during 1947 and 1948. Another forest seed, the *paracaxi*, is also collected in February. The seeds from this plant are allowed to soak in water for about eight days and are then cooked over a slow fire. The oil that is thus extracted brings about $2.50 (cr. $50) for a can of twenty liters; it is used both as a lubricant and for the manufacture of soap. Other vegetable oils, such as those derived from *patúa*, *andiroba*, and *copaíba* trees, are also exported.[18] Wild cacao is found

---

[18]In the 1980s during a timber boom, the near complete harvesting of the virola and andiroba trees led to the depletion of ucuuba and andiroba oils (made from the seeds of the trees) in the municipality and loss of the small, but useful income these seeds provided.

in the Amazon forest, and collector families spend time harvesting the seeds. Collectors may fell hardwood trees, such as *andiroba* and *virola*, in certain limited areas to be sold for lumber. Timbó vine, used for insecticides, brought a good price to the collector until recently, when synthetic products such as DDT replaced it on the market. *Buçu* palm leaf may be cut and sold for thatch. Common firewood is always salable along the Amazon mainstream to the numerous wood-burning steamers. Animal pelts, such as that of the deer, of the jaguar, and of wild pigs, bring in small sums to the collector families. In addition to these supplementary extractive products, many collectors plant small gardens during the dry season with quick-growing crops such as beans, corn, melons, and pumpkins. Without these additional sources of income and of food, collectors could not maintain themselves. In fact, the rubber industry of the Amazon Valley seems destined to a slow death. It is a strange phenomenon that, in the native home of rubber, industry cannot compete with the rubber plantations of Asia nor with the synthetic rubber industry of the industrial West.

Even plantation rubber has not, to date, proven to be commercially successful in the Amazon. Long ago rubber trees were planted in small quantities in various localities of the Valley. In Gurupá more than two hundred trees were planted near the edge of the town some forty years ago. Today the trees are rented out by the municipality to individuals to be exploited. Although it is a comparatively easy and comfortable job to collect the latex, the production is not particularly lucrative, for the trees do not produce so well as the wild hevea. The Ford Motor Company attempted to exploit Amazon rubber on a plantation basis on a large scale. In 1924 Ford was granted extensive concessions on the Tapajós River at Fordlândia and at Belterra. Several million rubber trees were planted on the two plantations. After World War II, however, the Ford Company resold the plantations to the Brazilian Government for a relatively small sum after spending millions of dollars on equipment and on rubber cultivation. The failure of this great private corporation after more than fifteen years indicates some of the difficulties inherent in the plantation rubber industry in the region.

The major difficulties of the Ford concessions were not tropical disease nor climate. In both Fordlândia and in Belterra, modern hospitals provided up-to-date medical care. In both concessions modern sanitation provided health conditions superior to those in the average

Brazilian city. Housing conditions, both for the plantation workers and for company officials, were excellent. The major difficulties seem to have been the problem of adapting the native rubber tree to plantation conditions, and the problem of securing a stable supply of labor. When the rubber trees were planted in close proximity, they proved to be much more vulnerable to their natural insect and disease enemies. To secure a disease-resistant rubber tree on their plantations, the Ford Company hired specialists who had previous experience in Asian plantations. They found it necessary to graft the native tree with a plantation variety imported from the Asian rubber groves. Most of the rubber-producing trees on the Belterra concession in 1945 had a native

FIGURE 3.6 | *João Pombo.*
Photograph by C. Wagley 1948.

Brazilian root system, an Asian trunk, and a native leaf system. Rubber planting was thus a complex and a costly process. Second, the Ford concessions suffered from a lack of labor. Despite favorable living conditions on the plantations—the schools, the hospitals, modern housing, availability of foods, and other facilities not generally found in the Amazon Valley—rubber workers would not remain in sufficient numbers to work the large plantations efficiently.

The Amazon rubber collectors are known for their nomadic way of life. In general, they are attracted into, or forced into, rubber collecting with the hope of making a quick profit after a season or two. Few consider rubber collecting as a lifelong occupation. Consequently, the

FIGURE 3.7 | *Jorge Palheta.*
Photograph by C. Wagley 1948.

rubber gatherers go to little trouble to build permanent improvements or adjuncts for their physical comfort. Because the collectors generally occupy land for which the trader for whom they work has some sort of title, they hardly bother to build a permanent house; and because their income is low, they accumulate few material possessions. Only their debts keep them from moving on, seeking always for a more favorable situation after a season in one locality. The rubber gatherers whom we knew had a feeling of instability, a desire to flee, and a vague hope of striking it rich. Their seminomadic habits and their "strike-it-rich" attitudes, generated by the social and economic system of the rubber industry of the Valley, are not conducive to long-term employment on commercial plantations. Recruits to the Ford concessions, paid at the low normal rate for day labor in the Amazon, soon moved on to look for a rich rubber field where they might build up a reserve in a year or two. Amazon plantations, dependent on an uncertain labor supply,

FIGURE 3.8 | *Pará family—Standing left to right: Bibi, Zeca; seated: Senina, Feliciana, Beija; squatting: Irac007 Paiva Ramos, Irene Dias Calvacante, Raimundo Pará do Carmo (Parazinho).*

Photograph by C. Wagley 1948.

cannot compete with those in Africa nor with those in Asia, which may call on enormous populations for labor. Only if Brazilian Government agronomists are able to produce a Brazilian tree better adapted to plantation conditions, and if a stable labor supply becomes available in the region, can the Amazon Valley look forward to developing rubber as a lucrative industry.[19]

IV

The rubber industry, however, has influenced Amazon society in many ways. The social system of large areas of the Valley, especially where rubber collecting is still (or has been) the basic economic pursuit, results directly from the commercial system related to the rubber industry. Throughout a large part of the Valley, the structure of the rural neighborhoods is determined, to a large extent, by the credit system, the economic dependence on the trader, and the vague landholding system that has developed out of the rubber-collecting industry. Furthermore, relationship of the rubber-collector neighborhoods to the wider community and to the city is, in turn, determined by the credit and the trading system of the wild-rubber industry. The commercial system by which rubber collecting is organized is controlled at the top by the exporter-importer companies of Belém and Manaus (*aviadores*). These large companies send out merchandise on credit to local traders (*seringalistas*), and they purchase rubber and other

---

[19]The problem of labor instability and worker turnover experienced at Belterra and Fordlândia was repeated at the Jarí tree plantation in the 1980s (see Hecht and Cockburn 2011) and, on a lesser scale, by the timber and palm heart extraction firms in Gurupá during the 1980s and 1990s. An alternative explanation of such widespread behavior in the Amazon might focus on the most compelling historic reason for people worldwide to enter into wage labor—a lack of direct access to land, resources, and tools needed for survival (Wolf 1982). Because the ribeirinhos of the Amazon typically have access to land and resources (but not always tools), they lack sufficient enticement (or coercion) to work full-time in wage labor, particularly on the level offered in Amazonia (low wages, poor working conditions). Without the incentive of restricted access to land and resources, the population systematically chooses to work for wages for short periods of time for immediate goals, then return home to their agroextractivist lifestyle, which, although challenging, is more appealing than wage labor. Even when wages are higher and working conditions better (as Wagley suggests for the Ford concession), this preference prevails.

products in return. These supply houses and exporters are owners of the riverboats that regularly ply the mainstream and tributaries, providing, in many cases, the only means of communication between trading stations and the towns and cities of the region. In turn, the local traders supply necessities to their customers, the rubber collectors, and they purchase from them the results of their collecting. Each is in debt to the other—the collector to the trader, and the trader to the import-export firm. Each advances merchandise to the other on credit. And, needless to say, in such an uncertain business the large exporters of Manaus and Belém are in debt to banks and rubber importers in Rio de Janeiro, London, and New York.[20] In rubber-collecting zones a rural neighborhood is formed by traders and their collector-customers who live scattered near the rubber trails and who come periodically to the trading post, which is the center of the neighborhood. Such a neighborhood has contact with the outside periodically through the visits of the steamer owned by the company of which traders are customer debtors.

In addition to debt, land tenure reinforces the exporter-trader-collector dependency relationship. Legal titles for land are often confused and precarious in the Amazon region. Titles have been issued for land at various periods by the state governments: some of them are legally valid; some of them give the "owners" rights only to the exploitation of rubber or to Brazil nuts on the land; and some of them, although indicating full ownership, are worth only the paper on which they are written. In any case, it is control over the land, and not legal documents, which in practice generally determines "ownership" of the land. Traders generally establish their *barracão* (trading post) at the mouth of a small river or tributary. The banks of the river and the rubber forest inland from the stream are thereby "owned" by the traders or by absentee "owners" from whom the trader rents. Their collector-customers inhabit and exploit the lands back from the river controlled by the trading post. Enormous areas in whole river valleys were thus controlled by single individuals and by export companies during the rubber boom. In these areas the "owners" had absolute control over the lives of the people within their domains.

Just upriver from Gurupá, for example, the family J. J. Andrade Ramos "owned," until less than a decade ago, all the land between the

---

[20]This system is known as aviamento.

two great rivers extending north of the Amazon mainstream to the Guiana borders. This area covered two county-like municipalities. With this domain there were two towns, both municipal seats, and there are several smaller settlements, which grew up around the company trading posts. The Andrade Ramos company owned its own steamboats and exported its products directly to southern Brazil and abroad. State and federal police powers hardly reached into their domain, for armed company employees "kept the peace." It was a common legend in Belém that during the early decades of the twentieth century, most of the prisoners from the jail were sent upriver to end their days in semislavery for the Andrade Ramos'. On one occasion, some years back, the workers on the Andrade Ramos domains revolted. They overpowered the armed guards, took control of a large riverboat, and sailed for Belém. In the Belém harbor, however, they were met by state police and, according to several reports, returned upriver to work out the rest of their lives in the most distant rubber trails in the Andrade Ramos territory. Nowadays, the Pereira Silva lands have been divided into several large properties, as have most enormous rubber territories throughout the Valley; but old "Colonel" Andrade Ramos still controls enormous tracts of land, and he is much feared by people in the Gurupá community, who tell of how his men controlled the rubber collectors on his property with the lash and with the rifle.

The relationship between the trader owner and the collector as it existed during the heyday of the rubber boom has been described by many writers. The contemporary Portuguese novelist Ferreira de Castro (1935), in *A Selva,*has described the brutality and the absolute life-and-death control of the trader over his collectors. Euclides da Cunha (1944), whose precise and colorful observations of the rebellion of a handful of Brazilian religious fanatics against the Brazilian federal forces in northeastern Brazil has become a national classic,also visited the Amazon during the early days of the rubber boom. In a brief essay, he gives a detailed picture of the recruiting of labor in the drought-stricken northeast region of Brazil and the debt-slavery system in the Amazon. According to Euclides da Cunha, the proprietors of rubber forests sent agents to the northeastern states who enlisted men for rubber gathering in the Amazon Valley. As soon as the new collector left his native community, he began to owe his *patrão* (employer). "He owed the steerage passage as far as Pará, and the money he received to prepare for the trip." Then his debt began to mount steadily. He was charged the cost of his passage up the Amazon into one of its tributaries to the trading post. There he was supplied with utensils for collecting latex, a gun and some ammunition, food to carry him through the collecting season, and some quinine to cure his almost certain malaria. All these things were charged to him at high prices. Euclides da Cunha calculates that at best the new rubber worker would owe the trader owner some 2,090 milreis[20] before beginning work. He also estimates that under the most favorable conditions the new collector might realize 2,000 milreis during the first year. Under ideal conditions the recruit might double his production the second year and thus pay off his debt and have a profit; but, inevitably, idleness caused by fevers, the cost of replacing tools, inactivity during the heavy rains, occasional splurges at festivals, and inexperience made necessary additional credit advances and added to the collector's debt. "It is evident," Euclides da Cunha wrote, "that the collector able to free himself by luck is rare" (Cunha 1941:23–24).

The trader owner of the trading post was protected by "law" in the days that both Euclides da Cunha and Ferreira de Castro described for the Amazon Valley. These "laws," which guaranteed to the traders the payments of the advances that they made to their collectors, were embodied in the "Rules of the Rubber Fields," a systematized agreement among the owners of rubber lands as to their relations with their debtor collectors. The "Rules" were formulated to prevent collectors from escaping and to keep them in debt. According to the "Rules," an owner might impose a fine on a collector for cutting a tree too deeply when "milking" the tree or for using a hatchet more than "four palms" wide in the process. The "Rules" stated that collectors might not make purchases at any other trading post than the one in which they made them credit advances. If they did, they might be fined 50 percent of the cost of the objects purchased. The collectors might not leave the employment of the trader to whom they were in debt without complete liquidation of their accounts. To prevent escape, traders established their principal trading stations at the mouths of tributaries, where guards, armed with .44 rifles, watched day and night for collectors who might try to escape downriver. Even if a collector was able to bypass the guards by fleeing overland through the tropical forest or by slipping downriver in the dark, the agreement among the traders prohibited their giving refuge to the fugitive. Each trader was obligated by the "Rules" to capture escaped debtors and to return them to their creditor traders. If by considerable luck a collector fleeing from debts reached Belém or Manaus, the collector might be arrested by the police to be returned upriver to the employer creditor. The "Rules" were not government decrees, but the owners of rubber fields and the traders put constant political pressure on the government to help them enforce the "Rules of the Rubber Fields" as if they were formal law.[21]

After 1912, with the end of the fabulously high rubber prices, both the commercial system and debt slavery related to the rubber industry began to disintegrate. The rubber "barons" lost their absolute political power along with their wealth. International scandals called attention to the "slavery" of the Amazon rubber collector. Traders without credit from the exporter were often glad to allow their collectors to leave. Yet even today essentially the same system of debtor-creditor relations persists, although in a somewhat milder form, throughout a great portion of the Valley.

Even in the farming area of the community of Gurupá, a similar pattern exists between the agriculturalists and the local traders and storekeepers. Most of the inhabitants of the farming neighborhoods are the *fregueses* (customers) of a specific trader or of a town storekeeper. The farmers who live along the Igarapé Jocojó and along the Igarapé Ribeira, for example, are traditionally the customers of the Casa Borralho in Gurupá. Most of them are in debt to Dona Diná Borralho (see Figure 3.4), who advances them food and merchandise, and she buys their surplus farm produce, if any, from them. Dona Diná has titles that give her "ownership" to most of the land bordering these small streams. Both Dona Diná and her brother-in-law, Oscar Santos, who is manager of the Casa Borralho, complain bitterly that "our customers trade elsewhere." They consider it unfair, almost illegal, for other traders to purchase manioc flour or forest products from their customers and for their customers to make purchases elsewhere. Still, their "customers" come to Gurupá after dark to sell their manioc flour to another store or they go upriver to another trading post, situated on the Amazon bank, to sell and buy. "I tell them of their debts and of the (rights to use) land and they are ashamed," said the manager of the Casa Borralho. He also threatens to remove them from the land and he limits their credit. But Dona Diná also knows that her "titles" to the

---

[21]The milreis was the old monetary unit equivalent to the cruzeiro.

land are of doubtful legal validity, and she would not attempt to evict farmers, many of whom have occupied the land for twenty years or more.[22] Furthermore, because farmers have less to sell to traders than the rubber collectors, they depend less on purchases from the traders, and it is more difficult for the traders to maintain control over their farmer customers than it is to maintain it over the collectors.

In the rubber-collecting area of the municipality of Gurupá, the traditional trader-customer relationship still functions as a very strong social and economic bond. The trading post is the center of a rural

---

[22]Despite the stories about the Andrade Ramos family, for the majority of rubber tappers in the lower Amazon a history of small-scale landownership enabled many tappers to work their own rubber trails and produce food. This allowed them to stay out of permanent debt to merchants. In Gurupá, for example, a large and powerful latifundiário class did not develop as it did in many neighboring municipalities. Gurupá's merchants did acquire large tracts of land (by purchase, foreclosure, intimidation, or invasion) on the várzea where the rubber trees were concentrated, but much land remained in the possession of small landowners. As indicated by the 625 land title registrations recorded between 1880 and 1910 in Gurupá, most landholdings were a quarter or a half league in dimension (between one and four kilometers). In terms of rubber trails possessed, only 1.5 percent of land registrations recorded over 100 trails, while 61 percent reported 10 or under. One rubber trail on the average contained between 80 and 150 individual trees and covered a 3–5 square kilometer area (Barham and Coomes 1994b:45). In Amazonian terms, a large estate consisted of 100 trails or more, whereas a small holding, usually owned by a family of humble origins, consisted of 10 trails or less (Weinstein 1983:172). The reason Gurupá did not develop a full-scale latifundiário pattern was because of the early entry into rubber extraction by many small- and medium-size landowners before the large aviador houses gained sufficient power to appropriate land (Weinstein 1983:47).

Even though Gurupá's land tenure structure mitigated against the extremes of debt-slavery abuses reported in other areas, landowners did exploit workers. Techniques common in Gurupá were prohibiting rubber tappers from planting crops, expelling individuals from land when caught trading rubber to regatões or spending too much time on subsistence activities, and manipulating trade that left the rubber tappers in persistent poverty. As in the entire Amazon, rubber profits seldom trickled down to the lowly extractor (Weinstein 183:70). Yet, a combination of Gurupá's history of small landownership, its proximity to Belém for trade, and the availability of unclaimed terra firme for agricultural production insured that many Gurupaenses had access to land, food, and alternative trade that aviadores and seringalistas could not monopolize as they did in more remote areas of the Amazon. This history is an important consideration when considering why Gurupá was able to develop a successful resistance movement against the political and economic powers in the 1980s—discussed in Chapter 8.

neighborhood in which the inhabitants are all customers of the trader. These collectors are socially and economically tied to the trading post, which serves them both as a market and as a social center. An example of a typical collector neighborhood is that surrounding the trading post of Francisco Felix, lying directly across the Amazon channel from the town of Gurupá. His trading post is situated at the point where the small Rio Urutaí flows into the Amazon. Francisco Felix has twenty-one customers, that is, the people from twenty-one scattered households who trade only at his store. A list of the names of the family heads of these households is posted on the door of his store. The rubber trails that these customers work are "owned" by Senhor Felix. He does not have a valid title to the land, but he does have documents showing that he purchased the *seringais* (rubber fields) from a former owner who had received a concession from the state government to exploit rubber in the area. More important than documents, however, is the fact that people of the community recognize Senhor Felix's "ownership" of the land. Each of the twenty-one families has received credit advances from Francisco Felix, and a study of his books indicated that he advanced an average of about $100 (cr. $2,000) to each family for the collecting season. Several of these customer families have debts of several years' standing.

Francisco Felix's customers live at various distances from his trading post. Six houses are situated on the Amazon mainstream and the others are up the Rio Urutaí. Each house is spaced some three hundred to eight hundred meters from the other and is built at a point on the river that gives access to two, three, or more rubber trails. As compared to the larger rubber trading posts on the upper Xingú, Tapajós, and Madeira rivers and those in the District of Acre, Francisco Felix's has a small number of customers. In the more productive districts, fifty to sixty or more families are often thus attached to a trader.

It is traditional throughout the Amazon Valley for the customers of a trader to come to the post on an appointed day (*quinzena*) to deliver the rubber they have collected and to stock up on supplies. The *quinzena* at Francisco Felix's post, and generally in the Lower Amazon region, takes place on the average of once each month rather than at regular fifteen-day intervals. The *quinzena* usually takes place just before the arrival of the *Union*, the wood-burning riverboat of J. Fontes Company of Belém, which supplies Francisco Felix with trade goods and which purchases his rubber and other produce. The *Union* ties up for a few hours at the wharf in front of Senhor Felix's post around the twentieth of each month. For a few hours there is fevered activity while the sailors unload supplies and while the rubber and other products are weighed and loaded aboard. But the busiest day of the month at the post is the day before the arrival of the steamer, when most of the customers and their families come to trade. Francisco Felix sends out a message to his customers setting the date for this trading day in accordance with the schedule of the *Union*, which is anything but regular in its sailings. But people do not limit their trading to the one day, and each Sunday a few customers gather at the post to trade, to drink, and to visit. But the *quinzena* each month is an occasion when all wish to be present. It is a day both of trading transactions and of recreation for the family, comparable to Saturday afternoons in a small American town.

In June of each year on the day of St. John, Francisco Felix invites all of his customers and their families to the trading post to hear prayers for the saint, to eat at his expense, and to dance out the night. For Senhor Felix is especially devoted to St. John, who, he feels, protects his trading post. His customers look forward to the annual festival, and Senhor Felix's friends from other trading posts also attend. On his birthday, the trader offers a party with drinking and dancing for his *freguesia* (customer group). The trading post has a large veranda opening up on the dock. There is a storeroom where the merchandise is displayed and other storerooms where the produce is kept for shipment. In addition, there are the living quarters of Senhor Felix's family, including a large salon used for visiting and for dancing on festive occasions. The structural form of a typical barracão indicates that it functions both as a market center and as a social center for the rural collector neighborhood. And Senhor Felix is, at the same time, the creditor employer of his customers and the social leader of the neighborhood.

In turn, commercial relations also determined Senhor Felix's social relations with the big city. He is a customer of the large wholesale import-export company, J. Fontes of Belém. The supplies and merchandise, such as kerosene, canned goods, kitchen utensils, candles, lamps, knives, hoes, manioc farina, dried fish, cloth, machine-made clothes, and other items which he carries in stock, are furnished on credit by J. Fontes Company. Against his debt, the company discounts the rubber and other products which he ships on the Union. Like his own collector customers, Senhor Felix seldom sees actual cash. Sometimes he sells some rubber secretly for cash to a *regatão,* one of the itinerant boats that poach on the regular company customers, just as his customers may trade secretly elsewhere. Sometimes he earns cash by selling to collector customers of other traders who pass by his post. But generally Senhor Felix deals only with his own customers and his own creditors. When he needs funds for a trip to Belém or for some other occasion, he draws cash against his credit with J. Fontes. The company often pays his bills for him with other city firms. Two years ago, when Senhor Felix's wife needed glasses, she traveled to Belém on the *Union.* J. Fontes Company sent her to an oculist, charging the doctor's bill and her passage to Senhor Felix's account. Once, many years ago, he tried to settle his account with J. Fontes Company, and asked to be allowed to deal with them on a monthly cash basis. He soon found that they were not interested in short-term accounts. Even in years when rubber brings high prices and when Senhor Felix has a surplus to his account, he does not withdraw his profits but allows them to remain on deposit with the company. "J. Fontes does not care if my account is paid up," he explained; "they want the rubber I send them." In the Amazon traders make more profit on the resale of the products purchased from their customers than from what is sold to them despite the high prices charged. Similarly, J. Fontes Company realizes more from the export of rubber than from the merchandise they sell to the traders.

The commercial system of the Amazon is no longer maintained by the old "Rules of the Rubber Fields," nor by the police and the .44 rifle as it was during the first decade of this century. Yet the obligations of the collector to the trader and the trader to the import-export firm have remained essentially unchanged as the basic relationships that channel commercial and social relationships within the region. The strength of the traditional system is an important element to contend with in any attempt to modify economic and social conditions in the Valley. Attempts during the last war to sell supplies directly to the traders, shortcutting the import-export firm, and to collect rubber directly, were doomed to failure by the pressure of the long-standing credit and social relationships between the traders and the big city company. To break away from their only source of credit and regular supplies—often their only source of communication with the outside—did not seem rational to the traders. Attempts to form cooperatives and to extend government credit to rural Amazonian populations often clash with this system of relationships, for cooperatives would do away with the traders. And yet even this Amazon commercial system can be helpful in introducing new innovations. New ideas, new forms of technology, and new instruments may be introduced through the city firms, to their traders, and finally to the collectors and farmers in distant areas of the Valley.[23]

V

Many of the basic problems of humanity's adjustment to the tropical environment of the Amazon community may be seen in the ways in which the people of Gurupá earn a living. The two principal occupations of the community, subsistence farming and the collecting of native products of the forest, are those characteristic of large areas of the Amazon Valley. It is apparent that neither of these occupations will alone furnish any more than a bare subsistence for a family in Gurupá. Even by combining collecting and farming, it is possible to maintain only a low standard of living.[24]

---

[23]Looking back in time from 2013, although Dona Diná may have never expelled workers from her lands, many of her peers did; and her successor at the Casa Borralho did as well. Wagley's account of the patron-client system here contrasts sharply with the narratives recorded between 1980 and 2013 (see Chapter 8). Following the consciousness-raising campaigns on human rights and land rights by the Catholic Church and bitter struggles over land in the 1980s, most people in 2013 reflect harshly on the abuses of the patron-client system.

[24]Early in 1943, when it looked as if wild rubber might be crucial to the Allied war effort, administrators were told that malaria was seriously impeding the collection of rubber and that there were no specifics available in the distant parts of the Valley to treat malaria. Several million tablets of Atabrine (an antimalaria drug) were quickly sent by air freight to Manaus. Then there was the problem of how to get the drug quickly and cheaply into the hands of the rubber gatherer. There were also the problems of transportation to the high tributaries and of the high prices that would certainly be charged for the precious drug if sold through the normal channels. It was decided to offer Atabrine gratuitous to the import-export firms with the understanding that it would be furnished free to the trader and, in turn, the collector. The drug was made quickly available, even in the distant high tributaries of the Valley, through the mechanism of the relationship of the city firm, local trader, and the collector.

[24]Ten lines were omitted that critiqued subsistence agriculture—without the benefit of more recent research on the potential of sustainable development through horticulture and extractive activities.

In addition, rubber collection actually seems to be a barrier to the production of an adequate food supply. Rubber and other forest products provide people with the necessary cash or credit without which they would be unable to purchase the numerous necessities that must be imported from outside; but at the same time, these collecting activities for export direct the efforts of a large part of the population away from food production. The return they receive from collecting does not bring sufficient income to purchase the food and other material necessities, which must be imported from outside the region. The emphasis on an extractive economy and collecting raw materials for distant markets since the beginning of European settlement has impeded humanity's effectual adjustment to the Amazon environment more than the physical environment.

Improvement of social conditions in the Amazon depends, of course, on the development of a more lucrative and more efficient economic basis for Amazon society. Agriculture must be modernized and adapted to local conditions so as to provide an adequate food supply for the present population; and this is even more urgent and crucial if immigration into the Valley is contemplated. The old collecting industries, such as those of Brazil nuts and wild rubber, must be so organized that they will provide an adequate livelihood for the Amazon producer—or they must be abandoned. In addition, new cash crops must be sought that may be produced on a commercial basis in the Amazon soil and for which there is a stable and lucrative market.

Economic change in Gurupá depends on improvement of transportation and communications, wider and more efficiently administered credit facilities, the removal of trade barriers, and the availability of modern technological equipment—all of which are determined beyond the frontiers of any single community. In other words, the improvement of the economic system of Gurupá will depend on national and international trends and policies. Yet it is in the local community that national or international policies and trends deal with concrete human situations and affect the lives of the people.

CHAPTER 4

....

Social Relations
in an Amazon Community

I n the small Amazon community of Gurupá, as in all human societies, people are ranked in prestige. In Gurupá social rank depends
on a combination of criteria, some of which are fixed at birth—such
as one's sex, race, and family membership—and others, such as occupation and education, which are left to individual choice and initiative
and that depend, too, on the available opportunities and the capacity of
a person to make use of them (Linton 1936:113ff.). Because Gurupá is a
small and isolated community, the distance between the highest and
lowest individual in the social scale of prestige is not so great as it is in
a large city or in a society with a more elaborate social structure. The
system of social rank is nonetheless an important aspect of Gurupá's
social life. There was a time, however, when the difference between the
lowest and the highest in social rank in Gurupá was greater. In the first
centuries of the town's history, those who were born of Native American
or mixed-blood parentage in the "village" quarter of the town carried
the stigma of their slave parents. Individuals were born as slaves or
as freemen. Mobility upward was extremely infrequent. During the
rubber boom the economic difference between the rich rubber merchants and the miserable rubber gatherers made social distances great.
At that time there was an "aristocracy" in Gurupá. Families such as
that of the baron of Gurupá were proud of their Portuguese ancestors.

They educated their children in the large cities of Brazil and Europe. They were wealthy in land, and they participated in the political and social life of the wider Amazon region. Such people traveled frequently to Belém and to Manaus, and they received visitors from other communities. They formed the *alta sociedade*—the aristocracy. As landowning merchants, they controlled economic and political life, occupying all of the public positions of the municipality. Such people as Coronel Filemeno Borralho, a wealthy merchant who came to Gurupá from Maranhão; Flaviano Flavio de Batista, who was a land-owner, the *intendente* (mayor) of Gurupá, and a political leader recognized and respected in Belém; and Dr. Joaquim Nobre, the judge, a graduate of the Law School in Belém who maintained his legitimate wife and children in Belém and a second family in Gurupá, were representative figures of this class. Class lines were more strictly maintained in the days of these aristocrats before the rubber crash. A member of the lower class would not sit down in the presence of one of these *brancos* (whites), as they were called. There were always two rooms of dancers at any party, one room for the lower class and the other for the aristocracy. In Gurupá, as in most Latin American communities, strong class distinctions between the colonial aristocracy and the people of aboriginal and slave origin persisted into the twentieth century.

Nowadays only a few descendants of these aristocratic families live in Gurupá. The few who do remain are relatively impoverished and have lost their high social rank. At the end of the rubber boom, most of the aristocratic families moved away one by one. Their successful children left to study in Belém or in South Brazil. Such men as the Jewish physician, mentioned earlier, never returned after they had completed their education, even though their parents stayed for a time. Today, except for the public health physician of the SESP, there is not a single individual with a complete secondary education in town. Only the Casa Borralho of the strong commercial houses of the rubber times remains. Neither the traditional aristocratic families (who still control large landholdings in the Amazon), the professional class, the military, the Church officials, the industrial and commercial groups, nor the political leaders—who together form the contemporary upper class of the Amazon region—are present in Gurupá society today.

To the outsider, therefore, Gurupá may appear to be a homogeneous society of rural peasants, of people who differ little from one another in social rank. In Belém, upper-class people are apt to classify the people of Gurupá, with the exception of a few government officials stationed there, as ribeirinhos. Travelers from larger centers generally call on the SESP doctor; Dona Diná at the Casa Borralho; or on the mayor, a young man who was once a sailor in the Brazilian navy. City people recognize these people as roughly equivalent to the urban middle class. Visitors from Belém sometimes comment on the lack of upper class in Gurupá. They may remark that "the mayor is nothing more than a caboclo," or they may wonder at the high social position of Dona Diná, who is a dark mulatta and whose husband had strong African features (*negro* in Portuguese). Yet, as one lives and participates in Gurupá social life, it soon becomes apparent that people, within the confines of the community itself, are quite sensitive to differences in social rank. In fact, people are quite explicit and overt as to the different social strata in their society.

Such present-day distinctions in social rank result from the class system of colonial Amazon society, from the former servitude of Indigenous populations and imported African slaves, and from the social ascendancy of the Portuguese colonials. They also reflect the economic and social position of the various groups who inhabit Gurupá today. In their simplest form the social strata of Gurupá are, in the words of the people themselves and in order of social prestige:

1. The First Class (*Gente de Primeira*), or the "whites" (*brancos*), who form the local upper class;
2. The Second Class (*Gente de Segunda*), who are the lower-class town dwellers;
3. The farmers (*Gente de Sítio*), who inhabit the agricultural lands of terra firme; and
4. The Island collectors (*ribeirinhos da Beira*), the people who live in huts built on stilts over the low swamps and inundated islands, earning their living from a purely collecting economy.

It cannot be said that all Gurupá people are fully aware of all these categories. As the city folk tend to view Gurupá as a homogeneous society of small town peasants, the First-Class people of Gurupá are apt to view all the people below them in the social hierarchy as simply "the people," or as "caboclos." In turn, the town-dwelling Second Class indicate their superiority to all the rural population by speaking of them as "caboclos," and the farmers reserve this term for the Island collectors, to whom they feel superior. And finally, the Island collectors would be slightly offended if they were called "caboclos," for they make little distinction between themselves and the farmers.[1] The system of social stratification of Gurupá society differs, therefore, in accordance with the social position from which it is viewed. And, as will become apparent, socioeconomic differences are greatest between the First Class and the three lower strata. Among the Second Class, the farmers and the Island collectors, the lines of social discrimination are not clearly drawn; social mobility takes place with great ease, and economic conditions differ less than between these three groups and the First Class. In a sense, therefore, it is perhaps proper to speak of Gurupá as a society with but two social classes—an upper and lower class; but a simple twofold division would not fully express the social distinctions made by the people themselves.

To the few people who claim some relationship with the old Gurupá aristocracy, such as Manuel Pere Serra, the state tax collector, and Dona Inacinha, the schoolteacher, few people truly belong to the "whites" or the First Class. Dona Inacinha (see Figure 2.6) would accept only one family, that of Dona Diná Borralho, as high society or First Class. She would not even count Dona Deborah, widow of an important Jewish merchant, as First Class because her son lives "in friendship" (i.e., without benefit of Church or civil marriage) with a young girl whom Dona Inacinha herself raised. To Dona Inacinha dances today are not parties but "wild gatherings where young ladies of family are mixed with everybody." Senhor Pere Serra (see Figure 2.7) said that "formerly political posts were held only by First Class," and he pointed out the lowly origins of the present mayor as a sign of the decadence of Gurupá society. He felt that it was not proper to bring his family to public functions; and during our residence in Gurupá, Senhor Pere Serra did not attend any of the social affairs offered by the public officials. Even people of the lower classes recognize that there are few aristocrats of local origin left in Gurupá today. A woman of low status remarked, "The only real First Class in Gurupá today are people from outside." Except for two or three families of merchants, the group recognized as "whites" or First Class are composed of the mayor, the police chief, the federal and state tax collectors, employees of the SESP,

---

[1]The Island collectors use the term "caboclo" to refer to the tribal natives who inhabit the headwaters of the Amazon tributaries. The Amazon "caboclo," therefore, exists only in the concept of the groups of higher status referring to those of lower status.

and their respective families—all salaried officials and government employees.

Yet the lines of social cleavage between the First Class and the lower groups, between the "whites" and the "people," are still relatively strongly felt in Gurupá. As late as 1942, the "line" between the two groups was rather strictly maintained. During the celebrations on the birthday of a well-known political hero of the region, there was a parade and an afternoon of fireworks and public speeches that were attended by everyone, seemingly without distinction. But in the evening there were two dances. One, held in the public dance pavilion, was an open dance for the "people." There men danced in their shirt sleeves, and both men and women danced barefooted on the rough boards. In the home of the mayor, who was at that time Benedito Levi, a descendant of one of the Jewish families, there were dancing and refreshments for the "whites"—a group of some thirty people. A few young unmarried girls of good reputation but of Second-Class families were invited to the festivities of the "whites." One young lady of the Second Class came with her mother to the First-Class dance dressed in party dress and shoes, while her brother danced in the public pavilion. A man accepted as First Class attended without his common-law wife because she was not "of the First." It was explained that he had never legalized his marriage because his "companion" was not "of good family."

In similar festivals held in 1948, the "line" between the upper and the lower classes seemed less rigid. At a dance offered by the mayor in 1948 many people of the Second Class were invited and attended. There was some comment to the effect that the mayor would need their votes in the next election. The return of Brazil to a system of free elections after ten years of dictatorship did give the voter, regardless of class, more importance. Many Second-Class people, however, would not attend the mayor's party even though they were invited, because they "felt ashamed in front of so many important people." Others did not come simply because they could not afford shoes and the clothes for the party. And the Second-Class people who did attend parties were made to feel their lower position. The First-Class guests were offered seats, served coffee, and invited to drink beer in the back room with the host. Second-Class people were not invited to sit, and they were offered refreshments last. The expression *meu branco* (my white) is still heard with considerable frequency as a term of respect for rank in Gurupá, and lower-class people always stand up when addressing a "white" such as Dona Diná Borralho or Dona Inacinha. Between the upper and the lower strata, the lines of social discrimination are still clearly drawn.[2]

Social discrimination is not so great between the three lower class groups. In general the farmers live on the same side of the Amazon mainstream as the town, and they visit it frequently. Lower-class townspeople have good friends and many relatives among the rural fanners, and they participate in the many festivals offered by the rural religious brotherhoods. They realize that they are not much different from the farmers—for they, too, are apt to earn at least a part of their living from farming. Yet rural farmers lead an isolated life, and their standard of living is somewhat lower than that of the Second Class town dweller. Townspeople have a few advantages over the farmers: they can send their children to school and the health post is near at hand. Therefore, Second Class town dwellers tend, on the whole, to feel superior to their rural friends and relatives.[3]

Both the lower-class townspeople and the farmers, however, look with some disdain on the extractors, who earn a living from the collection of rubber and of palm nuts alone. Although in years when rubber prices are high, people from the town and from the farming zone move to the Islands to collect rubber, they are only temporary inhabitants of these isolated areas. They feel that they are different from those who permanently work at collecting. Such people are considered "hicks." When the male collector comes to town to attend the festival of St. Benedict or St. Anthony, he wears his white suit, which has been starched to the point that it stands up alone. "He brings his shoes, which he may not have worn for two years. He endures the pain caused by his shoes for most of the first day but he takes off his shoes to dance," the townspeople say with considerable amusement. "He steps on his dancing partner's feet, and no one wants to dance with a caboclo." During the second day of the festival, "the caboclo's feet are swollen;

---

[2]In 2013 parties and celebrations continue to reflect local class distinctions. One is typically included or excluded from the elite class festivities by a written invitation—which is presented at the door for entry.

[3]In 2013 this pattern is still very evident, and it is not hard to observe town folk treating their country fellows in mildly (and occasionally harshly) condescending and patronizing ways.

he is not used to shoes and he is not used to walking on the hard ground" (in contrast to the soft mud of the swamps). As everywhere else, people find the "hick" ridiculous, and those from the town of Gurupá and from the farming area think of life on the Islands and on the floodlands as slightly barbaric. They point at the numerous "shotgun marriages" performed by the police chief among the Island ribeirinhos and at the fights that occur at their dances as indications of their lower moral standards and general backwardness. The collectors participate so seldom in the social life of the town of Gurupá that our companions from town were never able to tell us the names of dwellers of the huts along the riverbank in the rubber-collecting areas of the community. Yet they knew by name each of the isolated dwellers in the nearby farming area. But the Island ribeirinhos do not treat the lower-class townspeople and the farmers with the same excessive respect and politeness that all the lower-class groups show in front of the upper class. "They [the collectors and farmers] are less civilized," said Nhenjuca, a Second Class town dweller, "because they are isolated and poor."[4]

II

The people of Gurupá classified about one-third of the residents of the town as "whites" or First Class and the remainder as Second-Class or lower-class townsfolk. In terms of the total number of inhabitants of

---

[4]Gurupá's class system continued to level out over the following six decades. By the 1980s the people I interviewed insisted there were no longer any representatives of the First Class. Sebá Costa Barriga, a retired subsistence farmer and midwife in her sixties, told me in 1985, "There are no longer First Class people in Gurupá. But there are people from the second and third class. Second class ... came in after the First Class people died off. Third class is the poor. The poorest of the poor have no certain job. The better off poor have nice houses" (Pace & Hinote 2013:170). Zeca Pará, the former prosecutor and friend/consultant of Wagley, shared this point of view, adding, "Today there are no more First Class people. There are people of the first selection (*gente de primeira seleção*) and second selection, who are lower. These divisions are not classes as before. The First and Second classes of old functioned by rigorously separating people. For example, dances were held in which class boundaries were not crossed. Today the First Selection is small, the second is big" (Pace & Hinote 2013:170). To this Zeca's wife, Beija, commented, "There are no social classes today. There is no separation within society. The difference today is only money" (Pace & Hinote 2013:170).

the Gurupá community, including the rural zones, this means that the First Class forms less than 10 percent of the total population, and the lower-class townsfolk form approximately 20 percent. Our rough census of the community area indicated that about 60 percent of the population were farmers (Gente de Sítio). Only about 10 percent of the inhabitants of the community were Island collectors because the bulk of the latter live outside the community area, in the Island region of the municipality.[5] There was some difference of opinion among our many Gurupá friends regarding the social position of a few individuals in the lower rungs of the First Class. Manuel Borralho, a young man of low-class origin, who had been raised by Dona Diná Borralho, for example, was given First Class status by several people only after some hesitation. And, as stated earlier, a few of the people of the First Class, such as Senhor Pere Serra and Dona Inacinha, considered the group of "real First Class" to be very few in number today. On the whole, however, there was remarkable agreement among our Gurupá friends as to which families were First Class and which by default belonged to the lower-class groups of the town and rural areas. A series of criteria, some of which were explicit in their minds and some of which were

---

[5]Since 2005 Brazil's class system has been in rapid flux. According to some models, the numbers of poor and very poor (class designations D and E) have declined from 51 percent in 2005 to 25 percent in 2010. At the same time a new middle class has emerged (C) and increased from 34 percent to 53 percent. There is considerable debate whether C really represents a middle class in its fullest meaning and whether it will be sustainable without easy access to credit in a growing economy. Nonetheless, in this scale, middle-class status is based on income and consumption of specific goods and services (employment of domestic help in the form of a maid, cook, or nanny; the possession of a car or motorcycle; private schooling; college degree; access to computers and broadband Internet; and monthly earnings over 6.5 minimum wages or US $2,050 (one minimum wage is supposed to pay the food and housing costs for a family of four—but it does not come close); and so forth—Oliveira 2012; Neri 2010; Poschman et al. 2006). Using these criteria, adjusted to the 1940s, Gurupá's First class (10 percent) would have corresponded to class C, Second class (20 percent) to D, and the subsistence farmers and extractors (70 percent) to E. By 2013, C1 (middle middle class) is around 5 percent, C2 (lower middle) around 15 percent, D (poor) approximately 66.1 percent, and E (very poor) 13.9 percent. In many cases the distinctions between C2 and D are not easily discernible, regardless if they are based on income, education, or other forms of class distinction. In other words, about 81 percent of the population is fairly homogenous in social class standing, even though local social hierarchies and power imbalances exist.

implicitly understood, were used by the people of Gurupá in placing people in their proper social class.[6]

An explicit and important criterion was occupation. Several writers have called attention to a so-called "gentleman complex" in Brazil. Physical work in the last century was limited to the slave-peon caste and to those recently freed, and after emancipation manual labor continued as a symbol of low social status. As people moved up in the social scale, they adopted the attitudes of the former landed gentry and slave owners, and an attitude of disparagement of any form of manual labor persists in contemporary Brazil. It is a social value that is shared not only by the descendants of the slave-owning families but also by the new middle and commercial upper class of the cities and by the people of innumerable small towns throughout the interior of the country. Even in Gurupá, a small and isolated town in the Amazon Valley, the work one does is an indication of one's social class. Because the people of Gurupá are not descendants of the slave-owning gentry (in fact, many of them are most certainly descendants of slaves), emancipation from manual labor is all the more important as a symbol of upper-class status. Of seventeen men who were classed as First Class in our household survey, none worked with his hands. All were public employees or earned their living from commerce. The group included such people as the state tax collector, the mayor, the vice mayor, and the owners of the three commercial houses. Although the wives of these men did some domestic work, most of their families also had servants. In contrast, of fifty-five Second-Class men included in our survey, all but two (clerks in the town hall) earned their living from some form of manual labor. The few artisans in Gurupá, such as the shoemaker and the carpenters, were considered Second Class. Even agriculture

---

[6]Detailed schedules covering family composition, income, expenditures for food, occupation, property, and so forth, were collected for 113 households in the Gurupá community. They provide a sample of over 30 percent of the total population (estimated at 350 households); this sample was distributed as follows: 17 households in the First Class, 55 in the Second Class, 31 in the farmer group, and 10 in the Island collector group. Difficulties of transportation made it impossible to make our sample of both rural groups representative of their numerical strength in the total population, yet I believe that our rather inadequate sample of the two groups indicates valid differences in living standards.

is a lower-class occupation. Only one family among the seventeen First-Class families had a manioc garden, and it had been planted by hired labor.[7]

The size of one's income and the standard of living that one is able to maintain are also explicit criteria used by people in Gurupá to determine the social class of an individual. All of the families who were considered to be First Class had this in common: they dealt in money. All of them had a relatively steady income from salaries or from commerce, and therefore had either cash or credit in the local stores. As one Second-Class man put it bluntly, "The 'whites' are those who have a little [money] saved in their trunks. The difference is that when I want a coconut I must climb a tree and pick it myself, but when they want a coconut they pay someone to pick it." Our survey of family incomes bore out the idea, which is widely held in Gurupá, that money is an important criterion of social position. The average cash income for seventeen First-Class families was approximately $75 (cr. $1,597.10) per month as against an average of only $23 (cr. $452.30) per month for fifty-five Second-Class families living in town.[8]

First-Class families were better housed, better dressed, and better fed than Second Class. In all cases, those who were pointed out as members of the First Class lived in a dwelling, classed as a house (*casa*), which was situated on the First or Second Street rather than in the palm-thatched huts (*barracas*) in which 75 percent of the Second-Class families lived. In the houses of the First-Class families there were 0.9 persons per room, while there were 1.2 persons per room in Second-Class huts. In the Brazilian Amazon, footwear (both shoes and

---

[7]In 2013 this disdain for manual labor (Wagley 1968) continues in Gurupá. It was not uncommon for someone gaining additional income from timber or açaí extraction to invest in a dance hall, pool hall, or small store. In the mid-1980s, for example, I counted over two dozen dance halls for a town of approximately 3,000. On weekends the doors opened and music played, but in most halls, no one was inside. When asked why invest money in something that will not earn a profit, more than one owner commented, it is always better to try and work with one's mind than one's hands. I sit here and take money. I don't have to work in the roça.

[8]The monthly income for the First-Class families ranged from $25 (cr. $500) to $250 (cr. $5,000); of the Second-Class families from as low as $2.50 (cr. $50) to $85 (cr. $1,700). For 2010 equivalents, see footnotes 14, 15, and 17.

sandals) is an item of dress of special importance both socially and as a protection against hookworm.[9] The men of the First-Class families had an average of 3.3 pairs of shoes, while those of the Second Class had on the average only 1.8 pairs. First-Class women had an average of 3.6 pairs of shoes in contrast to an average of only 1.7 pairs for Second-Class women. First-Class homes were better furnished; they had more chairs, more linens, more kitchenware, more china, and more hammocks than the Second-Class homes. The few beds found in Gurupá are found only in houses of upper-class families. As in many out-of-the-way parts of the world, the sewing machine is an extremely valued object both for its contribution to household economy and for the prestige that it brings to the owner. All but three of the women among the seventeen First-Class families did own a sewing machine, while only eleven of the fifty-five Second-Class housewives included in our survey owned one.

The average monthly expenditure for food and other household necessities for the First-Class families was approximately $48 (cr. $962.20) per month in contrast to about $15 (cr. $207.20) for the Second-Class families of the town included in our survey.[10] The difference in cash expenditures between the two groups is somewhat offset, however, by the fact that many of the Second-Class families have gardens from which they harvest manioc for flour and sometimes a little maize,[11] and by the fact that many Second-Class men fish during the dry season. Yet these added sources of food scarcely balance such a wide margin of difference in basic expenditures. Certain foods never entered into Second-Class budgets. First-Class families regularly ate bread, canned butter,

---

[9]In 2011–12, when shown Wagley's 1948 photographs, people of Gurupá quickly pointed out how many individuals were shoeless. Most found this humorous and quite a few commented on how poor they must have been. Today, with affordable sandals and shoes readily available, the only shoeless people are children who wish to go barefoot. Still, when assessing one's dress, and presumably one's social standing, gazes will always focus on what type of footwear one is using—a likely holdover from the past.

[10]First Class family expenditures ranged from approximately $23 (cr. $455) to approximately $130.50 (cr. $2,609.50); Second Class family expenditures ranged from as low as $2.50 (cr. $55) to $45 (cr. $900).

[11]Twenty-two out of fifty-two Second-Class men were agriculturalists by profession, and sixteen of fifty-five Second-Class families had gardens to supplement their income.

and other imported foods, such as condensed milk, cheese, and guava paste—items that a Second-Class family might purchase once a year for a birthday or another festival. First-Class families purchased more beans, rice, dried meat, sugar, coffee, and other items that must be bought in one of Gurupá's three stores. Although even the average Gurupá upper-class standard of living is poor and inadequate, the differences both in income and in normal expenditures between the upper and lower class of the town of Gurupá set the two groups apart.

The standard of living of the two rural groups of the farmers and of the Island collectors is more difficult to measure because they depend so directly on their gardens, on fishing, and even on hunting for their food supply. Yet an analysis of their cash incomes and of their cash expenditures indicates that their living standards differ little from those of the lower-class town dweller. The average farmer family had a cash income of approximately $15 (cr. $301.90) per month, while the average income of the few collector families included was about $33 (cr. $661.30) per month. The higher cash income of the collector results from the sale of forest products, but it is offset by higher cash expenditures for food and other household necessities. The farmer families spent an average of about $10 (cr. $203.30) per month, while the collector families spent, on the average, slightly more than $24 (cr. $485.20) for purchased food and other necessities. The Island collectors are dedicated almost entirely to harvesting the natural products of the forest, and most of them lack even small manioc gardens for subsistence. Of the ten families of collectors for whom we took detailed budgets, only two had gardens. Such families must buy their own manioc flour.

One hundred percent of all rural families of the Gurupá community (both farmers and collectors) live in palm-thatched huts.[12] They have slightly less room than the urban lower class: 1.7 people per room for the farmer group and 1.5 persons per room for the collector group. In addition, rural people have fewer shoes and sandals than the town lower class: the men of the farmer group had an average of 1.3 pairs each, and the collector men had 1.5 pairs each. The women of the farmer families had 1.7 pairs of footwear and the women of the collector families 1.8. Only five women whose husbands were farmers had

---

[12]In 2013 it is rare to see a palm-thatched hut anywhere in Gurupá. The improved economy and availability of wood, brick, and tile building supplies allows nearly all to have at a minimum a wood-sided house with a tile or prefabricated corrugated roof.

sewing machines, but five out of ten collector families (with larger cash incomes) owned them.

Such statistics indicate that the two rural groups have a slightly lower standard of living than the lower-class urban groups. But the greatest difference in living standards is between the lower class as a whole (the Second Class of the town and rural farmers and collectors) and the upper-class "whites" or First Class. The lower-class people both of the town and of the countryside live on a semistarvation diet. Purchased foods and necessities such as sugar, coffee, salt, dried and fresh beef, kerosene, soap, and tobacco are used in small quantities and almost as luxuries. In 1948 day labor in Gurupá was paid only $0.75 (cr. $15) per day, and the price charged for any manufactured article was extremely expensive in relation to such wages or in relation to the prices paid for manioc flour, rubber, timbó roots, palm nuts, and other products that brought in cash or credit to the rural people. Thus lower-class people are generally in debt to the local commercial houses.

III

Although such statistical averages reflect closely the class cleavages of Gurupá society, the complex and interrelated factors that determine a standard of living and the human problems involved cannot be well described by statistics. Case histories of three families selected from our detailed studies of family budgets are, in the writer's opinion, more illustrative of the way the people of Gurupá live. These families were not the richest or the poorest of their respective socioeconomic strata; they were selected because they seemed representative of the average of each group.

The first, which we may call Family A, are "whites" or First Class. They live, characteristically, on First Street, but in a rather dilapidated adobe house. The family consists of a husband, wife, and three small children—two daughters and an infant son. The father is the secretary at the Town Hall, earning a salary of $75 per month (cr. $1,500). Their house has five rooms: a "visiting room" or parlor, two bedrooms, a dining room, and a kitchen. Baths are taken in the nearby river, and there is an outdoor privy installed by the public health service. The house faces directly on the street. Behind it is a long fenced-in backyard that contains twenty banana trees, fifteen pineapple plants, five coconut trees, and other fruit trees. The family also keeps twenty chickens in the back yard, more for their meat than for their eggs.

Family A's house is well furnished by local standards, although to the outsider it would seem rather empty. There are six wooden chairs, three tables, a china cabinet, four trunks for storing linens and clothes, two kerosene lamps, and a bed that is seldom slept in.[13] Like other families in Gurupá, Family A sleeps in hammocks, which may be seen rolled up against the wall during the daytime. Wife and husband sleep in one of the windowless alcove bedrooms, while the children sleep in the adjoining room. The kitchen, in the rear of the house, has a platform on which an open oven grill has been built for cooking. Kitchenware consists of four cast iron pots and various locally manufactured ceramic utensils. The dining room, which has the typical form of a partially open veranda, overlooks the backyard. It is used not only for meals but also as a general room for family living. Intimates of the family are received in the dining room rather than in the formal visiting room in the front of the house. In the china cabinet in the dining room are twelve plates; ten demitasse coffee cups with saucers; six large coffee cups with saucers for morning coffee; four water glasses; and ten knives, ten forks, and ten spoons.

For Gurupá, Family A is also relatively well dressed. The father has two cotton suits made for him by an itinerant tailor who comes to town about twice a year. He has three other pairs of trousers for everyday use. He has five shirts, four neckties, two pairs of shoes, and two pairs of open sandals; these he always wears about the house and sometimes even in the street. His wife has four "good" dresses, which she saves for festivals and for churchgoing. She has four older dresses and four pairs of sandals for everyday use. Each child has three "uniforms"—cotton dresses for the girls and one-piece cotton suits for the small son—and each has a pair of shoes, worn only on special occasions.

Except for the little food that they raise in their backyard, Family A buys all of its food. Like most Gurupá families, they have a charge account with one of the four commercial houses. They are customers of the Casa Borralho, where they spend a monthly average of $50 (cr. $1,000) in food and other "necessities." Most of this sum goes for

---

[13]Even the upper class in Gurupá prefers hammocks for sleeping. A bed is a prestige item, which, according to our informants, is used only for sexual relations.

Only in the 2000s did this viewpoint/practice changed as the price of beds declined and incomes rose. Still, beds tend to be hot and damp to sleep in, whereas hammocks are much cooler and dry out better in the rainy season.

such staples as manioc flour, coffee, sugar, fresh meat, salted and fresh fish, beans, and rice. Family A (like other First-Class families) also buys bread to eat for breakfast. They also often have canned butter, canned milk, and some sweets such as *goiabada* (guava paste) and *marmelada* (quince paste), the most common desserts throughout Brazil. The husband smokes ready-made cigarettes and now and again he drinks a bottle of beer or has a drink of *cachaça* at the Casa Borralho. Their account is seldom paid up; despite the fact that the husband has a regular salary, the cost of clothes, medicines, donations for the Church, and of an occasional party keeps them slightly in debt to the Casa Borralho. But it is considered good business in Gurupá to allow customers with a regular income to remain in debt, for they will feel obligated to continue purchasing from their debtor. Clerks at the Casa Borralho are rather liberal with Family A, urging husband and wife to make purchases beyond normal "necessities." Family A's way of life is not a comfortable one when compared to that of the more favored populations of the world, but for Gurupá it is considered almost rich.[14]

Our second example, Family B, is classified locally as Second Class, or lower-class town dwellers. Like Family A, it is composed of a husband, wife, and three children (two girls and a boy). But the oldest

---

[14]In 2013 a comparable analysis would find the following distinctions between the classes in Gurupá. The middle middle class (C1) families live in the town in the best housing. They are typically merchants with large businesses, landowners with valuable resources to extract, and professionals working in the hospital or court system. Only a few of this class are descendants of Gurupá's old elite. Most are recent migrants to the community or offspring of poorer families that rose in class standing with the municipality's improving economic fortunes. They will have bank accounts in Belém and have access to credit. As consumers, they will own motorcycles and maybe a car; have computers (only 3.5 percent of households in Gurupá have a computer according to IBGE [2012]) and smart phones with Internet access; subscribe to satellite television with dozens of channels; and dress in the latest urban middle-class fashions. Their homes will be fully furnished; there will be beds for all. They are likely to have maids and nannies. Their children increasingly earn college degrees (according to the 2010 census, 246 people in Gurupá have a college or advanced technical degree). Their incomes will typically be above 6.5 minimal salaries (R$ 4,040 or USD $2,050). According to the 2010 census, 5 percent of the population are in this income category—with 10 households (0.18 percent) earning monthly incomes above 20 minimal salaries (R$ 12,430 or USD $6,308).

The lower middle class (C2) families will also live in town and have good housing. In their ranks will be merchants with smaller businesses, landowners of medium size holdings, and lesser paid civil servants. They will have bank accounts in Belém

child, a twelve-year-old boy, helps in the garden and is a real economic asset to the family. Family B lives on Third Street in a palm-thatched hut. The father is a day laborer earning only $12.50 to $15 (cr. $250 to cr. $300) per month in cash, but this income is augmented by the produce (mostly manioc) from his garden, which he plants on land belonging to the municipality and cultivates with the help of his son and his wife. In addition, during the summer months, Senhor B fishes, both to add to the family larder and to sell. Some years, when rubber prices are high, he spends a month or so as a rubber collector in the Island region of the municipality. Family B also has a few chickens (ten hens), and their yard contains banana, papaya, and other fruit trees. Unlike Family A, who lives almost exclusively on salary, Family B depends to a great extent on farming, fishing, and collecting for a livelihood.

Family B's material standards are markedly lower than those of Family A. Their *barraca* has only three rooms: bedroom, dining room, and kitchen. There are a dining table and two wooden benches; they have two straight-backed chairs to be used by guests. A wooden box set on legs serves to store food and dishes. There are two trunks to hold the family clothes, and a single kerosene lamp provides illumination for the whole house. The family has only six plates, six demitasse cups and saucers, six spoons, two dinner knives, two water glasses, and a few odd pieces of china. Each member of the family has a hammock, but the children must sleep in the dining room. The husband has one full suit and two pairs of trousers. He owns two shirts, one for work and one for dress. The wife has one good dress for special occasions and two old dresses for everyday wear. The husband, the wife, and the older boy have shoes, which are kept carefully in the trunks. On a normal working day all go barefoot. The younger children have only one change of

---

and have some access to credit. They may own a motorcycle, but less likely a car. Some may have computers, but typically they will not have Internet service except what they can receive on their cell phones. They will have television, but only a dozen or so channels to choose from. Their clothes are less expensive, but still fashionable. Their homes are furnished, but with less expensive chairs, tables, and sofas. Although they may have beds, they will also use hammocks to sleep in. Domestic help is more likely to be for special occasions and not for daily chores. As a result, they will perform certain types of manual labor, both at home and beyond. Their children are less likely to earn a college degree, but will have a chance to try if motivated. They often earn 4 or more minimal wages (US $ 1,270) per month. In the 2010 census, households earning in this category represent around 15 percent of the population.

clothes for everyday use, but the older boy has extra pants and a new shirt for dress-up occasions.

Family B also are customers of the Casa Borralho, but the clerks do not urge them to make additional purchases. Though their gardens produce enough manioc to provide flour for their own use, in addition they spend, on the average, almost $10 (cr. $195) per month for other basic foods, such as fresh meat (2 to 4 kilos per month), coffee, sugar, rice (2 to 3 kilos per month), beans (1 to 2 kilos per month), and salt. They rarely consume such luxuries as canned milk, sweets, cottonseed oil, bread, and butter. Their diet is remarkably meager. They eat only one solid meal each day—midday dinner. The family goes to work or to school each morning after only a small demitasse of black coffee and a handful of *farinha* to last them until midday. Their diet is, as José de Castro writes regarding Amazon diets in general, "sparing, scanty, of startling sobriety. What a man eats during one whole day would not be enough for one meal in other climatic zones which form other habits" (Castro 1946:65). Family B obviously suffers from malnutrition. The children have stomachs swollen from hookworm, and the entire family are frequent visitors to the health post. Three children born to the couple have either died at birth or before reaching one year of age.

Like most families in Gurupá, Family B is in debt. Although their small income exceeds normal monthly expenditures, they splurge from time to time. During a drunken spree, the husband ran up a bill of $10 (cr. $200) for *cachaça*; on another occasion he and his wife accepted responsibility as one of the sponsors of the festival of Nossa Senhora das Dores. The food, liquor, and fireworks for the festival cost them over $20 (cr. $400). They were able to persuade the Casa Borralho to give them credit for new clothes for the festival of St. Benedict in 1947. Because they are always in debt and because the husband enjoys going to the Casa Borralho frequently for conversation, Family B tends to buy in quite small quantities: one small package of matches, a half-bottle of kerosene, or a half-kilo of beans. The standard of living of the Gurupá lower class is close to a bare minimum of existence.[15]

---

[15]In 2013 the working class (D) is the largest segment of the population (66.1 percent of households). They live both in town and in the interior. Their housing is adequate (wood and concrete blocks). They include small store owners, government blue collar workers, and a wide range of agroextractivists. They may scrape enough funds together to own a motorcycle and many will own a small motor boat. Computers are

Yet the rural groups discussed earlier, the farmers and the collectors, live in even greater poverty. The problems of these rural people vary somewhat according to their occupation. Collectors, without a garden to supply their families in manioc flour, must buy almost all their food. Farmers, with little cash or credit at the commercial houses, must depend almost exclusively on their gardens and on fishing and hunting to feed their families. The case of one farmer family will illustrate the very minimum existence of this rural lower class. This family, Family C, lives in a hut in Jocojó. There are four people in the family: a husband, wife, and two children, neither of whom is old enough as yet to be of help in the garden. Both the husband and his wife work in the fields, but the heavier tasks are performed by the husband. During a part of the year, the husband earns some income from collecting rubber or timbó root in the nearby forest. In 1947 he had a surplus of almost one thousand kilos of manioc flour, bringing the family the sum of $80 (cr. $1,600). He earned another $20 (cr. $400) in rubber collecting. This was the total cash income of the family.

Their hut is almost bare of furnishings. The kitchen has a table and two wooden boxes that a trader gave them. A wooden bench takes the place of chairs. The husband and wife keep their few clothes in a painted tin trunk.[16] The house is lighted with three small kerosene containers (*lamparinas*), which produce considerable black smoke and have little effect on the darkness. The wife has only one small metal pan and two cheap ceramic pots for cooking. Although they have three forks, the family generally eats only with spoons. There is a tin

---

rare, and Internet access, when they can afford it, is either at one of the few cyber cafes or through a cell phone. Not all families will own a television set (95.9 percent of urban households have a TV, but only 48.7 percent in the interior possess one—IBGE [2012]), but they will be able to watch programs in friends and neighbors' houses. Their clothes are basic, often reflecting region instead of national styles. Their homes are more humbly furnished, with chairs and stools occasionally in short supply, leaving people to sit on the floor. Beds are less common, whereas hammocks for sleeping and sitting are customary. Manual labor, including all household chores, is the task of the family. College education is unlikely, and even completing secondary schooling is a rarity. Income ranges from 1 minimum wage to 4, but during peak harvest periods for açaí or timber, they many earn much more.

[16]This type of tin trunk is used throughout rural Brazil both to carry belongings and as a coffin for children and infants.

plate for each member of the family. They own five demitasse cups and saucers for coffee and two water glasses. Both the wife and husband have individual hammocks, but the children share a hammock for sleeping.

Family C spends, on the average, $6.75 (cr. $135) for food and other necessities each month. They are the customers of a trading post at the mouth of the tributary on the Amazon mainstream. Prices at this trading post are even higher than in Gurupá stores, and Family C receives little for its money. Their purchases are normally limited to sugar (4 kilos per month), salt (1 kilo), a liter of kerosene, a small piece of tobacco, coffee (2 kilos), two boxes of matches, three kilos of sun-dried beef, and two bars of rough laundry soap. Fresh meat, except that which results from the hunt, is eaten only when they visit Gurupá or during a festival when a pig is butchered. Beans, rice, bread, *goiabada*, and other foods that are common in Brazilian homes are for them rare luxuries. The few clothes they have are exceedingly expensive; a piece of poor cloth for a woman's dress costs as much as $5 (cr. $100), and the cloth for a man's trousers about $3.75 (cr. $75). Therefore Family C has a minimum of clothes. Neither the husband nor wife has shoes; he has only one suit for festivals, and she has a good dress, which is carefully guarded for special occasions. Their everyday clothes are old and ragged. Their small son, who is eight years old, runs nude about the yard, and the daughter, who is ten, has two rather ragged dresses.

Family C, like Families A and B, is in debt. The trader from whom they buy lays claim to the land on which they plant, and he also owns the rubber trails from which the husband collects latex. The trader advances them food and merchandise against the manioc flour and the rubber, which they turn over to him. Rarely do they have any cash at all. Sometimes they get cash by selling a pelt or an *alqueire* (30 kilos) of manioc flour to an itinerant trading boat. When they wish to contribute to the annual festival of St. Peter at Jocojó each year, they must give rubber or garden products. Although rural workers in Gurupá provide a large part of the food for their families from their own gardens, or by hunting, fishing, and collecting edible fruits from the forest, the price of foods that must be bought, such as rice and beans, is beyond their purchasing power. Most rural families eat badly most of the time and face periods of semistarvation. The low social status of the farmer and collector families of the rural neighborhoods of Gurupá results primarily from their low economic condition.[17]

Despite these marked local differences in living standards between the upper and lower classes, Gurupá lacks the great contrast between the extremely rich, with their great ostentation and luxury, and the extremely poor, which is so characteristic of the large urban centers of Brazil. Compared to the rural farmers, collectors, and the town Second Class, the Gurupá "whites" seem wealthy indeed; but in larger perspective, even the upper class, except for the owners of the Casa Borralho, are poor. In short, the entire community of Gurupá has a remarkably low standard of living, especially when compared to a small town of equal size in the United States or in France.

IV

Although social rank in Gurupá is closely correlated to economic position, many other factors contribute to it. There are individuals classified as First Class who have lower incomes than others who are classed as Second Class. There are also people recognized as Second Class with sufficient income to be placed in First Class but lacking in the other qualifications necessary. Raimundo Gonçalves, for example, who has a salary from the federal government as foreman at the recently constructed airport at Gurupá and who employs people to plant large manioc gardens, is classed by everyone as Second Class. Dona Inacinha, the schoolteacher, although she lives in a rather large house on First Street, has an income only one-fifth as large as that of Raimundo

---

[17]In 2013 the poorest group in Gurupá (E) makes up 13.9 percent of the municipal's households. They may live in one of the swampy or otherwise rundown sectors of town or in the vast interior. Housing is substandard, frequently made of old and rotting wood and occasionally may be roofed with palm-thatching. They are unemployed or underemployed—holding part-time low paying jobs in extraction (açaí and timber) or low-skilled labor (such as hauling loads in human-powered carts) and frequently lack land for roças. They may rely on the government antipoverty programs to make ends meet, and with such funds avoid prolonged periods of hunger. Nonetheless, their children are likely to suffer from stunted growth and undernutrition. Homes are minimally furnished, beds are a rarity, and clothing may be old and ragged. Primary-level education is rarely completed. Income is often below ½ minimum wage.

Gonçalves. She earns hardly enough to eat even poorly; but in any list of the "whites" of Gurupá, Dona Inacinha's name is always one of the first three or four to be remembered. The reasons why Dona Inacinha is invariably assigned to the upper class and why Raimundo Gonçalves is always classed as Second Class are noneconomic in nature. They are differences in family, in education, in achieved positions within the community, and in personal characteristics. In Gurupá, as in other human societies, the criteria of social rank tend to cluster; that is, an individual of superior economic position is apt also to be a member of a superior family, with a better education, and with a position of leadership in society. A poor person is more apt to come from a family of lowly origins, to have less education, and to find it difficult to achieve a position of leadership. It is a combination, an individual rating by multiple systems of ranking, that gives and individual her or his final status.

The cases of Dona Inacinha and Raimundo Gonçalves illustrate the weighing of a variety of criteria. Dona Inacinha comes from a "good family"; she is a descendant of the baron of Gurupá. Although her father was poor, she spent her childhood in companionship with Dona Diná Borralho and the other girls of the First Class. She was sent to Belém to finish her primary schooling. Although her married life has been insecure (she has been widowed three times by death), she has always maintained a moral life. She made a great effort to educate her two sons, both of whom attended secondary schools in Belém. It was perhaps the unlucky fate of her marriages that turned Dona Inacinha's interest to religion. She has achieved a position as religious arbiter and leader of Gurupá. When the Brotherhood of St. Benedict fell apart, the records were left with her. When Gurupá no longer supported a padre, Dona Inacinha began to lead prayers at Vespers and on Sundays in the church. Whenever a visiting padre comes to Gurupá, Dona Inacinha invites him to stay in her home. The priest stationed in a nearby town asked Dona Inacinha to take charge of the Gurupá church. Gradually farmers and rubber gatherers, who wished to make offerings to St. Benedict, began to bring them to her house, asking her to add their names to her list of donors. It is said that at one time Dona Inacinha had more than "one hundred *contos*" (approximately $5,000) in her hands from offerings to the church. With these powers deriving from her position as religious leader, Dona Inacinha also became something of a social arbiter. She criticizes the manners and the morals of the townspeople, and they fear that she will pass on her opinions to the padre. It was Dona Inacinha who reported to the padre[18] that the dancing at the annual festival of Nossa Senhora das Dores celebrated by a small brotherhood in Gurupá was "nothing but a wild party." With the padre, she opposes the small brotherhoods in the rural zone. As religious leader, Dona Inacinha has achieved a social position in Gurupá much superior to that of her immediate family.

Raimundo Gonçalves, on the other hand, comes from outside. He moved to Gurupá only five years ago from the Upper Amazon. Though he is literate, it is obvious from his handwriting, spelling, and vocabulary that Raimundo has had only a year or two of schooling. No one knows anything about his family, but it is clear that he does not descend from aristocracy. First, he does manual labor. In supervising the weeding of the airfield, Raimundo sometimes works alongside the day laborers; and in his gardens, Raimundo and his wife will help to clear fields or to peel manioc tubers for making flour. Second, although Raimundo had a good income by Gurupá standards, sufficient to support his wife and eight children, he continues to live on Third Street. When Raimundo came to Gurupá, he moved into a hut. Little by little he improved it until it was better in appearance and in construction than many First Street dwellings. Yet its location is Second Class and it is still a hut. Third, Raimundo and his family continue to behave toward "whites" in a manner that indicates that they are Second Class. He is respected for his hard work and economic position by both the First and the Second Class, yet Raimundo and his wife are retiring and humble before upper-class people. He is apt to remove his hat when talking with Manuel Pere Serra, and his wife is embarrassed in front of Dona Inacinha. It is their way of being polite. Finally, although Raimundo and his family have better clothes than the normal Second-Class family, he likes to walk barefoot; and his wife seldom puts on her shoes or her better dresses. There is no need, therefore, to consult a family genealogy to know that Raimundo comes from the "people."

These criteria—family, education, manners, and behavior—are of little importance in differentiating between the various strata that form the lower class of the Gurupá society, that is, between the urban lower class, the farmers, and the collectors. As stated earlier,

---

[18]In this case the padre was Dom Clemente who went on to become the bishop of the diocese.

townspeople of all classes expect rural dwellers to be less polished in their manners. Townspeople criticize the morals of the rural collectors and farmers. They tell with mixed admiration and criticism of the leader of the village of Jocojó, João Pombo, who has for years lived openly with his legal wife and with his mistress Ermina, by whom he has several children. They tell stories of the ribeirinho who found that he might marry twice, once in the Church and once according to civil law. They point out the frequency, in rural neighborhoods, of marriage carried out on the order of the police after the complaint of the father of a minor girl against her lover. In addition, because schools are not available to them, people in the rural neighborhoods are overwhelmingly illiterate. Still, the line between the lower-class town dweller and the rural population, and between the fanner and the collector, is not so sharply drawn. Many people who are collectors move into one of the farming areas, and people from the farming areas have moved to the Islands to collect rubber during years when rubber prices were high. Many townspeople have lived in the rural zones. To a great extent, the difference between these lower strata is a question of occupation, income, residence, and living standards. But the difference between the "whites" and the lower strata is one of deeply ingrained attitudes and behavior patterns that must be learned and practiced if one is to pass from one group to another. Mobility upward from one strata of the lower class to another is relatively easy; there are no serious barriers to it in group consciousness or in the behavior expected of the members of each stratum.[19]

---

[19]In Pace and Hinote (2013:170–71) we asked people how they distinguish social rankings, to which respondents provided three general qualities or traits. First is money, although, it is the least important of the three. Bena Costa, a boarding house proprietor, commented, "Any caboclo can sell land and have some money. But he will spend it and end up poor again." Sebá Costa Barriga remarked that most important is knowledge and training so that people have the know-how to improve themselves and find solutions to problems. She noted that education is part of this, but gaining a profession is the most important goal. Second is job selection. People distinguished between manual labor (i.e., working with one's hands) and using one's knowledge to direct others to do manual labor. In this context, having a business is considered ideal and prestigious. Others work for theproprietor who collects the profit. The third is prestige. People are of higher standing if they are well-known (*conhecido*). Inlcuded here are individulas with political power as well as those with large social networks—such as patrões (plural of patrão) with many clients, or godparents with lots of godchildren. In each of these cases the family name can help elevate or reduce a person's status.

Movement from the lower class into the upper class, however, is difficult and infrequent. Educational opportunities are almost totally lacking for the rural population, and the lower classes of town find it difficult to maintain their children in school even for the three-year course. For any further education, only those of a superior financial position are able to send their children to Belém, or upriver to Santarém, where schools offer a complete primary education and the secondary course. Economic improvement is more difficult for the rural population than it is for the lower-class town dwellers. The persistence of subsistent agriculture, the low prices paid for farm products and the relatively high prices of all imported objects, the rigid commercial system based on debt, and other difficulties make it very improbable that an individual will rise in the economic scale. Furthermore, should members of the lower class gain some education and be able to escape the almost inevitable trap of the debt system and improve their economic position, then they are faced with the necessity of learning new manners and new ways of behavior. Such individuals would also find the memory of their low family origin a barrier to upward mobility. In Gurupá society, and in Amazon society as a whole, mobility upward from the lower class into the upper class is a difficult feat. As in other rigid class societies, and especially in small towns, the memory of low origin is an almost impossible barrier to overcome. Generally, the only way for an individual to rise in the social hierarchy is to move away to another town.

The tragic story of João Coimbra, who made a majestic effort to rise both economically and socially, will serve to illustrate the difficulties of social mobility. João was born of poor parents in the agricultural zone near Gurupá. His parents moved into town when he was a small child, and João was able to attend school for almost three years. He is therefore literate, although he reads and writes with some difficulty. He is at present about thirty-five years old; he is married and has one daughter. As a young man, he was known in Gurupá as a hard worker, shrewd, and honest. He has worked as a day laborer, as a rubber gatherer, and as an employee of Liberato Borralho, owner of the Casa Borralho, who seems to have become rather fond of him. Some ten years ago, with Liberato's financial help, João was able to purchase a small farm situated on the Itapereira Tributary, about a half-hour's walk from town. His land had three rubber trails, some lowland near the Amazon, and some terra firme for manioc. By working the land with the help of his brother-in-law Jorge Dias, by collecting rubber from his trails, and by working as a day laborer on the construction of the health post, João was able to pay for his land in a few years. During the first years of World War II, when rubber was high and the price of manioc flour was relatively high, João actually had credit or *sobra* (something left) on the widow Borralho's books. There came a time when the state government took steps to form an agricultural cooperative, which would allow local farmers to purchase much-needed tools and sell their produce at better prices. João was a leader in the group that attempted to establish the cooperative. He had plans to purchase machinery for exterminating the *saúva* ant and machinery to produce manioc flour. João had his three children in school, and his family was relatively well dressed. He was on his way up the ladder—at least economically.

But the cooperative failed for lack of official support. In 1942 João's seven-year-old son died, and the entire family came down with malaria. Since then his wife has been chronically ill. Because of sickness in the family, João missed many days of work; he was not able to plant as much manioc as in former years, and he had to leave the exploitation of the rubber trails to his brother-in-law. After one bad year, he was again in debt. By 1948 rubber prices had fallen, and although João and his brother-in-law had planted large manioc gardens, João was still in debt. People said that a ghost had put a curse on João's house, for his second son died in 1947 and his wife continued to be ill. He still had his land, but João's entire attitude in 1948 was one of defeat. He discussed at length the impossibility of anyone "improving one's situation" in Gurupá. His dream of becoming a landowner and a merchant, of visiting Belém and of educating his children, seemed an impossibility. João was a bitter man.

Yet Gurupá people seem to believe in success stories. At least, they tell of cases in which a simple sailor or a rubber gatherer became a wealthy and important man. Elíos Veiga, for example, told of his own son-in-law who, according to his account, became an important trader on the Tapajós River. This son-in-law, José Dias da Silva, was a poor sailor who worked aboard one of the numerous river steamers that ply the lower Amazon. He worked his way up to become a steward aboard. Then, through the help of his godfather, Manuel Paiva, the Portuguese owner of a large trading post near Gurupá, José moved to a better job aboard the motorship Moacyr. He appeared in Gurupá from time to time, generally for his holidays. During one visit he courted and married one of Elíos Veiga's daughters. As he became better known in Belém, he was able to secure merchandise on credit from one of the large commercial houses, and he set himself up as a trader on the Tocantins River. He was successful, and now he has a high social position in a small Tocantins town. His godfather, according to Veiga, has invited José Dias da Silva to return to Gurupá several times. His godfather offered him the use of a large tract of land with rubber trails, but "he would not work on another man's land; he would return only if he could buy his own land and have his own trading post," said his father-in-law.

All local success stories of economic and social mobility relate how successful young people were successful elsewhere, but not in Gurupá, through the help of a benevolent godfather, relative, or employer, or by some other stroke of luck.[20] Migration to the city of Belém or Manaus, or to another small community in the Amazon Valley, not only erases the memory of low family origin but also makes it possible for a people of lower-class family to establish a new set of relationships, escaping those people of the upper class toward whom they have habitually deferred. A few children of Gurupá are known to have been successful in the large cities. These few, however, evidently have little desire to return to their hometown even for a visit. There is a well-known physician in Belém who was born and who spent his first few years of life in Gurupá. He has not visited the town in over twenty years. Successful children of Gurupá in the large cities are rare, however; social barriers in the cities are also rigid, and Gurupá is unable to furnish young people with a solid early education as a basis for economic and social ascension. Most migrants from Gurupá to the large cities of Manaus and Belém become factory workers or low-paid laborers, members of the urban lower class.

The difficulties of economic and social advancement in Gurupá society reinforce the belief, so common throughout Brazil, that only a stroke of luck can lead to economic success. Only by winning in the lottery, by a lucky break in business, or by discovering gold buried centuries ago by missionaries is a person able to gain wealth. Lottery

---

[20]In the discourses recorded between 1983 and 2011 (see Pace and Hinote 2013:171), social mobility is always placed within the context of obtaining a suitable profession, whether through training or education. Once obtained, though, the assumption is that a person will have to move away because there are so few jobs in Gurupá. Social mobility, therefore, requires geographical mobility. Gurupaenses in general do not believe that hard work leads to social mobility, especially for the agroextractivists.

tickets are rarely sold in Gurupá nowadays, and *jogo do bicho* (a sort of numbers game, played throughout Brazil, in which animals are drawn instead of numbers) has not been played in recent years in the town. Both forms of gambling, however, are very much a part of Gurupá culture. People would like to buy a lottery ticket or "draw an animal" if they were available. They tell of friends who won in the "animal game" or in the lottery in the big city.[21] Above all, Gurupá folklore is full of stories of hidden treasures. There are "real-life" stories of people who spent years digging for treasures revealed to them in dreams. Liberato Borralho, who was for many years Gurupá's most important merchant and probably its wealthiest man, is said to have gained his start in life by finding a buried treasure. According to the story, Liberato dreamed one night that there was a pot of money buried just in front of his house. The dream revealed the exact spot, even the depth of the pot of money. Liberato heard the words, "The money is there for you." He went to the spot at night and dug up the money, but he did not tell anyone about it at the time. People knew of his luck because one of his employees saw him counting his fortune. Soon afterward Liberato had a mass celebrated in the church. But Liberato's luck did not stop with the finding of hidden treasure. He was able, because of his money, to marry Dona Diná Borralho, the daughter of a wealthy merchant, and to inherit from her father. In Gurupá people have little credence in becoming wealthy by slow accumulation of money. They believe in luck; or, as the Gurupá saying goes, "Whoever gets rich either inherited or stole."[22]

V

Brazil is well known throughout the world for its racial democracy. Throughout the country racial prejudice and discrimination are relatively subdued, in comparison to the situation in the United States of America, South Africa, and most of Europe. This does not mean that race prejudice is entirely lacking or that physical characteristics are not

---

[21]With improvements in Internet service, in the early 2010s Gurupá residents could play the national lottery. Jogo de bicho betting has been common since the mid-1980s as well. Both forms of gambling draw long lines in Gurupá just as in the rest of Brazil.
[22]Stories of finding lost treasure are still common place in 2013. The most popular ones involve rumors of finding gold stolen and buried by the Cabanos during the Cabanagem revolt.

symbols of social status and thus barriers or aids to social mobility. It does mean, however, that race relations are essentially peaceful and harmonious.[23] The Amazon Valley shares the traditional Brazilian patterns of race relations. Yet the attitudes in regard to different racial groups and the relations between racial groups in Amazon society reflect the distinctive aspects of Amazon history and regional society. Throughout most of Brazil, Indigenous populations rapidly gave way to imported African slaves as the major source of labor. Thus, the descendants of African slaves came to form the majority of the lower classes in contemporary society. Native Americans, as the memory of their early slave position in colonial society faded, became romantic figures; and it is today a point of pride for many aristocratic families in South Brazil to number Indigenous populations among their forebears. In the Amazon, on the other hand, colonists were not wealthy enough to purchase many African slaves. The few Africans who did reach such communities as Gurupá during the colonial period must have been valuable property, individuals to be instructed and treated with great care—or they were already free.[24] In the Amazon the majority of slaves were always Indigenous groups. Commerce in Native slaves, which began

---

[23]Wagley was strongly influenced by his friend and colleague Gilberto Freyre and his notion of racial harmony in Brazil (see Freyre [1946] and Wagley's [1946] review of Freyre). Since the 1950s, however, much research into Brazilian race relations, as well as current events, point to a more complex—and repressive—state of affairs (see Telles 2004). In the 2000s the Brazilian government implemented a series of civil rights laws to outlaw racial discrimination, including setting quotas to allow people of color access to key Brazilian institutions (e.g., government employment, education). Racism is now understood as a long-term social problem in Brazil that still affects millions of people.

In January of 2013 during a Federal University of Pará undergraduate course on sociology held in Gurupá, the university professors took the class by boat to the quilombo community of Gurupá-Mirím where they heard a full day's worth of testimony from community members about problems of racism in Gurupá. Needless to say, narratives on race relations in the 1940s versus those of 2013 were very different. After considerable discussion (on the national as well as local level) and consciousness-raising on the part of the Catholic Church, a critical understanding of race relations and racism has emerged in Gurupá.

[24]As documented by the 1980s research of Kelly in Chapter 2, Gurupá's African slave population—owned by military personnel from the fort's garrison and prison, along with government workers stationed at the tax collection post—reached as high as 31 percent in 1783, then fell to 14.5 percent in 1856 (320 individuals), and finally 7.7 percent in 1872 (Kelly 1984:143, 308, 346).

early in the colonial period, evidently continued in the Amazon well into the nineteenth century. W. E. Bates describes Indigenous slavery quite specifically in the middle of the nineteenth century. In the small village of Egá on the Upper Amazon, he saw enslaved "individuals of at least sixteen different tribes; most of whom had been bought when children of native chiefs. This species of slave dealing although forbidden by the laws of Brazil is winked at by the authorities." Bates' own assistant "ransomed" two native children who had been torn from their families, and Bates tells us how both died within a short time after their arrival at Egá despite his effort to doctor them (Bates 1930:278 ff.). Indigenous slavery persisted in the upper tributaries of the Amazon even into our own century. Slavery is therefore a relatively recent phenomenon in the Amazon Valley, and the descendants of Amazon Indigenous slaves occupy a low socioeconomic position, comparable to that of African descendants in other areas of Brazil.

In Gurupá all three ancestor groups that make up the Brazilian population—namely, the European, the African, and the Indigenous populations—are represented. All possible crossings of the three groups have taken place to such an extent that classification of the population of Gurupá as to ancestor origin is difficult, if not scientifically impossible.[25] [Using phenotypic categories to ascertain some measure

---

[25]The concept of "race" in Wagley's time, as well as today, is very problematic for anthropologists. Wagley actually worked hard during his career to expose the ideological creation of race, that is, racial classifications are based on social constructions of groups of people that are far from scientific, systematic, or rational (see Wagley 1959). In 1998 the American Anthropological Association Executive Board posted its official position on race. "With the vast expansion of scientific knowledge in this century . . . it has become clear that human populations are not unambiguous, clearly demarcated, biologically distinct groups. . . . These facts render any attempt to establish lines of division among biological populations both arbitrary and subjective. . . . Historical research has shown that the idea of 'race' has always carried more meanings than mere physical differences; indeed, physical variations in the human species have no meaning except the social ones that humans put on them. . . . 'Race' thus evolved as a worldview, a body of prejudgments that distorts our ideas about human differences and group behavior. . . . The 'racial' worldview was invented to assign some groups to perpetual low status, while others were permitted access to privilege, power, and wealth. . . . Given what we know about the capacity of normal humans to achieve and function within any culture, we conclude that present-day inequalities between so-called 'racial' groups are not consequences of their biological inheritance but products of historical and contemporary social, economic, educational, and political circumstances."

of heritage], however, the population of Gurupá appears to be about 15 percent European, about 50 percent mixtures of Europeans with Africans and Indigenous peoples in various degrees, about 25 percent Indigenous or Native American, and about 10 percent African.[26] [None] of those classed as European, African, or Native American are genetically pure; they are classified according to apparent physical characteristics (Wagley 1952:122). Our general observations in Gurupá, as well as the historical evidence, indicates that the Indigenous population genetic strain predominates in this mixed population.

The people of Gurupá have their own categories by which they classify their fellow citizens as to physical type. The most frequent ones used are *branco* (white) for those of apparent European physical type; *moreno* (brunette) for mixtures of various types; *caboclo* for those of apparent Indigenous physical characteristics; and *preto* (black) for those of apparent African physical type. The term mulato, so often used elsewhere in Brazil, is only used in Gurupá in the feminine gender to refer to an attractive woman (e.g., *uma mulatinha bonita* [pretty little mulatta] or *uma mulata boa* [good mulatta], but having the meaning of "a well formed wench"). As in most of Brazil, the term "*Negro*" is seldom heard, and then only in anger. Against anyone who has physical traits suggesting African ancestry, the label *Negro ruim* (bad black) is a powerful insult. The term *pardo*, which is so often used in Brazilian newspapers and in official census data to include people of various racial mixtures who are not clearly African, Indigenous, or European, is not used in Gurupá except by a few government officials.

The most important criterion for arriving at such classifications in Gurupá is the quality of the hair and the amount of body hair. The branco has thin straight hair and a heavy beard. The caboclo has black coarse hair. The male has "three hairs on his chin for a beard and his hair stands on end despite all efforts to comb it." The kinky hair of the preto is described as *quebra pente* (break-a-comb); people laugh when they tell how such hair strips the teeth from a comb when the preto tries to comb it. Other criteria that are sometimes used as indicators of

---

[26]In classifying 202 adults as to phenotypical appearance, the results were as follows: 50 percent *mestiço* (mixed), 17 percent *branco* (European), 23 percent *caboclo* (Native), and 10 percent *preto* (African). An independent census carried out by the health authorities of 305 Gurupá people listed 71 percent as *pardo* (literally "brown"), 19 percent as "white," and 30 percent as "black."

racial types are a flat nose and thick lips, which are signs of African ancestry; and slant eyes, indicative of Indigenous parental stock. Skin color is frequently mentioned, but the common diagnostic trait is hair. Gurupá people say that skin color and facial features are not trustworthy: "They fool one."

The general rule of thumb for Brazil—"The lighter the skin, the higher the class; the darker the skin, the lower the class"—may be said to apply in Gurupá. The majority of the Gurupá First Class are in physical appearance either Europeans or mestizos (mixtures) with predominantly European ancestry. The majority of the lower-class groups (the urban Second Class, the farmers, and the collectors) are in physical appearance mestizos with predominantly Indigenous or African ancestry, or they are of apparently unmixed Indigenous or African physical type. We collected data on the racial appearance and the social class of 202 Gurupá adults, the fathers and mothers of the families covered in our family studies referred to previously. Of the First Class, 53 percent (or 16 people) of the total were classified as brancos ("whites"), 44 percent (or 13 individuals) as morenos (mixed), 3 percent (or 1 individual) as caboclo (Indigenous descent), and none as preto (black). Of the 172 people in three lower-class groups taken as a unit, about 10 percent (or 18 individuals) were classed as "white," 51 percent (or 89 individuals) as mixed, 27 percent (or 46 individuals) as caboclo, and 12 percent (or 19 individuals) as preto, or black.

In Gurupá the descendants of the Indigenous and African populations continue to occupy the lower positions in the social hierarchy. Despite the relatively large population of freemen in the Amazon Valley of Indigenous and African ancestry in the nineteenth century, those inhabitants of Gurupá with Indigenous, African, and mestizo physical characteristics are derived ultimately from slave ancestry. As a group, they have not, during the last half-century, been able to rise in the social hierarchy. In Gurupá, where the effects of mass education and industrialism have not as yet been felt, Indigenous and African physical characteristics are still a symbol of low social status and of slave ancestry. European physical appearance is a symbol of aristocratic, slave-owning descent.

Yet there are individuals of all racial types in all social strata. The mayor of Gurupá, who is, of course, classified as a "white" or First Class, has the copper skin color and the high cheekbones of an Indigenous individual. The widow Dona Diná Borralho, the individual who has perhaps the highest social position in Gurupá, is a dark mulatta. Her husband was African Brazilian. The local porter and the town drunk, Jajaba, at the other extreme of the social scale, is clearly of European descent, having light pigmentation and a heavy beard. His father, some old people remember, was a Portuguese immigrant. There are other cases of dark mestizos and even a few "caboclos" in the upper class and of European physical types in the lower-class groups. The people of non-European physical types who figure in the upper class are numerous enough to indicate that racial characteristics are not immutable barriers to social advancement. Social position and class membership are economically and socially determined. Physical race is an important but uncertain diagnostic of social position.

Perhaps because of the enormous variety of different racial types in their society, the people of Gurupá seem acutely conscious of physical characteristics. When one wants to describe a specific person, it is usual to do so by saying "*aquele branco*" (that white) or "*aquele preto*" (that black), and so on, in about the same way that we might say "that short fat fellow." The relative lack of racial prejudice or discrimination does not mean that people are unaware of physical appearance. On the contrary, they seem more conscious of minute details of racial characteristics than people in the United States.

Eleven local people were asked to classify, as to physical type, twenty well-known individuals, selected from different social strata, according to the fourfold classification—branco, moreno, caboclo, and preto. The town drunk, the leader of the annual Boi Bumba pageant dance, the schoolteacher, a day laborer of the town hall, and others well known to everyone were included in the list. For a few individuals in the list whose physical characteristics were clearly African or European, there was general agreement as to their physical type. For example, Alfredo Dias, the pilot of a launch stationed at Gurupá, whose hair, facial features, and black skin leave no doubt that he is of African descent, was classed as preto by nine people, although two thought that he should be called a moreno despite his marked African traits. Agreement was also fairly general for those whose social position and physical characteristics, in a sense, coincided. The adopted son of the widow Borralho was a branco for ten people and a moreno for only one. He has a light complexion and a heavy beard.

On the other hand, people do not always agree on the racial classification of people whose physical traits were not so clear-cut, who were obviously of mixed racial descent, or whose physical characteristics conflict, so to speak, with their expected social position. Thus, Dona Inacinha was found to be a branca by five people and a morena by six. The vice mayor was classed as a branco by three, a caboclo by three, and a moreno by five people. He is a rather portly man whose mixed ancestry is clearly of all three racial stocks, but his appearance is more that of an Indigenous-European mestizo. In classifying Jajaba, five people out of eleven classified him as a caboclo, despite his marked European features, which the other six took into consideration in calling him a branco. "How can Jajaba be a branco?" one informant exclaimed, referring to his low social position. Conversely, Dona Diná Borralho was classed as a morena by nine people, while two others placed her as a branca. Dona Diná had a "white father and a black mother," one man reasoned, "but her money whitens her skin." He implied that if Dona Diná were of low social rank she might even be classed as a preta. The conflict between race appearance and expected social position reminds one of the Brazilian expression, "A rich Negro is a white and a poor white is a Negro," and of the story told by Henry Koster, the nineteenth century English traveler to Brazil. When Koster asked if a certain high official (captain-major) was not a "mulatto man," his informant replied, "He was but he is no longer." When Koster asked for an explanation, his informant replied, "Can a *capitão-mór* be a mulatto man?" (Koster 1816:391). Social position tends in many cases to override observable physical characteristics in the classification of individuals in terms of "race."

A series of stereotyped concepts and cultural values persists in Gurupá, reflecting the social position of people of different racial stocks in the colonial society. Light complexion and the fine facial features of the European, for example, are considered beautiful. In the slave society of the past, it was an advantage for children to inherit the features of their European fathers rather than the Indigenous or African features of their slave mothers. In Gurupá, mothers frequently boast of the "fine nose, the light skin, and the fine hair" of their children. Again, as Freyre has emphasized, the Portuguese male seems to have been especially attracted to the Indian and even the African woman; this attraction, according to Freyre (1946:11 ff.), seems to have its roots in the idealization of the Moorish beauty. Gurupá men consider the morena, varying from dark brunette to mulatta, to be the most attractive feminine type. They like the "long straight hair of the Tapuia"

[Native American], the regular features of the European, and a dark skin. On the other hand, women prefer lighter men. In colonial times it was to the advantage of the Indigenous or African woman to be the concubine or the wife of a European. Emilia, a young girl of Indigenous-Portuguese descent, made it quite clear that she would not marry a black "even if he were perfumed." She would like to marry a "light moreno." Yet Marcos Dias, the twenty-year-old son of the African Brazilian Alfredo Dias, who is a dark mulatto, was considered handsome by many women "in spite of his color and his 'bad' [kinky] hair."

Yet despite their stated preferences, people actually seek mates of approximately the same physical type. Of 82 married couples known to us in Gurupá, 56 couples were of the same physical type—that is, both brancos, or both pretos, and so forth. The other 26 couples in which husband and wife were classified in different physical categories were marriages between people of those categories that were nearest in pigmentation. They were all marriages of a branco with a moreno, a dark moreno with a preto, or a preto with a caboclo. There were no marriages, for instance, in our sample, between a preto and a branco. Marriages between people of the same physical type or between people of approximately the same skin color are not determined by any restrictions against interracial marriages. They result from the fact that in Gurupá people tend to marry roughly within the same social stratum. Because people of a social stratum tend to be generally of similar physical type, marriage in one's own social stratum results in marriage between people roughly similar in physical type. That marriages between people of different physical type are not prohibited, or even discouraged, was attested by our Gurupá informants, who remembered numerous cases of branco men marrying women of Native American or African physical type and of pretos and caboclos marrying branco wives. In Gurupá, whatever segregation exists is based on social class rather than on physical or socially defined race.[27]

The fixed ideas that the people of Gurupá maintain regarding the innate abilities of people of each "racial" category also reflect the position of each of these groups in colonial society. In Gurupá, people

---

[27]In 2013 people in Gurupá understand "race" to have a greater impact on social relations than might have been understood in the 1940s. Nevertheless, marriages among people of different so-called races are actually more common in 2013 than what Wagley observed in the 1940s.

say that the branco is always "good at business," and a man who is physically a branco arriving in the community would be considered per se "intelligent and well educated," obviously a persistence from the time when most Europeans were landed aristocrats, owners of great rubber-producing forests, or important officials from the capital. Our informants in Gurupá told us with some amusement of strangers who were brancos but who came dressed in poor clothes and who were found to be illiterate. In asking for a favor, people in Gurupá are apt to address others as "*Meu branco!*" (My white!), a term that indicates high respect.

As in other parts of Brazil and, for that matter, other parts of the New World, people of mixed African and European parentage (the moreno of Gurupá and the mulatto of other regions) are considered treacherous, irascible, and difficult to deal with. Especially those with light skin, "who seem almost branco," are thought to have *mau génio* (bad character), a term used to indicate an irritable person whose mood shifts easily to anger and not to describe a person's moral character. No one in Gurupá liked one of the public health physicians, a dark mulatto who spent almost three weeks there waiting for a boat to take him to his post. At first, several families invited him to visit them and men sought him out for conversation, for he was a doctor and thus a visitor of considerable prestige. But people soon found him to be abrupt and somewhat overaggressive. He was critical of Gurupá, complaining that it was a dull town. The attitude of the townspeople soon changed. "When a dark moreno becomes a doctor," one man said, "he is proud and he tries to act like a white." People will often overlook their fixed concepts of the different physical types, but when there is reason to criticize a person they soon fall back on such concepts to justify their feelings.

The number and variety of the stereotypes held in Gurupá in regard to the preto seem strangely out of keeping with the small number of African descendants in the present population. There is a veritable aura of prestige tied to the "old blacks" (*os velhos pretos*, as they are called). It was a group of "old blacks," people say, who were the leaders in the famous brotherhood devoted to St. Benedict, the most famous and most miraculous saint of the whole Lower Amazon area. It was the great devotion and the ability of these "old blacks" that made the brotherhood of St. Benedict in Gurupá such a strong one. "The old blacks began to die and the 'whites' began to take part in the devotion to

St. Benedict" is the way in which people of all racial groups explained the relative decadence and disorganization of St. Benedict's brotherhood today. Furthermore, the small village of Jocojó is said to have been inhabited almost entirely by "old blacks," although the people living there today have about the same appearance as the rest of the people of the Gurupá community area. This explains to people of Gurupá why the annual festival on St. Peter's day is always so well celebrated in Jocojó, and why the brotherhood devoted to this local saint is still so strong. "It is due to the knowledge and the devotion of the 'old blacks of Jocojó,'" people say.

The preto is also known as a fluent conversationalist and a good storyteller. People say that the "old blacks" who lived in Gurupá over a generation ago knew more stories than anyone else and told them better; and a local saying has it that "whoever talks a lot is a *Negro*." Maria, the light morena who is the wife of Nhenjuca, is an excellent storyteller, and people directed us to her at once when they heard that we were interested in hearing traditional legends and myths of the Amazon. "She tells so many stories that she is almost a preta," we were told. Others who told us stories would often say that they had heard them from an "old black" who was long since dead. And they pointed to Roque, a very black preto who was very articulate about his experiences as a rubber gatherer in the upper reaches of the Amazon tributaries, and who indeed told stories very well, as an example of the black storyteller. People excused Roque's somewhat doubtful veracity by saying that he was a "preto who liked to talk."

In Gurupá people of African descent are known, in addition, as particularly witty and crafty. And the African Brazilian male is thought of as especially potent sexually. He is assumed to have large genitalia and is therefore thought to be much appreciated by women of all racial groups. A series of pornographic stories told in Gurupá among men illustrate all these qualities of the African. In several of these stories, a black man is having a sexual affair with a white woman, the wife of his master—or of his *patrão* (boss) if the story is placed in modern times. The stories revolve around the skill of the African slave in tricking his master, who suspects the affair but is unable to discover the pair together. Men tell of the sexual exploits of pretos of their acquaintance and of their greater sexual abilities. The African woman and the dark morena are also considered to have greater sexual appetites than the cabocla or the white woman. But the craftiness of the African Brazilian is not limited to situations involving his sexual exploits. There are stories of how pretos outsmarted their masters who would punish them for not working, and how the African Brazilians equalized matters with a trader patron who overcharged them for the goods they purchased.

The stereotypes of African descendants as good storytellers, and of the African as especially potent sexually, are similar indeed to stereotypes regarding the African Americans encountered in North America. Furthermore, a series of jokes, many of which are pornographic, are told in the North American South about the African American (Myrdal 1944:39). Undoubtedly, these similar stereotypes result from the background of African slavery that is common both to southern North America and to northern Brazil. But here the similarity ends. The picture of the "old black" as a good storyteller in Gurupá is not that of Uncle Remus who mildly recounts folk tales to a younger audience. In Gurupá the picture evoked is that of the colorful raconteur of stories of all kinds, both for the family and for the ears of men in the bar.

The stereotype of the sexual ability of the African male may well arise from sexual envy on the part of non-African males in Gurupá, as it seems to in the South of the United States. But it does not serve, as Gunnar Myrdal (1944:108) indicates, for the North American South, "as part of the social control devices to aid in preventing intercourse between Negro males and white females." This very situation is part of the plot of many "off-color" stories, and both legal marriages and extramarital sexual affairs between dark males and lighter females are commonplace occurrences in Gurupá. Nor do the stories told about the African Brazilian serve the function of "proving inferiority" (Myrdal 1944:39); on the contrary, they have the function of proving a superior quality, namely, craftiness. In Gurupá these stories are not told by a white caste about an inferior caste: they are stories told by people of various racial hues about their fellow citizens. In Gurupá the stereotypes held in regard to Africans show then in a favorable light. To be sure, they show the blacks as inferior to the whites, but they have many attributes that are highly valued in Gurupá society.

Yet at the same time people in Gurupá disparage the African Brazilian in a rather warm and humorous manner. They know and make use of widespread Brazilianisms that disparage and belittle the African American, such as, "If the black does not soil when he enters, he does when he leaves" (Wagley 1952:122; Pierson 1942). But these sayings are apt to be used by pretos about themselves and by people in a light joking manner to chide their intimate friends of obvious African ancestry. Nhenjuca, for example, whose mother was a well-known "old black," often blamed his own bad habits on his African ancestry. "I talk too much because I am a preto," he said, to the amusement of his visitors. "I would put an end to that race of people" (the African), he ad libbed into the lines of a folk play in which he had an important part, "but the devil of it is, I also come from the same quality." Nhenjuca's complaints about his African ancestry always brought laughter, for people knew that he was proud of his mother. No one in Gurupá, to our knowledge, is ashamed of African ancestry; and the prestige of the "old blacks" is high in Gurupá tradition.[28]

The stereotypes that the people of Gurupá hold regarding the *tapuia* or the caboclo (Native American physical type), on the other hand, are not so favorable as those referring to the African Brazilian.

---

[28]By 2000 alternations in Gurupá's racial classification system began as recognition of African and Indigenous ancestry grew in the community (Pace & Hinote 2013: 168–69). For the former, this emergent awareness is tied to claims of land entitlement tied to African-slave heritage. This right was established by Brazil's 1988 Constitution, Decree 68, which guaranteed ethnic minorities, including groups descended from African slaves or quilombolas, the right to own the property on which they subsist. Through the hard work of the local population, the Catholic priest, rural union, and the NGO FASE-Gurupá (see Chapter 8), 85,468 hectares—or nearly 10 percent of the municipality—was registered as quilombo and granted to the local residents by the mid-2000s (Treccani 2006:607). Being part of a quilombo, however, necessitates some form of African ancestry recognition. When I talked to members of quilombo communities in 2001 and onward, they spoke self-consciously, if not embarrassedly, about being *negros* in a positive sense (a stark reversal from what people told Wagley in 1948). For example, in a conversation with Doca de Castro, an agroextractivist in his forties from the quilombo Maria-Ribeira, he stated, "I am *negro*." Continuing on he said, "Twenty-five years ago I would have been embarrassed to admit being *negro*. People then, and now, use the term *preto*. Our African and slave ancestry was always hidden and no one spoke of it openly" (Pace and Hinote 2013:169). In this same conversation, Jean-Marie Royer, a French anthropologist who conducted research in Maria-Ribeira in the 1990s, observed that acknowledgement of of slave descent and being a *negro* occured only in the context of land offers. Paulo Oliveira from FASE concluded a year earlier that people in the quilombos were not so much developing a cultural awareness of being *negro* as they were developing a political awareness that the land is theirs because their ancestors were slaves (see Pace and Hinote 2013:169). Since the rush for land under quilombo status has subsided, I have noted a gradual decline in the use of *negro*. In its place people once again use preto. But I have also heard the new term *quilombolo* or *quilombola* used, which focuses on slave descent with a less overt declaration of African descent.

Caboclos appear as good hunters and fishers. They have a special sensitivity for the habits of animals and they know almost instinctively where and how to hunt or fish. No one can remember a famous hunter who was not a "caboclo with but three hairs on his chin." Veiga was known in his earlier years as an excellent hunter. He was born and raised in the rural district near Gurupá where he learned very early to hunt, but people attribute his skill to the fact that "he is *tapuia*." These concepts are harmless enough, for skill at hunting is something useful and to be admired in Gurupá. Still caboclo and *tapuia* are used in a sense of dispraisal; people do not use them when speaking directly to people of Indigenous physical characteristics. "It is not a hard word," said Veiga, who was pointed out as a typical representative of this physical type, "but it makes a person sad."

The term, as stated earlier, has a double meaning—one indicating low social status and another indicating Native American physical characteristics. Furthermore, most of the stereotypes associated with caboclos or the tapuias are derogatory. Caboclos are considered lazy: "They do not plant gardens, but live from the sale of a little rubber and by fishing for their meals." Caboclos are thought to be timid because they live isolated in the forest. "They prefer to live like animals, away from others, deep in the forest," one man said; caboclo, however, is thought to be tricky and exceedingly suspicious. A popular local saying has it that "the suspicious caboclo hangs up his hammock and then sleeps under it." Commercial men say that the caboclos must be watched in any business deal; they will insert a rock in the core of a large ball of crude rubber to increase its weight when they sell it to the trader. They will sell *timborana*, a vine that resembles the true *timbó* from which insecticides are produced, but that has no value, to the unsuspecting trader. Such stereotypes regarding the caboclo are not limited to people of that physical type (Native American) but are often aimed at all rural collectors. As most people point out, the rural collectors are in the great majority tapuias or caboclos in a physical sense, but even town dwellers of this physical type are thought to share their timidity, laziness, ability at hunting and fishing, and trickiness.

People of Native American descent, unlike those of African descent, do not like to be reminded of their native ancestry. The children playing in front of a Gurupá home were heard many times teasing the housewife of "caboclo" physical type. They called her *tapuia* and *índia*, and she would reply in anger, "Go away, your parents are Indians themselves."

In the Amazon the Native American, even more often than the African, was the slave in colonial society. In the opinion of the European, the Native was a nude barbarian and of less prestige than the more expensive African slave. Today, Indigenous physical characteristics are therefore a symbol not only of slave ancestry but also of a social origin lower than the African's in colonial times.[29]

VI

In the great metropolitan centers of the country, there are already indications that discrimination, tensions, and prejudices between people of different racial types are emerging (Bastide 1952; Costa Pinto 1952).[30]

---

[29]The term caboclo has likewise undergone change. In 1948 Wagley found that caboclo had a narrow definition associated with Indigenous heritage. By the 2000s the term's use expanded in a uniquely regional fashion to label mixtures of blacks, whites, and descendants of the Indigenous populations (see Pace and Hinote 2013:166–67). In other parts of the Americas the term *mestizo* (European and Indigenous mixtures) is frequently used for this group, although it does not normally include people of African descent. In Brazil there is a label referring to African and Indigenous mixtures known as *cafuzo*, but it is not a widely used term and does not include Europeans. Both *cafuzo* and *mestiço* (the Portuguese word for mestizo) are not commonly used in Gurupá.

For example, while in the quilombo of Jocojó in 2002 I queried Mauro, a subsistence farmer in his early thirties, whether there is any Indigenous blood found among the people of Jocojó. As described in Pace and Hinote (2013:167) he replied yes, you can see it in their faces. I continued, asking how he classified these people in terms of race. Mauro answered there is no special word for Indigenous features. I asked if caboclo meant *índio* (Indian), to which he responded no. I next asked if a caboclo is a negro. He said that they are the same thing with only the hair being different, straight versus kinky.

In an ironic twist, the derogatory term caboclo can be used to disavow both Indigenous and African heritage. In 2002 Alfredo Gomes da Costa Filho, a Church functionary in his late fifties, explained to me that, "until very recently we considered Indians to be *bichos* (beasts) from the stories we heard. No one wanted to identify with them. We called ourselves caboclos instead" (Pace and Hinote 2013:168). In a parallel fashion, people have denied or been unaware of their African ancestry. In 2002 Gabriel, a 72-year-old religious leader of Jocojó, told me that until recently no one in his family knew of their African slave heritage. He explained: "No one called themselves *negro* or descendants of slaves. That would be an insult. We saw ourselves as *pretos*, *morenos*, and *caboclos*, but never as *negros*" (Pace and Hinote 2013:168). In both of these cases, caboclo is a neutral term in the same manner as are preto and moreno—which refer to colors and features and not necessarily, orexplicitly , to 'race'.

[30]Sixteen lines were omitted from this page that maintains Gurupá's racial democracy as a model for the future.

There is the danger [or promise] that, when a large number of people of African and Indigenous ancestry improve their educational and economic position, they will challenge the dominant position of the "whites" (even though they are also of mixed ancestry), with the result that race will be emphasized as a criterion of social position. Furthermore, as such rural Brazilian communities as Gurupá become more closely tied to the Western industrial and commercial world, they will be exposed to a different ideology regarding race relations. After all, the technicians, the administrators, and even the scientists are the products of a civilization that has in the last four hundred years taught racial inequality. There is a danger that along with their useful techniques, instruments, and concepts they may teach racial inequality.

The social class structure of the Brazilian Amazon region is clearly a drawback to be overcome by any program aiming at social and economic change. The *alta sociedade*, that is, the descendants of the colonial landholders of the rubber barons, and of successful commercial families, are content with the status quo. They look with suspicion on any program that might result in basic changes in Amazon society. They have been able to draw sufficient wealth from extractive industries to allow them to live in Belém and Manaus or even abroad. They have been able to educate their children elsewhere. Any program of economic development and technical assistance would inevitably have to deal with these "aristocrats" and with the growing middle class of the Amazon region, made up of the professional groups, the public officials and civil servants, the office workers in commercial companies, and the like. In Gurupá any health program or agricultural program would have to be channeled through the First Class because they are the government officials and the commercial leaders of the community.[31] Any initiative that depends entirely either on this "middle class" or on the regional aristocrats would have but a limited influence on the region. The Gurupá upper class and the regional middle class share many of the social values of the old landed gentry. Upper-class Brazilian urbanites look down on the inhabitants of the small towns and know little about the so-called interior. The ideal of any state or federal employee who is unfortunate enough to be stationed in a small town in the

---

[31]Between the 1980s and 2000, as will be shown in Chapter 8, the traditional elite of Gurupá was removed from power, allowing development projects in the 2000s to be channeled directly through the rural workers union and the NGO FASE-Gurupá.

"interior" is to be transferred to the city. Like the urban upper and middle class, the Gurupá First Class holds manual labor in dispraisal. They know little about the problems and the values of their lower-class fellow citizens, the Second-Class townspeople, the rural agricultural-ists, and the collectors of forest products. The chasm between the upper and the lower strata in Amazon society is a wide one. Innovations introduced through these upper-and middle-class groups tend to ignore the mass of people in the lower strata of Amazon society.

Social rank in all human societies is based on a combination of birthright and individual achievement. Despite many changes since colonial times, Amazon society still places an emphasis on birthright, and there are few opportunities for individual achievement. The highly crystallized class system that has persisted since the colonial period is changing with extreme slowness. But, as educational and health facili-ties and economic opportunities are made available to a larger segment of the population, the emphasis will shift from position ascribed at birth to social positions that are achieved. This will bring about a rear-rangement of the Amazon social hierarchy and will result in individual maladjustments and disappointments. That is the price that the people of Gurupá will have to pay for "progress." But modification of the tra-ditional class system will also allow a fuller utilization of the human resources of the Amazon Valley.

CHAPTER 5

....

Family Affairs
in an Amazon Community

The large and closely knit family is one of the most important institutions of Brazilian society. When Brazilians speak of *minha família* (my family), they generally refer to a large group consisting not only of the husband's relatives but also those of his wife. They are apt to call the more immediate unit "my wife/husband and children" (*minha mulher/meu marido e filhos*) reserving the word "family" for the larger circle of kin. The family often includes first, second, and even third cousins. First cousins are called "brother cousins" (*primos irmãos*), whereas second and third cousins are simply "cousins." The term for "uncle" and "aunt" may also be extended to mean one's parents' cousins. Over a hundred relatives may form the family of a middle-class Brazilian city dweller, and a member of the traditional aristocracy may be able to count literally hundreds of relatives. In such large circles of kin, intimacy is greater among those who have a close degree of kinship. An inner circle of aunts, uncles, and "brother/sister cousins" usually has the more frequent and devoted relationships. For many Brazilians social life is lived mainly within this widely extended family. There are birthday parties, baptisms, graduations, funerals, and other occasions on which the family gathers, and there are weddings at which one garners a whole new circle of family connections. In Rio de Janeiro, São Paulo, and even in the Amazon cities of Belém and Manaus, crowded urban conditions make for dispersal of these large family groups throughout the city; yet constant visiting, the telephone, and frequent family gatherings keep the group intact.[1] At any crisis in the life of one of the family members, others gather to offer help and sympathy.

Gilberto Freyre has described the role of the large patriarchal families in the colonial life of the northeastern coastal region of Brazil. In the rural society of colonial times, the aristocrats lived on the plantation surrounded by married sons and daughters and their children, by a few distant relatives who had come to depend on them, and by slaves—all members, in a way, of the family. Marriages were alliances between large families, and marriages of first cousins or of uncles with nieces were frequent (Freyre 1946:261). Often, an effort was made to steer a younger son into the church so that the family chapel might be in the hands of a priest who was a member of the family. Political affairs were dominated by family loyalties. The family was so important in colonial society that, in Gilberto Freyre's (1946:261) words, "The family and not the individual, much less the State or any commercial company, was from the sixteenth century the great colonizing factor in Brazil, the productive unit, the capital that cleared the land, founded plantations, purchased slaves, oxen, implements; and in politics it was the social force that set itself up as the most powerful colonial aristocracy in the Americas. Over it the King of Portugal may be said, practically, to have reigned without ruling."

In the Amazon region families were not so wealthy or powerful as the great patriarchal groups of the colonial northeast. Nevertheless they were very important in politics, in economics, and in the social life of the region. Even today most Amazon commercial companies are family owned, and family connections are important in politics. After each election the bureaucracy is apt to be crammed with the relatives of newly elected officials. The family is the focus of social life. A visitor in Belém or Manaus may find people somewhat inhospitable because most social events take place within the family circle. Once accepted by a family, however, visitors' social life may then become quite intense. They will be introduced by a friend to relatives, by these relatives to

---

[1]There is a tendency in Rio de Janeiro for relatives to purchase apartments in the same large cooperative apartment building.

others, and perhaps even be given letters of introduction to members of
the family in other towns.

II

People of all social classes in Gurupá share the Brazilian ideal of a large
and united family group. They speak of important families and they are
conscious of the role of family connections. Yet in Gurupá families
are not nearly so large as they are among the urban middle class and the
aristocrats of the region. Frequent emigration to Belém, to distant
rubber fields, and even to other regions of Brazil results in a loss of contact with relatives. Among the upper and middle class of Brazilian cities
with their superior economic conditions, people migrate less frequently
than in rural communities. Whenever possible, Brazilians stay within
reach of their families. In Gurupá, however, with one or two exceptions,
everyone has a relatively precarious income and at any time may feel the
need to move away in search of more favorable and stable circumstances.
Without wealth or property, or even economic stability, relatives can be
of little help to other relatives. The large Brazilian family is therefore less
often encountered in rural communities such as Gurupá.

In such a town everyone has relatives who have moved away. Even
Manuel Pere Serra (see Figure 2.7), a descendant of one of Gurupá's
"best families," is the only one of four brothers now living in Gurupá.
He had just returned there in 1948. One of his brothers is a civil administrator in the Brazilian army; another has a position in Rio de Janeiro;
and the third "could never settle anywhere, but worked with a commercial company in many places until he died in Belém" a few years
ago. Pere Serra's mother and sister live with him in Gurupá, and he has
an uncle (his mother's brother-in-law) and a first cousin who are
owners of a trading post not far from town. Nowadays these are his
only relatives in the community; most of his family lives in Belém or
elsewhere. In his father's time, when Gurupá was more prosperous, the
family was important politically and exceedingly numerous, if the genealogy that he gave us may be trusted.

Elíos Veiga, a Second Class town dweller, also has many relatives
who have long since left Gurupá. His family was a large one consisting
of five sons and two daughters. But when Veiga was about ten years old,
they moved from Gurupá to Monte Alegre, where they lived for a few
years. Two of his brothers remained there with an uncle and an aunt

when the family returned to take up farming near Gurupá on the Igarapé Itapereira. He still has family, he says, in Monte Alegre. Another brother left later to collect rubber in the rubber fields of the Upper Amazon and has never returned. His older brother married late and left no descendants. But Veiga has several "nephews and nieces," children of one of his sisters. Anastacio Veiga, the best known flute player in Gurupá, is his cousin, and through Anastacio, Veiga has several other relatives. Veiga is the father of five daughters and one son; two daughters married and stayed in Gurupá, but the others have moved away to Belém, to Santarém, and to the Tapajós River with their husbands. His only son left Gurupá long ago and seldom writes. Veiga considers himself, however, to be a fortunate man; he says that he has a "large family." He was able to count as many as twenty-five relatives within the Gurupá community between close and distant kin. But, as compared to the widely extended family groups of the middle and upper class in Belém, his family is small.

In the farming district of the Gurupá community, however, the kinship circle is somewhat larger than among the town dwellers. Income from farming in the Amazon is amazingly low, yet farming is still a relatively stable occupation. From their gardens people are guaranteed a minimum subsistence, and they are less dependent on cash for foodstuffs than the city dweller or the rubber collectors. Farmers are thus less often forced to migrate, and they have large and extended families—closer to the Brazilian ideal than those of the poor townspeople. In the farming village of Jocojó, genealogies showed that kinship formed a complex web of relationships among the inhabitants. Talentino, one of the leaders of the village, had four married sisters and their husbands and children as neighbors. Furthermore, his wife was the niece of João Pombo (see Figure 3.6), the most important man of the settlement, and thus he was tied to Pombo's large group of relatives. He was also related, through marriage, to Teodosio, another head of a large family in the settlement. Of the total population of slightly more than one hundred people, this one man, Talentino, was related by kinship to well over half. And João Pombo could claim relationship to over eighty of the villagers through direct descent or through marriage.

The Amazon rubber collectors, as already mentioned, are famous for their nomadic habits. They move about frequently, hoping to escape from debt and to find rubber trails where conditions are better than the one in which they work. The collector, therefore, often leaves relatives behind, and in the rubber-collecting neighborhoods of the Gurupá community, even more so than in town, the family is small. Sometimes a father lives and works with his sons, or sometimes two or more brothers will exploit a group of contiguous rubber trails; but in general the collectors are people with few, if any, relatives. In this sense they are not average Brazilians. The economic instability of rubber gathering does not provide a basis for a large kin group. Only among more settled farmers do people in Gurupá have the security of widespread kinship bonds.

In keeping with Brazilian ideals, however, relatives are no less united in Gurupá than elsewhere in the country. In normal social relations in Gurupá, one is aware of moving within small circles of kin. For example, soon after our arrival in 1948, we became quite friendly with the farmer Jorge Palheta (see Figure 3.7). When we needed someone to clean our house, he recommended a cousin. Later he introduced us to his brother-in-law, João Dias. Jorge became one of our most trustworthy sources of information on farming techniques and the problems of the small farmer in Gurupá. His mother-in-law, Dico Dias mother, received us at once in her simple home and gave us unsparingly of her time, teaching us local folklore. Whenever we traveled in the vicinity by canoe, Dico Dias half-brother was always ready to arrange for a canoe and, if necessary, paddlers for us. Both Jorge Palheta and João Dias had a few distant relatives (a "cousin," an "aunt," or an "uncle") in the rural neighborhoods, and we were always received at once by them.[2] Likewise, in the village of Jocojó, João Pombo asked his family to receive us well, and thus the majority of the villagers welcomed us into their homes. Elíos Veiga said that we might always call on his family. As elsewhere in Brazil, kinship is an important mechanism in Gurupá for channeling personal relations.

III

As in most of the Latin world, the people of Gurupá extend their relationships beyond the kinship circle by means of ritual co-parenthood.

---

[2]In the 1980s Jorge Palheta likewise extended his kinship network to my wife Olga and me. Through him we worked with and befriended his daughter, Cecília Palheta, who was Gurupá's first woman mayor. With Cecília's wide range of connections we gained access to all government workers for interviews and were frequently afforded free transportation throughout the municipality.

Because their kinship circle is, for Brazilians, not large, the people of Gurupá perhaps make even more frequent use of such ritual relationships than do the inhabitants of the big cities. It is almost as if they compensated for their relatively small number of kinsmen by doing so. Like most Latins, the people of Gurupá are Catholics. In accordance with Catholic ritual, the parents of a child invite a man and a woman to serve as sponsors at their child's baptism. The sponsors become godfather and godmother to the child, and the same rite establishes a strong relationship not only between the godchild (*afilhado*) and its godparents (*padrinhos*) but also between the parents of the child and the godparents, who become *comadres* (co-mothers) and *compadres* (co-fathers) to each other. This three-way relationship—between godparents with their godchild, between parents with their child, and between parents with the godparents—is one of considerable importance in most of Latin America and in many Latin countries of Europe. Godparents accept responsibility for the child materially and spiritually. Children owe especial respect to their godparents—"even more than to their parents," as one person in Gurupá explained. The parents and their co-fathers and co-mothers have, ideally, a relationship of mutual respect, of mutual aid, and of intimate friendship. They help one another and lend financial and moral aid to one another. It is considered incestuous for a co-mother and co-father to have sex relations; thus individuals of different sex, related to one another in this way, may have friendly relations without being suspected of sexual misbehavior. It is a common sight in the Amazon region to see two men embrace each other, using the common salutation, "*Como vai, meu compadre?*" (How are you, my co-father?), and to hear a man politely say, "*Minha comadre, Maria.*" Children kiss the hands of their godparents, asking for "a Blessing," and the godfather or godmother answers, "*Deus lhe abençoe, meu filho*" (God bless you, my child).[3]

In the upper- and middle-class groups of a large Brazilian city, *compadresco*[4] relationships are often used to extend further an already extensive kinship circle or as a way of reinforcing the existing bonds with a particular kinsman. For example, the director of a company might invite a close business associate and spouse to serve as godparents to

---

[3]In 2013 these patterns continue as described by Wagley.
[4]Compadresco (adjective) and compadrio (noun) are the terms used for the constellation of relationship between the parents, godparents, and godchild.

his child; or the director might invite a wealthy or politically important cousin and spouse to serve. In the former case, he establishes new ties both for himself and for his child; and in the latter, he strengthens his kin ties to his cousin. In addition, throughout Brazil there is generally a ritual sponsor (godparent) at confirmation;[5] and at marriage both the bride and the groom invite a couple as their *padrinho e madrinha de casamento* (godparents of marriage). Thus a Brazilian child might normally, in the course of its life, acquire godparents at baptism, another godparent at confirmation, and godparents at marriage. He or she would also share, in a sense, the marriage godparents of the spouse. An individual by the time of marriage might expect to be related to at least seven people by ritual sponsorship. In addition, any adult might also expect to be invited several times to serve as godparent of baptism, of confirmation, or of marriage, thus adding considerably to the number of individuals with whom ritual kinship ties are extended.

The force of these *compadresco* relations, added to family and kinship ties, are felt profoundly in Brazilian social, economic, and political life. Co-parents extend political and economic favors to each other and to their godchildren. It is common to refer to someone who is protected politically by an important figure as an *"afilhado politico"* (political godchild). A much more durable political maneuver than "kissing babies" is to stand as godparent for children at baptism. An old and practiced politician in the Amazon region, for example, kept a notebook in which he entered the addresses and birthdays of his three to four hundred godchildren. They were strategically scattered over the entire state, and both his godchildren and his co-parents were certain voters and excellent political campaigners for him.[6]

In such communities as Gurupá, where so many people are economically insecure, the compadrio system seems to have proliferated.

---

[5] A male acquires a padrinho and a female a madrinha.

[6] In the rural areas of north Brazil, compadrio relationships are not "stripped of their importance and reduced to a mere formula of address" as indicated by Antonio Candido (1951:308) for the central and southern parts of the country. My own experience, even in such urban centers as Rio de Janeiro, leads me to believe that although compadrio relationships are perhaps less strong, and certainly modified by industrial urban conditions, they still have important functions in Brazilian society. A godparent is no longer "a second mother or father," but she or he passes on favors, if convenient, to godsons, even in large towns and urban centers.

For in addition to *compadres*[7] of baptism, in Gurupá and throughout the Amazon region, there are also "*compadres de fogueira*" (co-parents of the fire). Both on St. John's Day and on St. Peter's Day in late June, it is customary throughout Brazil to build large bonfires around which the festivities of the season take place. Paper balloons are launched, fireworks are set off, sweet potatoes are roasted, and special songs of the season are sung. Along the Amazon, as the bonfire burns down into embers, one may also garner new co-parents, godchildren, or god-parents, as the case demands. A man invites a good friend, or an important man who might help him, to become his co-father. A youngster asks an adult to become his godfather or godmother. The relationship is established by a simple rite. The two, with the fire between them, pass their clasped hands over the fire three times, and recite an oath in unison. This oath, of which there are several versions, is as follows: "St. John said, St. Peter confirmed, that Our Lord Jesus Christ ordered us to be co-parents in this life and in the other also."[8]

Such relationships established "over the fire" are not as binding as those established at baptism. Some people caught by an undesirable invitation go through the rite out of politeness. They sometimes elect to ignore the relationship later on. On St. Peter's Day in 1948, for example, a young married man was invited by three young girls to become their godfather. He accepted, explaining that it would be bad manners to refuse. Later he treated the relationship as a pleasant joke, calling each of them "my godchild" when he met them, and then, after a few weeks again addressed them formally by name. Others, however, take such relationships more seriously, and co-parentship by fire can be as intimate and stable as that formed by baptism. João Pombo, to cite one example, invited a man from Gurupá to become his co-father several weeks before St. John's Eve. The two men arranged to spend the festival together, and that evening they went through the rites of becoming

---

[7]The term compadre is used here generically to refer to the constellation of relationships of the system, namely, compadre, comadre, madrinha, padrinho, afilhado, and afilhada.

[8]São João disse,
São Pedro confirmou,
Que Nosso Senhor Jesus Cristo mandou
A gente ser compadre
Nesta vida e na outra também.

co-fathers of the fire. Afterward, they treated each other with the same respect, the same mutual support, and the same cordiality as if one had sponsored the baptism of the child of the other. The possibility of extending one's bonds of ritual kinship at St. John's and St. Peter's Eve increases the number of people within the *compadrio* circle of any individual enormously.[9] Most people in Gurupá make use of this mechanism to widen their circle of secure interpersonal relations.[10]

The strength and the degree of intimacy of *compadrio* relationships depend on several factors—on the continuity of frequent association of the individuals concerned, on whether or not the continuation of such ties is of material or social value, and on the personal inclinations of the individuals involved. In many cases noted in Gurupá, individuals have lost touch with their godparents or co-parents; frequently, we were told of a sponsor at the baptism of a child who later moved away and never again wrote letters or returned to visit. Yet in other instances, where there was a reason to continue the relationship (if the sponsor was a merchant or a politician, for example, to whom numerous relationships throughout the region would be valuable), the godparent did not forget the godchild and the co-parent. Several of our friends in Gurupá told us of their godparents or co-parents who had moved to other towns or to Belém and who sent presents on each birthday. Whenever these co-parents pass through Gurupá, they visit with their godchildren and co-parents. *Compadrio* relationships between people within the community, however, tend to be close and intimate. The relationship between two old friends, between two cousins, between traders and customers, or between neighbors who are co-parents is generally a warm, stable, and respectful one. If they live nearby, the godchild visits the godparents daily, asking them for their "blessing." Godchildren run errands for their godparents and are given small

---

[9]In the mid-1980s my wife Olga and I "passed over the bonfire" of Saint John with Zeca Pará and his young son Esteven to establish fictive kinship ties. The next morning Zeca knocked on my window shutter (we were neighbors) and with a smile on his face addressed me as "compadre" and proceeded to ask for a loan of 100 cruzados, which was now his right to do (see p. 157). Zeca passed away in the 1990s, but when visiting Gurupá we still look for and greet Esteven, now in his 40s, married with five daughters, as a godson of the fire.

[10]Sometimes, people also "confirm" their kinship or their previously existing co-parent relationship "over the fire."

presents and sweets.[11] Presents are forthcoming from the godparents on birthdays and at Christmas. Godchildren become intimates in their godparents' homes, and they come to look on their godmother and godfather somewhat as a "second mother and father." Co-fathers lend each other small sums, they cooperate with each other in cooperative work parties, they aid each other in house repairs, and they are apt to spend many leisure hours together. Co-mothers cooperate in manufacturing manioc flour, watch out for each other's children, help each other in preparing the large meals on birthdays, and visit each other often. There is freer visiting, without fear of jealousy, between couples tied to each other by *compadrio* relationships than between neighbors or even distant relatives, for sexual relations are unthinkable between a co-father and his co-mother.

Nhenjuca and his wife, Anna, have a strong *compadrio* relationship with Ernesto and his wife, Maria. For years the two men had called each other co-father since they had passed over the fire on St. John's Eve; in addition, they were good friends and neighbors, both living on Second Street in Gurupá. Then, a few years ago, Ernesto and his wife invited Nhenjuca and Anna to serve as sponsors at the baptism of their adopted son, thus strengthening and reaffirming their established friendship and existing relationship. Nhenjuca and Ernesto plant their gardens cooperatively and they have pooled their resources to build a large fish trap. The two women work together each week preparing farinha, and sometimes Nhenjuca and Ernesto help their wives in the task. When Ernesto and Maria undertook to serve as sponsors for the festival of Santa Maria, celebrated by a religious brotherhood in one of the rural neighborhoods, Nhenjuca and Anna spent most of a week helping their co-father and co-mother prepare food to be served at the festival. Nhenjuca lent Ernesto approximately $5 (cr. $100), and Anna lent Maria cooking utensils and cups and saucers for serving coffee. Nhenjuca and Anna attended the festival, working throughout the day, helping their co-parents to serve the many guests. The two

---

[11]On many afternoons between 1984 and 1986 I would watch from my window as Zeca Pará would greet his many godchildren as they passed by. He claimed to have several hundred. Whenever he had an errand to run but did not want to leave the house, he would simply wait a few minutes until a godchild would walk by, at which point he would ask the individual to run the errand for him. I never saw a godchild deny his request.

couples visit each other almost daily, and each is aware of the family difficulties and troubles of the other. Maria sent for Nhenjuca at once when her husband got drunk and was jailed; Nhenjuca knew of his co-father's weakness for rum and was able to persuade the police officer to release Ernesto in his care. Each of these four people has other *compadrio* relationships, both by baptism and by fire, but the bond between the two couples has been singled out among all of them as the most intimate of all. Like the formal structure of kinship, the institution of compadrio offers a form through which intimate and secure interpersonal relationships may be channeled; but, as in kinship, the potentiality of the relationship may not be fulfilled. Neither co-parents nor cousins need have especially close or friendly relations, and certain kinsmen or certain co-parents are always more closely associated than others.

Nhenjuca and Ernesto and their families make use of the full potentialities of the *compadrio* relationship in living out a cooperative and intimate friendship. These two families are lower-class townspeople. Both have approximately the same income and approximately the same social status in the community. Their *compadrio* relationship is therefore a reciprocal one strengthened by mutual aid. Neither co-parent has any special power to protect the other, nor has Nhenjuca wealth or political power through which he might be of any special aid to his godson. Many co-parents are, like the ones discussed previously, members of the same socioeconomic stratum and class. On the other hand, the *compadrio* relationship is perhaps more frequently established in Gurupá between individuals of different economic and social position— between members of the lower- and upper-class groups. Poor people feel that one way to garner some advantage for their children is to ask a trader, a public official, or anyone with prestige and a relatively superior economic situation to serve as sponsor at the baptism. Perhaps, also, the co-parent of higher status and greater wealth will favor and protect the poorer co-parent. In such cases the initiative comes always from the lower-class family, who invite the upper-class individual or couple to serve as godparents. That this form of *compadrio* relationship is more common in Gurupá is attested by the number of such relationships that people of different social classes reported in our household survey. The household heads who were classified as "whites" reported an average of 28.1 godchildren; that is, they were requested to serve that many times as godparents.[12] In contrast, the heads of families classified as lower-class townspeople (i.e., Gente de Segunda) had an average of only 4.2 godchildren.

In Gurupá the higher one's prestige and the greater one's wealth, the larger the number of godchildren and co-parents one tends to have. In fact, it almost might be said that the number of godchildren and co-parents that an individual can claim is an index of social position. The frequency with which an individual is invited to serve as a ritual sponsor or to pass over the fire on St. John's or St. Peter's Eve is a reflection of economic, social, political, and familial standing in the community. Dona Diná, owner of the Casa Borralho, whose income and social position is perhaps the highest of any individual in Gurupá, claimed 142 godchildren and over three hundred co-mothers and co-fathers, the fathers and mothers of these godchildren. Another strong commercial man of the community reported one hundred godchildren, and a rural trader had as many as sixty-five godchildren. Dona Inacinha, the schoolteacher who lacks financial support for her upper-class position, was able to report only sixteen godchildren. Not all of these numerous *compadrio* relationships reported by people of the upper class were with lower-class families; for among upper-class families too there is a tendency to invite someone as a godparent or co-parent who stands even higher in the social and economic hierarchy. In this way strong ties are established between important families of the community and of neighboring communities. But mainly, the *compadrio* system provides a means of cementing relationships between the various social strata of Gurupá society.

Compadrio relationships between individuals of widely different social strata are by nature not as close and intimate as those between people of the same economic and social position. The fact that Dona Diná has so many godchildren and so many co-parents means, of course, that the relationship is necessarily diluted and weakened by sheer numbers. In fact, Dona Diná cannot possibly remember all of the names of her godchildren and of her co-parents. She keeps a notebook in which, over the years, she has inserted their names to remember them all. On several occasions young men have appeared at the Casa

---

[12]These include godchildren by baptism as well as godchildren of the fire when the latter were recognized as godchildren.

Borralho announcing that they are godchildren of Dona Diná and of her late husband, Liberato. Dona Diná refers to her notebook (which is evidently not complete) on such occasions, questioning the young man about his age, the name of his parents, and when he was baptized. If she is reasonably certain that she or Liberato "stood for him" at baptism, she extends him the hospitality of her house and asks the manager of the Casa Borralho to advance credit to him if he wishes to collect rubber.

Co-fathers and co-mothers who are steady customers at the Casa Borralho are remembered well by Dona Diná. When they come to trade, they are offered coffee or a meal in her house. João Pombo, for example, the neighborhood leader on the Igarapé Jocojó, is Dona Diná's co-father. She and Liberato stood as sponsors at the baptism of João Pombo's eldest son. Whenever João Pombo comes to Gurupá, he eats a meal at Dona Diná's house. She respects her co-father and will not listen to the gossip regarding João Pombo's complex family affairs (he has maintained both a wife and a mistress for years). João Pombo sent his son to live with Liberato and Dona Diná so that the boy might attend school in town. For this he paid the boy's godparents nothing, and when the son finally returned to Jocojó to live, Dona Diná complained, half in jest and half seriously, "My co-father stole our godchild from us." João Pombo has brought many customers to the Casa Borralho, and he is a valuable co-father to the owner of the Casa Borralho. Nowadays the people of Jocojó tend to buy and sell at other stores and trading posts, and Dona Diná freely complains to her co-father for allowing "his people" to do so.

Many of Liberato's co-parents, Dona Diná explained of her late husband, always came to ask him how they should vote. Liberato is said by the people of Gurupá to have avoided politics and to have attempted to remain neutral during some of the rather violent political campaigns and elections that took place before 1930. Liberato always said that politics were bad for his business. Yet everybody says that local politicians always made friendly gestures to him. On one occasion he carried out a quiet but effective campaign against a candidate for mayor who offended him. Liberato, with his numerous co-parent customers, controlled many votes. Even today local politicians seek out the support of individuals with numerous compadrio relations, and such relationships also serve to cement commercial and political relations. It reinforces relations between traders and collector and farmer customers.

Between members of the same class, it is a reciprocal relationship of mutual aid; between members of separate social classes, it provides a "bridge" reinforcing their economic and social relationship by a personal bond validated by the Church and by tradition.[13]

IV

Unlike the large households of aristocratic plantation owners of colonial northeastern Brazil, with their numerous relatives and servants, described by Gilberto Freyre, most Gurupá homes consist of one nuclear family: a husband, a wife, and their children. Most people in Gurupá consider it a real disadvantage to be forced to live with relatives or in-laws despite the value placed on a large circle of kin. Several people told us that they would not like to live with their in-laws. Men, especially, felt that the sharing of a house with their wife's parents would only lead to trouble. A few people, as they do everywhere, realize the value of sharing a household with relatives and of having their help in household tasks and in caring for children. One young mother, for example, told us that she wanted to move away from Gurupá "to my mother-in-law's house" in another town on the Lower Amazon. "There I will be better off," she said. "She is a good midwife. She will help me with the children. There, if my husband does not behave correctly, his mother will help me talk with him." And in Gurupá there are households shared by several relatives that are as peaceful as one-family homes. Elíos Veiga shares his small house with his daughter and his son-in-law and their two children; and Dona Diná, owner of the Casa Borralho, has her unmarried younger sister, three adopted children, and her younger married sister with her husband and their children living with her. In the rural neighborhoods it is not unusual to find a married daughter and her husband,

---

[13]In 2013 the compadresco system continues much the same as described in 1948. Because there is no longer a First Class, people commented that few individuals had 50, let alone 100 godchildren and co-parents anymore. Yet even the generation currently in their 20s can expect 4 or 5 godchildren during their lifetimes. The rise of *evangélicos* (fundamentalist Christian groups), which make up 13 percent of the municipal population (IBGE 2012) and who do not support the Catholic tradition of godchildren/godparents, has lessened the practice somewhat in the community. For one reason or another, however, many evangélicos still end up with godparents, co-parents, and godchildren.

or even a married son and his family, sharing a house with the parents. But most people prefer to have their own homes and to be economically independent of their relatives.

In these one-family households the father is theoretically the absolute head. One of the main reasons why multiple-family households are thought to be unhappy arrangements is the belief that conflicts inevitably arise between the dominating males. To his immediate family a father's word should be law. No one should question his coming and going. Each evening he should pray before the small altar placed in the comer of one room of the house; he stands as he prays for the family while the wife and children kneel behind him. Only the father is thought to understand the family finances. He should make all purchases, even the daily groceries, and Gurupá stores are points of reunion for men who chat and have a drink as they buy the food for that night's dinner. Only men should make business decisions. A father should fully support his family, and a disparaging remark about a husband is to say "his wife is fishing"—that is, that she must work for food for the family. A man should be the father of sons, for sons are symbols of a man's masculinity. A husband and father is rather expected to have extramarital sexual affairs, and he may even have illegitimate children. Women smile and hint at the wicked and very masculine activities of their husbands. João Pombo, for example, is known as "a good father and husband," although everyone also knows that he has two families—one by his legal wife and another by a mistress who lives only a few kilometers away. Gurupá husbands are expected to be extremely jealous, sometimes beating their wives for any signs of flirting. Confronted with adultery, a husband would be expected to kill both his wife and her lover. One case, related to us, concerned the dual murder perpetrated by Joviniano Gomes several years ago. One night Joviniano returned from his garden and found his wife in her lover's arms. Joviniano "went blind" and killed both with a knife. Joviniano gave himself up to the police, and months afterward a judge and jury absolved him of any guilt. His wife was dishonest and "he was fully right in what he did," our informants said.

In keeping with this stereotype of the dominating and aggressive husband and father, the wife and mother in Gurupá should be mild, quiet, and passive. She should never talk too much, at least in the presence of her husband. She is a hard worker within the household, and even in the fields, if necessary. The wife never sits at the table with her husband for meals, but stands to serve him and any other men present. A wife should never participate in economic affairs. She is thought to be entirely dependent economically on her husband. Even Dona Diná, the well-to-do widow, would never set a price nor complete a business transaction. These are men's affairs to be carried on between men. Thus, when we discussed having our meals in her house, she agreed that we might do so but stated that only her brother-in-law would be able to set a price. In making studies of family budgets in Gurupá, it was always necessary to have both the husband and his wife present at interviews. The wife would know the amounts of food used in preparing dishes, but only the husband knew the prices they paid for food, clothes, and other items. Women are expected to be virgins at marriage and to know nothing at all about sex. Men feel that a wife should be taught what she knows about sex only by her husband; and during her life she must be absolutely faithful to him. Good wives should not be seen too frequently in the street, nor should they pay visits, even to feminine friends, too often without their husbands. Such freedom might cast some doubt on their moral behavior.

In Gurupá, as in all communities throughout the world, however, there is a great distance between the ideal and reality—between what people say they should do and what they do. Yet such ideal patterns of behavior, regarding the ideal father and husband and the ideal wife and mother, determine to a large extent actual behavior. Such ideals provide a set of rules toward which people think they should aspire—but never quite achieve. As elsewhere, there are few ideal husbands and few ideal wives. Few men are able to be the dominating central figure of their nuclear family, and there are few women who are able to be the quiet, passive figures of the ideal picture. Most men go through the motions, publicly issuing orders to their wives and children; and women serve their husbands meals, especially when there are visitors. Women refrain from commercial activities, asking men to buy the groceries, and they avoid meeting men in the streets. In public, both sexes act the roles that their society assigns to them.

In the intimacy of the family, things are different. Men and women talk over business deals. Women actually know prices well. Dona Diná, despite her public protestations to the contrary, is the real power at the Casa Borralho; and her brother-in-law, who is the manager, discusses business with her frequently and often waits patiently for her decisions. Nhenjuca even gives his money to his wife, Anna, to keep for him.

Only in public does Nhenjuca hold the family pocketbook, for Anna tells him what to buy at the store and gives him money for the purchases. With the exception of a few office holders, who have salaries, and a few storekeepers and traders, most men need their wives' help to make a living. Among the lower-class groups of the town and of the rural neighborhoods, most women help their husbands in the garden at such jobs as planting and harvesting, and they do most of the task of manufacturing manioc flour. There are many women who even collect rubber, taking over a husband's rubber trail when he is ill or indisposed. Women sometimes even do the job of smoking the latex, and most rubber gatherers' wives fish while their husbands make the round of his trails.

Women even hold a few public jobs in Gurupá and participate in its business life. Dona Filomena is an office worker at the health post. The post office in Gurupá has a postmistress, the wife of the state tax collector. Dona Inacinha and her cousin are the schoolteachers. Dona Senina, the wife of Bibi Pará (see Figure 3.8), is a notary in charge of civil records. Women also participate in business. The baker's wife took an active and equal part in his business; and although women do not normally sell from behind the counters in stores, Dona Deborah, the wife of Gurupá's only remaining Jewish merchant, always took part in the buying of merchandise and the selling of products to the city exporters. After her husband's death she managed the business until her son was old enough to take over.

Widows are especially capable in what is ideally the man's world. Dona Verissima, whose first husband died over ten years ago, is known as a leader in one rural neighborhood. She is a major producer of manioc flour. For several years she hired men to clear gardens for her on the banks of the Igarapé Bacá, and she was able to make a living for herself, a small son, and her adolescent daughters. Now the daughters are married and the son is an able-bodied young man. Her son and her two sons-in-law still work with Dona Verissima clearing and planting gardens, and she and her daughters work hard at the manufacture of manioc flour, which they sell at the trading post. It is well known that Dona Carita directs the activities of her family group and of the hired workers; the flour they produce is known as "Dona Verissima's *farinha*." The actual sale of the flour, however, is made by one of the sons-in-law.

Dona Feliciana, the mother of Dico Dias, is also a leader in her family circle (see Figure 3.8). During her life she was married twice.

Both of her husbands died leaving her with children to support. She has raised four children by dint of her own economic enterprise. She worked as a domestic servant for the local public officials and she and her children planted gardens. As the children grew up, they contributed through their work in the garden and by taking temporary jobs in town. Three of these children continue to live in Gurupá and they tend to follow Dona Feliciana's directions in most economic affairs. On one occasion, when an inquiry was made as to whether her twenty-year-old son might be willing to work paddling a canoe for a three-day trip, she replied for him in his absence. "He will agree," she said. "I shall send him tomorrow morning ready to travel."

It is well known that widows tend to dominate their children. This is true of Dona Verissima, of Dona Feliciana, of Dona Diná, and of Dona Maria. The mother of José and Bibi Pará, Dona Feliciana, took the wages of her unmarried son when he worked with the public health services, returning to him only what she thought he should spend. Dona Diná holds absolute sway over her twenty-seven-year-old adopted son. He works in the Casa Borralho without regular pay, receiving only what she decides he needs for spending money. She provides him with clothes and food. He is said by gossips to "steal enough for his pleasures." Dona Diná watches over his affairs to the best of her ability. When she heard that he was having an affair with a woman from one of the rural neighborhoods, she refused to allow him to visit that neighborhood. She also sent word to the woman to stay away from town. Both of the Pará brothers complained that they remained in Gurupá only because of their obligations to their widowed mother. Both said that as soon as she dies they will move away. Bibi complained that he once had a good job in a bar at a resort near Belém and that he would never have returned to Gurupá if his mother had not written him demanding that he do so. Both Bibi and Zeca, who are thirty-eight and forty years of age, respectively, feel they must follow her wishes.[14]

Other people in Gurupá told us of how "strong" their mothers were. They described a picture of family life in which an old widowed mother came to dominate the family scene. Nhenjuca, for example, remembers that his mother, Efigenia, had nine children; and although only three boys lived to be adults, "We respected her and always did

---

[14]Dona Feliciana lived to be 100 years old. Neither Bibi nor Zeca ever left Gurupá, ever after her death.

what we were told." She was crippled in one arm, having been burned severely with kerosene when she was a child. "But she worked to raise us," explained Nhenjuca. He hardly remembers his father, who was constantly traveling to the rubber fields before he died. Efigenia was an excellent cook, and as such she worked for the "whites." She was severe with her sons and made them serve as "slaves for St. Benedict," performing tasks for the Church and for the saint's festival. She made them attend school and she arranged odd jobs for them, collecting the pay. "She died at eighty-eight years of age when a vampire bat bit her on the toe," Nhenjuca told us, with considerable admiration for her longevity and strength of character.

Elíos Veiga also remembers his mother as the central figure in his family and the dominant figure in his early life. He said, quite bluntly, "She was the head of the family. When my father was alive she decided everything with him. After my father died, my older brother, Paulo, helped her. She did nothing without consulting him." The other children came to see her "when they were called," and they "stood when they talked with her." Each morning she asked that they come to stand before her and "ask a blessing," and each evening at vesper she prayed for her family—even before her husband died. Elíos' mother even decided when the time had come for him to marry; and she made arrangements for his first betrothal, which Veiga later, however, broke off. When he did marry, he took his wife to live in his mother's house and he and his elder brother lived near their mother, working with her until her death.

The picture of family life acquired from observation of the facts of family affairs and from the life stories told by people of Gurupá differs strikingly from the ideal picture of family relationships. Rather than the dominant male controlling and fully supporting his family, a woman is just as often the central figure of the household. Few men in Gurupá are as aggressive, even in the moment of discovered adultery on the part of their wives, as the picture of the dominant jealous Latin male has it. Casemiro Fonseca, to mention but one case, did nothing violent, although his wife carried on an affair quite openly. He finally made her leave to live with her lover. "It is a sad story," he told us. "She did not behave correctly, and I feel sorry for our children, who live with her, because they are not learning to read and write." Casemiro had lost face; he knew that men laughed at him as a *cornudo* (cuckold), and he continually refused to allow his wife to return to him. Still, he did not resort to violence. Despite the Latin and Brazilian ideal of the dominant male—the macho, as they like to say—in such societies as Gurupá the women must share a great portion of the responsibility and authority in the family. When men are absent, as they often are in societies where the economic situation is insecure and unstable, women have no choice except that of taking over. When men are away for months working in the rubber fields, or when they migrate looking for work, leaving their families behind, women tend to become the dominant figures within the family. The ideal roles of behavior that are held in Gurupá are those of the old landed gentry of Brazil. They were only possible for full realization in the stable plantation society of the nineteenth century and among the aristocrats of Brazilian cities—never by the majority of the Brazilian people. Such ideals are obviously out of keeping with the reality of Gurupá society, just as they are also impossible in the modern urban life of Rio de Janeiro and São Paulo.[15]

---

[15]Since the 1980s there have been considerable changes in gender roles in Gurupá (Pace 1995). Most notably, many women have been employed in the legal and medical fields and have served in politics. During the last three decades, women have worked as mayor, vice-mayor, council-member, judge, prosecutor, doctor, and dentist, as well as having leadership positions in the rural workers union and the fishers union. There are a number of reasons for this development. First is a national trend of greater numbers of women than men entering the medical and legal professions. Second is a regional inclination to place women professionals in Gurupá because of its relative safety (i.e., low violence) and its proximity to Belém (so women can be close to their families). Third is a local trend of increasing female participation in the rural workers and fishers union following various empowerment campaigns directed by the Catholic Church (Pace 1995). As for women politicians, their successes are due to their political proficiencies, or in some cases, due to the support of a man (e.g., a spouse or mentor politician) who aids in their election with the goal of manipulating them— the 'puppet syndrome' (Blay 1981; Pace 1995). Cecília Palheta was recruited by José Vicente (Dona Inacinha's son), the virtual coronel of Gurupá during the military dictatorship, to run for mayor (see Chapter 8). After her victory, he attempted to control her political decision making. When she and her husband Chico resisted, a bitter feud developed that lasted until José Vicente left Gurupá.

At the same time that gender roles for women have expanded to traditionally male jobs in the public sector, there are powerful limitations and drawbacks. Cecília summed up the difficulties in terms of politics.

Women have not participated [in politics] as much in Gurupá. I was the first woman mayor, followed by Esmeralda. But there have been no more. There is currently only one vereadora [councilwoman]. In the past, most have served one term and then given up.

V

The difference between ideal and actual behavior patterns is also apparent in courtship and marriage in Gurupá. Throughout rural Brazil the ideal picture of courting is one of a formal set of arrangements finally leading to marriage. Girls should be carefully protected; they should never be allowed to be alone with men who are not close relatives. A mother should accompany her daughters to a party, watching carefully while they dance, never allowing them out of her sight. Young men should not call casually on a girl. Only after some secret understanding between the two reached by passing notes or through quick snatches of conversation during the promenade in the evening in the public square will a young man find some excuse to call at her house. After several visits from a young suitor, parents expect some formal declaration on his part. With the acceptance of a young man's proposal by the young lady and by her parents, the two become *noivos* (fiancés) and actual courting begins. Now that they are engaged, the young man may call on his fiancée, sitting with her in the parlor in the company of some member of her family. They may be allowed to walk in the public square in view of the populace. They may converse through the

---

Even in my case it was not easy. I was gone all the time and couldn't do the traditional things at home. My husband, Chico, at first complained about me being gone from the house. But I reminded him that when he asked for my hand in marriage, my father (Jorge Palheta) told him I am a person who will always be working and be outside the home. Each time Chico complained, I reminded him of that conversation with my father. Still, after our daughter was born, I was gone so much as mayor that Chico would joke and tell people he was the real mother. (Pace and Hinote 2013:131)

As Cecília suggests, even though rapid changes are taking place, many people in Gurupá continue to express traditional viewpoints on gender roles. In our surveys of the community, when asked about the gender appropriateness for different occupations and domestic chores, the common response was "appropriate for both women and men" for most categories. However, when we asked about household economics—should a husband stay home with the children if the wife earns more—51.7 percent of women and 0 percent of men answered yes. These types of answers, in conjunction with observations of most gendered activities, indicate a continued preference among many to assign male responsibilities to the public realm (despite women prominently employed there) and female responsibilities to the domestic realm—the so-called machismo-marianismo divide (Pace and Hinote 2013:134–35). It appears that folk views (the ideal) and actual behavior are very much in flux and frequently at odds with one another, not dissimilar to Wagley's depiction of 1948.

window—the girl leaning out of the window that opens onto the street and the young man leaning against the wall underneath. As their engagement continues, the young suitor may be invited to meals with his fiancée's family and he may visit with them after dinner in the dining room, where family life traditionally takes place in rural Brazil. Their engagement should be relatively lengthy, lasting for a year or two or even more. The young lady accumulates her *enxoval* (trousseau), and the young man works to establish himself economically so that he will be able to support a family.

In Brazil marriage is legally a civil affair. By law a marriage must be performed by a civil official before it may be celebrated in the church. There is thus, ideally speaking, a civil ceremony performed by a judge followed by a second ceremony on the same day (or next day) celebrated by the Catholic priest in the church. In rural Brazil, however, most people put greater emphasis on the Church ceremonies than on the civil ceremonies. A marriage is not fully recognized socially as a proper union until after the wedding in church. As in most of the Western World, the wedding ceremony is an occasion for considerable festivities, and there is often a reception at the home of the bride. Pictures are taken of the bride in her white wedding veil. Presents are given. Altogether, it is a high point in the life of any Brazilian girl. She is expected to be a virgin—even innocent of the facts of sexual life. Traditionally, the groom is considered to have been "finally caught," so to speak. Marriage is a point in his life where he has decided to "settle down" and to raise a family. He should have had considerable sexual experience during his bachelor days. The idea that a man marries to care for his sexual needs is not a logical one to most rural Brazilians.

This ideal picture of courtship and marriage is shared by most people in Gurupá, but only a few of the First Class come even close to carrying out the pattern described. As Dona Inacinha tells of her first marriage, it seems to have conformed rather closely to the ideal, and other people in Gurupá remember that her husband made formal arrangements with her parents, that she had a formal courtship that lasted almost a year, and that she was married both by the civil judge and by the padre. People do not doubt that she was a virgin at marriage; but they add that she was somewhat too lively as an unmarried girl. She "danced the samba in the public pavilion" when the drums beat for dancing during the festival of St. Benedict. This was considered doubtful behavior for an unmarried virgin of a good family. Other upper-class marriages described for us seem always to have fallen short of the ideal pattern in some way. When one of the high public officials of the municipality married in 1948, all of the proper forms were carried out, but it was rumored that the bride was not a virgin and that the groom was willing to overlook this inexcusable fault "because her father is rich." "The whole thing is a joke," said one townsman. In 1948 Pere Serra's sister was engaged to be married, and he was somewhat irritated because her fiancé had never taken the trouble to "speak to the family," that is, to make formal arrangements with her parents. Only a religious ceremony was planned, and the townspeople gossiped that the prospective groom, who lived in a small town downriver, was already married by civil ceremony. Of fifteen couples of the First Class interviewed during our household surveys, nine of them claimed to be married both by civil and by Church rites, three by civil code only, and three only by the Church. Of two or three of those claiming marriage both by civil and by religious ceremony,[16] townspeople informed us that civil marriage had been entered into long after the religious rites and even after children had been born. In others the religious rites had followed the civil rites and the consummation of the marriage by several months, because the Catholic priest visits Gurupá only two or three times a year.

Among the lower-status groups of the Gurupá community, both of the town and of the rural areas, marriage diverges more strikingly from the ideal or "normal" patterns of rural Brazil. Ninety-one couples of the lower-class groups (the Second Class town dwellers, the farmers, and the collectors) were interviewed regarding marriage. The marriages of all the couples interviewed were of at least several years' standing and apparently stable at that time. Of these, only twenty-two claimed both civil and religious rites at marriage. Eight couples were married by civil law alone and thirty-eight only by Church marriages. Twenty-three of the ninety-one couples admitted readily to consensual marriage, that is, they lived together "in friendship," without benefit of

---

[16]I have said "claimed" advisedly, for one cannot be certain of such statements without verifying them by records in the state capital or those in the hands of the bishop in another Amazon town. It is our opinion that if careful verification of all statements against both civil and Church records had been made, the figures would have shown more couples married by religious rites only and more couples living amasiado ("in friendship," by consensual marriage) in all strata of the society.

formal wedlock. Among those who reported formal marriages, many had lived "in friendship" for years before either the religious or civil wedding was celebrated. The greater frequency of Church marriages over civil ceremonies reflects the values of older people in Gurupá and in other Amazon communities. It also indicates, as most people in Brazil already know, that the Church in its zeal to sanctify consensual unions often marries couples before the civil rites have been performed. Young people in Gurupá are fully aware that the civil ceremony is legally binding, establishing obligations enforceable by the police, and there is a growing tendency for brides, and especially their families, to insist on a civil ceremony.

Throughout Brazil the idea is commonly held that men do not wish to marry. Several people explained that a young man does not willingly take on the heavy responsibilities of a permanent union and renounce the pleasures of sexual adventure. Sometimes the efforts of his own family are enough to push him into a marriage. Elíos Veiga told us that when his mother heard that he was visiting a prostitute in Gurupá and that he had become "sick" (gonorrhea), she called him to say that "the time has come for you to marry." She took immediate steps ordering him to speak to the father of a neighboring girl, asking her in marriage. As in many cultures, marriage is thought of in Gurupá as a way of settling a young man down. Generally, however, it is not the youth's parents who are able to persuade or force him into a marriage but the parents of a girl with whom he may have formed a liaison.

Gurupá fathers, probably from their own youthful experience, are quite certain that all young men have dishonorable designs on their daughters. They are equally sure, and certainly with less reason, that a girl cannot resist the advances of any man unless she is chaperoned. Daughters, therefore, must be watched with vigilance and all men who approach them eyed with grave suspicion. Young women in Gurupá have thus little or no liberty of action or movement. They cannot dance unless accompanied by an adult member of their family. They are not allowed to leave the house after dark. They cannot walk freely about the town or about the neighborhood even in the daytime, unless they do so in pairs or in groups. Needless to say, young women are irritated by such curbs. They tend to look forward to marriage as the only way of obtaining a minimum of freedom. They have little opportunity to be courted by young men and they are apt to do so secretly. The necessity of secrecy in courting, at least until the young man is ready to "officialize their courtship" by formally proposing marriage to her family, very often leads to a premarital sexual affair.[17]

A typical case is the personal history told to us by Maria Profeta, who now lives in Gurupá as a respected widow. Maria was in love with Raimundo Pará. She exchanged notes with him. She met him secretly to talk for a few minutes as she walked in the early evening to a relative's house. As arranged, he came to her house to visit her family, but her parents did not approve of him. They did not believe that he really intended to marry Maria nor that if he did he would make a stable husband. As in most tragic love stories, her parents forbade her to see Raimundo and they took to meeting secretly in the forest. He promised to marry Maria. "To force my father to allow us to marry," Maria gave herself to Raimundo. Shortly afterward, she became pregnant. Then she began to feel "morning nausea" and headaches, and her mother noticed that her menstruation did not occur. A *curandeira*, who gave herbal medicines for irregular menses, was called to attend her. The old woman immediately recognized that Maria was pregnant and forced a confession out of her. "Medicines will do no good," the old midwife reported to Maria's mother; "we must wait to see if it will be a dress-maker or a hunter!" Maria was "so ashamed that she wanted to die." The old midwife defended her, saying, "This happens to many young women, even the daughters of the 'whites.'" According to Maria, her father whipped her until she fell to the floor, and he called her all of the vile names in his vocabulary. "I felt relieved after the beating," Maria

---

[17]In our 1986, 1999, and 2009 surveys of Gurupá, we asked people's opinions about women and men flirting and perceptions on men and women frequenting bars. In the 2009 survey there was a marked shift toward greater acceptance of women flirting and being in bars. We then asked our key consultants what was causing these opinion changes , and all acknowledged the sway of telenovelas where women of all socioeco-nomic backgrounds flirt and visit in bars without any mention of impropriety or scandal. Seeing such conduct on television, our consultants deduced, makes it easier to accept it locally (Pace and Hinote 2013:133). This view is reflected in Divina's ob-servations about women flirting over the years. She is a 62-year-old housewife who has raised all her children in Gurupá. Divina declared that she is not happy with the changes and is glad she does not have to raise her daughters now. She complained, "Before you turn around they are with their boyfriends and pregnant. They are *na mata sem cachorro* (lost in the forest without a dog to guide them). Everyone says it is normal, though. My comadre (co-mother) even said to me the other day, look at all the girls on television who flirt and are fine. She doesn't see a problem with it" (Pace and Hinote 2013:133).

says today. Later she explained to her father that Raimundo had offered marriage but that they did "not want to be married by the police" (i.e., by order of the police). When her father sent for Raimundo, he came at once. Her father threatened him with arrest and even with physical violence. Raimundo promised marriage. For a time Maria lived on with her family. She was never cursed or disowned by her parents or by her godparents. She avoided walking in the streets to hide her condition, but soon everyone was aware of what had taken place. Maria continued working in the garden with her parents until her father would not allow her to do heavy work any longer. At first she avoided Raimundo because she "was angry with him" for not carrying out his promise of marriage at once. But finally Raimundo found a thatched hut and they took up residence together. Two or three months later, during the festival of St. Benedict, when the padre came to Gurupá, they were married in the church. Maria was within a few days of giving birth. The child was born and it was a girl. Her father became very attached to his granddaughter, and he was extremely sad when the child died two years later. Maria told us that she "intended to give the child" to her father, for he was more interested in the child than Raimundo was.

Like so many of these marriages, Maria's marriage to Raimundo did not last. Raimundo was soon called up for military service. He left to serve in Belém and never returned. Maria heard that he began "living with" another woman (she was also called Maria) whom he married later in a civil ceremony. Maria later lived for several years with another man but she was not happy. After a time, she left him. She decided "never to take up with another man." Today Maria Profeta is one of the leaders of a religious brotherhood and is much admired for her housekeeping abilities. She deviated from the ideal patterns of her society but in a direction in which women of her class are expected to deviate.

Marriages are forced on the groom in Gurupá with such frequency that it can almost be said to be normal behavior. During our last visit to Gurupá, in 1948, five marriages of couples from the rural neighborhoods were celebrated before the manager of the Casa Borralho, who also serves as the temporary justice of the peace. All five marriages, as it happened, were "by the police." Each had been arranged by the bride's father with the backing of the local police officer after the girl had been deflowered. In all cases the young man had agreed to the marriage only after the family had complained to the police officer.[18] Such a complaint is generally sufficient to bring about the marriage, for the girl is anxious for marriage and the young man has generally been attracted to her. Marriage satisfies the parents of the girl, and the community soon forgets the distasteful details. On the wedding day the bride wears a white veil if she can afford to buy or can borrow one, and the groom will spend considerable money buying drinks and food for friends celebrating the marriage.

In town, people say that three-fourths of the marriages among, farmers and collectors take place "by the police." Nhenjuca explained to us, citing innumerable cases of such marriages among our common acquaintances, that sometimes the cost of a civil marriage is a factor. The justice of the peace and the civil registrar (*tabelião*) do not charge fees when the marriage is ordered "by the police." If a couple marry "by request" (*de pedido*), then "they must work for almost a year to save money to pay," although the fee amounts to only about ten dollars. "If they marry 'by the police,' it is cheaper and they do not have this expense," said Nhenjuca. Not all cases of deflowering of a minor, however, are reported to the police officer.[19] In many instances, such as that of Maria Profeta, the couple have already agreed on marriage, and when the girl becomes pregnant a few tough words from her father are enough to bring about the marriage. The girl's family keeps the matter quiet. The couple then take up residence together and the marriage may never actually take place. Sometimes, years afterward, when several children have been born, such a couple will be married in a Church or civil ceremony. Many other consensual unions, however, are stormy and brittle affairs. In some cases there are bitter quarrels between the father and his daughter and her husband. Often the young man, who is forced into a marriage for which he has little desire, uses almost any pretext to break with his bride. As in the case of Maria Profeta, the husband finds some excuse to move away, looking for a more lucrative occupation and an excuse to leave his bride behind.

---

[18]The Brazilian penal code makes deflowering of a minor a prison offense, but it would be difficult for the Gurupá police officer to enforce this law. Often the girls involved are not legally minors (i.e., under 18 years of age). Thus, about all the police are able to do is to threaten the man with jail.

[19]The rather haphazardly kept police records of Gurupá showed only 41 cases of "deflowering a minor" for a ten-year period (1933–1943), although from local informants we heard of more than ten taking place in 1948.

The common-law marriage of Anna Botelho and João Inácio, for example, led to bitter quarrels with Anna's father. João Inácio and Anna had been having sexual relations secretly for several months when her father learned of their affair. Anna wanted to leave home to live with João Inácio, but the father refused to allow her to do so. One night João Inácio, accompanied by his four brothers, came "to get the girl." Her father resisted, and rather than harm him, the brothers left without her. The next day, however, Anna slipped away by herself in a canoe to join her lover. This occurred in January. In June she was still living with João Inácio, without a marriage ceremony having taken place. Her father complained to the police officer, who sent word that he would jail João Inácio unless the couple came to Gurupá for a civil marriage. In June, when João Inácio appeared alone in Gurupá, the police officer jailed him for twenty-four hours to frighten him, and the marriage was set for August. Most people doubt whether the couple will ever marry, for they live too far up a small tributary on the far side of the Amazon for the threats to have much effect. Anna's father, however, still rages at João Inácio and at his daughter. "She is nothing better than a prostitute," he told us, and he refuses to have her in his house. Yet when a younger sister was ill, Anna returned home to visit her. People told us that on this occasion she asked for a "blessing" from her father and received it. Although the father says that he will never receive either Anna or João Inácio in his house until they are married, most people predict that within a few months they will be on close family terms.

Men often resist civil or Church marriage with women with whom they are living in consensual marriage on the basis that they were not virgins when they met them. A man may even hesitate to marry the young girl who he is certain has given herself only to him. One man in Gurupá reasoned rather brutally that if a girl allows one man to have her without wedlock, then she may well do so again. She might therefore easily succumb to temptation as she did with him. Only in exceptional cases may a girl who is known "not to be a virgin" (*não é moça*, literally, not a girl) expect either a civil or a Church wedding. Likewise, a man who discovers that his bride is not a virgin on their wedding night may be expected to leave her at once. This happened to Pedro Silva, a sailor on the public health launch stationed at Gurupá. Pedro married Clara "with all the apparatus," as they say in Gurupá. He spent almost $125 on the wedding, including clothes for himself and his bride, fees for both the civil and Church ceremonies, and celebrations.

It was a voluntary marriage "by request." On his wedding night, however, Pedro found that Clara was not a virgin. "She had been used," he said. Next morning Pedro denounced his bride to her father and refused to live with her. After more than a year, Pedro was still disillusioned with women in general and would have nothing to do with Clara. Other cases were told to us of women who "had been returned to their fathers" because they were not virgins at marriage; and three women, now living by consensual marriages of long standing and who are the mothers of children by their common-law husbands, were pointed out as girls abandoned on their wedding night by their legal husbands. Only as long as she is a virgin may a girl hope for marriage according to the ideal pattern.[20]

The frequency of consensual unions in Gurupá;[21] the large number of marriages performed against the grooms' desires, often under police pressure; and the high value placed on virginity, and even the "act of returning a bride to her father," make for instability of marital relations.[22] Although consensual unions are recognized by the community,

---

[20]Those cultural attitudes and values are reflected in the terms used for women in Gurupá: *moça* is used for a woman of almost any age above puberty who is virginal and thus still marriageable; *rapariga* for any nonvirginal woman, ranging from a respectable woman living in consensual marriage to a prostitute; and *viúva* for a widow who was once married either by civil or religious rites.

[21]Of 3,360 people over 20 years of age in the municipality of Gurupá, according to the 1940 census, only 1,577 were reported as "married" and 190 as "widows" or "widowers." Of 5,124 people in the entire municipality listed as "single," only 3,721 were under 19 years of age, thus leaving 1,503 of 20 years of age and over. I am not aware of the criterion used for "marriage," but it was probably legal union. If so, this indicates that the number of people who enter marriage either on a consensual basis or only by religious ceremony amounts to almost 50 percent of the total population. Few people in Gurupá over twenty years of age live without some form of marital alliance. Women are expected to get married when they are 18 or 19 years old, and men by the time they are 20 years old, or slightly afterward.

Data from the 2010 census indicate that 56.7 percent of unions in Gurupá are consensual or common-law, 30.4 percent are religious, 3 percent are civil only, and 9.9 percent are both religious and civil (IBGE 2012).

[22]In 2013 there have been significant changes in marriage patterns and family composition in Gurupá. Shotgun weddings are rare (I never heard of one during my research years) even though teenage pregnancy rates are very high (29 percent of all births in Gurupá in 2009 were to adolescent girls, 18 years or younger—Instituto

people also realize that they lack both legal and religious sanction. Men desert their common-law spouses, or even wives whom they have been forced to marry, with frequency. The economic instability of the lower-class townsmen, of the farmer, and especially of the rubber collectors contributes to marital instability, and it is perhaps the fundamental cause of the reluctance of so many men in Gurupá to accept the responsibility of a legally sanctioned family. Economic necessity forces many men to leave the Gurupá community to collect rubber in the district of Acre or in another upriver rubber field; they often find themselves bound by debt or attracted to the new community, and they may never return. Others migrate to Belém, and even eventually to the metropolitan centers of South Brazil, seeking employment. Women are therefore often left with children to support by husbands searching for a better economic situation. Thus in Gurupá women often become the heads of families without adult males. Such women may have a series of common-law husbands during their lifetimes, each of whom moves on—or dies—leaving children for them to raise and support. Such was the case of Dona Verissima, Dona Feliciana, and Dona Efigenia, mentioned earlier, widows forced to take a dominant and active role as the heads of their families.[23] It is clear that the values and the ideal patterns of behavior held in Gurupá are not adjusted to the realities of Gurupá society.

Peabiru 2011). Use of birth control methods (condoms and birth control pills) are available, but not widely used for a number of cultural reasons (the preferred form of birth control is tubal ligation performed in the hospital after the second or third pregnancy). Single-parent families headed by young women do not carry the same stigma as in the past, in part because government programs like the *Bolsa Familiar* (Family Grant) provide funds for basic subsistence needs.

[23]T. Lynn Smith (1946:213) mentions the tendency for the frontier regions of Brazil to have a high ratio of males to females. There were as many as 171.3 males to each 100 females in the District of Acre in 1920 and 117.5 men per 100 females in the state of Amazonas in the same year. The Amazon Region is traditionally an area where men have come, leaving their women folk behind. This has been especially true during the years when rubber prices were high. Gurupá, however, is not a frontier community in this sense. The 1940 census showed a sex ratio about equally balanced between males and females (i.e., 3,557 males to 3,524 females) in the municipality. The rubber-producing zones, especially during periods of high rubber prices, attract male migrants; but in turn, the agricultural zone loses population by emigration.

VI

The picture that the people of Gurupá give of the proper manner of educating children and of the treatment of children by their parents is very similar in many ways to the one we are accustomed to in the Western World. Parents are supposed to love and to protect their children, and in turn children must respect their parents. Both women and men in Gurupá told us that they wanted children. Men want males, and they told us of the pride of a father in having a son to carry on the family name. Women profess to want a large family of children of either sex. Our friends in Gurupá pointed to the frequency of adoption among childless couples in the community as proof that everyone desires children. Parents seem proud of their children; they like to dress them in satins, laces, and ribbons. On the first birthday of her child, one Gurupá mother gave a party for her friends at which there was a huge cake with one candle, sweets and cakes for the guests, beer and rum, and dancing with music through the night for her friends and relatives. She was proud of her infant son. Theoretically, people feel that children should be given warmth, care, and protection. They do not believe in corporal punishment. Although they showed us the *palmatória* (small paddle) to be used to slap the open palm of a disobedient child, none of us ever saw one used. One man told us indulgently how he made such a paddle to frighten his little grandson and how the boy cut it up into pieces.

In Gurupá people say that children should never do heavy work, for "their bones are soft." Elíos Veiga felt, for instance, that boys should not be allowed to work in the fields with an ax or with any other heavy instrument until they were seventeen or eighteen years of age. He claimed that he did not allow his son to work in the garden until the boy was fifteen years old. Even then the boy did only light jobs such as planting and harvesting manioc. Not until he was eighteen, Veiga said, did he allow his son to help in the heavy jobs of clearing the garden site and of digging out the roots. Elíos' nephew, on the other hand, had to do heavy work "as early as fourteen years of age." For that reason "he never built his body," Veiga explained to us. Veiga also told us that his own mother made him study music (he learned the flute by ear) until he was almost twenty years of age, and she would not allow him to do heavy work. The same is true of girls; they should not carry heavy burdens until after they are married at eighteen to twenty years of age. Children should be protected from heavy manual labor and surrounded by affection. If they are given such treatment, later they will repay their parents. They owe the parents a debt and they should support the parents in their old age. In Gurupá, as elsewhere in rural Brazil, children are taught to ask a "blessing" of their parents each morning and evening; and an ideal child continues to ask a "blessing" of his father and mother throughout life and continues to submit to parental authority long after he is adult.

Such ideal patterns of the "protected child" and of the "respected parent," however, differ considerably from the norms of behavior. The idea that a child should not be allowed to do manual labor is essentially aristocratic. The insecure economic plight of most people in Gurupá, the instability of marital relations, and the resulting broken families do not create a situation favorable to protecting children. In a few upper-class families where there are servants, children are free from household tasks. In all upper-class families children are shielded from any manual labor—for that is a mark of lower-class status. People of all classes would like to achieve the ideal of protecting their children from work; but the best they can do is to indulge their children from time to time by spending relatively large sums for clothes, for presents, or for a birthday celebration. Actually, most children work hard, and begin to do so at a relatively early age. Girls, as early as six or seven years of age, carry water from the river for household use. They help in the kitchen washing dishes, grinding coffee, helping to cook, and keeping the house clean. Nhenjuca's daughter, who was eleven years old, helped wash clothes, did much of the ironing, worked with her mother in the fabrication of manioc flour, peeling the tubers, passing the dough through a sieve, and turning the larger wheel of the grater. Between her school hours (from approximately 8:00 a.m. to midday) and her numerous chores, Chiquinha had only a couple of hours, snatched at the end of the day, for play.

Boys are equally occupied. They generally begin working with their fathers in the garden when they are ten or twelve, and they may fish at night to help fill the family larder. Elíos Veiga, for example, criticized his neighbor, Raimundo Mendes, because he allowed his small ten-year-old son to paddle the canoe when the boy fished with his father and because he allowed the boy to fish alone until almost midnight. In most rural families small boys of twelve years of age commonly do a full day's work in the garden, and they often take the father's place in making the rounds of a rubber trail when he is ill. Above all, little boys are asked to run innumerable errands and to perform a variety of small tasks that adults find trying. The observation, made in jest by a Brazilian, to the effect that "the last slave in Brazil is the small boy," is valid for Gurupá. Adults keep boys from about nine to thirteen years of age busy scurrying about. "Fetch me my tobacco!" "Take this package home for me!" "Let Joãozinho fetch an umbrella for you. It is raining!" "Go to the garden and get the ax I forgot"—these are but a few of the innumerable orders given by parents, relatives, and even friends of the family to a small boy in the course of a day. Boys only have time to play if they can escape from adult company. For play, they therefore meet at distant parts of the town, late in the afternoon.

The frequency of adoption in Gurupá is, in fact, directly related to the usefulness of children. Many of our Gurupá acquaintances had *filhos de críação* (adopted children). Nhenjuca and his wife, who were childless, had adopted their daughter when she was but one year of age. Another childless couple, Ernesto and Maria, adopted an infant just before our visit in 1948. Domingos Almeida, one of the public health-center employees, whose wife was pregnant, also had an adopted son four years of age. Alvaro and his wife, Diquinha, whose house also served as the local *pensão* (boardinghouse) had two adopted children—a boy and a girl. Bibi Pará and his wife have an adopted son ten years of age. The schoolteacher, Dona Inacinha, had raised several adopted daughters in addition to her own two sons. Dona Diná, whose only son died a few years ago, had during her lifetime adopted twelve children. In 1948, three of her adopted children lived in her house under her care. These were a ten-year-old girl, Raimunda, whose parents, distant relatives of Dona Diná, lived in another state; Liberato, a boy eight years old, whose parents had died; and Catarina, a girl eleven years old, whose rubber-collector father had asked Dona Diná to take her to raise. In addition, Filomeno, who was a man of all work at the Casa Borralho, and Manuel, the clerk in the same store, were both adopted sons of Dona Diná and had been raised in her house. Her other adopted children were then scattered, some living in the rural areas and others in Belém. Practically without exception, all families with any financial stability in Gurupá had adopted children. In nearly all of the trading posts in the rural neighborhoods of Gurupá, the traders showed us their "adopted children."

These children are in general treated well. When they are adopted by a childless couple, they are treated as if they were the parents' own children. This was true of Nhenjuca and Anna's adopted daughter and of Ernesto and Maria's treatment of their adopted son. People in the Amazon region have a great respect for education. In most cases the foster parents see to it that their adopted children attend school, if facilities are available. People also feel that in addition to "instruction" (formal schooling), they have an obligation to give their adopted children "education," meaning training in manners, and they are strict with them, teaching them "respect" and formal manners. Foster parents also have the obligation to see that their wards have some religious training, and they insist that they pray each evening with the family. If possible they give them some formal religious education through the Church. Thus in Gurupá they send the children to vesper service led by Dona Inacinha and to catechism and to Mass when a padre is in town. It is also an obligation of the foster parents to "teach adopted children to work." Because such children usually come from a lower economic and social status than their foster parents, frequently from poverty-stricken families, they are given tasks involving manual labor—carrying water, cutting fire wood, washing out the house, and other menial tasks.

In upper-class Gurupá families, where there are both adopted children and the parents' own offspring, it is the adopted children who do the chores. Dona Diná's ten-year-old adopted son, Liberato, for example, had to watch over her small nephews. He spent many hours patiently rocking them in a hammock and watching over them in their play. During the few hours Liberato had free from school and from his younger charges, he was constantly dispatched on errands by his adoptive mother or by the manager of the Casa Borralho. The family whose backyard adjoined our own in Gurupá included an adopted son five years old. He was constantly occupied with chores—chopping firewood, carrying water, emptying bedpans, fetching his "grandmother's" scissors, and so on. The mother of the family scolded him constantly in a tone of voice that easily carried over into our house. From time to time his "grandmother" rapped the boy hard on the head because he was slow to learn, an act that is rare in Gurupá. Sometimes she threatened to return him to his father "if he did not correct his ways." In most upper-class households such adopted children are given a definitely inferior status in the family. Their position is midway between that of a poor relative and of an unpaid servant. In fact, in the city of Belém, it has long been an established custom for families of some means to "adopt" children from the small towns of the interior. They thus provide their homes a servant, and at the same time give a child some schooling and often training in a trade or craft. But in poorer families of Gurupá, all children must work hard. Thus the treatment of adopted children is no different than that of the offspring of the parents.

The frequency of adoption in the Amazon region is related directly to poverty and to the high mortality rates among the population. Human life is uncertain in the Amazon. It is not uncommon for malaria or another epidemic to cause the sudden death of a woman and her husband, leaving two or three minor children. Lacking public institutions, and without the backing of large circles of kin, other families must take the orphans to raise. As described previously, the uncertain economic situation of most men leads frequently to the disruption of marriage. Women abandoned by their husbands often find it necessary to "give away" one or more of their children. Sometimes poor farmers or rubber collectors have "more children than they can support," and they "give away" their children, hoping to gain material and educational benefits for them. Many travelers to out-of-the-way areas of the Amazon have been offered children. "Take the child back to your country [to Rio de Janeiro or to Belém], where he will get an education," said a woman near Gurupá, offering a cringing little boy, one of several small children. Dona Diná told us of a rubber gatherers who had traveled several days to give her their daughter because they had heard of her kindness and interest in her adopted children. They told her of their desperate economic plight and said that the little girl did not have enough to eat and that they had no possibility of giving her any schooling. They begged Dona Diná to take the girl, and would not let her refuse. When Dona Diná finally accepted, the couple left for an upriver rubber station never again to return.

As a system of caring for orphans and abandoned children, this system of adoption depends on the presence of a favored socioeconomic group able to assume the care of numerous children and on social conditions that make children useful members of the household. As these conditions disappear, as they have in southern Brazil and in the more industrialized nations, public institutions are provided. Yet in Gurupá, as elsewhere, adoption is also motivated by sincere parental yearnings for children. One childless couple of Gurupá's First Class, for example, asked a rubber-gatherer's wife, while she was pregnant, that they be given the child when it was born. The baby was given to them only a few days after its birth, and they were sad, they said, that it would be necessary to tell the child when it was older that it was adopted. Many foster parents remember their children with great affection even after they have left home. Dona Inacinha told us how much she suffered when her adopted daughter ran off with Samuel, the son of one of Gurupá's storekeepers. Dona Diná used every opportunity to send fruit, fish, and other presents to one of her adopted sons who had moved to Belém to work for an air-transport company. Likewise, many adopted children remember their foster parents with real warmth and respect.

One of the most striking cases of adoption in Gurupá illustrates this sincere desire for children, as well as the rather free manner in which people "give away" their children. The case occurred only a few months before our visit to the community. Maria, a young woman of about nineteen years of age, was abandoned by her common-law husband after she had become pregnant. During the last few days of her pregnancy, according to the report of the public health doctor in Gurupá, Maria had serious hemorrhages. He was able to send her downriver hurriedly to the hospital in the delta region, where Maria gave birth prematurely to a child who at once died. Although she had no husband, and a child would have been a real burden to her, Maria was heartbroken. A woman in the next bed, who had just given birth to her seventh child, commiserated with Maria. Finally, the woman told her that she and her husband "could not feed so many" and offered Maria the newborn boy. To the surprise of the physicians (who were newly arrived from South Brazil), Maria accepted the child with alacrity. She returned proudly to Gurupá with her baby. For almost a year she worked as a domestic for one of Gurupá's "first families" to support the child. She then went to live "in friendship" with a young farmer who had manioc plantations near the Igarapé ltapereira, not far from town, telling us that he would "help support my son."

The frequent adoptions in Gurupá and the free way people allow their children to be adopted cannot therefore be explained entirely in terms of poverty or of the usefulness of children to their foster parents. Adoption has the same human basis in the Amazon as it does elsewhere. But, in many parts of the world, a mother who would give up her child so easily as the one mentioned previously would be considered lacking in maternal feelings, and in many societies even poverty-stricken mothers cling desperately to their children.[24] In the Amazon, the "giving away" of a child is understandable behavior motivated by the acquisition of benefits for the child. And in Gurupá the attitudes of foster parents toward their children differ from those of foster parents in other Western societies. In the United States of America, for example, foster parents are generally anxious to know something of the "antecedents" of a child considered for adoption, and they sometimes fear that an adopted child might "turn out badly" because of its biological heredity. In Gurupá people never predict that an adopted child may become a social deviant or be unsuccessful in life because of its parentage. More credence seems to be given to social environment than to biological heredity in Gurupá. Further, these attitudes toward adoption and toward allowing children to be adopted seem to reflect a fundamental attitude of parents toward children in Gurupá. People love children, but they can allow them to be taken by others when their own poverty makes adoption beneficial. People are able to consider and to love their children as independent personalities and not as projections of their own personalities and desires.[25]

VII

Knowledge of the family life of any society is of foremost importance to any program of planned social change. This is especially true of any program involving the modification of habits, values, or attitudes. It is within the intimacy of the family that habits, values, and attitudes are inculcated. Attempts may be made to bring about changes in a community, and in its individual members, through schools, through health centers, or by various governmental means; but if these efforts run counter to patterns of behavior and values held within the intimacy

---

[24]In Gurupá, no strong stigma, such as exists, for example, in the United States of America, attaches to illegitimacy or to the unmarried woman to force her to give up her child.

[25]In 2013 the tradition of raising *filhos de criação* has for all practical reasons ended for the younger generations. Lower mortality rates for women giving birth and for women and men in their 20s to 40s in general means fewer children are left parentless and in need of adoption. Lower social stigma attached to single-teenage motherhood and the ability to support one's children through government assistant programs also reduces the need for adoption. Only people in their 40s remember the tradition well.

of the family, they will have little chance of final success. Hygiene, for example, may be taught in the schools and the health center may carry on a skilled program of public education; but unless such knowledge filters into the family and is taught by the family also, it will tend to be accepted only "theoretically" and will have little effect on the lives of the children. Furthermore, the people carrying out such programs must be cognizant of the ideal roles assigned to the various members of the family as well as of the actual behavior of its members. In Gurupá, for example, the ideal pattern has it that the husband, controlling completely the family purse, does the family shopping. He therefore has an important voice in what the family eats, and any educational program aimed at establishing better food habits in Gurupá must educate both the husband, who buys the food, and the wife, who cooks it. Yet one must be aware of the disparity between the ideal and the normative behavior. In Gurupá wives have, in fact, greater powers over family affairs than the ideal pattern indicates, and many women are in reality the mainstays of their families. This means that any educational program calling for cooperation of the family group must aim at both the husband and wife.

Again, in laying plans and putting into effect any program of social change in a community or in a region, the different forms that a particular institution or a set of attitudes and values takes in the various socioeconomic groups must be considered. In the Amazon region the ideal form of the family, the ideal patterns of behavior for its members, and the values attached to family life are those of the aristocratic upper class of the region. Among the regional aristocracy—a class not present in Gurupá—these ideals are more nearly realized than in Gurupá. Among the descendants of the regional landholders, among the commercial class, among the political leaders and the higher bureaucrats, the large extended family with hundreds of relatives is a functioning institution that is basic to their social, commercial, and political relations. A knowledge of the surnames and the familial affiliations of one's associates is very necessary for successful participation at this level of Amazon society. If one knows that one's associates are a da Gama Martins or a Costa Azevedo,[26] much is at once explained in regard to their social, economic, and political position in regional

---

[26]These names are, of course, fictitious, but during a visit to Belém or Manaus one soon learns the surnames of the important families.

society. Such large families control the social, economic, and political life; and they have intermarried until a web of kinship unites large groups of people in business and government circles.

In the small towns and in the rural neighborhoods of the Amazon region, this widely extended and united Brazilian family is an ideal seldom achieved. Because people are poor, they lack the property and the common economic interests that tend to hold large kinship groups together. Kinsfolk move away and lose touch with one another. The poor townspeople, the small farmer, and the rubber gatherers of Gurupá have relatively circumscribed family circles. Lacking the security of a large kinship circle, they place great emphasis on ritual kinship. The lack of economic security in Gurupá has led to brittle marital relations that are in basic conflict with the ideals derived from the aristocratic tradition. Among these rural Brazilians, the family is indeed a weak link in their social system and the source of many of the community's social ills.

CHAPTER 6

People Also Play

In Gurupá the winter months of rain from January through April are tedious and monotonous. People are held at home by the hard winter rains. The streets of the town are muddy and sometimes even partially flooded. The river and the small tributaries are swollen and overflow their banks. Like the cold winter of temperate climates, the tropical winter of the Amazon region makes people in Gurupá stick close to home. And, as in the temperate zones, the end of the dull winter months is marked by a series of festivals. In fact, this analogy in the cycle of the climatic year assured the continuation of the old spring festivals of Portugal in North Brazil. In particular, the festivals of June (St. Anthony's, St. John's, and St. Peter's), which are so important in Portugal, were transplanted to the New World, where they now mark the end of the winter rains, just as in Portugal they mark the arrival of spring. In May and in June of each year in the Amazon Valley, as the rivers return to their banks and as the rains diminish in frequency, the season begins, and during the whole dry season there is a series of festivals in the Gurupá community that reaches a climax with the festival of St. Benedict on December 27th. Between June 13th, which is St. Anthony's Day, and December 28th, when the festivities for St. Benedict officially end,[1]

---

[1] Since the 1970s the dates for St. Benedict festival are December 9–28.

there are more than fourteen religious festivals in the Gurupá community. Only three of these festivals take place in the town, the others being celebrated in the rural neighborhoods. Although all of them are celebrated in honor of a saint, only two of them, St. Anthony's and St. Benedict's, are recognized by the Church. The others are considered "profane" by the priest who visits Gurupá periodically.

These "profane" festivals are organized in each rural neighborhood by religious brotherhoods (*irmandades*). These brotherhoods resemble the "Third Orders," which are so common in Brazil; but they are not beneficial associations and they are not subordinated to the official Church. Because they do not conform to Church rules, the Catholic priest opposes them. Yet, despite his opposition, these brotherhoods thrive in the rural districts. More than a mere association of the devotees of a particular saint, the brotherhoods give formal organization to the rural neighborhood. Because most of the inhabitants (both male and female) of a neighborhood are, at the same time, members of the brotherhood, the officers of the brotherhoods are also the leaders and the individuals of highest prestige in the neighborhood. The officers of a typical brotherhood are generally the *procurador* (attorney for the saint), the *tesoureiro* (treasurer), the *secretário* (secretary), the *zeladora* (keeper of the image), the *mestre sala* (master of ceremonies), and the *andador* (official in charge of the saint's errands). Each brotherhood is devoted to a particular saint. The brotherhood owns an image of the saint, a banner on which there is the symbol of the saint, and also the musical instruments—the drums, rattles, and *raspador*, or "scraper"—used by the *folia*,[2] whose obligation it is to go from house to house each year singing and asking for contributions toward the celebration of the saint's festival. The "saint" is housed in the residence of one of the officials or, by some of the better organized brotherhoods, in a small chapel. Members pay a small membership fee, usually no more than one *cruzeiro* (five cents) each year. There is a registry book in which the rules and regulations of the brotherhood, the names of the officers, the list of members, and, irregularly, the minutes and financial accounts, are inscribed. The principal function of these rural brotherhoods is the organization of the annual festival of the

---

[2]Folia, which has the literal meaning in Portuguese of rapid dancing to the accompaniment of the tambourine, is used in this region to mean both the group of musicians and devotees who seek contributions for the saint and for their activities.

saint to which they are devoted. This festival is sometimes anticipated by a *folia*. On these occasions, the officers of the brotherhood take the image of their saint in a decorated canoe to visit other neighborhoods and villages. As they travel, they stop at each house, where, to the rhythm of the drums, the rattle, and the scraper, they sing in honor of their saint and ask for donations. Such a *folia* may last as long as a month or as little as a few days.

The festival itself fills ten days, beginning nine days before the saint's day and ending the day after it. Although this lengthy festival is the responsibility of the entire brotherhood, individuals are chosen each year as judges (*juízes*) and as majordomos (*mordomos*) to take over the expense and the responsibility of the various phases. For each phase of festivities, there are two judges or two majordomos—a man and a woman, usually a married couple. The couple responsible for the first day of the festival, when an enormous votive mast is raised, are known as the judges of the mast. The judges of the festival are responsible for the festivities on the vespers of the saint's day itself. The majordomos, also known as *noitários* (owners of the night), organize the activities and the expenses of the days between the raising of the mast and the saint's day.

The majordomos are expected only to offer coffee and a small manioc cake to those who attend the *ladainha* (evening prayers). On the rare occasions when a dance is offered during the nine days preceding the saint's day (the novena), a flute and guitar played by two of the brothers provide the only music. But the costs of the judges of the festival are exceedingly high in terms of the average income of the people concerned. They are the sponsors of that part of the festival attended by the largest number of people. The actual saint's day is the climax of the festival, and it is fitting that the occasion be most elaborately celebrated. The judges must have food for all who come; they must purchase dozens of rockets; they must pay musicians to play through the night for dancing; and they must provide rum for at least the officials and more important guests. The average expenditure for a couple serving as judges of the mast is between $25 and $40; for a couple serving as majordomos, about $10; and for the judges of the festival, between $40 and $100 or more.

These rural festivals, although built around religious observances in homage of the saint, are lively social occasions for the whole family. Typical is that held in Maria Ribeira each year in honor of the patron saint, St. Apolonia. Maria Ribeira is a village-type neighborhood. There are some twelve palm-thatched houses clustered around an irregularly shaped plaza. In the plaza there is a large shed with open sides and a hard beaten clay floor, called the *ramada*, which is used for dancing during festivals. The local brotherhood does not support a chapel, and the image of St. Apolonia is housed in a portion of an official's residence. St. Apolonia's day is celebrated on August 28th in Maria Ribeira; following local custom, festivities are initiated on August 18th. On that day people from nearby and even from the town of Gurupá begin to arrive early in the morning for the raising of the mast. They come in canoes loaded to the gunwales with their small tin trunks containing their party clothes; with hammocks and other baggage; with food; and sometimes a bottle of rum. Each canoe load announces its arrival by shooting off fire rockets or simply by shouting. As each canoe ties up in the little port of Maria Ribeira, the men first hide their paddles securely in the brush, for it is well known that at the end of the day's festivities, or at dawn after a night of dancing, property rights in paddles are not respected by people in a hurry to return home. As more and more visitors arrive, separate groups of men and women may be seen going to bathing spots along the small stream. There they bathe leisurely, perform their toilet, and change for the late afternoon's and the night's recreation. Among the men a bottle is generally taken along; and as they change into their shoes, clean trousers, white shirts, and suit coats, they laugh and talk and have a few early drinks.

Such baths are repeated as often as twice a day during the festival. One of the strongest impressions an outsider takes away is the cleanliness of the people. There is a smell of clean clothes and of the natural perfumes from the Amazon woods. Even on a hot day it seems cool, for people are freshly bathed and dressed for each prayer service and for each dance. Only the cheap manufactured perfumes, with which men and women alike are apt to sprinkle themselves, mar the very pleasant atmosphere.

By noon the *folia*, made up of musicians and singers of the brotherhood, begin the round of the houses of Maria Ribeira itself. Earlier they have visited other neighborhoods asking for contributions. Now, they go from house to house asking for donations from the residents. Before each house, they sing a verse asking permission to enter. The lady of the house kneels before the image of St. Apolonia, takes the image from its bearer, and carries it into her house, placing it on a temporary altar improvised for the occasion out of a sewing machine or a wooden box. The housewife then kneels and prays to the saint. Following her prayers, the *folia* sing again in praise of the latter. The woman of the house then presents them with an offering—money, a chicken, a pineapple, a few pounds of manioc flour, or something else that may be auctioned on the saint's day. The official in charge of the brotherhood accompanies the *folia* to collect the offerings at each house. By sundown the *folia* have visited each household in the small village and the time has come for the official opening of the saint's festivals.

The festival officially opens with the raising of the mast. A pole about eight meters long has been prepared and placed in readiness a short distance away from the village in the forest. This mast is decorated with green leaves and with whole pineapples, which have been tied to the long pole at regular intervals along its entire length. At sundown, the mast is shouldered by a group of young men. Accompanied by the judges of the mast and the musicians of the *folia*, they carry it to a spot in front of the residence that serves as a chapel. There the long

FIGURE 6.1 | *Folia of São Pedro in the community of Bacá. Saint is under the umbrella.*

Photography by C. Wagley 1948.

FIGURE 6.2 | *Community of Jocojó and votive mast (center) between two masts offered as religious promessas.*
Photography by C. Wagley 1948.

pole is planted upright. Rockets are set off and the *folia*, followed by the judges and by members of the brotherhood, march around the mast several times, singing the praises of their saint. Following these ceremonies the saint's image is returned to the altar in the chapel, and the master of ceremonies calls everyone to evening prayers.

The evening prayers, and all other religious services during these festivals, are led by a lay member of the brotherhood. The leader of religious services is usually the master of ceremonies. A Catholic priest is never present, nor is his presence wanted. On one occasion, it was explained, the padre was determined to attend one of the festivals, despite all the difficulties that the brothers of the association had put in his way. They explained that there was little food and that the tributary would not allow travel in anything but a very small canoe, which would be uncomfortable for him. They could not promise him a decent house. Still he persisted in his determination to attend. So they sent a canoe that leaked so badly that the padre had to give up and turn back after several hours of travel. Had he been present, they explained, there would have been no dancing and no drinking at the festival.

At Maria Ribeira the master of ceremonies led the services in Latin, and each short verse was repeated by the members of the *folia*. Then a young woman led the prayers. When she had finished, the master of ceremonies continued to pray in Latin. This consisted of several repetitions of *miserere nobis* while the *folia* beat softly on the drums. This was the pattern, in general, of the evening prayers, which were held each evening during the entire novena, and of the other religious services held in the chapel on the saint's day. After the religious services were over, the group in the chapel formed a procession that moved to the pavilion. There the master of ceremonies invited the judges of the mast to be seated while the *folia* group sang a series of verses thanking the judges for providing the festival. The judges then opened the dancing. They danced a *"mão de samba"* (literally, "a hand of samba," but meaning "a dance") together and the festivities were under way. The drummers beat out samba time and everyone joined in. After the first dances, which must always be samba, an orchestra consisting of a flute, a guitar, one or two *cavaquinhos* (ukuleles), and perhaps a *sacudidor* (rattle) substituted for the drums. Dinner was served first to officials of the brotherhood, together with the judges, majordomos, and the *folia* group; then to the orchestra; and then in a series of tables to all the guests. Dancing continued throughout the night until dawn.

During the night the men slipped away furtively from time to time to their cache of rum for a drink—"to take the dust out of your eyes," as they explained. Rarely, however, did anyone drink to excess. Violent and noisy behavior is unusual. Women left the dancing at intervals to have a look at their children who were asleep in their hammocks hung around the edges of the dance pavilion or in nearby houses. Sometimes an adult relaxed into a hammock for a quick nap or a rest, but the noise of the music, the shuffle of feet over the rough boards, and the laughter and chatter of people continued throughout the entire night. The next morning, after a small black coffee and a piece of *beijú* cake, the visitors took their leave.

During the next eight evenings of the novena, there were evening prayers each afternoon at sunset. The majordomo of the day provided rockets to be set off just before and after the prayers, as well as coffee and cakes for the participants. Only twice during the novena did the majordomos pay for music for dancing, and this lasted only a few hours. The days of the novena were lively, but generally only a few visitors were present. The people of Maria Ribeira were busy preparing for the climax of the festival.

On August 27th, the day before St. Apolonia's day, more than a hundred visitors from other rural neighborhoods and from the town of Gurupá arrived during the morning and early afternoon. As evening approached, the *folia* group took the image of St. Apolonia from the chapel and placed it in a canoe highly decorated with paper banners and flags. It was time for the "Half-Moon," a nautical procession of canoes that weaves in and out, forming a figure eight in the stream in front of the village. The *folia* group, carrying the saint in the leading canoe, played their drums and led the singing. Rockets were set off in profusion. Following the Half-Moon, the *folia* group carried the saint's image to several houses where visitors were staying to ask for additional donations. By eight o'clock the master of ceremonies had announced evening prayers. After the services, which were more elaborate than usual, a *círio* (a procession in which each participant carries a candle) was formed. It moved slowly from the chapel to the dance pavilion. That evening the judges of the festival danced the first samba while others watched. The social dancing in the pavilion that followed was especially animated, continuing throughout the entire night and until the sun was well up in the sky the next morning. And on that day, after a brief rest, the dancing started up again. It was the morning of St. Apolonia's day, and dancing extended throughout the morning until about mid-afternoon.

More people were present on the vespers of the saint's day than on the first day of the festival when the mast was raised. The dinner given by the judges of the festival, which was served with the aid of their co-parents and close relatives, began as early as 9:00 p.m. and continued with consecutive tables throughout the night. Some visitors were not invited to the table until well after midnight. Four pigs were killed and great amounts of manioc flour, sugar, coffee, and rum were consumed. Including the cost of the musicians, who played throughout the night and the next day, the cost of the festival to the judges was well over $100 (cr. $2,000). The judges, a husband and wife, had made a vow that they would undertake the responsibility. The husband had planted a large garden the year before to provide manioc flour for the occasion and he had raised the pigs in anticipation of the feast. He was certain, however, that with St. Apolonia's protection he would be able to repay the debts he had contracted at the trading post to provide rockets, coffee, sugar, kerosene, and other articles. He had also borrowed money to pay the musicians. It is a point of honor for the judges that nobody goes without food and that there is music as long as people wish to dance—even though in doing so a judge may acquire debts that will take two or three years to repay.

About mid-afternoon, the master of ceremonies stopped the dancing to announce the auction to sell off the objects and the food that had been donated to the saint. The officers of the brotherhood conducted the auction. One of them, a person noted for his wit, served as auctioneer, and another took note of all sales. Bunches of bananas, pineapples, bags of manioc flour, a pedigree hen, a bottle of rum, a shaving kit wrapped in tissue paper as a "surprise," two cakes in brightly colored boxes, and numerous other small items were auctioned off. On this occasion the proceeds from the auction were only $2.50 (cr. $50), but at times people are known to compete ardently for desired items (especially for "surprises"), raising the bids far beyond any expectation.[3] The funds go to the brotherhood to be used in repairing and decorating their small chapel. Following the auction, the officers of the brotherhood retired to select the sponsors for next year's festival. Candidates for judge of the mast, for majordomos, and for judge of the festival had already been approached. Some of those present had made vows to the saint, and they came forward volunteering to serve. In Maria Ribeira, in 1948, the selections were easy, for Dona Diná Borralho, who attended during the last days, offered to take the obligation of judge of

---

[3]At an auction held in the town of Gurupá of donations contributed for a health club, people bid as much as $2.50 for a watermelon, $1.00 for a pineapple, $3.00 for a simple cake, and so on. Competing with each other, people bid far more than they could afford.

In 2012 an auction in town celebrating a neighborhood's patron saint resulted in bids for simple cakes as high as $26.00 (45 reis). By contrast, bids for simple cakes during the festivals of Saints Antony and Benedict often double this amount. As in the 1940s, competitive bidding in the 2000s often leads to outlays of cash beyond what bidders can reasonably afford.

the festival for the next year. Another merchant and his wife agreed to be judges of the mast, and other couples accepted as majordomos for the nights of the novena. The names of these new judges and majordomos were copied into the minutes, and at evening prayers the new judges and majordomos were asked to stand along with that year's sponsors so that all might see them. Dancing began again after the evening religious services, and as usual lasted until morning. The last night was considered the high point of the festivities, and a few additional visitors came only for the dancing.

The next morning people began to leave. A few stayed for the felling of the mast, which took place in mid-afternoon as a symbol of the end of the festivities. While the *folia* sang to the rhythm of their percussion instruments, men stepped up to take a swing with their axes at the mast pole until it was finally cut down. People then removed the foliage and made it into brooms to be used in a symbolic sweeping of the plaza and of the homes of the officers of the brotherhood. When this had been done, canoe-loads of people started for home. They floated slowly down the tributary, paddled leisurely up or down the Amazon, and then up the small streams where they lived, to return home. They paddled slowly, for they had used considerable energy dancing for two nights. Some had hangovers. After such a festival, both the visitors and their hosts sleep throughout the next day.

During the summer months, a typical family of the Gurupá community might participate in several of these rural festivals, which are held in nearby neighborhoods. In the concentrated village of Jocojó alone, there are four during the summer. No one needs an invitation to attend a festival, for one always has friends, relatives, or co-parents in each neighborhood. Townspeople also attend and, as in the case cited previously, they often serve as judges or majordomos for the saint's festivals in the rural neighborhoods. People seldom go to festivals held outside the area of the Gurupá community. They believe that dances in more distant neighborhoods often turn into *farras* (wild parties) with drunkenness and numerous fights. Within the community area, however, the festivals are attended by "our own people." Such festivals not only provide recreation for town and rural inhabitants of the area, but they also serve to bring unity to the community. They bridge a gap in social relations between the people of the town and those of the rural zones. Both the brotherhoods and the festivals they sponsor are important social institutions in the community of Gurupá.

II

....

The patron saint of Gurupá is St. Anthony, the patron saint of Portugal. But the saint who is most loved, most famous, and most worshiped is St. Benedict, known in Brazil as the "black saint."[4] The image of St. Benedict in Gurupá is famous throughout the Lower Amazon. He is known as a special protector of rubber gatherers. In Gurupá St. Benedict is considered "the people's saint," whereas St. Anthony is the saint of the First Class and the "whites." The latter, selected by the Iberian founders of Gurupá, did not find favor with the people who came to make up the bulk of the population—the Indigenous, the mestizos, and the African descendants. Yet, because St. Anthony is the official patron of the town, the Catholic priest encourages his devotion; and with the full support of the padre, St. Anthony's day in June is one of the major festivals of the town. The festival of St. Benedict, however, celebrated in December, is by far the most important and the best attended festival in Gurupá. It is a festival famous throughout the entire region.

About a generation ago, the festivals in honor of these two saints were organized by brotherhoods similar to those that exist today in the rural neighborhoods. The brotherhoods of the town were richer and larger in membership than those in the rural districts of today. Both the Irmandade de São Benedito and the Irmandade do São Antonio maintained cemeteries in which the members were buried. These are still in existence.[5] In keeping with the social position of the people devoted to each saint, the Brotherhood of St. Anthony was made up of "whites" and First Class, whereas the Brotherhood of St. Benedict consisted of the "people"—the town Second Class, the farmers, and the rubber collectors. Especially were *os velhos pretos* (the old blacks) devoted to St. Benedict, and they are said to have been the leaders in the brotherhood. Today both brotherhoods exist in name only. Each year before the festivals of St. Anthony and St. Benedict, an announcement

------

[4]As mentioned in Chapter 2, the Portuguese military established St. Anthony as the patron of the Fort in 1623. Later the St. Joseph Capuchins of Mercy, a Franciscan charismatic order, came to Gurupá and likely established St. Benedict as an important saint. Both Saints Anthony and Benedict are Franciscan saints (Leite 1943:134–36).
[5]In 2013 both of these cemeteries are in poor states of repair. Although they are routinely weeded by the municipality, as is the Jewish cemetery, time has taken a toll and many of the graves are poorly marked or unmarked.

is printed listing the officers of the brotherhood sponsoring the festival and the names of the judges and the majordomos. The Catholic priest is always listed as attorney for the saint for both brotherhoods. The other officers are always people of some official position, such as the mayor, the schoolteacher, or the federal tax collector, or important merchants. The judges and the majordomos are always the same each year, and all are of the upper strata of Gurupá society. The festivals are actually organized by Dona Inacinha, the devoted schoolteacher, with the help of a few other upper-class ladies. The cost of the festival is met to a great extent by a collection made among the townspeople. Substantial donations are expected from the merchants of the town, who stand to profit by them. The names of those who contribute most are listed as majordomos of the brotherhood. Actually, however, these associations have ceased to exist; there is no membership body, and the directorate consists only of the upper-class sponsors listed on the printed announcement.

Of a once strong brotherhood, only the *folia* group of St. Benedict remains as an organized body. The *folia* is composed mainly of lower-class mulattoes and African Brazilians, descendants of the "old blacks" once so devoted to St. Benedict. There is a master of ceremonies, an official in charge of saint's errands, and musicians (drummers, a rattle player, and a scraper), all of whom learned their duties and the traditional verses and songs from men who held the positions when the brotherhood was an organized association. These members of the *folia* of St. Benedict feel that the image of the saint belongs to them: "It has been taken away from us by Dona Inacinha and the padre." Nowadays, the padre no longer allows the *folia* group of St. Benedict to take the image out of the church. The long journeys throughout the Lower Amazon on which they once took their saint, singing his praises and collecting contributions, are now reduced to a short procession through the town, supervised by the padre and Dona Inacinha. Only on the actual saint's day is the *folia* group allowed to follow behind their saint's image in the procession. The *folia* may not nowadays go from house to house carrying the image and asking for donations, nor may they play and sing inside the church as they once did. The festival of St. Benedict, once directed and organized by the brotherhood, has now been expropriated by the official Church (Galvão 1952).

The festival of St. Anthony is rather a formal affair. The Catholic padre, who comes to Gurupá for the occasion, does not believe in mixing religion with pleasure: thus the recreational aspects of the celebration are minimal. In form the festival follows the pattern described for rural festivals. In the past there was the day of raising of the mast followed by a novena for the saint ending on the saint's day. A mast is seldom raised now, but the upper-class devotees still celebrate a novena. On St. Anthony's Day, there is a Mass and a procession. Numerous baptisms and marriages are performed, for this is one of the two days of the year when a Catholic priest is certain to be present in the town. Several hundred people are generally attracted to Gurupá for the occasion. Business is brisk in the town stores, and the merchants put up a few stands to sell soft drinks and sweets. Sometimes a dance is furtively organized, against the wishes of the priest, by some of the townspeople. There is generally an auction where the few gifts offered to the saint are sold. According to Dona Inacinha, the festival of St. Anthony "does not pay the expenses of decorating the church."

On the other hand, the festival of St. Benedict not only pays for the decoration of the church for both festivals but also provides the cash to pay for repairs on the church throughout the year. Because St. Benedict is the special protector of rubber gatherers, most collectors donate the first day's harvest of each season to their saint. In a normal year this amounts to more than one thousand pounds of crude rubber. Boats passing by Gurupá fire off rockets in honor of St. Benedict and frequently stop to offer a donation to the saint. Both the townspeople and the rural dwellers of the Gurupá community present gifts to their favorite saint during the year in return for his favors. As St. Benedict's festival approaches, the voluntary offerings increase. They consist of rubber, a calf, manioc flour, chickens, pigs, and almost any salable product. Dona Inacinha receives the offerings and lists them in a book with the name of the donor and, later, the amount they bring in when they are sold at auction on St. Benedict's day. In two years Dona Inacinha was able to pay the expenses of decorating the church for the festivals and to accumulate approximately $2,000 (cr. $40,000) used for repairing the church. "St. Anthony lives in St. Benedict's house and at St. Benedict's expense," people complain. Dona Inacinha considers that these funds "belong to the Church," and she makes an accounting of them to the padre, but the people feel that the money belongs to their saint.

In the past, St. Benedict received even more donations than he does now. During the years of the rubber boom, the saint's annual income was fabulous in terms of Gurupá's economy. In those days the brotherhood sent the *folia* group with the saint's image on two long trips to collect contributions and offerings. The saint's image was placed on a temporary altar in a large sailing vessel manned by members of the brotherhood. They sailed almost 125 miles upriver, stopping at each settlement or trading post, singing and praying to their saint, and collecting offerings. Returning to Gurupá, the group unloaded their cargo of rubber, cattle, pigs, manioc flour, and other gifts and then proceeded downriver, returning only on the eve of the raising of the mast to inaugurate the festivities. The return of the *folia* was always anxiously expected, and the stories of the miracles performed by St. Benedict on these expeditions are told with pride by older men. Nowadays, "because the padre no longer allows the image to go out of the church with the *folia*," one devotee explained, "St. Benedict is poor."[6]

In the past the celebrations for St. Benedict, like those for St. Anthony, followed the traditional pattern of the raising of the mast, the evening prayers during a novena, the social dancing, a Half-Moon nautical procession, the *folia* group playing in front of each residence, and the cutting of the votive mast and the sweeping of the houses. St. Benedict's festival differed from those held today in the rural zones only in that it was more elaborate and attended by many more people. Today many

---

[6]The tensions between the Church hierarchy and the laity over the Saints' celebrations continued into the 1970s at which point the Bishop Eurico Kräutler issued a list of provisions to regulate the patron saint festivals in the Prelature of Xingú (which includes Gurupá). Among these, all religious festivals must be organized and approved by the parish priest; all indecent dancing and alcohol abuse are prohibited; and all festivities must be suspended during the liturgical celebrations and must end by midnight. If these provisions are not followed, he stated, the Church will prohibit the use of chapel and the Holy Image and will not provide a priest for the celebration (see Lopes 2004:25). Despite the clampdown, in Gurupá there was a notable shift in the organization of the saint festival of Saints Anthony and Benedict that favored the poor. In 1972 Padre Giúlio Luppi began appointing members from the newly forming *comunidades ecclesiastical de base* (ecclesiastical base communities) or CEBS—who were mainly the poor rural agroextractivists—to the Festivals' Boards, not the traditional wealthy families or civil servants of the town. This was part of an emphasis to include the poor and marginal members of society in the religious life of the church, which also involved their political and economic enfranchisement outside of the church. In other words, the religious nature of the festival was being combined with the politico-religious message of Liberation Theology (see Chapter 8). As part of this process, the Church in Gurupá increasingly accepted the lay traditions of the saint festivals prohibited in the previous decades.

FIGURE 6.3 | *Folia for Saint Benedict. Performed on Wagley's request.*
Photograph by C. Wagley 1948.

phases of the saint's festival are abbreviated, even omitted, because of the greater controls of the Catholic Church.[7] As before, however, people begin to gather by December 1st, and the crowd increases each day until December 8th, when the mast is raised. At least one thousand visitors from the rural districts and from neighboring municipalities attend the inauguration of the festival. By December 25th and 26th, during the climax of the festivities, there are generally more than two thousand people in Gurupá—almost four times the normal population of the town.[8] To feed the many visitors, there are stands in the streets serving foods, açaí juice, sweets, and soft drinks. In every Gurupá household there are guests and even paying boarders. Other people sleep in the boats that bring them; and still others, braving the possibility of rain, hang their hammocks outdoors under the trees.

---

[7]Wagley's festival dates reflect the old schedule before the revisions in the 1970s.

By the 2010s, all ritual components have been restored to the celebration, including dancing in front of the Saint in the church.

[8]In 2012 the festival of Saint Benedict attracted an estimated 10,000 people, doubling the population of the town.

Each night there are dances. Admission to these dances is five cruzeiros for men. Ladies enter free of charge. The music is furnished by an orchestra consisting of a flute, a guitar, a ukulele, and a scraper. And every night and all day long during the last days of the festivities, there is samba dancing in the pavilion to the beat of drums. The samba,[9] as danced on this occasion and at the rural festivals, differs from the characteristic Brazilian samba of the city, both in tempo and in the movements of the dance itself. The old-style samba of Gurupá is danced by couples, but the partners dance apart without touching each other. Their steps are short and shuffling; their bodies are stiff with only the arms swinging for balance. The tempo is fast, and the drummers are replaced at intervals; the dancing is almost continuous. Samba dancing in the pavilion is traditional during St. Benedict's festival, and people gather to "dance a hand" and to watch the better dancers. Order is kept by the *folia* group, the remnant of the brotherhood, who do not allow men to dance with their hats on and forbid drinking in the vicinity. The pavilion is a central attraction of the festival, but nowadays people are beginning to prefer the *baile pegado* (joined dancing), as modern social dancing is called, and these commercial dances attract many visitors away from the pavilion.[10]

Under the direction of the master of ceremonies, Benedito Torres, a descendant of one of the "old blacks," the *folia* of St. Benedict still meets to practice in the evenings for several weeks before the festival. There are several good drummers as well as players of the scraper and of the rattle. All of them know the *versinhos* (quatrains)[11] to be sung on each specific occasion during the festival. They still hold forth in front

---

[9]In 2013 the dance is called *gumbá* and is said to have been handed down through the centuries by Gurupá's African slave population and its descendants. The dance is now considered an important part of the community's cultural heritage.

[10]In 2010s the dances take place in several of Gurupá's large dance halls, typically with a disk jockey playing the latest techno-brega and well as regular brega and carimbó. Live performances usually involve a singer from Belém, backed up by a keyboard synthesizer or two playing techno-brega—accompanied by an electronic light show. Another innovation that is part of the secular celebration for Saint Benedict is the "beer bath" (*banho de cerveja*). In a demarcated area on Second Street, people pour beer on one another as sport, using great quantities in the process.

[11]These quatrains are introduced by the leader, the master of ceremonies, who is known for his good voice. The instrumentalists join him in the refrain. An alvorada, to give but one example, has the following words:

of the church on the occasion of the raising of the mast, and from time to time during the festival they sing an *alvorada* (morning serenade) at the break of day and at sunset an Ave Maria. Only on the vespers of St. Benedict's day, however, do they sing in front of people's homes asking for donations. The padre allows them to carry only the *esplendor* (the saint's crown) as a substitute for the image itself. On December 24th the *folia* sings for the Half-Moon procession, occupying the first canoe with their saint and accompanying the image back to the church. Afterward they sing its praises from the church doorway. In Gurupá, Christmas is hardly celebrated at all, except for a midnight Mass. It is overshadowed by the climax of the festivities for St. Benedict, which continue from December 24th through the 28th. On the 24th there are the processions and the singing of the *folia* group, and on the 25th there is samba dancing. The activities of the *folia* group are nowadays suspended on Christmas day at the request of the padre. Early on the 26th there is an early Mass for St. Benedict, and in the afternoon the traditional auction of the donations to the saint begins. This generally continues well into the next day. Samba dancing and social dancing are continuous on the 26th and 27th. On December 28th the mast is cut down as the *folia* group sings again. The leaves used to decorate the mast are much sought after by townspeople and visitors alike as medicine. A large crowd rushes to gather them as the votive pole falls. The custom of sweeping out the houses of the judges and the majordomos at the end of a festival is still maintained in the town of Gurupá, although these people are sponsors in name only. On New Year's Eve, after the influx of visitors is over, the merchants offer the townspeople a dance "because they have made a great deal of money." Coming just before the heavy rains of "winter" begin, St. Benedict's day is the climax of the year.[12]

Alvorada! Alvorada!
De manhã de madrugada
ainda o folião canta "Madrugada"
Grande tino tern o galo
para cantar "Madrugada!"

[12]In the 2010s the festivals of Saints Anthony and Benedict are well organized and well attended events, much closer to the celebrations during the rubber boom than what Wagley observed in 1948. Much of the success has come from the Church's reorganization, through the tenets of Liberation Theology and the organization of CEBs (discussed in Chapter 8), which has both incorporated and reinforced the

III

The festivals of June—St. Anthony (June 12th), St. John (June 24th), and SS. Peter and Paul (June 28th)—are among the most characteristic and traditional of Brazil. Like most traditional elements of Brazilian national culture, the northern portion of the country preserves these celebrations in their characteristically Brazilian form. Throughout North Brazil, St. Anthony's, St. John's, and St. Peter's are the occasion for numerous social gatherings and celebrations, following customs inherited from Portugal but modified in the process of adaptation to new conditions. On these occasions there is always the large *Fogueira de São João*, the bonfire around which a Brazilian family and their friends gather to eat sweets, roasted sweet potatoes, manioc cakes, and other traditional delicacies. Around the bonfire it is traditional to set off firecrackers, rockets, and fireworks and to send up paper balloons into the night. Old folksongs are sung. In cities and towns these days are occasions for dances and parties. In the larger metropolitan centers, such as Rio de Janeiro, Recife, and Belém, people come to parties and balls in costumes of rural dress—in simple gingham dresses and in trousers similar to blue jeans worn with cotton shirts and straw hats. These festivals, especially St. John's, are characteristic of the rural countryside and of small towns, and it is traditional for city folk to dress as country people and to imitate old rural tradition, just as in North America we dress as country folk at square dances.

In Gurupá, as in other communities of the Amazon Valley, the festivals of June are celebrated in their characteristic and traditional manner. St. Anthony's, as noted earlier, is an important religious festival.

---

religious brotherhoods. As Robson Lopes (2004:54), a former priest of Gurupá observed, there was a reciprocal relationship between the brotherhoods and the CEBs in the 1970s. As the brotherhoods began accepting the CEBs' proposals to combine faith (prayer, reflection) with social and political action, the parish and lay leaders were building on the brotherhoods as the core of the grassroots organization. Lopes (2004:54) maintains that if, on one hand, the brotherhoods found a broadening of their activities by assuming the parish catechetical services, on the other hand the CEBs have found fertile ground among the brotherhoods to sow Liberation Theology.

In 2013 there are lively and well attended Saints festivals all over the municipality that are sponsored by private families, CEBs, or brotherhoods. Many will raise a votive mast, dance the traditional gumbá, conduct the land and fluvial processions (Half-Moon), pray the novena, recite payers in Latin, and in the end hold a dance after the cutting down of the votive mast (see Lopes 2004:35).

Thus there is little merrymaking on this day. On the eve of St. John's and of St. Peter's, however, there are bonfires in front of most Gurupá homes. Few fireworks are set off because only rockets are available locally and these are used mostly for religious processions. But people gather around the bonfires visiting and singing. On these occasions people seek co-parents over the bonfire, widening their circle of personal security. Generally there are social dances in the town. In the village of Jocojó, St. John's Day is celebrated by the brotherhood of the neighborhood. During these days, also, the *Boi Bumba* company, and on occasion a group enacting the *Cordão de Passarinho* (The Bird Chain), enliven the scene. *The Bird Chain* has not been enacted in Gurupá for several years; it is a rather mild tale of a bird that was killed by a hunter and brought back to life by a fairy. It was always played by a company of young girls and young men recruited from the better families, and it was never very popular among the people. Everyone prefers the *Boi Bumba*. This traditional folk comedy is performed by local actors in many towns of North Brazil and in almost every Amazon community during this season of the year. Even in Belém numerous companies enact the *Boi Bumba* during June and July.

Everyone knows the plot. It is the story of the shooting of a cowboy's favorite ox by a simple farmer. Old Francisco, as the farmer is called, is the central figure in the drama, and he is usually dressed in the garb of a northeastern backwoodsman. In Gurupá, Francisco, a comic character, wears a mask with a notably long nose. The head cowboy and his companions cry over the ox's death and try unsuccessfully to capture Old Francisco. Finally, the head cowboy calls in the Indians, played in Gurupá by younger men who are decorated with paint and red macaw feathers and who each carry a bow and arrow. After these caboclos (the term is used to signify Indians) are baptized, they are sent out to capture Francisco. Because they are famous warriors, they are able to do so. The cowboy demands that Francisco cure his ox, so Francisco calls the "doctors"—Dr. Rum, Dr. Woodtick, and Dr. Medicine. The latter gives the ox (at least in the Gurupá version of the play) a purgative of peppers, wood ticks, rose leaves, and various other herbal medicines. Then he orders Old Francisco to look under the ox's tail to see if the purgative is working. As Francisco looks, the purge suddenly works. The ox rises full of energy and life as the play ends.

In the past, Gurupá supported two or three companies who played *Boi Bumba* during the festival season of June. In those days there was

FIGURE 6.4 | *Boi Bumba. Paulo Ferreira de Freitas is sixth from the right.*
Photograph by C. Wagley 1948.

a competition (*desafio*) among them for the most luxurious costumes
and the originality of the actors. Formerly each company had a *curral*,
something like an open-air theater. Nowadays there is only one company, and it performs in the open street. This company, known as the
Deuce of Diamonds (*Dois de Oiro*), is led by Paulo Ferreira de Freitas
(see Figure 6.4), whose position is called the *amo de boi* (owner or at-
tendant of the ox) or sometimes the *mestre de boi* (master of the ox).
Paulo also plays the important role of the head cowboy. In 1948 Paulo
had just returned to Gurupá after several years' absence, motivated by
his irritation at being jailed when he drank too much during a performance. For the performances of 1948, therefore, Paulo had to train several new actors. During his absence several regular performers had
moved away. He began rehearsals in early May, teaching his actors
their lines from a notebook into which the entire play had been copied.
He carefully explained their roles with the wisdom of many years of
experience. Several actors, however, had played the same part year after
year. Nhenjuca, for example, who played Old Francisco, and Paulo
himself were old hands at their respective parts.

The lines of the play are both sung and recited. They are similar to those used by other *Boi Bumba* companies, but Paulo has written many of his own variations into his version of the play. Furthermore, the actors often elaborate on their lines or ad lib in accordance with the occasion. Nhenjuca, who is known for his wit, is famous for his improvisations, and he overacts constantly. He explains coyly, for example, that his wife Catarina (played vulgarly by a man) caused him to shoot the ox: "She is pregnant and would eat only fillet of ox." A high point in the play is the exchange of insults between Francisco and the Indians. Sings Francisco:

> I don't like Indians
> even if they are my relations;
> For Indians have the habit
> of stealing all one's possessions.[13]

And the Indians answer in chorus:

> Whoever wants to catch Chiquinho
> need only make a fire in his sight.
> For Chico has the habit
> of always asking for a light.[14]

These are traditional lines, and they are always good for a laugh no matter how many times the audience has heard them. But the brightest moments come when Nhenjuca departs from his lines and comments on a local matter or singles out someone in the audience as the butt of his ready wit. "The only thing that is useful about the SESP," he remarks as the physician approaches, "is DDT." As an American

---

[13]In Portuguese it makes a neat little verse:
> Eu nao gosto de cabolcoos
> nem que seja meu parente.
> Todo caboclo tem de costume
> de roubar os teréns da gente

[14]"Chiquinho" and "Chico" are nicknames for Francisco. In Portuguese, the native Brazilian's reply reads:
> Quem quizer pegar Chiquinho
> Faça fogo no caminho.
> O Chico tem de costume
> ascender seu cachimbo.

anthropologist was sighted, he ad libbed, "I am also an American and Americans can't be blacks."[15] The ox itself comes in for considerable fun. It is constructed of papier mâché and starched cloth stretched over a bamboo frame. It has horns on its crude head and is decorated with garlands of bright paper flowers. The words "Deuce of Diamonds" are painted on its sides. Two young men play the ox, and as usual the head sometimes gets out of coordination with the hind parts, to the great amusement of the audience. A particularly hilarious performance was given one evening when the two young men under the ox were slightly intoxicated, stampeding about and chasing the young women in the audience.

The Deuce of Diamonds Company plays almost each night from June 11th, the vespers of St. Anthony, until after St. Peter's festival on June 29th. Each year their leader invites someone of prestige in Gurupá to serve as sponsor of his *Boi Bumba* company. In 1948 the sponsors were Alvaro and his wife, Diquinha, the owners of the Gurupá boardinghouse. It was in their house that the company rehearsed and the sponsors paid for the construction and decoration of the ox. The company's first performance of the year took place in the street in front of Alvaro's house. Following the first performance, any who wish may invite the company to perform for them in front of their dwelling. All First-Class families feel obligated to request one performance, and many other families are anxious to have them play at their homes. On certain evenings, especially on the three saints' days, the company performs several times. In payment, the host at whose home the play is performed offers the company a donation, "the tongue of the oxen," as it is called. The "tongue," generally wrapped in an envelope, varies from fifty cents (cr. $10) to $2.50 (cr. $50), depending on the financial position of the family. And it is considered proper to invite the principal performers into the house after the play ends for a glass of beer, a glass of sweet homemade liquor, or even a drink of rum. A large audience gathers at each performance. The host brings chairs and offers refreshments to his close friends, to relatives, and to co-parents. Others crowd about in the street watching the performance.

The funds collected as donations from these performances are not paid to the performers. Each performer pays the cost of his own

---

[15]Nhenjuca is a dark mulatto, but he calls himself a preto (black). He makes fun of the so-called weaknesses attributed to the African descent.

costume, and participates for the pleasure the acting gives him.[16] Antenor Palheta, for example, who played the role of an Indian, spent over $5 (cr. $100) for the materials for his costume and lost several days' work as an employee of the health post to take part in the play. The donations given to the company go to the sponsors, who thus recoup the cost of the construction of the ox and the other expenses (such as drinks for the performers during practice). Furthermore, the funds collected from performances are expected to pay for a party offered to the performers and to their many friends on the day of the *matança do boi* (slaughter of the ox) following the final performance of the season. At this party the sponsor kills the ox with a knife and the guests "drink its blood"; that is, the sponsor by tradition punctures a barrel of wine placed under the ox, and the wine (ox blood) is caught in jars to be consumed by the participants. In Gurupá wine is expensive, but at least one bottle must be spilled before beer and rum are substituted. There is music and dancing at the "slaughter" party, which usually takes place just after St. Peter's Day in late June. The exact date for the party depends on the pleasure of the company's sponsors. The *Boi Bumba* is a much appreciated part of the festivals of June, but by late June people are somewhat bored by the repeated performances. Each year in May, however, they look forward with renewed enthusiasm to June and to the *Boi Bumba*.[17]

---

[16]Compatible with the Gurupá ideals of feminine behavior, women do not participate in the Boi Bumba. A man, as indicated previously, enacts the only feminine part in the play. Young girls did participate in The Bird Chain, which was mainly an upper-class affair closely supervised by their families.

[17]As best as I can tell, the Boi Bumba witnessed and photographed by Wagley was the last one ever presented in Gurupá. In the 2000s it has been replaced as a source of entertainment by the *quadrilhas* (a type of square dance that is structured around a mock wedding). Many of these quadrilhas, however, are competitive contests that require significant expenditures of money and months of practice. In Gurupá, the quadrilha competitions may be between different public schools, or between rival dance squads in town or from neighboring towns (Gurupá usually has four of these dance teams). The squads consist of twenty to forty youths who drill for months in preparation for the festivities. Their costumes are expensive elaborations of stereotypical rural folk dress, although other themes can be used. The dances are flamboyant, meticulously choreographed, and performed to regional music—preferably brega and forró. The expense, time, work, passion, and camaraderie involved in the quadrilhas equals that of the Carnaval dancing blocks in other parts of Brazil (Pace and Hinote 2013:165).

IV

In addition to these regular festivals and holidays, families in Gurupá offer parties, dinners, and dances for their friends and relatives throughout the year. One manner of entertaining one's neighbors and relatives is the work party for clearing gardens in the early summer. The cooperative labor, the large lunch, the drinking, and sometimes a dance when the work is done turn hard work into recreation. The majority of these social gatherings, however, are offered, as in most of Brazil, on the occasion of a wedding, a baptism, a first communion, and especially on birthdays. Throughout Brazil birthdays are important occasions to be remembered and celebrated by one's family and friends. In the cities people receive telegrams and visits from friends and relatives. Housewives keep a notebook listing the various birthdays and take care not to forget them. On the birthday of any one of its members, many Brazilian families expect visitors late in the afternoon. Relatives and friends come bringing their children; and even though a small child's birthday is being celebrated, adults pay the family a visit. There is a table sumptuous with tiny sandwiches, cakes, pastries, and such traditional sweets as *bala de ovo* (balls of eggs), *trouxinhas de noiva* (brides' little packages), *toiçinhos do ceu* (pieces from heaven), *olhos de sogra* (mother-in-law's eyes), and *bombocados* (good mouthfuls). Soft drinks, chocolate, and tea are also served. Children run about in their best clothes, stuffing themselves with sweets from the table. The late afternoon reception is often extended into dinner when a buffet supper with wines is served, and sometimes there may be dancing in the evening for younger members of the family. When families cannot afford such elaborate entertainment, there is a lunch or dinner in honor of the anniversary, with several plates served with beer or wine. No matter how modest the family, a birthday in Brazil is an occasion for entertainment.

The people of Gurupá, like other Brazilians, go to considerable expense and work to celebrate birthdays. If the family can afford it at all, there is some kind of a commemoration for each member of the family. The food served in Gurupá is not as elaborate or as plentiful as that offered in the upper-class homes of Rio de Janeiro, but many of the traditional delicacies and sweets are present on the table. Midday lunch is a common manner of celebrating a birthday; sometimes people offer a party at night with music for dancing and a table of meat-filled pastries and sweets with *guaraná*, beer, wine, liquors, and other beverages. On such occasions people are apt to be excessive and ostentatious in their hospitality. They spend more than they can afford, often going into debt heavily to offer a *festa* or a lunch at which nothing is lacking. Always at such luncheons and parties, the hosts ask to be forgiven for the poor quality and the lack of quantity of the food served, while going to extremes to offer more than the guests can consume. People are exceedingly hospitable in Gurupá, but their hospitality is never really modest and unassuming.

On the first birthday of her adopted son, for example, Maria, the young unmarried mother whose history was mentioned earlier, had musicians play a morning serenade for the infant. She and her friends set off several rockets in the child's honor early that morning. She gave a large luncheon for more than twenty friends, with beef, duck in tucupí sauce, numerous other dishes, and a variety of beverages. In the afternoon visitors poured into her small house. Later she paid the local orchestra to play for dancing until after midnight. At the time Maria was working as a domestic in the home of a state government employee, and her income was hardly as much as five dollars per month, including food. She went in debt almost fifty dollars for the festivities. Though people felt that Maria's behavior was extreme, and they could not understand why the stores allowed her so much credit, everyone admired her hospitality and her free-handed way of doing things.

On another occasion, Alvaro offered a luncheon for his wife, Diquinha, on her birthday. It was to be a small luncheon for a few friends, Alvaro announced, but he invited twenty-three guests, selected only from among the First Class. The mayor, the federal tax collector, the secretary of the municipal government, the public health physician, and other local notables were invited. Friends of lesser importance and his neighbors were invited to a festa with dancing that same evening. Although the luncheon was given in her honor, Diquinha did not sit at the table. She and her sister worked steadily all of the day before and throughout the morning preparing. The table at lunch was literally smothered with beef, with duck in tucupí sauce, with fish, and other edibles. Numerous bottles of beer were opened, and more than a dozen bottles of wine were consumed. There were three desserts. The meal was followed by flowery toasts and speeches. Each male guest rose to speak in honor of Alvaro and Diquinha, offering felicitations for her birthday. Finally Alvaro spoke, asking to be forgiven for his limited hospitality, and toasted his guests. At four o'clock, after more than three hours at the table, the guests departed to fall into their hammocks to sleep, only to be invited to return that evening for dancing. The cost of the luncheon and of the evening party that followed was the equivalent of several months' income for Alvaro and Diquinha.

Some fifty or more guests came for the *festa* at Alvaro's that evening. A local orchestra played *choros*, *marchas*, and sambas until well after midnight. People came in their best clothes; and although it was a warm evening, men danced in their coats. Mothers came escorting their daughters. The women sat in chairs and on benches on one side of the room, and the men stood in a group on the other side. As each dance began, the gentlemen crossed the room to invite the lady of his choice to dance. Everyone behaved with rigorous formality. About ten o'clock the ladies were invited to partake of *pasteis* and vermouth, which had been laid on the table in the dining veranda. Later the men went to the table to drink beer, and vermouth mixed with rum. Afterward the party became livelier. Zeca Pará announced a quadrille (a square dance), which he "called" in a mixture of Portuguese and confused French—the manner he had learned from his father. After an hour of the quadrille the guests seemed to have relaxed, and dancing in couples was resumed. Everyone spoke of Alvaro's and Diquinha's party as *muito alegre* (very lively), but compared to other birthday parties offered by Gurupá families living on Third Street and living in the rural neighborhoods it was obviously a rather ceremonious affair. At some of the parties given by people of lower social status, dancing continues until dawn and neighbors and friends drink frequently to their hosts' health and to many more birthdays. Birthday parties are perhaps the most frequent type of social gatherings held in Gurupá. They satisfy a basic human need of response from others and considerable recreation for all who attend.[18]

---

[18]In 2013 birthdays continue to be important events, marked by parties in which individuals of all ages are invited. My wife and I had the pleasure of attending one of the last birthday parties for Zeca Pará in the late 1980s, following closely the description given here in 1948. More recent celebrations may be just as elaborate, depending on the financial abilities of the family. Going into debt for parties is not uncommon. Serving food, and lots of it, is still an essential element of a good party. Cakes, whether homemade or bought in one of several bakeries in Gurupá, are elaborately decorated and accompanied by birthday candles. They may be light and sweet made

V

In the city of Belém, Gurupá is known as a dull town. People from the city passing Gurupá on a river steamer, or even after visiting there for a few days, wonder how people can live in such a humdrum community. There are no movies. The town does not support a social club where the upper class might hold dances and congregate in the evening as do many larger Brazilian towns and cities. The occasional Sunday afternoon soccer matches between the two recently organized local teams are of little interest to Brazilian urbanites, who are apt to be impassioned fans of a professional team that plays for thousands of spectators in a huge stadium. Even the pre-Lenten Carnaval, which Brazilians of the cities celebrate in such a colorful and joyous manner, tends to be relatively dull. A few members of the upper class dance in the streets in weak imitation of the dancing they have seen in Belém; and on one night during Carnaval, there may be a ball limited to upper-class participants.[19] As compared to the annual *círio* in Belém, even the festival of St. Benedict provides little excitement. As in most small towns, the pace is slow in Gurupá and the forms of amusement are few. The way people entertain themselves would seem quaint and old-fashioned to most city people.

The people of Gurupá, however, do not find their community dull. They seek pleasure, as they understand it, by means of their traditional forms of recreation. Although recreation is an important aspect of community life everywhere, in the Amazon Valley, where a sparse

---

of flour, or the heavier and less sugary macaxeira (manioc) cakes. The host's traditional apology for limited hospitality is often repeated despite the abundance. On more than one occasion when we had our daughters with us in Gurupá, on their birthdays our Gurupá friends would make sure to throw a party with plenty of cake and soft drinks, even though they subsisted on limited incomes. Birthdays, even for foreign friends, were just too important not to celebrate.

[19]Possibly due to television exposure ever since the 1980s when people have been able to watch the national pageantry and pandemonium in real time, Gurupá's Carnaval is today better organized. There may be a couple of blocos (dance blocks) parading around with an assortment of drums. The new tradition of a "beer bath" will also take place on designated days. Yet, the celebration is much weaker than the saints' festivals and the June festivals (on the surveys it consistently ranked below Christmas as well). It does not help that Carnaval falls in the middle of the rainy season where daily deluges dampen everyone's spirits.

population is spread over an immense area, recreational gatherings are of even greater importance in breaking the solitude of human existence. Furthermore, in Gurupá people do not seek pleasure alone but mix their pleasure with their work. They organize work parties and they drink and sing as they work. Their saint's festivals and their birthday parties provide the basis for important group and individual incentives. People will spend all of their savings, or go into debt, to serve as a sponsor for a saint's festival or to offer an elaborate birthday party. And recreation is closely related to their religion and to the social organization of their community; the rural religious brotherhoods have as their principal function the celebration of a saint's-day festival and are also basic social units in the rural neighborhoods. Any educator, technician, or administrator charged with planning or implementing a program of social and economic change should take into consideration the meaning and the function of these traditional forms of recreation in Gurupá society.

In opposing the neighborhood brotherhoods and festivals, the Catholic priest and the official Church organization are combatting an important social institution, unaware of its great potential value to themselves and to the community. It is well known that the cooperation of community leaders is necessary in any program of community action. The officials of these rural brotherhoods are important leaders in the rural neighborhoods. Their cooperation would be of the utmost value to the Church or to any other organization dealing with community problems. The brotherhoods of rural Gurupá might easily be given new and additional functions; the leaders of these neighborhood organizations might, for example, be persuaded to support programs in health, in agriculture, and in education. The Brazilian government and its various administrative agencies should be aware of these leaders and their power. In fact, in any effort to stimulate the relatively weak sense of community cohesion in Gurupá, it might even be advisable to attempt the reorganization of the decadent town brotherhoods dedicated to St. Benedict and to St. Anthony. Such associations could furnish a basis for community organization in a form already well known to the people.[20]

---

[20]As mentioned earlier, the current priest who has been in Gurupá since 1971 and who carefully read *Amazon Town*, has done this to great effect (see Chapter 8).

One frequently hears city dwellers and people from abroad complain that the Amazon ribeirinho is lazy. Such people cite their experience. "When caboclos are paid higher wages, they will work fewer days," they say.[21] They complain that the ribeirinhos neglect their gardens and neglect rubber gathering because of the "wild parties" at religious festivals. Unquestionably, the season of festivals is the time when new gardens must be cleared and planted and when rubber is harvested. Amazon festivals, therefore, conflict with the season of most intensive economic activity; but as long as the present economic patterns continue, the people will necessarily divide their time during the dry summer months between work and play. Such festivals, however, are major economic incentives. In the Amazon people are anxious to improve their material life, but even more important to them is the prestige and the response from others that they receive when serving as sponsors for a saint's festival or as hosts to family and friends at an elaborate birthday party. To earn the money for such purposes, people work to earn more than their minimal necessities. Material improvements such as radios, electric fixtures, mechanical farm tools, cheaper clothing, and imported foods are generally not available to the Amazon rural workers, or are beyond the scope of their earning power; therefore, such material improvements provide little incentive.[22] When

---

[21]In 2013, as açaí and timber extraction wealth mounts for some agroextractivist households in Gurupá, people also have begun to work less. Rather than interpreting this behavior as irrational, illogical, or simply laziness, the behavior can be understood in terms of the consumption–labor balance principle first formulated by A. V. Chayanov (1986). Developed to explain the behavior of Russian peasants in the early 20th century, Chayanov proposed that subsistence farmers work only as hard as they need in order to meet their subsistence requirements, but beyond that have no incentive to produce surpluses. If sufficiency is surpassed, they reduce their labor, thereby reducing drudgery. Sahlins (1972) used this concept in his definition of the domestic mode of production and the original affluent society for tribal societies. In the context Wagley raises the issue—that is, stimulating development in the Amazon—the model argues that the peasant survival strategies are systematically different from capitalist enterprises (they maximize total income, not profit) and that without some form of culturally appropriate "incentive" (or the more historically common resort to repressive measures such as coercion, expropriation of land, or excessive taxation), increased production is not likely.

[22]In 2013 access to cell phones, motorcycles, motorboats, and processed food create incentive for consumption; but with the current extraction boom and the falling prices for these products, consumption is obtainable without working as long or as hard as in the past.

people are deprived of their own forms of recreation and hospitality, as they are in many Amazon communities, there is little desire to accumulate beyond their immediate physical needs. People do not value material improvements alone, and such intangibles as recreation and hospitality may be valued as highly as a better material standard of living. It is just such incentives and values that are often overlooked by "practical" administrators responsible for programs of economic development.

CHAPTER 7

....

From Magic to Science

I n our own civilization scientific and naturalistic explanations have gradually replaced magical and supernatural explanations for phenomena and for events. This basic change in our worldview began centuries ago and is still taking place with ever increasing velocity. Only a relatively short time ago, rainfall was thought to depend on the supernatural, and malaria was believed to result from bad air or bad "humors." Magical means and prayers were used to ensure sufficient rainfall for the crops. Often harmful precautions, such as sleeping in a room tightly closed to keep out night airs, were used to prevent malaria. Nowadays rainfall is attributed to natural causes and can even be produced by scientifically controlled experiments. Today it is known that the anopheles mosquito transmits malaria; science has shown us how to contain the disease through containment of the insect. Similar examples might be taken from almost any sphere of our way of life. As the field of science expands, the segment of human experience depending on magical or even "common sense" explanation is steadily reduced.

This process of change has not taken place with equal velocity in all segments of our culture, nor is it as complete at any time as it might be. Even in our large metropolitan centers, magical beliefs persist in the face of the most modern scientific concepts. We avoid using the number "13" in public buildings and some of us still do not walk under a ladder. Science has not fully penetrated "downward" to great masses of people nor has it diffused "outward" to those living in marginal areas of our civilization. In London, Paris, New York, and Rio de Janeiro large numbers of people have a very vague idea of the bacterial concept of disease. In out-of-the-way portions of any Western country, countless magical folk beliefs persist regarding agriculture, health, and other aspects of human affairs. Lacking a knowledge of soils, of plant genetics, and other scientific principles of agriculture, the farmer sees a relationship between the phase of the moon at planting and the success of a potato crop, and a mother relates the illness of her child to the stare of a stranger who she concludes must have "an evil eye." Both science and magic depend on cause and effect. In magic, however, the relationship is by analogy, a fabrication of the human mind, whereas in science the relationship is in the natural world and can be experimentally determined. Thus, as greater scientific knowledge becomes available, magic and fortuitous relationships established by tradition slowly give way before scientific knowledge. But magic does not give way easily to science. People do not give up their traditional beliefs with ease even in the face of more rational explanations, because their own experience validates their view of the universe. They hesitate to take over the new and untried. Therefore new concepts, to be accepted, must be introduced in comprehensible terms of the worldview of the people concerned. Without a knowledge of this worldview, the social innovator may have difficulty in introducing what is considered rational thought.

Brazil, with its cultural heritage formed out of the fusion of the cultures of Europe, of Africa, and of the Native American, has its very distinctive set of folk beliefs and magical practices. The Amazon region, isolated for so long from the centers of technology and science, has retained many folk beliefs and magical practices from all three of those cultural backgrounds. There are medieval Iberian beliefs that have persisted long after they disappeared in Portugal. Numerous concepts and customs of Indigenous origin are retained today by the Amazon rural population. And despite the relatively few African slaves who came into the region, African custom has also influenced Amazon folk belief. In many cases the origin of a particular set of beliefs may be easily assigned to one of the three cultures. For example, the concepts and practices surrounding shamans, or pajés, as they are called in the Amazon, are clearly of Indigenous origin. But other elements and complexes seem to have their origin in more than one cultural heritage. They seem to be fusions of beliefs and custom from two or all three of these traditions and to have taken new forms distinctive of Amazon folk culture. The belief in *Matinta Perera*, a person who becomes a dreadful ghost at night, to cite one example, is probably a merging of the European belief in werewolves with Amazon native concepts of dangerous forest spirits. No matter what their origin, Amazon folk beliefs are an important aspect of the worldview of the rural inhabitant of the region. Such beliefs, and the customary behavior associated with them, often determine the acceptance or rejection of scientific concepts crucial to technological change in the Amazon Valley.

II

The people of Gurupá, like most other Brazilians, are largely Catholic. There is one Jewish family of Moroccan origin, the remnant of a group that settled there during the rubber boom. There are only five or six *crentes* (believers), as Protestants are called, among all the inhabitants of the community.[1] This homogeneity in religious faith is an important factor in creating solidarity and uniting people of various social classes and of all races. The regulations of the Roman Catholic Church provide people with ideal patterns of behavior for many life situations. Ideally, all people meet on an equal basis in the Church. In Gurupá, however, there is no resident priest. The sacraments of the Church are available to the members of the community only when the padre from an upriver community visits the town during the annual festivals of St. Anthony and St. Benedict. Confession, communion, mass, baptism, confirmation, marriage, and the last rites may be performed only on these occasions. Furthermore, the parish priest, when he visits the community, is an outsider. In many Amazon communities he is apt to be a foreign missionary—a Franciscan from Germany, a Salesian monk

---

[1]The 2010 census indicates this religious balance has changed somewhat. Roman and Orthodox Catholics make up 80 percent of the population, whereas *evangélicos* (principally conservative evangelical Christians, although the category in Gurupá also includes groups such as Jehovah Witness and Seventh Day Adventist) account for 12.8 percent (a much lower rate than the national average of 22.2 percent). Nonbelievers make up the remaining 7.2 percent (IBGE 2012). Despite this change, to date there has been no significant religious strife between the groups.

from Italy, a Dominican from France or, in recent years, a Maryknoll Father from the United States. The priest who visits Gurupá regularly is German, and his severe concept of Catholicism makes it difficult for the people to accept him fully. But even in the past, when the padre who attended the Gurupá church was a native Brazilian, there was considerable suspicion of him. Men suspect a priest's motives when he closets himself too long in confession with their daughters and their wives. They suspect him of using the funds of the Church for his own purposes. Thus in Gurupá, as in many Brazilian communities, the people have little connection with the official Church. Men, especially, are apt even to be antagonistic toward it. Although any padre is respected ex officio, and wields considerable power, priests are generally not strong leaders in most Brazilian communities, as they so often are in other Latin Catholic countries.[2]

The religious activities of Gurupá, as of many other Amazon communities, are left mainly in the hands of the people themselves. Leadership and direction are provided by local devotees. Dona Inacinha, the schoolteacher, cares for the church, leads evening prayers, and teaches the catechism to children. In the rural neighborhoods it is the religious brotherhoods, described in an earlier chapter, who organize and promote religious activities. In all Brazilian communities, there are always *beatas*, women devotees such as Dona Inacinha (and sometimes a few *beatos*, their male counterparts) who are the important religious leaders in their communities. Such women "live in church," people say. They are the religious, and often the moral, arbiters of their community. In Gurupá, Dona Inacinha is the treasurer for the Church, receiving donations to the saints. She gives most of her time and attention to religious affairs, even mixing religious instruction with her regular lessons in the school. Some people laugh and say that she is attempting to make up for sins committed when she was a young lady, and a few malicious gossips cast some doubts as to the nature of her relations with the padre. It was said, half seriously, that a former padre was the father of her second son. But Dona Inacinha, ignoring gossip, looks over her flock and complains of their lack of religion and of their "profane" religious activities.

The lack of control by the formal Church organization over the religious life of Gurupá does not mean that its people are unreligious.

---

[2]As will be shown in the next chapter, all this has changed in Gurupá with the spread of Liberation Theology and the rise of CEBs, which began in 1971.

On the contrary, they profess to be "good Catholics," and in their own way they are. But the content of their religion includes many local variations of archaic Iberian beliefs, which, although not in direct conflict with contemporary orthodox ideology, often overshadow many of its main precepts. God and Christ are worshiped, but more important in local religion are the Virgin and the saints. Furthermore, local devotion focuses on those saints whose images are found in the local church and in the small chapels in the rural neighborhoods. St. Anthony, St. Benedict, St. John, St. Apolonia, and the Virgin are identified by the people with their local images. Each saint is considered a local divinity. St. Anthony and St. Benedict, whose images share the main altar in the town church, have even been seen walking at night in the streets. Nhenjuca's father told him of seeing the two saints strolling one night under the mango trees of First Street. They were dressed as monks, and they walked in the direction of the church. He saw them enter. A light went on inside and then the church was dark again. The next day he went to the church and inspected the images; both St. Anthony and St. Benedict had sand on their feet. On another occasion a soldier saw two men walking in the street late one night. When they did not halt at his command, he fired. They did not stop, and he recognized them as the saints. The next day the keeper of the church found a bullet hole in the image of St. Anthony.[3] Other images of the same saints in nearby towns are not thought to be identical. The church in Arumanduba has a St. Benedict, but "it is not the same as ours," said an Gurupá informant. "It may be the son of the one that stands in our church. Ours is a pretão [a big black], and he never smiles as does the little one" (in the Arumanduba church).[4]

---

[3]These stories are told as passionately in 2013 as they were in 1948.

[4]The story of St. Benedict's life, as told in Gurupá, pictures him as of dark skin and as "a slave in the house of our Lord"—of the same color and status of the ancestors of most of the lower-class people. One story has it that Benedict worked in the Lord's kitchen and served the table for the Lord and the other saints. He was sorry for the many beggars who came to the kitchen door, and he gave them bread. The other saints told the Lord that Benedict was stealing. The Lord hid himself behind a door, and when he saw Benedict go out with a parcel containing bread for the beggars, he ordered him to open it. Benedict was frightened and said that his parcel contained flowers, and when he opened it, the bread had changed to flowers. The Lord was pleased. "He was a good employer, and he lectured the other saints for gossiping."

To the people of Gurupá, the saints are protectors, benevolent powers to whom they may go for help and protection. Adultery, theft, murder, and other crimes are not punished by the saints, and people seldom feel the need to ask forgiveness for such sins. These are matters controlled by the law and by public opinion, and they are judged by secular standards. The proper attitude toward the saints is *respeito* (respect); and the only sin punished by them is "lack of respect." By this, people mean that the saint must be offered prayers, must have his or her day celebrated in the appropriate manner, and must be offered vows that must be fulfilled. No one in Gurupá could remember when a saint had punished anyone for breaking one of the Ten Commandments, but everyone could remember instances when punishment was meted out for not fulfilling a vow. The vow [also known as a *promessa* or promise] is the principal means of securing the saint's protection or aid in a crisis. In a sense even the *ladainhas* (evening prayers), the processions, and the other collective ceremonies carried out in honor of the saint are vows. The community, the neighborhood, and the brotherhood of devotees have a standing vow to perform them to ensure the welfare of the group. Without these ceremonies the protection of their saint would be withdrawn. Most vows in Gurupá, however, take the form of individual contracts. Devotees promise, for example, that if their children are cured of a serious disease they will offer a novena or will serve as judge for the saint's festival day. One man promised St. Lucia that he would offer her a novena each year if she would help him stop drinking. He asked that she strike him blind if he ever again touched alcohol.

Another example was related by Nhenjuca. When Nhenjuca was a small boy, he suffered from a large open sore caused by an insect bite. His mother, a very devout follower of St. Benedict, offered Nhenjuca as a "slave of St. Benedict" if he got well. The open infection had resisted cure for three years; but six weeks after his mother's vow, Nhenjuca was cured. As a slave of St. Benedict, Nhenjuca must all his life offer a day's work each year for the saint, performing such tasks as repairing the church or even cleaning the pavilion where the dancing is held on St. Benedict's day. In Nhenjuca's youth, the slaves of St. Benedict were subjected to rigid discipline. If they did not work or pray to their saint, they were ordered by the leaders of the brotherhood to kneel with bare knees on a jagged rock to ask penitence. To offer a son or a daughter as a slave of St. Benedict was a very serious vow in the past, and it is rare nowadays.

One seldom hears in Gurupá of the more exotic and dramatic vows that are so common in other parts of Brazil. In the arid northeastern region of the country, it is common for people to vow to walk hundreds of miles, sometimes as long as for twenty days, to visit famous and miraculous shrines such as those of the Born Jesus da Lapa or of São Francisco de Canindé. Individuals of high social status make a vow to walk barefooted in the candle procession of the Virgin of Nazareth in Belém. They sometimes crawl on their knees up the 365 steps leading to the Church of Our Lady of the Rock in Rio de Janeiro. In Gurupá vows are apt to be less extravagant. One vows to make a donation, to serve as a judge for a festival, to pray a novena, or to offer an *ex-voto*, a present to the saint in the form of an effigy of the organ of the human body that the saint has cured.[5] In Belém and in other large centers of northern Brazil, replicas of arms, legs, heads, fingers, breasts, and even internal organs are cast in wax to be offered to a saint in fulfillment of a vow. In Gurupá such replicas are carved out of wood. Until the German missionary priest had them removed as profane, carvings of various parts of the human body were found on the altar of the Gurupá church.[6]

Delinquency in fulfilling a vow arouses the saint's anger. It shows lack of respect. The saint expects a return for favors and protection. Instances are told in Gurupá of people who were punished because they did not carry out their vows. João Mendes, for example, promised to give his own weight in crude rubber to St. Benedict if he were cured of his headaches. João Mendes was cured; but the next year, when the *folia* came to his trading post asking for donations for St. Benedict, he modified the terms of his vow. He said that he had promised only the "weight of the saint" (i.e., the image) in rubber. No one questioned João Mendes' statement. But when the image of St. Benedict was placed on the scales with the rubber that João gave, it was found to weigh as much as João Mendes himself. The saint had performed a miracle.

---

[5]In 2011 I observed several individuals walking on their knees for part of the processional route for Saint Benedict. A caretaker assisted (patterned on the caretakers of Belém's Círio—the largest religious procession in the world), sliding portions of a cardboard box under the devotees' knees as they progressed down the street.

[6]In 2013 ex-votos are still commonly offered to Saint Benedict. The Church stores many of these in a closet to the rear of the Church. There is some talk of creating a museum in the Church to display the pieces—a very different attitude than the one taken by the priest in 1948.

FIGURE 7.1 | *Ex-votos offered in fulfillment of vows (promessas) to Saint Benedict.*
Photograph by C. Wagley 1948.

St. Benedict had forced João Mendes to fulfill his original vow. Another man, who had promised the saint a steer, presented the smallest and thinnest from among his herd. As the canoe carrying the image left the ranch, the strongest beef in the herd broke away and started swimming after it. The members of the *folia* took the second steer into their canoe. They understood that St. Benedict was dissatisfied and had punished the man by making him give two animals instead of one.[7]

---

[7]These stories of the saints' wrath have continued through the decades. In the 1980s the owner of one of the main riverboats serving Gurupá—*Fé em Deus* (Faith in God)—made a point of sailing in the Meia Lua as payment for Saint Benedict's protection throughout the year. However, participating in the fluvial procession meant losing a week's worth of revenue because the boat could not make its usual run. To make more money, the owner skipped the procession one December. The next year, the boat was struck by a series of mechanical problems causing the owner considerable financial hardship. Everyone reasoned it was the saint's punishment for not sending the boat to the Meia Lua. The next year Fé em Deus led the fluvial procession, and continued to do so until the boat no longer made the trip past Gurupá.

Sometimes the saints are not so mild in punishing broken vows. They send sickness, they cause damage to one's garden, and they send bad luck in business dealings. Sometimes the slighted saint sends a warning. Once when the image of St. Benedict was being sent on a large river steamer to Abaeté, where there are specialists in repainting images, the ship's captain placed the saint in the hold as he would any baggage. Shortly after leaving Gurupá, the pilot found that he had no control over the rudder. The steamer was caught sidewise in the river current, and the crew felt certain that the boat would crash into the bank. A man from Gurupá, however, remembered the saint and informed the captain of the saint's powers. The image of St. Benedict was hurriedly removed from the ship's hold and placed on an improvised altar in one of the cabins. The boat began to steer accurately at once.[8] The saints cure ills, give good crops, protect the rubber collector on the trail, and safeguard boatmen against the dangers of navigation. They help people find lost objects, aid young women in securing husbands, and return wandering fathers to their wives and children. They perform a multitude of other benevolent deeds, but they are also jealous of their rights, expecting a return for their favors and protection.

As in all Latin American communities, certain saints are believed to have special attributes and powers. St. Anthony is a *casamenteiro* (a marrying saint) who is especially appealed to by women wanting a husband. St. Christopher, as elsewhere, protects travelers. St. Thomas favors the farmer. St. Apolonia is a patroness of teeth, aiding people with toothaches. Our Lady of Sorrows protects women in childbirth, and St. John and St. Peter are favorable to lovers. St. Benedict, as mentioned earlier, is the special protector of rubber gatherers, and each year many rubber collectors donate their first day's harvest to their protector. In addition, almost every individual in Gurupá has a saint who has proved to be especially indulgent to him or to his family. Each household has at least one small image, or sometimes a large picture, of the saint or saints who are its special devotion. Our Lady of Sorrows is Maria Profeta's. She appeared to her one night in a dream when

---

[8]In 2007 Benedito Dias, a retired manioc farmer and son of Dona Sebá the midwife, told me that working on one's Saint's day can be hazardous. He had an acquaintance that did such, going to his roça instead of honoring the saint. On that day a tree fell on the poor soul and killed him. Benedito reasoned it was punishment for not revering the Saint.

numerous families in Gurupá were ill with fever. Because of Our Lady's protection, neither Maria nor her family became ill during the epidemic. As a result, Maria and her friends have organized a small brotherhood to honor her. Nhenjuca has the special protection of St. Lucia, the saint who helped him break away from rum. Many people feel that their special protector is the saint of their birthday or the saint whose name they carry. In fact, people name their children after the saint who they feel is their special guardian. In Gurupá the number of Beneditos and Beneditas attests to the fame of St. Benedict. Indeed, even though they are devoted to another saint, everyone in Gurupá turns now and again to St. Benedict. Rather than St. Anthony, the official patron of Gurupá, people feel that it is St. Benedict who really protects the community, and his fame extends far and wide. Stories of St. Benedict's cures are legion. The number of presents that appear before the image, the amount of the donations offered each year, and the influx of people to attend St. Benedict's festival are evidence of the widespread devotion to the saint in the entire Lower Amazon. Not a day passes in Gurupá without the noise of skyrockets, set off by a passing boat, in honor of St. Benedict.[9]

III

In addition to this body of Catholic belief, the people of Gurupá believe in supernatural powers and perform magical practices of aboriginal origin. The Portuguese learned how to survive in this new land and how to exploit the strange environment from the native peoples, but in the process they acquired many aboriginal beliefs. These were perpetuated in the new culture formed as Indigenous groups were detribalized and dominated by the newcomers. Thus the worldview of the Amazon mestizo and the ribeirinho came to be an intricate blend of native and European ideology. And it is not surprising that those aspects of native religion that dealt with the forest, the mighty river, the fauna, the flora, and the activities of humans in exploiting their environment are today a part of the folk belief of Gurupá and other small Amazon communities.

---

[9]In 2013 boats and barges passing by Gurupá on the Amazon River continue to send off skyrockets to honor St. Benedict.

The religious system of the Tupí tribes who survived conquest and who influenced Amazon folk culture so strongly, did not stress highly organized rituals led by a priesthood, as did the religions of the more complex native peoples of Mexico and Peru.[10] Theirs was a loosely constructed religion without a well-defined pantheon or a highly systematic religious ideology. The origin of natural phenomena and of useful arts was ascribed to a series of mythical culture heroes. One of them, Mairá-Monan, taught humankind the techniques of agriculture; and another, Monan, created the sky, the earth, the birds, and the animals. Still another, called Tupan, who was later identified by Christian missionaries with the Christian God, was a secondary figure accounting for lightning, thunder, and rain. These ancestor figures were not worshiped as active supernatural forces. Instead, a series of forest spirits and ghosts of the dead were believed to bring bad luck, sickness, defeat in war, and general misfortune; and it was this category of supernaturals who had to be pleased, placated, and controlled. One of them, Yurupara, described as a dangerous forest goblin, was equated by Christian missionaries with the Devil. He was believed to attract hunters deeper and deeper into the forest until they were irreparably lost. Another was Curupira, a small human-like creature with feet turned backward, who protected forest animals and punished hunters. The Tupían peoples were deathly afraid of the spirits of the dead, and believed that they took the form of animals—a toad, a bird, or a lizard—and roamed abroad at night.

These native religious beliefs clashed inevitably with the ideology of Christianity, which offered other explanations for the origin of things. The missionaries set about eradicating pagan beliefs and teaching the people the orthodox Catholic concepts. The names of the Indigenous culture heroes disappeared and in their place came God, the Devil, and the saints. But the European colonists and missionaries of the seventeenth and eighteenth centuries themselves believed in werewolves, witches, and demons; their own view of the supernatural world was in many respects similar to that of the Native Americans.

---

[10]As mentioned in Chapter 2, the Brazilian Amazon was likely the home of a number of socially complex chiefdoms. But during conquest, disease, warfare, and enslavement reduced their numbers by more than 90 percent in most estimates. The Indigenous religious beliefs that survive in today's belief system can only be at best a remnant of the once multifaceted belief system of this devastated population.

Because the forest demons and malevolent ghosts referred to a new and strange world and did not directly contradict orthodox Catholic ideology, it was not difficult for the colonists and the missionaries to add dangerous and fearful entities of the forest and the river to their own cargo of magical belief. The new demons and ghosts, as described by the Indigenous populations, corresponded roughly with those of medieval Iberian belief. Thus the native and the European worldviews reinforced each other and blended together to form the worldview of Amazon folk culture.

The Tupí-speaking Indigenous populations of the Amazon forest depended on their shamans, whom they called *pays*, to protect them against the demons, to cure sickness, and to relieve them of the misfortunes caused by the spirits. These shamans were characterized by personal traits that set them off from the laity. They are said to have been highly excitable and of nervous temperament. In communicating with the spirits that they controlled, they went into trance states, even into cataleptic seizures. These trances were induced by swallowing large quantities of tobacco smoke and by dancing and singing to the rhythm of a gourd rattle. The Indigenous populations believed that all disease had a magical or supernatural cause. Sickness resulted from punishment by a forest spirit or by a ghost or from the malevolent magic of sorcerers. The shamans cured such ills by massage, by blowing tobacco smoke over the patient's body, and by sucking out the small object (a bone, a stone, or even a lizard) induced in the body of the patient by the offended supernatural. Shamans had tremendous powers over their people. After 1500 there were several revivalistic movements among the Tupían tribes led by shamans who promised a return to "the mythical land of the culture heroes," where people need not work and where they were assured of eternal youth (Métraux 1927:1–45). Several groups migrated up the Amazon to points above the mouth of the Rio Negro to escape the European and to search for this mythical land.

Shamans may even today be found among the mixed populations of the Amazon. In fact, they practice today among the Amazon rural population throughout most of the Valley. They control, as in native times, ghosts and the dangerous spirits of the forest. People have continued to believe in the supernaturals, and it is to be expected that religious practitioners able to cope with these powers would be necessary. They are found in Santarém; Óbidos is a well-known center for them; and even in the working-class districts of Belém and Manaus men calling themselves pajés practice a mixture of aboriginal and modern spiritualistic belief. No pajés live and work today in the town of Gurupá, but there are several in the surrounding rural neighborhoods. People from town sometimes seek their advice and ask them to perform a cure. Sometimes they persuade a pajé to come secretly to town. Secrecy is necessary because a physician stationed in Gurupá several years ago undertook a campaign against the pajés, charging them with practicing medicine without a license. One of them was jailed. As a result, the pajés nowadays practice secretly, in fear of the authorities. In turn, the latter claim that the pajés are "superstitious barbarians and uneducated," and criminals to be driven out of the community. Most people deny they have ever sought the help of a pajé. Still, a few pajés who live in the rural neighborhoods of Gurupá are well-known figures, and they are always busy. A municipal official was known to have gone to one of them for a cure. In fact, the pajé is feared and respected both by the town and by rural people, and in general the authorities close their eyes to his activities.

None of the shamans living in the Gurupá community, however, is a great pajé. The great ones, everybody in Gurupá agrees, lived about a generation ago. They were called *sacacas*. Such famous men as Joaquim Sacaca, who was said to have been a Native American born on the Upper Rio Negro; Fortunato Pombo, who lived in the neighborhood of Jocojó; and Lucio, who died about ten years ago, were pajé sacacas.[11] These powerful shamans had numerous spirits with whom they were on a familiar basis, and who helped them in their cures; they were also able to travel enormous distances under water and to remain under water for days, even weeks. Their capacity for traveling and remaining under water distinguished these *sacacas* from the less powerful pajés who serve the people of Gurupá nowadays. People say that the *sacacas* wore the skin of a giant water snake (*cobra grande*) during their travels under water. They each had particular places on the riverbank, called "ports," from which they embarked into the enchanted kingdom in the depths of the Amazon River or on their underwater travels. The port, for example, of Joaquim Sacaca was a log covered with thorns on which only he could walk barefooted. Another *sacaca* used a hollow log as

---

[11]I do not know a translation for the term sacaca, although it is a name given to an Indigenous tribe that once inhabited the Island of Marajó, from which famous shamans may have come.

a tunnel to enter the water. Fortunato Pombo frequently visited other towns. He traveled from Gurupá to Santarém in a few minutes, and in an instant he would make an underwater trip to towns further down the Amazon. Joaquim Sacaca would often hear Luandinha, a female spirit said to have been a large water snake, call him, and he would disappear to spend a few hours with her in the depths of the Amazon. People saw bubbles rising to the surface as he descended to the bottom to join her. The spirits addressed Joaquim as "Father," and people said that the pajé *sacacas* did not die. According to local folklore, they lived forever in an enchanted kingdom under water just as the shamans of the Tupían tribesmen lived on in a mythical land in the west.

It is said in Gurupá that great pajés may announce their future capacities by crying aloud in the womb. As a small child a pajé is unlike other children; he or she—for women may also be pajés—suffers from tantrums and seizures. Such individuals show early signs of supernatural powers. As a boy, Fortunato Pombo loved to wander along the riverbank shooting at shrimp and small fish with his toy bow and arrow. One day he disappeared. His mother found his shirt hanging on a pole close to the pier, and she was certain that he had drowned. She wept for three days, but at the end of the third day Pombo appeared again. At first he would not tell of his experiences. Then he told of the companion spirits he had seen in the depths of the water, and of the food, and of the large, beautifully painted *tauari* (cigar) that he had been offered, but that he did not accept for fear of never returning.[12] By twelve, Fortunato had already performed a cure. One day, while paying a visit with his mother to a dying boy, Fortunato announced that the boy would not die. He picked a few herbs in the back yard and ordered his mother to prepare a medicine for the boy to drink. Remembering Fortunato's earlier visit to the depths, the mother did as he requested. Shortly afterward the sick boy recovered, and thereafter Fortunato's fame as a pajé and curer spread.

Other pajés do not announce themselves quite so early. Often the parents of children who show signs of possessing such powers do not want them to become pajés and take preventive steps. They may take

---

[12]The Orpheus in Hades theme involving the danger of taking anything in the underworld for fear of not being allowed to return reoccurs in all stories told of the underwater visits of Gurupá shamans.

a child who shows such symptoms to a pajé and ask that he dispel the spirits attracted to the child. Others, who wish the child to become a pajé, take the child to a well-known pajé who will establish the relationship between the spirits and the child. If one of these two procedures is not adopted, children showing such symptoms may not be able to withstand the spirits, and they may die. Nowadays people profess, at least, that they do not want their children to become pajés. The pajé is persecuted by the authorities, called "pagan" by the padre, and publicly criticized by the upper class. But often the individual cannot escape. Dona Benta, for example, told of her daughter who became a pajé despite the efforts of an old pajé to send the spirits away. The pajé was not certain of the results of his cure and warned the parents to watch the girl carefully when she reached the age of about fifteen. The girl led a normal life until she was sixteen, when her father died. The shock caused her to take to her hammock, crying and moaning in grief. Then, filtering through the moaning of her daughter, Dona Benta heard a man's voice saying that his name was Nerto, a spirit from the depths. Other voices joined that of Nerto, and speaking through the girl each one announced its name. Some of them were females and others were males. Afterward, the daughter told of conversations she had with her spirits. She was able to foretell the future and she performed several miraculous cures. People advised Dona Benta to take her daughter to a well-known pajé for instruction, for it was dangerous to deal with spirits without knowing how. Dona Benta did not allow her to receive full instructions from the pajé for fear of the police and in fear of public opinion. People are convinced that the girl's death several years later was caused by "being taken away by her spirits."

Sometimes the symptoms appear later in life. Elíos Veiga told us of his surprise when his eldest daughter suddenly showed such symptoms when she was over twenty years old. The young woman had been having serious headaches. At night she cried and sometimes moaned in her sleep. Several praying women and blessers, women who add to these methods by a variety of herbal remedies, had tried to cure her headaches, but none was able to help her. Then one night she rose from her hammock and ran pell-mell toward the river. She would have plunged in if her father and brothers had not held her back. Her compulsive behavior occurred several times before Veiga decided to call a pajé. The pajé was able to send the spirits away temporarily, but they soon returned. The young woman soon married, moving away to

Belém, and there she became a pajé. Rumors from Belém have it that Maria José, as she is called, is now a well-known pajé and spiritualist medium in a working-class district of that city.

Although there have been many changes since aboriginal times, modern Amazon shamanism shows the remarkable persistence of Indigenous religion despite more than three centuries of Christian influence. Like the Indigenous shamans before them, modern Amazon pajés have a retinue of spirit helpers; they have powers of divination, they become possessed and fall into a trance, and they cure. Nowadays their friendly supernatural powers are mainly "spirits from the depths of the river" with modern Brazilian names, a saint, or an "Indian" (i.e., the ghost of an IIndigenous shaman) rather than the old Tupían demons of the forest or ghosts. Today alcohol is used, together with tobacco, to stimulate the trance. Pajés may dance and sing holding a sacred rattle in their hand, as the Tupían pay did; or they may make use of a bunch of red parrot feathers, a wand of herbs, or even a crucifix for the same purpose. But the old techniques of curing—namely, the process of blowing clouds of tobacco smoke over the patient's body, of massaging, and, in the end, of pretending to suck a small object out of the patient's body—remain essentially the same.

One of the members of our research party was treated by a pajé named Satiro Ronato de Lima (see Figure 6.1—the man to the far left playing the raspador or scraper). Satiro is not a powerful pajé. He has not been practicing many years. Ascendino and Maria de Lourdes, both of whom also live within the Gurupá community, are better known. Satiro's methods are not as traditional as those of the better known pajés, but he began his cure in the traditional manner. He prepared a table by covering a small box with a white cloth. Then he placed on the table several long cigars prepared from locally grown tobacco rolled in the bark of the *tauari* tree. Next he fumigated a glass by blowing clouds of smoke into it; then he filled it with white rum. Satiro then asked his patient to lie in a hammock stretched near his table, and he began to sing, calling each of his spirit helpers by name. Suddenly one of them possessed him, and his voice and his posture immediately changed. The spirit helper was obviously a female, because he began to sing in high falsetto and his movements were dainty.

At this point Satiro might well have made use of his divinatory powers, for pajés, while they are in a trance, announce who their next patients will be and may even read the mind of the patient being treated. Ascendino, for example, read the thoughts of one of his patients: "You believe that I am ignorant and you do not believe in me," he said. The patient was embarrassed but admitted that what Ascendino said was true. Satiro, however, did not make use of such powers. He began to smoke, to drink frequently of the rum, and to sing in the voice of his "companion," who, he announced, was Mariquinha—a female from the depths. He left us and went down the path from the house to the nearby stream. There, standing in the water he called other companion spirits. Though Satiro did not use a rattle, he held a wand of twigs in his hand; with this he made the sign of the cross over himself and over his patient when he returned. He blew tobacco smoke over the patient's body and massaged the patient's back where the latter had complained of pains. Ascendino or Maria de Lourdes would have sucked with their mouths near the painful area. Finally, Satiro announced his diagnosis. The pains were not the result of witchcraft performed by an enemy; thus he did not have a beetle or a small piece of bone to show. (On another occasion a pajé announced that he had removed a beetle placed in his patient's body by witchcraft, blew into a glass filled with rum, and then quickly covered the glass with a saucer. The next morning a large black beetle was found floating in the rum.) Satiro, however, said that his patient's pains were from natural causes— an *ataque de ramo frio* (attack of cold twigs), and he recommended a special diet and a series of herbal remedies. Finally, he dismissed his spirit helpers and returned to a normal state. Afterward he complained of being exhausted.

Satiro is still learning his profession. Though he wanted a rattle very badly, he told us that first he must have the power to travel under water. In the depths he expects to receive his maraca (rattle) from the very mouth of a giant water snake. A more powerful pajé told Satiro that he also needs a "virgin mirror"—one into which no one has ever looked—so that he could see his spirit companions without danger to himself while traveling under water. He has tried unsuccessfully several times to buy such a mirror, but someone always looks over his shoulder as the box containing them is opened in the store. Satiro is certain that he will one day be a strong pajé. He apologized because he could not as yet distinguish all his "companions" one from another. "In the beginning," he said, "it is like a forest in which one knows there are rubber trees. But, because a trail has not yet been opened, one cannot see the rubber trees or how to get to them. Later on, when a trail has been opened, one knows them tree by tree." He believes that he will one day be able to travel underwater and visit the great water snake and that he will have an "Indian" among his companion spirits as does Maria de Lourdes and Ascendino. Perhaps Satiro will even become a *sacaca* with all the prestige of those great men of a generation ago.

The modern shamans of Gurupá have been influenced by Catholicism and, as the reader might suspect, to some extent by spiritualism, which is practiced in the large cities of Belém and Manaus. Yet most pajés make a distinction between spiritualism and true *pajélança* (shamanism). They say that the spiritualistic mediums from the city work with "spirits of the air" vaguely thought of as disembodied souls, whereas the true pajé works with "beings of the water." The pajés do not distinguish so sharply between Catholicism and shamanistic belief. In curing they freely use Catholic and pseudo-Catholic prayers; they make the sign of the cross; and a saint may be included among "companion" spirits.

All pajés protest with great vigor that they are good Catholics and stanch devotees of their particular patron saint. But in the Amazon Valley, unlike the situation among the Indigenous populations of Peru, Guatemala, and Mexico, there has not been a thorough fusion between Catholicism and the remnants of the native religious rites. Instead, belief in pajés and their spirits exists simultaneously with Catholicism and the cult of the saints. The two sets of belief, shamanism and folk Catholicism, do not oppose each other. Each serves a different purpose. The saints protect the general welfare of the community, and through the mechanism of vows, they give favors and even cure. Shamanism deals with magical influences; it cures illness due to malignant supernaturals and to witchcraft.[13]

---

[13]In 2013 only one "pajé" exists in Gurupá—in the rural neighborhood of Carrazedo. He is actually a curandeiro and CEB leader in the Catholic Church who uses the nickname of Pajé.

As Wagley suggested, most of the traits and practices associated with the pajés of old are now part of the repertoire of Umbandistas and Spiritualists who interact with or are possessed by Indigenous sprits. People in Gurupá are aware of the differences between Umbanda, Spiritism, and true pajalança and will tell you there are no true pajés in Gurupá anymore.

IV
....

Like the beliefs surrounding the pajé, the series of dangerous super-naturals who inhabit the forest and the river, about which people in Gurupá tell, are also mainly of Indigenous origin. As in shamanism, old Indigenous religious belief has been modified by, and fused with, analogous European concepts that the Portuguese brought to the Amazon. A few people in Gurupá protest that these spirits and super-naturals do not exist, particularly the upper class, who have heard out-siders scoff at such ideas, calling them superstitions and "the nonsense of the caboclo." Especially in the presence of city people, the more so-phisticated members of the Gurupá community are ashamed and pre-tend to laugh at such ideas. But in reality almost everyone in Gurupá, even most of the upper class, retains some credence in these dangerous supernaturals. When it was reported, for example, that the giant snake with luminous eyes had been seen in the river near Gurupá, none of the upper-class doubters would go out in a canoe at night. Far from being old superstitions now discarded, belief in these old Indigenous-European supernaturals is alive in Gurupá today.

Many of these powers are related directly to hunting and fishing—to the exploitation of the natural environment. This is true of Anhangá,[14] a ghost or demon who hunts people in the forest, according to the reports of hunters and rubber gatherers. Anhangá appears to them generally as an *inhambu*, a forest fowl, but it may take the form of almost any animal. However, because the Anhangá so often takes the form of an inhambu, the latter is considered *visagento* (magically malignant). The only differ-ence between the normal inhambu and the inhambu Anhangá is its actions and the white down breast feathers and the red head feathers characteristic of the Anhangá. Both Jorge Palheta and Nhenjuca have met up with Anhangá in the form of the inhambu fowl. Jorge Palheta and some companions were camped deep within a forest cutting timber when they heard a thin whistle, which came nearer. Finally, it seemed to issue from right above their heads inside their hut. Jorge Palheta recognized the sound as that of the Anhangá. He sprinkled himself and his companions with holy water, frightening the Anhangá away.[15]

----

[14]Anhangá in língua geral and the native Tupí language means "ghost" or "shadow."
[15]He did not explain just why he was equipped with holy water, but men do often take a bottle of holy water with them on long trips just for such contingencies.

Nhenjuca's experience was more according to pattern. He had been hunting inhambu fowls with unusual success. Each afternoon, after working in his garden, he would hunt for a few hours, almost always killing a bird or two. One afternoon, however, he saw an inhambu Anhangá; before he recognized it, he shot. The bird fell on Nhenjuca's head, and it was so heavy that he was knocked unconscious. He was lucky, he told us, that the Anhangá did not "steal his shadow," which would have made him very ill. Nhenjuca gave up hunting. His narrow escape thoroughly frightened him.

Like the inhambu, monkeys, especially the guariba, or howler monkey (*Alouatta caraya*), are to be feared in the forest. The guariba is also a *bicho visagento* (magically malignant animal). Certain guaribas, with the same appearance as any normal animal, have powers to "steal a person's shadow." Antonio Dias, a rubber gatherer, told of an encounter with a guariba monkey that was malignant. One day Antonio heard his name called as he walked alone deep in the forest. He turned to see a large howler monkey advancing on him. Antonio fled in panic. Women are especially afraid of the guariba, who they believe will invade their houses to rape them. Many people believe that such malignant animals are the same as the "mother of the animal" (*mãe de bicho*), a supernatural that protects the animals of each species against hunters or fishermen who kill too many of them. These mothers punish hunters or fishers by stealing their shadows.

The most famous of the forest spirits, however, is the Curupira, a small human-like creature whose feet are turned backward. Curupiras live deep in the forest, from which their long shrill cries are often heard. They are said to be especially fond of rum and tobacco. They attract hunters deeper and deeper into the forest, until they are lost and never return. The Curupira can imitate a human voice. They call out to rubber gatherers or hunters who believe the voice to be that of a companion and thus are drawn off their paths. Everyone in Gurupá knows of the Curupira, but no one in town has ever encountered one.[16]

---

[16]In the 2010s we interviewed several people who testified to seeing the Curupira. For example, Filomena Gonçalves Dias recounted how one day she and her husband Benedito were walking to their roça on Igarapé Itapereira when one came out of the forest and jumped in front of her. She said "It was a little thing, short, black, with real hard hair (kinky), but hairless skin—it was naked. It was like a person, but it was not." Filomena yelled and it disappeared. Pajé also related his encounter with the

In the rural neighborhoods a few men have heard them call out in the forest, but no one has actually seen one. However, people tell many stories of their grandfathers meeting the Curupira face to face. Elíos Veiga told one, as he heard it from his grandfather, who was already an old man when Veiga was a youth. In those days the Igarapé Arinoá was bordered by an impenetrable forest. It was "a place of Curupiras." According to the story, a newcomer arrived in the Gurupá community. Elíos' grandfather told him of the wild game that might be found in the upper reaches of the Igarapé Arinoá, and the man decided to go hunting there. He went armed with a "cross of holy wax" hung about his neck and a supply of holy wax in his ammunition bag. Later the hunter told of his encounter. As soon as he beached his canoe on the first night, he saw the Curupira. It was a dark creature "no bigger than a child," and "like a small caboclinho" (i.e., like a little Indian). But the Curupira could not come close to the hunter, for the holy wax repelled him and kept him at a distance. The Curupira asked the man to remove the cross from his neck; and when the hunter did so, the Curupira closed in. The stranger knocked the Curupira to the ground with a hard blow, but with a simple move the Curupira threw the hunter so high into the air that his leg was broken when he fell. The hunter grabbed his ammunition bag, which contained holy wax, and the act saved him. The Curupira was made harmless, but he did put the stranger to sleep with a powerful *catinga* (bad smell). When the man awoke he was floating downstream in his canoe, a magic arrow by his side. From that day forth, the hunter was an excellent shot, never missing his target. Since those times, the Curupiras have left the Igarapé Arinoá. As people have moved in, they have retreated deeper into the forest.

Curupira. He said in truth he did not know if it was a curupira or a spirit because, he explained, at one time it is a curupira and at another time it is a spirit. Pajé continued, "The ancestors used to say that deep in the forest there are springs of the rivers where you can find a mother of animals (*mãe de bichos*), and the mother of that is the Curupira. When people go into the forest, near these springs, they hear its strong shrill whistle and shouts, people yelling without anyone answering. You hear it hitting pieces of wood together, thump, thump, thump. And when you go to the sound, there is nothing there." Pajé maintains he has seen it twice in the form of a person. For him, it exists in Gurupá.

In the 2009 survey 47.5 percent of respondents said they believe the Curupira existed (Pace and Hinote 2013:173–74).

Unlike the Curupira, the giant snake (*cobra grande*) is still seen even by Gurupá townspeople. The giant snake is believed to be one of the constrictors, a *sucuriju* or a *giboia*, which has grown larger and heavier than normal and has supernatural qualities. A giant snake may be 135 or 165 feet in length. It is so large that "the furrows which its body leaves as it crawls about become creeks." Such giant snakes are believed to live in the deepest parts of the river. Thus many people think of them as the *boiúna*, the giant snake of which some pajés have spoken. Sometimes a giant snake appears on the surface for everyone to see. For an entire week during our 1948 visit to Gurupá, no one dared fish at night because a giant snake had appeared on two successive nights in the river just in front of the town. Two fishermen had actually seen its great luminous eyes closing in on them as they sat in their canoes. They went to their hammocks sick with fright. Giant snakes usually appear on stormy nights during the winter or rainy season. "Its eyes shine like the spotlights on a river steamer." In fact, people say that sometimes a giant snake becomes "an enchanted river boat." Such a ship was seen several times by Marinho de Abreu Pae, who was the *trapicheiro* (public dock keeper) in Gurupá for many years. A "*cobra grande navio*" (giant-snake ship) came directly upriver toward the public pier with all lights ablaze. When it came close it turned back downstream. Another informant, a rubber gatherer who was traveling to Gurupá in a canoe, confirmed Marinho's statements. He was resting at an old abandoned *barracão*, he explained. He heard the beat of a river boat's engines. Then he saw the ship approaching the abandoned pier. It was a big boat all lighted up, and "a man in red clothes" was standing at the steering wheel (probably the Devil). Then suddenly it sailed away in the direction from which it had come. The connection between the enchanted ship and the giant snake was never fully explained by the people of Gurupá, but all of them felt that they were manifestations of the same dangerous power.[17]

---

[17]In 2012 José Sousa, son of Edgar and Isabel, who is an agroextractivist living on Marajoí River, commented that although he knows science says the cobra grande doesn't exist, he and his family have seen it. He said it was about five thirty in the afternoon, his mother was picking lice out of her granddaughter's head on the dock, and his father was inside writing. He went on the dock to talk to his mother and then looked to the river where he saw a tree trunk floating downstream with something on it. He told his mother, "If someone were hunting deer, there is a deer right there passing by." He said he was just fooling around with her, thinking it was just a tree

Another dangerous apparition is Matinta Perera. Whereas Curupira and Anhangá inhabit the deep forest and giant snakes are of the river, Matinta Perera appears in the town itself. It is appropriate, therefore, that the beliefs relating to Matinta Perera are mainly European in origin. The description of Matinta Perera is much like the Old World concept of werewolves. Some say in Gurupá that Matinta Perera is always a woman, but others say that it also appears in male form. It is agreed that people become Matinta Pereras through their own destiny. Such people are unaware of their fate at first. But then they begin to have nightmares, grow thin, and take on a yellowish skin color. Matinta Perera appears at night in the streets or near people's homes, always accompanied by a coal black bird that is Matinta Perera's pet. Some people say that they "leave their heads at home when they go out." All people are afraid of it because it "steals your shadow," bringing illness and even death. One may capture such an apparition, however, by reciting prayers and locking the door as Matinta Perera approaches. The next morning, the person who is Matinta Perera will be found seated in human form on the doorstep. Or one may attack Matinta Perera with switches. The next day the person will have welts on the face. One of our friends in Gurupá claims to have captured one by the first method about ten years ago. The young woman who appeared on our friend's doorstep the next morning was arrested and jailed by the police.

The freshwater dolphin, which inhabits the Amazon Basin, is called the *boto*; is also enchanted and is thought to be endowed with magical and supernatural powers. The people of the Amazon have

---

trunk. So Isabel looked and said it isn't a deer but a tapir. He looked again and said, "no it is not a tapir, it is a snake." They called for Edgar to come with a gun. José continued: "The head of it was enormous and we noticed its teeth poking out of its mouth like horns." The snake submerged before Edgar could get off a shot, making no waves whatsoever. "Even though science says the cobra grande does not exist," José reiterated, "we all saw it."

In another example in 2012, Giancarlos Pessoa, an 11-year-old school boy in Gurupá, told of a cobra grande that appeared a couple of days before on the Igarapé Bacá where it enters the Amazon River. He said the snake almost ate a man and two children who were in a canoe. He said, "They escaped, but the man was so scared they had to take him to the hospital to calm him down. This same snake passed in from of the river boat Rodrigues Alves just yesterday with lots of people seeing it. It was an enormous snake."

In the 2009 survey, 82.2 percent of respondents expressed a belief in the existence of the cobra grande (Pace and Hinote 2013:173).

noted a series of physiological similarities between the dolphin, which is a mammalian, and humans, and likewise many physiological differences between the dolphin and fishes. There are two types of botos recognized in Gurupá—the large *vermelho* (red) and the *tucuxi*, a small black one. The latter is considered to be somewhat benevolent. It is said to save drowning people by helping them ashore, and it frightens away the large red botos when they attack a canoe or bathers. Despite the good reputation of the smaller black boto, however, people feel that it is better to avoid all botos, both red and black. They are all creatures with high magical potency.

In fact, almost the entire body of the boto may be used for some magical or medicinal purpose. The skin may be dried to prepare a fumigation used to treat snake bite or the wound of a stingray. Another treatment consists of grating the teeth or a bone of the boto into a powder to be placed inside the snake bite or in the wound. A tooth of the dolphin hung around an infant's neck will cure diarrhea. The boto's ear made into a charm to be tied around the wrist of a child will guarantee good hearing. The fat from the boto is an important ingredient of a preparation for rheumatism, and the meat of the animal is thought to be a specific cure for leprosy. The brain is extremely potent and dangerous. A small piece—"enough to fit into the hole of a needle"—placed in a dog's food will make the animal an excellent hunter and immune from panema. The same amount given to a human will allow the giver to gain control over the victim just as a person controls a good hunting dog; but a slightly larger portion of the boto's brain placed in a people's food will drive them crazy and cause the brain to wither away. The penis and the left eye of the boto may be dried and grated to form a powerful aphrodisiac. A powder made of *carajuru*[18] and the grated penis may be spread on a man's penis just before coitus. It is thought to cause such a large and continued erection that the woman will reach orgasm many times and "almost go crazy over her lover." A man who uses this preparation will be able to have the woman whenever he wishes her. The left eye of the boto also may be grated into a powder and used as a magical love potion to be placed in a woman's food by a man who desires her. According to many people, the socket of the left eye may be dried to be used as a "sight" through which a man may peer

---

[18]A wild plant, *Arrabidaea* sp. A red liquid is extracted from the leaves.

at a woman whom he desires, causing her to become impassioned of him.[19]

The boto has strong sexual associations in the minds of the people of Gurupá and of other Amazon communities. The animal itself is thought to have great sexual potency and magical powers. It is said that fishermen have had intercourse with boto females that they killed on the beach. The sexual organs of the female are strikingly similar to those of a woman, and they give a man such intense pleasure, it is said, that if his companion does not pull him away he will die in continued intercourse. In Gurupá, however, people think that the human female must be protected from the advances of the male boto. Women are thought to be unable to resist a man if they are tempted; thus, in the same way that an unchaperoned girl in Gurupá often falls prey to a human lover, she also cannot resist the male boto. It is believed that the male boto may appear in the form of a handsome young man, generally dressed in a white starched suit. He appears unannounced in homes to seduce women, especially virgins. Sometimes he may take on the likeness of a husband and have sexual relations with the wife, who is unaware of the deception. The boto male in human form can only be discovered by the fact that his feet are turned backward on the body.[20] In any case, it is impossible for women to resist him. But, as women continue sexual relations with a boto, they become thin and yellow, and may even die if the relations are not interrupted. If a girl gives birth to the boto's child, it must be immediately "returned to its father" (i.e., thrown in the water) so that the boto father will not harm the mother.[21] Numerous cases of illegitimate children have been charged to the boto in the Amazon region.

---

[19]A rather amusing Amazon anecdote hinges on this belief: A young city dweller traveling on a large river steamer fell in love with a young lady aboard. Passing the town of Santarém, he bought the eye socket of a boto and decided to sight the young lady through it. As he attempted to do so, however, she moved out of range and the burly captain stepped into view. The young man spent the rest of the trip avoiding the amorous attentions of the captain.

[20]In 2013 the most common version of exposing the boto is to have the creature remove its hat, which will expose the blowhole on the top of its head.

[21]There were no local cases of infanticide for this reason known by our Gurupá informants, but several cases have occurred in the lower Amazon region in the last decade. One well-known case reached the courts in Belém. Both the pajé, who had advised the mother to kill her child, and the mother were charged with murder.

Nhenjuca told us of a friend's wife who was seduced by a boto. The friend, who lived in a rural neighborhood near Gurupá, was accustomed to fish at night. One night while he was away a handsome stranger came to his house and seduced his wife. The stranger returned night after night. The husband was not suspicious, but then he noticed that his wife was becoming overtired, and that her color was a sickly yellow. Then he began to notice that each night as he went off in his canoe to fish, a boto followed him for a distance, surfacing frequently and then suddenly disappearing. The husband became suspicious, and one night he returned early and rushed to his house. As he entered, he thought he saw a man running to the water's edge making a snorting noise as the boto does. The next night, when the boto followed him he shot at it. He saw a red stain of blood on the surface and he was sure he had killed the boto. The wife began at once to gain weight and to lose her yellow color; but the poor husband, Nhenjuca related, became ill with a fever and died a short time afterward, bewitched by the boto lover of his wife.

Several instances of boto men seducing, or attempting to seduce, virgins have taken place in Gurupá. Raimundo Dias told us how a boto man seduced his sister who died a few years ago. They lived at the time in a hut near the river. For several nights the whole family heard a strange whistling, as if someone were calling. One evening his sister began to sing a strange, unintelligible song. They rushed to her room. She was nude, and struggled violently with them in an attempt to jump into the water. Raimundo saw the flash of a white figure as it entered the water and then he heard a boto snort out in the river. Raimundo's father rubbed the girl's body with garlic, a substance offensive to all botos, and she became calm. People believe that the boto men want to take women with them to the depths, and this seems to have been the case with Raimundo's sister. She could not be saved, however, for she had lived with her boto lover too long, and she died soon after he left her.[22]

The boto is especially attracted by a menstruating woman. Women therefore should not travel by canoe in this condition. If they do, boto males will follow and try to upset their canoe. Sometimes women need not even be menstruating to attract them. A woman should never look at the botos when they surface near a canoe in which they are traveling.

---

[22]If a girl sticks her boto lover with a pin, he will become disenchanted, remaining a human male and never returning to his boto form.

If she does, the boto will try to take her away. Only by sticking a knife into the bottom of the canoe, cutting the water with a large cutlass, or rubbing the stem of the canoe with garlic or garlic vine will the boto males be forced to leave the canoe alone. Other people add that the boto cannot stand the smell of pepper. In Gurupá people who live on the edge of the river sometimes burn garlic and pepper when women in the house are menstruating, to keep away male botos. The boto, more than any other animal, is "enchanted," and the male is a dangerous sexual competitor to humans. At each great festival, some people say, two or three boto men attend, dancing with the girls and finally seducing them.[23]

V

To the visitor the people of Gurupá seem unusually preoccupied with disease and with the dangers of pregnancy, childbirth, and other physiological processes. They spend a large proportion of their incomes on patent medicines such as *Saúde da Mulher* (a preparation to ease the pains of menstruation), Carter's Little Liver Pills, and other concoctions that may be found in almost any store or trading post. Everyone knows a long list of herbal remedies and innumerable folk methods of treating disease. In any long conversation with a person from Gurupá, the subject of disease and of cures and remedies is almost certain to come up. In our notebooks we wrote down hundreds of local specifics, numerous methods of treating the sick, and many ways to avoid catching disease. Until a decade ago Gurupá (and most other Amazon rural

---

[23]In the 2010s boto stories are common and widespread. Pajé described the male boto in human form as always dressed in a white shirt, white pants, and a hat on the head. It is always close to 40 or 50 years old. "This is what people here have seen," he said. "We have consulted with each other and this story of the boto here is consistent." Pajé's own encounter occurred on the walkway linking the houses of Carrazedo. He saw a person all dressed in white, but when he directed his flashlight in its direction, the creature jumped into the water. He then saw it floating in the river; it was the boto. In another example, Artúlia Lourenço from Mojú remembered she once was paddling upstream in a canoe by herself while she was menstruating. Soon she saw a very large boto below the canoe. "His big eyes were staring at me—I was very afraid. I knew that people say the boto gets mad at women menstruating. This, I am sure, happened to me. Luckily I got to shore before anything bad happened."

In the 2009 survey we found that 56.4 percent of respondents believed the boto can transform into human form (Pace and Hinote 2013:173).

areas) lacked scientific medical assistance almost completely. From time to time a physician from Belém stopped over in the town, attending patients and dispensing medicines. On occasion a male practical nurse was in attendance at the health post that was maintained for short periods by the state government. Until 1942, when the SESP stationed a physician in Gurupá and provided him with up-to-date pharmaceuticals, the people of Gurupá depended almost entirely on patent medicines, household remedies, herbal specifics, and their own folk practitioners for protection against disease and physical accidents. With their poor diets, without adequate public health facilities or medical assistance, without a scientific knowledge of the transmission of disease, and living in an environment that is amenable to disease, the people of Gurupá have always suffered from ill health. It is no wonder that they are preoccupied with the subject.

The concept of disease held by the people of Gurupá is, in a sense, dual in nature. They believe in natural causes, and are often quite willing to accept a physician's explanation of the cause of illness; but they also believe that disease is caused by the dangerous forest or water spirits, or is even the result of punishment by a saint. Their own folk medicine reflects this dual concept. The pajé cures by magical means, by removing an extrusive particle with the help of his friendly spirits; but he also advises special diets and herbal medicines. Similarly, though people pray to their patron saints asking for their intervention in a cure, they also take patent medicines and local remedies. Many of the Gurupá beliefs regarding the treatment of disease have a sound basis in observed fact, but others are based on supernatural and magical concepts. Some of the methods of treatment and medicines used by Gurupá people and by local practitioners are at least scientifically well grounded; but many others are actually harmful to the patient. Still, whether good or bad in the light of modern scientific medicine, the people have been able to survive in the Amazon environment for several centuries.

Birth is a dangerous process. Although statistics are not available for the number of women who die during childbirth or for the number of stillborn children, numerous cases of deaths in childbirth were related to us. Almost all women told of losing children at birth and of abortions.

In Gurupá most births are attended by a *curiosa* (or *parteira*), as midwives are called. There are four professional midwives in town and but half a dozen others in the rural neighborhoods. These old women, who attend at the birth and who generally remain in the home caring for the mother and child for eight days, charge on the average $2.50 (cr. $50) for the first child and as little as $1.00 (cr. $20) for the succeeding births. During these days the midwife is fed, of course, and the husband is obliged to send a canoe to fetch her and later to return her to her home. Most midwives are old widows, such as Dona Joaquina Costa, who have had several children of their own and who live in the home of a relative during the short periods when they are without a client. Most of these midwives are also gifted with powers to "bless," and they know numerous prayers that are used like incantations to aid their clients. Midwives also advise their clients during pregnancy and on feminine hygiene during menstruation.

Women do not like to discuss menstruation, but the old midwives are remarkable repositories of knowledge about menstruation and other aspects of feminine hygiene. It was mainly from them that we learned about these aspects of Gurupá life. Men considered women to be unclean during menstruation, and sex relations during such days are considered dangerous to the health of the man.[24] Women are told not to take baths nor to wash their hair while menstruating; and they should avoid eating acid fruits such as oranges, lemons, and mangos. Above all, they should avoid streams and rivers for fear of the *caruara*, a spider-like arthropod living near the water's edge. The smell of menstrual blood irritates the *caruara*, several midwives explained, which shoots the woman with invisible arrows as she passes. She will have painfully swollen legs and arms as a result. Morena Coimbra was once hit by the *caruara* during her menstruation, and she told us of the treatment that the midwife prescribed. She was told to rub herself with an ointment made of the leaves of several trees mixed with the oil from the nut of the *araticu* and *andiroba*. The midwife also "blessed" her (i.e., touched her head while uttering a prayer) to drive the *caruara* away. Women also ask the midwife for herbal remedies against severe colic during menstruation and against excessive flow or abnormal suspension of the menses. For the latter, among other specifics, Dona Joaquina prescribes a brew made of *abuta* roots,[25] the pulp of a gourd,[26]

---

[24]Some men believe that they may contract gonorrhea during intercourse with a menstruating woman.

[25]*Menispermaceas* sp.

[26]The gourd known as buchinha (*Lufa operculata*). The pulp of the fruit is said to contain a strong alkaloid. See Le Cointe (1947: 81).

and coffee leaves to be taken twice a day. Some midwives also know methods of anti-conception and methods of producing abortion, but most people feel that midwives are seldom successful at either. One of them told us that she knew a prayer that would *atalhar* (block) a woman. She had used this prayer for a woman who lived on the Igarapé Itapereira. The woman had had three twin births and did not want to conceive again. This midwife also prescribed teas made out of *carapanaúba* bark (*Apocináccas*),[27] green *ananás* (wild pineapple), the pulp of the gourd, and quinine bark to induce abortion in case her patient conceived in spite of her prayer.

Most midwives claim that they can predict whether a pregnant woman is carrying a male or female child. One of the four who live in the town of Gurupá told us that she could tell the sex of the child by the way the pregnant woman walked. "If she puts her left foot forward first as a woman does, then it is a girl, but if she starts on her right foot as a man does it is a boy." All midwives warn the expectant mother and her husband (if they do not already know) not to touch the meat and the fish caught by others. They might cause the hunter or the fisher to have panema. She tells the pregnant woman to be careful in church, for the smell of incense will cause her to faint.[28] Pregnant women should not eat a "twin" banana (i.e., two fruits joined) for fear that the birth will result in twins. During pregnancy, however, women may continue to work preparing farinha and even carrying heavy cans of water from the river. Except for the few restrictions and dangers mentioned previously, pregnancy is considered a relatively healthy period. As soon as the woman feels birth pains, her husband calls the midwife. When the midwife lives a considerable distance away, she often comes early to wait for the birth. Some women prefer to give birth in the hammock. They take a semisitting position with their legs dropped over the side. Often the midwife, or even the husband, supports the woman under her shoulders as she sits in the hammock, which is split underneath so that the midwife can secure the child from below as it is born. Most midwives, however, do not like their patients to use the hammock. They prefer a pallet prepared on the floor out of straw mats and sheets. Women have more support, they say, *para dar o puxo* (to give the pull),

---

[27]This bark is also said to contain a strong alkaloid (Le Cointe 1947:123).
[28]Fainting in church can therefore be quite embarrassing, especially for an unmarried girl.

or to exert force at each contraction. As the birth pains come, the midwife massages the woman's abdomen and her thighs and makes her flex her legs. If the birth is difficult, she gives her teas and *garrafadas* (i.e., preparations made out of various herbs, barks, and roots generally soaked in rum). During one difficult birth, Dona Joaquina spread a beaten egg mixed with sugar over the woman's abdomen and gave the woman the same mixture internally to give her strength. She uses a mixture of several palm oils with the leaves of wild plants as an ointment to relieve the birth pains.

Prayers and incantations are also used by the midwife to help a woman through a difficult birth. As soon as the child is born, the midwife cuts the umbilical cord "three fingers away from the child and three fingers away from the mother" and ties it with a string. She anoints the ends of the cord with an oil of palm and rubs the child's navel with tobacco juice. Formerly the infant was not bathed at this time for fear of the "illness of the seventh day" (infection of the umbilical cord). Now it may be bathed in warm water. If a child is born "asleep" (seeming to be dead), the midwife takes some olive oil or any palm oil on her fingers and spreads it over the infant's throat and chest. Then, with a rattle or any two pieces of metal, she makes a noise to "awaken" the child. To cause the placenta to drop Dona Joaquina blows into the mouth of a bottle. Most mothers are wrapped with a long sheet just after the birth "to hold them in place," and to prevent *mãe de corpo* (prolapse of the uterus).

Following the birth there is a long period of convalescence during which the mother must respect numerous postnatal taboos. The convalescence differs in length, depending on the sex of the child. It should be forty-five days for a male child and forty-two for a female. During the first eight days of this period, most midwives advise their patients to remain in the hammock and, if possible, in a dark room. The remaining days should be spent at home avoiding heavy duties, if possible, and observing many dietary restrictions. During the first eight days, for example, she may eat chicken but not the variety with black legs and no feathers on its neck, which is common in Gurupá. She may eat a porridge made of rice flour and of manioc flour; and the large plantain, if it is well cooked, is not harmful. The mother should take mainly teas made from various medicinal herbs to drink. Even after the first eight days the mother must avoid certain foods that are felt to be strong or harmful, such as eggs, pork, citric fruits, beans, fish without scales, and most game. The meat of animals that are reproducers is considered harmful, especially those that might have been in rut when they were killed. But veal and the meat of castrated animals is considered less strong and not dangerous. During the entire period of convalescence women should not bathe in the river. After fifteen days or so, she is allowed to wash herself in a basin of water, but if she were to bathe in the river before the entire convalescence were over, she would be thought to be in danger of being impregnated by an electric eel or a large constrictor.

Some midwives advise husbands to observe eight days of convalescence after their wives give birth. During this time the father should not perform heavy work. He might cause the child to have "body aches," according to the midwives. But few men believe that this very modified form of couvade is really necessary, and few observe it.

Childbirths attended by midwives are not particularly clean or sanitary. Recently, the physician of the public health service has been able to persuade at least those midwives who live in town itself to come to the health post for some instruction in elementary hygiene. He has asked them to boil water and to have the sheets, towels, and the abdominal binding of the mothers sterilized and to boil their scissors before using them. These new ideas, if the midwives in town may be believed, have been adopted. The health service has given each midwife a small handbag equipped with surgical scissors, gauze, adhesive tape, mercurochrome, and surgical thread. They are asked to report all births to the physician for purposes of vital statistics. One old midwife rebelled against these ideas. She was horrified when the physician suggested that a mother be given orange juice and eggs before the end of her forty-two days of convalescence, and she continues to follow the traditional concepts and methods. But the other midwives seem to be proud of the recognition given them. Recently they have called the physician more frequently to aid them with difficult births.[29]

As in childbirth, most cases of illness or accident in Gurupá are treated by local practitioners and by traditional methods of folk medicine. There is a large daily attendance at the health post established in

---

[29]In the 2010s midwives receive training in the municipality's hospital. Combined with the frequent use of the hospital for births, and the presence of both a speed boat ambulance and even emergency airlifts out of Gurupá to Belém, mortality for mothers during childbirth, as well as infant mortality rates, have drop appreciatively.

1942 by the SESP where the physician now offers consultations each morning. Townspeople are getting the habit of going to the post whenever they are ill and even request the physician to come to their homes in the case of an accident or of grave sickness. People from the rural districts, even beyond the area included in the Gurupá community, come to the health post for consultation. There is no charge for the physician's services or for the medicines he dispenses; but, because the physician's primary function in the community is that of a public health officer, and because he has two other towns in his district, he has relatively little time to give to medical assistance. Furthermore, despite the line of people waiting each morning for consultation at the health post, the SESP cannot reach the entire urban and rural population in this enormous district. Nor are the majority of the people in this area accustomed as yet to seeking medical care. Despite the presence of the physician and despite his growing importance, people still seek out their pajés or their *benzedeiras* (literally, "a blesser," but used to mean "one who blesses") and *rezadeiras* (literally, "a prayer," one who prays) for treatment of illness.[30]

These practitioners, the blessers and the prayers, may be of either sex, but most of them are women. Like the pajé, they generally have some especially endowed power to cure. Their powers, however, manifest themselves in a milder form than those of the pajé. Such power is evident in successful diagnosis of illness and in successful treatments. Their treatments consist both of prayers, used as incantations, and of herbal medicines. Their prayers, which they know by memory and which most of them keep secret, are specifics for headaches, colds, diarrhea, fevers, and other common diseases and ailments. Such prayers only have power for the particular practitioner who uses them. A few blessers are specialists. One of them is famous for the cure of snake bite. But most of them have an extensive knowledge of herbal remedies, and even numerous patent medicines available at the local stores, which will cure a large variety of diseases. In the town of Gurupá, there are at least a dozen of these practitioners, and there is always at least one in each rural neighborhood.

---

[30]In 2013 the hospital staff still attends long lines of the sick and injured every morning. As mentioned in Chapter 2, the facilities in Gurupá have improved, but are still substandard by international standards. As a result of problematic health care, most people still use home remedies and local healers to maintain their health.

Many of the medicines prescribed by the blessers and prayers are common household remedies that may be applied by anyone with the knowledge. Women more frequently than men know the names and the uses of these plants. "Men always ask their wives," one man answered when we asked him to explain the medicinal value of a plant. In the back yard of almost any Gurupá home, a flat box set on stilts, called a *jirau*, may be seen in which a series of plants are growing. These plants, sometimes mistaken for decorative flowers, are medicinal herbs—in a sense the family medicine chest—which have been planted or transplanted to be handy in the case of need. In addition, in almost every Gurupá household there are bottles of medicines prepared from roots and barks of native trees soaked in rum. People also keep a sack of their favorite herbs, barks, and roots handy in the house. Others may even be purchased at the local stores and trading posts. There are the *urubu caá* (*Aristolochia trilobata*) leaves; peppermint leaves; *japana branca* bark (*Eupatorium ayapana*); locust-tree bark; *pracaxi* bark (*Pentaclethra filamentosa*); the sap of the *caxinguba* tree (*Ficus*); avocado-tree leaves; *manjericão* (*Ocimum minimum*) leaves; and literally hundreds of other plants, barks, and roots known to have medicinal properties. These medicines are used in a variety of combinations, depending frequently on the training of the practitioner who prescribes it. In general, however, they are prepared and used as hot teas, as infusions mixed with rum, as medicines, as *suadores* (to bring on perspiration), as fumigations (to produce smoke that is thought to be curative), or as baths. Others are taken as tonics, and still others to produce vomiting and as purgatives.

A Gurupá blesser is able to prescribe literally hundreds of detailed recipes for these preparations. The leaves of the aromatic *manjericão* plant are used to make a tea to treat a common cold or a cough. The juice from the bark of the *pracaxi* tree mixed with a little water, passed through a piece of cloth, and left out at night to catch the dew is a strong emetic that is used to treat intestinal worms. To prepare one strong purgative, "take nine seeds from the *piãoseiro* tree (*Jatropha cureas*), cut them in half, throw away the skin around the seeds, crush one-half of each seed, and extract the juice that should be taken with a small cup of coffee." For sore eyes, "grate the root of *japuí* and mix it with maternal milk—or, if this is not available, with the white of an egg to be placed over the eyes." Rheumatism may be treated with "a hot bath made of sugar-cane stalks or of *manjericão* leaves that have been left to soak in the sun for three days and to catch the dew three nights." Whooping cough is treated "with *aturiá*[31] leaves mixed with a few drops of kerosene." "Lizard fat mixed with a liquid formed by soaking corn cobs, orange and lime leaves and dried *sabugueiro* flowers (*Sambucus nigra*) in water" is a remedy for measles. All of these teas, emetics, purgatives, and baths in general require a convalescence during which one must avoid certain foods, exposure to sun or rain, and performance of heavy work. After taking the purgative of *piãoseiro* described previously, one may not eat fish for two days nor should one be exposed to rain, sun, or dew. After any purgative the patient should avoid looking at any green foliage until after the first bowel movement. After most remedial baths, purgatives, and emetics, those foods classified as strong must be avoided. So entrenched is the idea in Gurupá that every medicine must have its rules of convalescence that the physician there has found it very difficult to persuade his clients that the medicines he dispenses need not involve special diets, rest, and other taboos.

Not all of these medicines are specifics for disease, but many of them may be taken as preventives, or to give strength to the individual for particular purposes. Women take baths into which they mix the *cumaru* bean[32] to make their husbands jealous. A preparation made from the *umaparanga* root will give good luck in business. There are also infusions taken to avoid the bad effects of the "evil eye" and to drive away the vampire bat. A hot bath of the house of a *cupim* (termites) mixed with sweet herbs from the forest is a preventive against witchcraft. Other teas and herbal medicines are taken to protect women during their long postnatal lying-in period and to prevent children from catching childhood diseases. There are several aphrodisiacs, such as the root or the bark of the *marapuana* tree[33] mixed with rum or a powder made of the dried penis of the coati[34] taken in water. In addition to internal medicine there are plasters and methods of treatments. Yaws and tropical ulcers are treated, for example, by placing a plaster

---

[31] A spiny plant with long leaves that grows on the low banks of the river (*Machaerium lunatum*).

[32] The tonka bean, Coumarouna Dinata Aubl.

[33] This tree is called catuaba (*Bignoniaceae*) outside Amazonas, and its bark is widely used throughout rural Brazil as an aphrodisiac or a "nerve" tonic.

[34] The coati (*Nasua nasua*), an animal resembling the raccoon, "never has a soft penis," people explain.

made of a baked lemon mixed with rust scraped from iron over an open sore. The milk of *apuí* plant (*Guttiferae*) mixed with black pepper forms a plaster for any sore arm or leg. Ulcers from syphilis are cured by salve made of silver nitrate (secured in the local store) and the white of an egg, or a piece of copper may be placed over the ulcer and tightly bound next to it.

Numerous formulas are also known for fumigations. People fumigate to cure a disease, to prevent catching a prevalent disease, to drive away *assustamento* (fright), to free individuals and objects of panema, and even simply to bring happiness into the house. A few traditional housewives "fumigate their homes each week." Dona Inacinha, the schoolteacher, does so each Saturday; and Dona Feliciana Pará, also an upper-class housewife, fumigates her house every Friday. They vary the formula according to the purpose. A formula for prevention of any disease that is epidemic is "the nest of [a certain] bee mixed with the seed of *Oxí* and the dried leaves of the *parapará* tree." This mixture is burned in a broken ceramic bowl. The fumigations, according to several people, should always begin at the front of the house, progressing room by room back to the kitchen, and afterward the ashes should be thrown in the direction of the setting sun. Fumigation is not as much used nowadays in Gurupá as it was in the past. Many people use it only for treatment of panema, but many formulas are known, and fumigation remains a traditional method of Gurupá folk medicine. Amulets and charms with powers to cure and to protect are also included in this body of belief. *Almofadas* (literally, "pillows") are formed by placing various formulas and objects in a small sack to wear around the neck. A "pillow" of jacuratú[35] feathers will protect children from illness, and the teeth of the alligator or the fresh-water dolphin protect children from the evil eye and from diarrhea. A bracelet made of the "Tears of Our Lady" (small red and black seeds of a tree) protects a child against animals that might steal its shadow, against diarrhea caused by teething, and other evils. This body of belief involving disease, misfortune, accidents, and magical danger is very vast indeed in Gurupá. The native practitioners—the pajés, midwives, blessers, and prayers—have a wider range of knowledge than the layman, and they have personal capacity to cure that is manifest in the power of their prayers. But all people in Gurupá (especially women) have a wide knowledge of their folk medicine.

---

[35] A variety of the jacú (*Penelope jacquacu*), a large forest fowl.

The preoccupation with medicines is a never-ending interest to the people of Gurupá. It is an aspect of life emphasized in their culture.[36]

VI

The worldview of the people of Gurupá and other Amazon communities is in process of transition.[37] With modern communications and with the technology that we have nowadays at our command, the process of change in Gurupá is more rapid and more drastic. It does not occur gradually. The physician in Gurupá uses penicillin to treat syphilis, pneumonia, and other illnesses rather than lizard fat, roots, and leaves from plants; and he cures without the added help of prayers and incantations. From a concept that malaria is caused by taking a bath or drinking stagnant water, the people of Gurupá are suddenly told that the disease is transmitted by the anopheles mosquito and that their homes must be sprayed with DDT. A patient may be treated one day with a strong purgative made of barks and roots of the forest and the next day with a sulfa compound or with penicillin.

The people of Gurupá, like human beings everywhere, are quick to recognize the advantages of such efficient technologies. They are quick to realize that penicillin is a more effective medicinal than their own "home remedies." But they are slower to accept the scientific concepts that lie behind the spraying of their houses and other innovations.[38]

---

[36]In 2013 people still use a wide variety of home remedies. *Jiraus* are still found in backyards—often an old canoe filled with dirt placed on simple scaffolding. Alternatively, people use wooden boxes that are bottomless placed on the ground and filled with dirt for their plants. In an interesting twist, a Cuban-born physician who has worked in Gurupá for many years introduced many to medicinal plant healing practices from her country. Gurupá's second priest, Padre Bento, also maintains an active interest in medicinal healing and has exchanged knowledge and plants with many in the municipality.

[37]Twenty-six lines were omitted from this section that overstate the successes of science (e.g., the use of DDT) and underestimate the value of traditional belief systems.

[38]Wagley's research in Gurupá was during the very beginning of applied anthropology and development anthropology. Since that time researchers have learned valuable lessons about overestimating the infallibility of "science" as well as underestimating the long-term adaptations of traditional peoples. They have also learned to include in their development calculations the impact of political, economic, and ideological biases as well as contemplate as critically as possible who really benefits from development initiatives.

A new element that is introduced into a culture does not immediately replace the older element. New methods and new ideas must be integrated into the matrix of the preexisting culture, and in the process the culture and the view of the world of the people are modified. New methods may be imposed from outside, but the change is never complete until the new methods are integrated into the conceptual scheme of the people concerned.

There is an often repeated saying in Brazil: "Believe in the Virgin and run"; in other words, one should not rely on faith alone. People in Gurupá follow this old adage. Some have accepted the new scientific ideas coming from the outside, but at the same time they fear giving up their traditional beliefs and practices. Many continue to have more faith in their native practitioners and medicines than in the physician. In a crisis they will "give him a try." Mariano Gomes, for example, who was the secretary to the municipal government a few years ago, boasted a secondary education. He was one of the most prominent supporters of the health post and of the benefits of modern medical science. But when Mariano became very ill, he went both to the physician at the health post and to Ascendino, a pajé, for treatment. The pajé came secretly to Gurupá to diagnose his illness. He said that Mariano was sick because of witchcraft, which "the doctor does not know how to cure." Cases of people with apparent faith in science resorting to magical procedures are exceedingly frequent. And most people in Gurupá seek help from their herbal remedies, from their native practitioners, and from the supernatural before they turn to science. One of the most frequent complaints of physicians practicing in the Amazon region is the state of their patients when they finally seek their help. They are dehydrated from the use of strong purges and from violent vomiting. They have been given numerous herbal remedies, and they have lost strength from rigorous diets. For most people, for reasons of economics, distance from medical facilities, or, simply, lack of faith in science, modern medicine is a last resort.

Between the two systems, between folk traditions and science, there are bound to be conflicts. The doctors, aware of the clash between the two systems, have driven the pajés out of town to practice secretly in isolated rural areas. Without understanding the local concepts of dangerous foods and the necessity for convalescence after any medicine, physicians are irritated when their patients refuse to take citrus fruits, eggs, and other "strong" foods and refuse to give them to their children. The people are worried, even angry, when the physicians laugh at their superstitions and when they advise women to break their post-natal taboos exposing them to illness and supernatural dangers. The doctors do not always know of panema or of *caruara*, for example, and if they do learn of these concepts, they are apt to thrust them aside as the ignorance of backward people. Engineers are angry when their Gurupá labor force refuses to work on August 1st and August 24th, unaware that these are believed to be *dias aziagos* (days bringing bad luck).

By knowing the folk beliefs of the people with whom they are working, the physician, the engineer, or anyone bringing new ideas and methods into a folk society would be able to avoid many conflicts. The beliefs concerning health and disease held by the people of Gurupá are part of their view of the world, which includes the cult of the saints, their belief in forest and water spirits, their faith in pajés and the midwives, their dependency on prayers and incantations, and their knowledge of herbal folk remedies. These many beliefs and practices fuse magic with empirical knowledge. It is still fundamentally a magical view of the world, even though scientific knowledge is encroaching on magic with increasing velocity.

CHAPTER 8

A Community in an Underdeveloped Area: The Struggle for Liberation and Sustainable Development

By Richard Pace

If there is anything approaching a universal law for human cultures, it is the fact that change is inevitable. Cultures are never static. Even small-scale cultures that appear to use technologies that date back thousands of years (such as foraging or horticultural ones) are not frozen in the past. Typically they use what has proven to be productive, sustainable, and satisfying with seemingly minimal modification. But it is a certainty that they have experienced change through innovation and diffusion, as they may have borrowed religious beliefs from neighboring groups, altered marriage patterns in response to demographic pressures, or even engaged in periodic wage labor and consumed products produced in industrialized centers. The lower Amazon region, with Gurupá as one part of that area, is no exception to this "law" of change. Even though subsistence farmers in 2013 may spend the day processing manioc in the same manner their ancestors did centuries ago, they will likely finish the day's work in time to return home and turn on their televisions to watch the nightly *telenovelas* (a type of soap opera very popular in Brazil). On the walk home, the younger generation may even take out cell phones, once in range of the reply tower, and check the Internet for any Facebook messages.

Over a span of 60 years since Wagley's pioneering work on Gurupá was first published, there have been massive changes not only in communications technology, but in environmental adaptation, economics, politics, religion, and worldview as well. Many of these changes are as dramatic as they are unpredictable. They include a rancorous struggle over land ownership and extractive resources, political upheaval, the emergence of a powerful religious movement entwining spirituality with the quest for social justice, and a rural workers union movement battling the established power holders to organize their fellow agroextractivists to secure their land rights. Following these changes were a series of innovative sustainable development projects, a boom in açaí extraction, and rising standards of living. In 1987 just as many of these changes were just beginning, Charles Wagley exclaimed at my dissertation defense, "I no longer know Gurupá." The comment was as much an expression of nostalgic lament of an era gone by as it was a disquieting recognition that global processes, with both their positive and negative consequences, had forcefully reached his "little Amazon community."

At the same time, as much as Gurupá has changed and will continue to change, there is a core of practices, patterns, traditions, and beliefs that persists. This core is recognizable in form and understandable in its expression or exercise over time. Wagley has vividly captured much of its essence in the preceding chapters. In the footnotes spread through this book the manner and extent of its continuation is highlighted. This core sets the stage to understand how cultures are sustained in the face of change. It is also the cultural context that must be taken into consideration when designing, directing, or assessing development projects intended to improve the lives of people throughout the Amazon region.

Two very important initiatives undertaken to improve the human condition in Gurupá during the last three decades have consciously built on the community's core of practices, patterns, traditions, and beliefs to affect change. The first is the movement for social justice through the Catholic Church. Working with the religious brotherhoods spread throughout the municipality and through the collective labor traditions in place for centuries, the movement has organized famers and extractors to overturn the abusive patron–client system, claim moral and legal rights to land, and form labor unions and political parties to defend a dignified livelihood. Building on the organizational successes of the Church movement, the NGO FASE-Gurupá and the rural union have incorporated the rich environmental knowledge

FIGURE 8.1 | *View from fort.*
Photograph by R. Pace 2012.

FIGURE 8.2 | *First Street 2013. Compare to Figure 2.2.*
Photograph by R. Pace.

FIGURE 8.3 | *Second Street 2010. Compare to Figure 2.3.*

From *Amazon Town TV: An Audience Ethnography in Gurupá, Brazil,* by Richard Pace and Brian P. Hinote, 2013. Reprinted by permission of University of Texas Press.

FIGURE 8.4 | *Town Hall 2010. Compare to Figure 2.4.*

Photograph by R. Pace.

FIGURE 8.5 | *Procession for St. Benedict.*
Photograph by R. Pace 2011.

FIGURE 8.6 | *Meia Lua procession for St. Benedict.*
Photograph by R. Pace 2011.

extant in the rural population to design sustainable develop projects that enhance agricultural production and the extraction of forest commodities while maintaining rainforest cover and biodiversity. FASE and the union have also labored endlessly to establish legal title to land, which, in several cases, required rewriting Brazilian land statutes. The successes of both initiatives are now incorporated into the curriculum of an innovative rural school (*Casa Familiar Rural*—Rural Family House), ensuring an educated and socially and environmentally aware group of new leaders for the community (Magalhães 2009).[1]

Gurupá in the early 2010s is enjoying an economic prosperity not matched since the height of the rubber boom in the 1890s. It is driven by a surge in açaí extraction and a range of economic and political reforms that more evenly distribute the new wealth. Obtaining this new prosperity, however, has required much struggle and sacrifice. Notwithstanding the success achieved so far, the struggle is hardly over. The latest round of threats comes from the building of the Belo Monte Dam upstream from Gurupá on the Xingú River. The dam will be the third largest hydroelectric complex on the planet. It is predicted to create massive environmental, economic, and public health problems. All the while, not even one kilowatt of energy from the dam is planned to reach Gurupá. The changes brought by the dam construction will surely test the strength of Gurupá's rural union, political parties, and Church, as well as the continuity of the successes obtained so far.

II

From 1948 until 1964 the economic conditions in the Lower Amazon Region and in Gurupá remained precarious. Continued economic depression and the onset of two-to-four digit inflation rates created long-term threats to subsistence farmers and extractors' livelihoods. Edgar Pantoja da Sousa, a former agroextractivist from Marajoí River, now in his 70s, described life during this period. He began by noting natural rubber commerce had begun to fail with the introduction of

---

[1]The school has been in existence for 12 years. It combines both elementary and secondary education with innovative technical courses in agroextractivism for the várzea. It has been a vital element in the spread of technological innovations developed by the rural union, FASE, and the local population.

synthetic rubber. This left only *timbó* and *cipó* (vines used in basket making) as marketable extractive products—neither of which paid well. People survived on manioc farming—which also never paid well—along with growing tobacco, beans, corn, and sugar cane for home consumption. "It was very difficult to buy anything of value; even material to make clothes was too expensive for most." Edgar continued:

> *Everyone lived on the patrão's land and the dependence was total. It was the patrão who ordered people to do agriculture, saying where and what to plant. It was the patrão who ordered people to vote for this or that politician. It was the patrão who sold the goods, the cloth, and medicine at inflated prices that were so hard to afford. People were always in debt to the patrão. Overseers were always watching so that no one diverted the production of the patrão to another buyer. You had to be faithful to your patrão despite the underpayment for produce and overcharging for goods.*

Edgar lamented, there was no school on the river. At the time, he said, "People lived in complete ignorance." Isabel Silva Viana, wife of Edgar, added that there was much malaria at the time. People did not know where it came from, but they all had it. Tearing up, she said her father likely died of malaria. "They never knew for sure since there was no doctor. He simply came down with a high fever and passed away."

With economic depression and high inflation disrupting the regional economy, Gurupá's economy began a painful transformation. Many of the trading posts scattered around the interior of the municipality were hard hit with poor earnings. They were unable to extend credit to their *freguesia* (customers) over the customary one to three months. Trading post merchants had to cut their stocks of merchandize, increase prices, and impose monthly payment of debts. This resulted in a significant loss of commerce and customers and eventually led to the closing of nearly one-half of all Gurupá's major trading posts by the 1980s. Gone were many of the rural trading posts, such as Francisco Felix's on the Urutaí River and the large one owned by the Pires Serra family in Paraíso. In town many trading posts closed, and the Casa Borralho, now under the direction of Dona Diná's brother-in-law Oscar Santos, was greatly weakened and in the process of a steady decline.

The loss of trading posts meant the elimination of debt obligations for the freguesia. In a sense, losing one's patrão "freed" a family of the economic burden of debt-peonage and might even leave it in control of land. But at the same time, the closing of trading posts deprived the farmers and extractors of their only viable access to imported goods. For these families freed of debt, but now lacking a patrão, a harsh period ensued, characterized by underemployment and periodic bouts with hunger, especially for those lacking land adequate for planting gardens. Even for families who managed to maintain a patron–client tie with one of the remaining trading posts, the depressed economy, poor earnings from agricultural and extracted products, asymmetrical exchange relations with merchants, and inflation left them increasingly deeper in poverty. Filomena Gonçalves Dias, a former manioc farmer from Bacá, was a teenager during this time and remembers how hard things were. "It was difficult to get money," she reminisced. "If you came to the town to sell manioc flour, you were only able to buy a few goods because your manioc was not worth much. You did not buy more, since you didn't have credit or a patrão to finance your purchases." Edgar Souza told of the loss of the last trading post on Marajoí River. As bad as the trading posts were, he explained, "Once they were gone there was no one left that could sell even a box of matches. For you to buy a kilo of sugar or a box of matches you had to go to the town of Gurupá or to the entrance of Marajoí River, where people had a store. But there was no transportation, no motors for the boats; everything required paddling a canoe that could take days. It was very difficult."

At this point in time the worse predictions Wagley made in *Amazon Town* seemed to hold sway. Life was precarious and misery was widespread. Many individuals, unable to eke out a living, were forced to emigrate—a common pattern Wagley described in Chapters 3 and 5. One measure of emigration is indicated by a survey we conducted in 1985 of people born in Gurupá. The survey revealed that 56% of the sample had siblings living in other municipalities. In other words, over half the families could not afford to stay together due to the depressed economy. Jorge Palheta, the former manioc farmer who later entered politics, becoming first a council member and eventually mayor,[2] recounted how the 1950s and 60s were times of travel for men. There was no work in Gurupá, he said, so men left. River transportation

---

[2] The Town Council Hall or *Câmara* in Gurupá is named after him.

was relatively cheap, so they ventured far. They found work as hired hands on cattle ranches on the Xingú River, agricultural laborers for the Japanese colonies in Monte Alegre, rubber tappers for the plantation system attempted at Fordlândia and Belterra on the Tapajós, Brazil nut collectors on the Trombetas, jute cutters in Almerím, and subsistence agriculture and rubber workers in Oriximina. Jorge stated, "They worked very hard. But when they returned home, they usually brought only meager remittances."

Wagley captured the state of affairs after his short return trip to Gurupá in 1962 with an ominous warning in his 1964 epilogue to *Amazon Town*:

> *The lethargy and backwardness of Gurupá, and all similar communities, is a threat to the world, not just to Brazil. People cannot continue to be illiterate, hungry, badly clothed, ill-informed, sick, and deprived of the minimum facilities of a modern community without seeking in desperation for some formula to provide them with rapid change during their lifetime. Today, Gurupá is in communication with the outside world and open to outside influences. The people of Gurupá want the things they have seen or have merely heard about. They will not remain passive for long. (1964:311)*

III

April 1, 1964, marked the beginning of a radically different phase in the history of Gurupá, as in the rest of Brazil. On this date of infamy the Brazilian military regime overthrew the civilian government and established a repressive dictatorship that lasted until 1985. During this time the regime aggressively pursued a policy of economic growth through the diffusion of Western industrial capitalist technology, institutions (minus the emphasis on a democratic government), and values, frequently financed with foreign loans and investments. As a form of modernization theory, the policy did result in a great increase in industrial output and wealth generation. Yet the wealth was concentrated among a minority of Brazilians just as poverty for the majority increased. Political repression, torture, and executions (often through "disappearances") were used widely to eliminate any opposition (Skidmore 1988).

The Amazon region fit into the military's designs as an exporter of raw materials to furnish much needed revenue to finance industrial development in the Southeast and, later on, to help pay the surging international debt created by this process (Bunker 1985:93). The regime was also concerned with integrating Amazonia more tightly with the rest of Brazil for geopolitical concerns. Geopolitical threats, whether imaginary or real, included the possibilities of territorial intrusions from neighboring countries as well as the potential rise of insurgent movements committed to overthrowing the military government (Morais and Silva 2005).[3] Toward this end the dictatorship built roads into the rain forest, constructed new settlements for settlers, built military posts, and initiated a gigantic land giveaway (the largest in modern world history) to encourage private and corporate investment in the region (see Bunker 1985; Moran 1981). Also critical to the military's blueprints was the cultural and ideological integration of the country—also a safeguard against anti-regime social movements. The military government invested heavily in mass communication, especially television, as an effective technology for nation building and political control (Skidmore 1993).

The most prized development projects, and the most robustly subsidized by the military regime, were large-scale ventures in mineral, gold, and timber extraction. The military government also encouraged and subsidized extensive cattle ranching, despite its poor economic returns and its devastating environmental impact (see Hecht and Cockburn 2011). As the generals built new roads into the Amazon frontier, which included the terra firme lands away from the rivers and floodplains, most areas experienced a heavy spontaneous migration of subsistence farmers. These farmers came from the Northeast and South, where environmental factors and land ownership concentration created by the commercialization of export-oriented agriculture forced them to seek new land (Foweraker 1981; Bunker 1985; Hall 1997; Hecht and Cockburn 2011). They were joined by other small farmers from the Amazon who were likewise looking for land. Once on the frontier, the

---

[3]The most cited example was the Araguaia guerrilla movement (1972–75) in which approximately 80 rebels attempted to create a Marxist revolution from bases in southern Pará. The Brazilian military destroyed the movement with massive force. All those who were captured were subjected to torture followed by extrajudicial killings (Morais and Silva 2005).

migrants occupied unowned public lands to produce subsistence crops and extract forest resources with a small marketable surplus.

Conflict between the subsistence farmers and large commercial enterprises followed. The commercial enterprises began an aggressive campaign to expropriate properties from migrant farmers or any other peasant or Indigenous group on contested land. The use of intimidation and violence was widespread (Martins 1985, Schmink and Wood 1992), with thousands of farmers expelled from their land by private militia (*pistoleiros*) frequently working in conjunction with local police. Techniques used by these henchmen to drive out farmers included threats to property and lives followed by destruction of property, kidnapping, torture, and assassination. Lawlessness prevailed throughout the region as the military regime failed to protect small-scale farmers from violence and land expropriation on the part of large enterprises. This neglect persisted until the cycle of land appropriation by politically powerful landowners and business enterprises was complete (Foweraker 1981:124; Amnesty International 1988:62).

Even though Gurupá was not targeted for any major development project during the military dictatorship, it was affected by the regime's need to generate revenue through the extraction and export of natural resources. Beginning in the late 1960s, following generous incentives provided by the military government, timber firms, palm heart extraction firms, and commercial fishers began to enter the municipality and remove large quantities of natural resources. Their activities quickly led to confrontations over rights to land and resources with the local agroextractivists. As on the frontier, the firms in Gurupá relied on a variety of tactics to resolve problems—including the use of intimidation and violence to remove people from the land. Unlike the frontier, there was no heavy spontaneous in-migration, in large part due to the lack of a road to Gurupá. Nor were there any deaths associated with the social conflict over land and resources. Yet, the processes paralleled one another in creating high levels of agitation that increasingly radicalized agroextractivists into political action (see Pace 1992, 1998).

In the case of timber, the military government offered subsidies, tax breaks, and land concessions to companies willing to extract in the region. Several national and international timber firms set up in Gurupá and began extracting. Soon Gurupá experienced an economic boom as timber exports soared from 10,548 cubic meters in 1950 to 669,000 cubic meters at the height of the boom in 1985 (IBGE 1956;

IDESP 1989). The timber extraction firms on occasion brought in workers from other municipalities to harvest trees, but more frequently hired locally. The firms either contracted workers through their own agents, called *gatos* (cats), who paid workers in cash, or they used the municipality's remaining trading posts to secure men—and sometimes women—using the traditional patterns of patron–client ties through debt-peonage.

Many *gatos* who worked in the municipality of Gurupá and bought timber for Brazilian, Japanese, American, and Belgium companies complained they were handicapped by the lack of access to merchandise provided to workers. Wennuildo Flavio, nicknamed Minerio, was one such agent from Minas Gerais working for a national company. Mineiro explained that his job was especially difficult because the workers always wanted cash advances as well as supplies of food, clothing, and other goods. His company could not comply logistically, and, as a result, he suffered from persistent labor turnover that greatly cut into his personal profit (Pace 1998:118–19). By contrast, the remaining trading post merchants easily provided the workers with their demands for advances and merchandise. For example, Oscar Santos and his son Antônio from the Casa Borralho, Dona Inacinha's son José Vicente de Paulo Barreta Mello, as well as several others, worked closely with the timber firms and through their financial support were able to fortify their faltering trading posts and expand their clientele. Oscar Santos, for example, told how the timber boom helped him to increase his freguesia to 300 people—almost as high as it had been for the Casa Borralho in the rubber boom (Pace 1998:116). With the possibility of accruing outstanding debt through transactions in the trading post, these merchants were able to retain their workers over longer periods of time.

At the same time the old debt-peonage system was experiencing a mild revival, the boom economy and unprecedented flow of cash in the local economy allowed some timber extractors to earn enough to pay off all debts. Whereas they could still obtain goods and food on credit or by barter through the trading posts, they had the option to receive the balance of their earnings in cash. By opting for cash payments, these extractors avoided entering into further debt relations. They could then shop around in a growing number of retail stores being established in town. In this way they could avoid the extensive price manipulation of the trading post, which in Gurupá was often 100 percent higher than prices in coastal cities such as Belém (the retail stores would inflate prices by only 50–60 percent). With the savings, these extractors and their families began consuming imported manufactured goods, imported canned foods, and medicine and converted their housing materials from palm-thatch to wooden board sidings with tile roofs. The cash economy thus not only improved extractors' standard of living and raised consumerist expectations, at least temporarily, but it also reduced the merchants' traditional control over customers. This was an important milestone in Gurupá's political economy, one that signaled significant erosion in the trading-post dominance and a turning point in the patron–client system.

The extraction of timber was not a peaceful process in Gurupá. Strong tensions arose over the ownership of the widely scattered trees[4] growing on large expanses of land that lacked precise demarcations. Up until this point in time, most of the land in Gurupá had never been surveyed (see Treccani 2001, 2006, for an exhaustive analysis of Gurupá's land tenure system from colonial times until the present day). There was no need because the value of land was in extractable resources, primarily rubber and cacao, rather than in the land itself. Land titles in the municipality reflected this pattern and typically defined only the possession of resources, such as the number of rubber trails or cacao trees on the land, rather than detailed geographic locations. In many cases land titles overlapped, especially ones that only mentioned locations along river fronts but never described back boundaries to properties. Titles to the same land were also issued to different people by different government agencies. In some cases titles were fraudulent or completely missing.

The result was ambiguous and overlapping claims to trees, leading to disputes adjudicated in Gurupá's court or through threats of violence exchanged in the depths of the rain forest. In most cases, large landowners and trading-post merchants prevailed over small landowners and occupants of land (many of whom had gained control of properties as trading-post merchants abandoned the area in the previous decade). Their success came from superior financial resources and access to lawyers, their political connections (including support of timber extraction firms, the municipal government, and police force),

---

[4]This is an ecological adaptation that protects each species of tree from the tropical forest's abundant pests and diseases. For more details, see Moran 1993.

and their ability to hire *fiscais* or guards that frequently acted as henchmen or private militia to intimidate and evict residents. This conflict
greatly raised tensions throughout the municipality.

A second form of conflict linked to timber extraction occurred
when Brumasa-Bruynzell Madeiras,[5] a large multinational timber enterprise, purchased 95,708 hectares of land on the Great Island of
Gurupá to harvest timber in the 1970s. The sale of the land was legally
questionable, but the firm's financial resources, experienced lawyers,
and political connections enabled it to win most court cases challenging the purchase. Once in possession, the company evicted some
occupants from the land, but in general employed people living there
as a source of cheap labor to extract timber. These residents were instructed to cut only certain woods and deliver the logs to the company
headquarters. Residents were not allowed to clear new areas for slash-
and-burn gardens, which would destroy valuable timber. They had to
continue farming old areas despite diminishing crop yields. Moreover,
the company did not set up a trading post to finance the residents with
food and tools or to give loans for medical or other emergencies. Instead, the company paid cash wages that were significantly lower than
other firms operating in Gurupá.

People soon found these conditions intolerable. Benedito Lima,
who lived on Báquia Preta River with his wife and two young children,
commented bitterly that Brumasa's wages for timber extraction were so
low they barely paid for one's survival. Because he could not clear land
for a new roça, his agricultural produce was inadequate for his family.
Imported food was hard to obtain due to the distance he had to travel
to the nearest store. He criticized the company for refusing to offer any
form of credit to help people like him in times of need.

As a result of these conditions, residents of the Great Island of
Gurupá retaliated against the company in a fashion commonly used
during the rubber boom of the 19th century (Weinstein 1983:102;
Hecht and Cockburn 2011:185). Timber was cut and sold illegally to
noncompany buyers who paid higher prices and often offered credit.
On discovery of the practice, the company reacted with punitive measures. It hired private militia to intimidate residents. People from the

---

[5]Under the leadership of Brazilian business tycoon Augusto Azevedo Antunes, the
Brazilian and Dutch company extracted timber to produce plywood in an extensive
area in the Marajó region.

Great Island of Gurupá reported physical beatings, threats at gunpoint, and destruction of property on the part of the company's henchman. Gurupá's small police force was frequently dispatched to the area, not to stop the extralegal violence, but to evict occupants. These tensions continued into the 1990s, at which point the company abandoned the land once it had been stripped of its valuable timber.

Overlapping with the timber boom was a lesser boom in palm heart extraction. Since the 1950s Brazil has become one of the world's largest producers of palm hearts for international markets. Large scale Amazon extraction of palm hearts began in the 1970s as reserves of the trees in the South and Southeast of Brazil were depleted by predatory extraction (Oliveira 1991:127–131). In Gurupá, where the local species of palm hearts (*Euterpe oleracea* Mart) grows in natural stands along the waterways, the first processing unit was established in 1973 with a larger one in town set up in 1977. From that point on, municipal extraction increased greatly from 60 tons in 1978 to a peak of 4,840 tons in 1989 (IBGE 1984; Oliveira 1991:131). Similar to timber extraction, palm heart firms typically hired workers through local trading posts or, alternatively, imported them from neighboring municipalities to work for cash wages.

As with timber extraction, palm heart extraction quickly lead to ownership disputes created by the inadequate and confusing land tenure system. Unlike timber extraction, conflict over palm heart extraction was further complicated by the dual use of the palm. Not only does it produce palm hearts, but the tree also produces açaí—a palm fruit that grows in caches near the top of the palm. The fruit (actually the mesocarp that surrounds the seed) is mixed with water to make a porridge-like drink eaten with a spoon. It is often sweetened with sugar, or mixed with manioc flour, tapioca, and even fish. Açaí is consumed locally as a staple. It is often referred to as the "milk of the Amazon," and its consumption may take on a near-addictive quality for some. In the 1980s, açaí was sold for export to neighboring municipalities only when there was a surplus harvest.

Palm hearts, on the other hand, were rarely consumed locally; nearly all were extracted for export to the south of Brazil or overseas. Palm hearts are produced from the apical meristem growing tip of the tree. To harvest palm hearts, the extractor must cut down the tree. This process eliminates açaí production until regrowth can occur from the base clump in usually three to five years. Making matters worse, extraction firms in Gurupá repeatedly clear-cut areas that diminished regrowth potential and improperly harvested palm hearts by topping the tree, which prevents any regrowth from the base clump (see Brondízio 2008). In the 1980s each palm tree harvested produced the equivalent of .05 US cents. By contrast, açaí fruit produced about $5.00 US per year. Large landowners, however, traditionally did not have exclusive rights to açaí, which was typically collected and consumed by the agroextractivists. If landowners wanted revenue from the tree, they had to cut it down for the palm heart. If they did this, the loss of açaí eliminated an important nutritional supplement and much needed source of income for many rural families.

One example among many of the hardships created by palm heart extraction occurred along the Marajoí River, near the eastern border of the municipality. Along 50 kilometers of the river and its tributaries, approximately 200 families organized into three communities made their livings from the extraction of forest products and subsistence agriculture. By the late-1970s the palm heart plant in Gurupá was interested in stands of palm hearts located there. To entice the residents to extract, the plant sent representatives to the interior and offered a motor for a boat if a family would use it to cut a minimum of 20,000 palms, with the landowner also getting a portion of the profits. Edgar Sousa remember this well, saying at first his family thought this was great way to get a motor for their boat because people living along the river were so poor. To pay off the motor, however, they typically had to extract more than the 20,000 palms, particularly if the motor needed repairs or they used more fuel than planned. Therefore, once a family started extracting palm hearts and using the motor, they could not stop— entrapped in debt just as all other economic pursuits controlled by patrões (plural of patrão).

In the end the rewards for cutting palm hearts were never that good and did not compensate for all the labor expended, nor for all the environmental harm done. Edgar said that after 10 to 15 years of extraction, the river was stripped of the palm and açaí (90 percent of the açaí/palm hearts were removed from Marajoí by the mid-1980s; FASE 1997). Then the palm heart processing plant closed and left town. Marajoí River, once so rich in açaí, now had to ship in poor quality and bad tasting açaí from other municipalities if they wanted the fruit. Making matters worse, there was no more game in the forest (driven off by extractors); and the river was polluted from careless extraction activities, which reduced fish stocks.

On the Great Island of Gurupá palm heart extraction followed similar patterns. With the arrival of the palm heart plants in Gurupá, as well as with extraction firms cutting palms for plants in other municipalities, the large landowners claiming the Island's land saw a chance to earn much desired revenue. In no small part their yearning for palm heart profits came from the need to pay back taxes on the land. Because land title in Gurupá was always questionable, paying taxes was key to establishing land claim if legally challenged in court. Manuel do Carmo de Jesus Pena—an extractivist who grew up on the Mojú River and now heads the Casa Familiar Rural school—reported that the occupants of the land on the Great Island later learned that none of the landowning families had legitimate title to the land. He remembered vividly at the time how he and his family were indignant that the patrões felt they had rights to the açaí. He and his fellows on Mojú River looked on with acrimony as the large landowners contracted a variety of extraction firms to quickly work through the stands of palm heart using wantonly nonsustainable harvesting methods. For many communities near Manuel do Carmo's home, their açaí was lost.

A third assault on Gurupá, which began in earnest in the 1980s, involved export-oriented commercial fishing. Financed by the state (Superintendência de Desenvolvimento da Amazônia or Superintendence for the Development of Amazônia—SUDAM), the goal was to feed the growing urban populations as well as earn foreign revenue for balance of payment problems through export to the international market (Loureiro 1985:148). As the fishing fleets entered the municipality's waters, few residents of Gurupá were involved in the process and almost none of the fish ended up in the local market (Oliveira 1991:155). Some Gurupá residents did participate in commercial shrimp production. Shrimp production usually involved traditional social relations of production through a trading post, although commercial buyers also paid cash to shrimpers (Oliveira 1991:160).

Conflict erupted between local fishers and the commercial fishers as stocks diminished with overharvesting. There were no restrictions on quantity, type, or size of catches or on the type of nets used by commercial fishers. They typically discarded fish not commercially valuable, causing high rates of mortality. Discarded fish ranged as high as

70 percent of all fish caught (Oliveira 1991:153). Although there are no scientific studies for Gurupá, residents acknowledge a drop in fish caught for local consumption. The flash point, however, was not in the main channel of the Amazon River, where the vast fluvial expanse made it hard enough to simply detect fishers, let alone regulate them. Rather, confrontations escalated in the seasonally flooded lakes and ox bows rich in easily netted fish as dry season waters receded. Local subsistence fishers relied heavily on the lakes for livelihood, and for fishers living nearer town, much of their surplus fish were sold to the urban population.

The extraction and fishing booms promoted by the military government to finance their development plans in the Southeast led to quick profits for a few in Gurupá; but in terms of a long-term development perspective, it also led to the depletion or reduction of key resources vital to local livelihoods. Although resource depletion has historically disrupted Gurupá's economy on numerous occasions (see Bunker 1985:60–65), the cumulative effect of centuries of natural resource misuse peaked in the 1980s with the disappearance of marketable species of timber, along with associated oleaginous seeds (sold to trading posts or used to make medicinal home remedies), açaí, and fish. Each of these was critical in generating cash income and/or as an important source of nutrition for agroextractivist population.

IV

The military regime's broad development plans required far-reaching political shifts at the national as well as local levels. For the Amazon region as a whole, this involved the loss of regional political autonomy and the transfer of all strategic policy decision to the national level in Brasília (Bunker 1985:124). The military dictatorship methodically undercut the power of the traditional Amazon elite through federally regulated appointments to local political offices; federal appropriation of "commons" land totaling almost two-thirds of the legal Amazon region; the creation of new economic enterprises directed by the state or large corporations, which ended traditional extractive and exchange monopolies; and the establishing of National Security Areas under military control including all of southern Pará, Jarí, Manaus, and parts of Rondônia (Martins 1985; Bunker 1985; Hall 2000). As a result of these measures, the powerful groups that emerged in the Amazon were totally dependent on the "initiative and support" of the military government and big corporations investing in the region (Bunker 1985:82).

In Gurupá during the period of military rule, José Vicente de Paulo Barreta Mello, son of Dona Inacinha, twice served as mayor. He used his political skills and ties to the new regime, along with his newfound wealth from timber extraction, to become the virtual coronel (municipal boss) for nearly 18 years (see Petit 1996). During this time period he did the military government's bidding by facilitating the extraction of Gurupá's resources by multinational and national enterprises and by containing local opposition to regime policies. He used his political influence to sway resource conflicts in favor of timber and palm heart extraction firms. He swiftly marshaled the municipality's small police force to evict people from land once legal decisions were reached. At the same time he grew wealthier, by local standards, leading to widespread allegations he misappropriated municipal funds (a common allegation against politicians in Brazil). Due to his behavior he lost political legitimacy among the agroextractivist population and eventual lost influence among his political allies as well. By the 1980s, when the military regime initiated its policy of *abertura* (political opening) in a slow return to democracy, he had lost most of his power base and became a principal focus around which the population rallied in protest (Pace 1998; Oliveira 1991).

In the early years of the military dictatorship, there was only fragmented opposition to the political and economic pressures imposed on the population in Gurupá. Most resistance was in the form of clandestine sales of extracted resources, refusal to leave property until forcibly evicted, and unsuccessful court challenges. By the mid-1970s, however, organized opposition to the military regime began to emerge in the municipality. At this point the Catholic Church became a major player in the political landscape. Unlike the Church of the 1940s described by Wagley—with infrequent visits by clergy and conservative stances often in opposition to the local folk culture—the Church of the 1970s commiserated passionately with the plight of the common agroextractivist. Led by an Italian Priest Giúlio Luppi (see Figure 8.7), the Church advocated Liberation Theology. This perspective emphasized Christian teachings on social justice—focusing on the poor and disenfranchised sectors of society—and strongly encouraged the oppressed to organize politically and defend their basic human rights (Berryman 1987; Boff and Boff 1986; Gutiérrez 1971).

FIGURE 8.7 | *Padre Giúlio during St. Benedict procession.*
Photograph by R. Pace 2011.

Liberation Theology is part of a global movement in the Catholic Church based on the teachings of Vatican II (1962–1965) and the second general conference of Latin American bishops in Medellín (1968). These meetings ushered in a new emphasis on lay participation in Church activities along with the explicit goal of achieving social justice for the poor and marginalized (Levine and Mainwaring 1989:210). The theology intertwines traditional goals of spiritual salvation with earthly concerns of alleviating material suffering (e.g., hunger, illness, discrimination, repression, and other burdens created by poverty and political intolerance). Proponents reason that religious influence only makes sense when the basic human conditions of life are being met (Bruneau 1982:50). Blame for the severe level of material suffering and disenfranchisement in Brazil were linked to the policies of the military regime and the "structural sins of capitalism" (Gutiérrez 1971). Supporters of Liberation Theology called for social and political enfranchisement of excluded sectors through social reform and/or revolution (Follmann 1985:79).

The Vatican II and Medellín reforms reached Brazil as large sectors of the population suffered sharply deteriorating economic and political conditions. These included substantial declines in wages and standard of living for the working class and a rise in mass detainment, torture, and assassination of political opponents—all consequences of the military regime's modernization policies (Skidmore 1988). When progressive Church members began to speak out against these abuses in the name of social justice, the military regime attacked and slandered them in an unrelenting campaign of demoralization (Martins 1985:24; Branford and Glock 1985:140). Particularly in the Amazon region, Church members suffered intimidation, incarceration, beatings, torture, deportation, and even murder in numbers unparalleled in Brazilian history (Martins 1985:58). These attacks, plus the military regime's historically unprecedented exclusion of the Church from its traditional advisory role in government decision making (Salem 1981:35), radicalized the Church and led to a direct Church–state standoff.

In Gurupá, the standoff first took the form of Church condemnation of local inequalities during weekly masses and Church-related meetings (e.g., Catechism Week, Agricultural Workers Meetings, and Women's Week). The priest, church laity, and other opponents of the dictatorship formed a coalition under the Church umbrella (all other avenues for social protest were systemically eliminated by the regime) to denounce the inequitable exchange rates for produce given by the trading-post merchants to their customers. The coalition urged agro-extractivists to circumvent trading posts altogether through the creation of independent cooperatives. It denounced land rights abuses by large landowners. The Church brought in legal experts from the Pastoral Land Commission to explain Brazil's land right statutes and the meaning of usufruct rights. They beseeched families threatened with expulsion to demand their usufruct rights or at least their indemnification rights for improvements made to the land. The local coalition also strongly urged participation in rural unions and, by the end of the dictatorship, political elections as well (Pace 1998:191).

The Church and its allies attacked local political corruption and suppression of human rights. The abuses of the local commercial, landowning, and political elite were targets of criticism. The mayor at the time, José Vicente, reacted angrily. Broadcasting from his home loud speaker system he labeled the Church, the priest, lay members, and other opponents of the dictatorship as communist radicals. He denounced the priest for stirring up class conflict. He threatened imprisonment to all who opposed the military regime. Alfredo Gomes da

Costa Filho, who worked as a Church catechist and was active in the opposition coalition, described the tensions in town. He said everyone had to be careful of what was said and who might be listening. He noted that opposition leaders were imprisoned in Gurupá's small jail on several occasions when they impeded extraction firms. The priest was imprisoned twice for interfering in domestic politics as a foreigner. Alfredo continued that everyone understood that there were implied threats of assassination, common occurrences in other parts of the Amazon. He maintained that only in the rural interior, away from the cadres of the military regime, could people speak freely. It is here that opposition organization took place.

In 1984 near the height of political tensions in Gurupá, I asked Alfredo how he and others in the opposition coped with fears of arrest, incarceration, and assassination (Pace 1998:209). Alfredo responded with a saying common throughout the region—a metaphor on how to survive against overwhelming odds. Alfredo began, "It is like walking in the deep forest when you are most vulnerable and you encounter a *bicho* (wild and dangerous beast). At that moment you must decide what to do. If you run, the bicho will catch you and kill you. If you freeze the bicho will eat you." Alfredo continued: "The only option you have is to confront the bicho, no matter the odds of success. That is what we have to do now, confront the bicho of oppression that has been in this land for so long. We have no other choice."

In addition to articulating Liberation Theology's ideological message, the progressive sector of the Catholic Church also promoted social activism through the formation of lay religious/political groups known as *Comunidades Eclesiais de Base* (Christian Base Communities) or CEBs. In Gurupá, 66 CEBs, or *comunidades* as they are more commonly called, were established throughout the municipality. In nearly each case, as mentioned in Chapter 6, they built on the traditional *irmandades* or religious brotherhoods organized to conduct festivals in honor of neighborhood patron saints. They continued these functions while at the same time organizing labor exchanges for mutual aid (*convites*) and establishing cooperatives for the sale of extracted and agricultural products and the purchase of medicine.

Some of the comunidades engaged in more overt political behavior. They joined together to boycott merchants' trading posts as they formed their own trading-post cooperatives. They physically blocked the evictions of their fellows from land through *empates* (literary meaning tying up) in which women, men, and children formed a human barrier to protect those who were threatened by henchmen and even the police.[6] They also used empates to prevent extraction of timber and palm heart from property contested by occupants of land. One such example occurred in the subsistence farming hamlet of Camutá located along the Pucuruí River (see Pace 1998:199–205). Thirty families eked out a living through manioc farming, timber extraction, and some hunting. Using the ideas from Liberation Theology, the hamlet was struggling to construct an agricultural colony (*colônia*) founded on communal rights to land and resources. To develop their agricultural community they relied on income generated from the extraction of timber that they sold to independent contractors working in the region.

Throughout the 1980s and into the 1990s, Camutá fought against frequent attempts by timber extraction firms to poach the timber stands located behind the hamlet. The community resisted. One of the community leaders, Dico Ferreira, rallied his fellows through his unwavering resolve that land and resources belong to those who work them (part of the Liberation Theology creed). Dico believed that social justice was best achieved if the people of Camutá harvested the timber and invested the profits locally in their agricultural colony rather than allow outside firms to export the profits to other parts of Brazil or overseas. He also maintained that Camutá's slower rate of extraction and care given to the cutting of timber roads, as compared to the careless work done by extraction firms, was a better environmental alternative that destroyed less of the noncommercial species while allowing more time for regrowth. This claim was later substantiated by FASE's (2002) research that demonstrated timber firms damaged on average 27 trees with diameters above 30 centimeters per hectare. The destruction comes from the construction of timber roads, work areas, and the felling of trees on top of other trees. Techniques used by the small-scale extractors, such as in Camutá, by contrast, damage only 11 trees per hectare.

To protect against intrusions by timber firms, the people of Camutá began patrolling the expanses of their territory, which, like most land in Gurupá, was not demarcated. When community members

---

[6]At the time people in Gurupá were not aware that the tacit was pioneered by the rubber tappers of Acre under the leadership of Chico Mendes. For a full account of the Acre struggle with cattle ranchers and the assassination of Mendes, see Rodrigues (2007) and Revkin (1990).

discovered illegal timber roads, they gathered their fellows to travel to the extraction site. Men, women, and children then confronted the extractors and impeded their work. Dico told of the fear and apprehension felt by the community members as they encircled the extractors in the forest. The community members were unarmed and their intentions nonviolent, but they were resolute on obstructing the timber extraction. If the extractors were armed or aggressive, the outcome could be perilous. But Dico calculated that the cost of not challenging the intrusions was just as dangerous in the long-term because the community would be robbed of a vital resource needed for its well-being. Dico smiled as he recounted that in each empate they found the extractors to be men from rural communities similar to Camutá. These men had little desire to fight their fellow ribeirinho families. In every instance, the extractors withdrew peacefully. Later Camutá would receive threats of legal action from the local judge on behalf of the timber firms. On one occasion they were imprisoned in Gurupá's jail for their actions. Dico explained, "We just kept on patrolling our land and using empates whenever there was a problem. No one at the time had legal title to the land. We lived and worked the land, so the timber was ours and we defended our rights to it."

As the comunidades in Gurupá grew in number and strength, they began to focus on reorganization of the rural workers union (*Sindicato dos Trabalhadores Rurais*), which was a key institution needed to establish legal rights to land for the agroextractivists. Up until that point in time the union was under the control of the conservatives in support of the local landowning elite and the military regime (Pace 1998:178). They purposefully kept the union from pursuing rural workers' rights to fair earnings vis-à-vis the trading-post merchants or usufruct and indemnification rights to land. To change the course of the union, the opposition coalition put together an election slate that, once elected, would aggressively pursue these matters. When union elections were near, members of the comunidades entered the union building unannounced one afternoon and discovered massive voter-registration fraud being committed by the outgoing union president, likely at the bequest of the large landowners and political appointees of the military regime. The opposition members realized that the forthcoming elections were being rigged and called for assistance from their fellows to come and secure the union and protect the evidence of fraud from destruction.

What followed in 1986 was an unprecedented and harrowing confrontation between conservative members backing the local elite and status quo and a much larger group who supported the opposition. The opposition coalition coordinated a 54-day occupation of union headquarters to protest the fraud and force government officials to investigate. Hundreds of supporters of the opposition from the interior mobilized to come and participate (see Figure 8.8). Isabel Silva Viana described the protests as an expression of unity, support, and camaraderie never experienced before among agroextractivists. For the first time the lowly farmer and extractor joined with others to "confront the bicho" of inequality, she said, using the regional metaphor. She told of how many families sent food so that no one occupying the union went hungry. People prayed together, sang songs together, and endured as the conservatives hurled insults, threats, and sometimes stones at the protestors. We had many leaders she said: Mamê Chico Evangelista, Moarcyr Alho, Bertila Almeida Ferreira, Dico Ferreira, Chiquinho Alves, Beijamin Gonçalves, Manuel do Carmo de Jesus Pena, Alfredo Gomes da Costa Filho, Pedro Tapuru Alves, Sebastião Pena, Osvaldo

FIGURE 8.8 | *Union occupation, Mamê Chico Evangelista addressing the audience.*

Photograph by P. Alves 1986.

Viana Serrão, Nelcindo Rodrigues de Jesus, Adelino Pantoja da Costa, João Nascimento da Cruz, and of course her husband, Edgar.

A large protest march was held in which 3,000 supporters walked through the streets of town—a mobilization of the population on the scale of the all-important Saint Benedict procession. The large landowners and their political allies were shocked at the size of the protest. They realized in no uncertain terms that unless the opposition was repressed immediately their days of local control, and their way of life, would end. They tried in vain to call in military police to end the union occupation, but apparently Gurupá was not of enough strategic importance to regional powers to merit intervention.

In the midst of the union occupation, the priest's boat—*O Livramento* (Liberation)—was stolen and sunk. The boat was an important symbol for the opposition as it was the principal means through which the Padre reached the vast rural population to spread Liberation Theology and assist in social organization. To the conservatives the boat symbolized all the challenges to landowners' power, and its destruction seemed to be the best way to demoralize the opposition. To the contrary, for 18 months after its sinking, the opposition movement fervently searched for the boat in the vastness of the Amazon River. When it was eventually found and pulled from the muddy bottoms of the river (see Figure 8.9), the people of Gurupá interpreted it as a miracle and a sign from Saint Benedict (the protector of river travelers and the poor in general). The priest and the opposition coalition were now understood to have the blessing of the Saint.

In the end, the opposition coalition took control of the union and easily won the next election. The union began systematic support for agroextractivists in their land struggles with landowners and extraction firms. The patron–client system that governed Gurupá for centuries fell apart, leaving only a bitter memory in the minds of many. With the union firmly in place, the opposition began strengthening the associated political party, the Workers' Party (*Partido dos Trabalhadores*) or PT, which was founded in 1981. PT steadily grew in influence, first electing *vereadores* (council members) and then mayors of Gurupá. By 1989 the support for PT had grown so strong in Gurupá that in the national presidential elections the municipality was the only one in all of Brazil to vote in the initial and runoff phases for the PT candidate Luiz Inácio Lula da Silva. Although Lula was unsuccessful in this election, he showed his gratitude by visiting the town—taking lots of pictures with his Gurupaense supporters. Lula later went on to win

FIGURE 8.9 | *Raising of the Livramento.*
Photograph by P. Alves 1988.

two terms as president of Brazil; and when he left office in 2010, he was
the most popular politician in the country.

V

By the 1990s environment concerns over holes in the ozone layer and
initial warnings on the impacts of global warming helped created anxious publics throughout the world. Within this new global environmental context, the repeated reports out of Amazonia documenting
decades of rain forest destruction and irreplaceable loss of biodiversity
drew increasingly vocal international criticism. These reports were
combined with grim predictions of global climate change, to which the
burning of the rain forest contributed. Preservation of the rainforest
was eventually framed in terms of maintaining a massive natural
carbon sink to blunt the worst greenhouse effects (Hunt 2007).

At this point something new emerged in the developmental discourses. Environmentalists joined with poverty alleviation specialists
to envision alternative development models (Barbosa 2000). The concept of sustainable development was born when economic growth was

tied to sustaining long-term use of resources with minimal disruption of ecosystems. At about the same time, the assault on rainforest people's livelihood through habitat destruction also surfaced as an important element in environmental struggles. Although global audiences were at first unfamiliar with the very existence of rainforest peoples (Indigenous peoples and agroextractivists), let alone their plight, when their livelihoods were redefined as "naturally conservationist" and their images recast as rainforest guardians,[7] international interest rose significantly (Hall 1997:99; Barbosa 2000:103). By the mid-1990s, an array of grassroots organizations, NGOs, Brazilian and international government agencies, universities, and international lending agencies began helping rainforest peoples protect their livelihood, which, in turn, would protect the rain forest. These groups provided resources for funding, legal aid, and lobbying to secure legal rights to land. They also provided expertise to assist in the development of pilot projects in extractive reserves, sustainable forestry, sustainable fishing, and sustainable agriculture (Hall 1997:33–35).

In Gurupá, the rural union working closely with Paulo Oliveria, who conducted his Master's research on labor organization in Gurupá in the mid-1980s, was able to take advantage of this new interest in sustainable development. Through Oliveira's leadership, in 1997, the NGO FASE-Gurupá (*Federação de Órgãos de Assistência Social e Educacional* or Federation of Social and Educational Assistance Entities) received a large grant from the European Union's Pilot Program to Conserve the Brazilian Forest designed to improve local standards of living while developing sustainable development projects that preserved the rain forest. Over the next decade FASE worked with the rural union and Gurupá residents to conduct dozens of pilot projects in sustainable forestry, fishery, agriculture, and environmental monitoring.

---

[7]The concept of rainforest guardian comes from research on rainforest peoples' traditional lifestyles, such as slash-and-burn agriculture, extraction of forest resources, fishing, and hunting, which suggests that rainforest peoples make their living while managing natural resources in sustainable ways and conserving (or even increasing) rainforest biodiversity over long periods of time (Sponsel et. al. 1996:23, Smith and Wishnie 2000:495–96, 514; Schwartzman, Nepstad, and Moreira 2000:1371). Research suggests that their various modes of subsistence may have the potential to create a higher standard of living than any other current Amazon development strategy (Posey and Balée 1989; Anderson et al. 1991).

FASE and the rural union helped regularize land titles and ownership claims in the municipality (a major task) and successfully developed a number of sustainable management plans approved by IBAMA (*Instituto Brasileiro do Meia Ambiente e dos Recursos Naturais Renováveis*—Brazilian Institute for the Environment and Renewable Natural Resources). These initiatives left Gurupá with extractive reserves, managed areas, and quilombos that protected 90 percent of the municipality.

One of the first undertakings by FASE was an international conference in 1998 on the commercialization of forest products produced in a sustainable form hosted in Gurupá. By FASE's account, 169 representatives from 20 countries attended the conference and discussed ways to produce marketable goods for international commerce while protecting the rain forest. The conference made a strong impression on the people of Gurupá and reinforced the value of maintaining rainforest ecologies. Pedro Alves—more commonly known as "Pedro Tapuru"—is a former agroextractivist from the Mararú River who is now employed by the Chico Mendes Institute. Pedro worked for FASE in the 1990s and remembered the conference. He described how FASE and the union had to scramble to find housing, food, and filtered water for so many different types of people speaking so many different languages. But the experience opened people's eyes in Gurupá. "We found out," he said, "how much the world valued our forest, and we learned we needed to take steps to preserve it for future generations."

Manuel Pantoja Costa, or "Bira" as he is more commonly known, was hired by Paulo Oliveira in 1997 to coordinate the project in Gurupá. Bira, the brother of Alfredo Gomes da Costa Filho, grew up as an agroextractivist in Gurupá-Mirím. Later he became a nurse in the municipal hospital where he worked for 20 years. Bira recalled that one of the first tasks he had to coordinate was the creation a forest inventory for all the properties in the municipality. The baseline data were essential to gage the sustainable development possibilities. To amass the information, Bira worked long hours in the countryside, communicating with his fellow agroextractivists and assisting the FASE technicians in all their logistical needs.

Following the completion of the inventory, the next step for FASE was to regularize land ownership. Bira explained: "Regularization meant sorting through and assessing all claims to land, then obtaining the proper documents to legally register it with a government agency.

This process did not always result in a land title, but it did guarantee land rights for the family that works it." At this point the attorney Girolamo Treccani (who wrote his dissertation on Gurupá's land tenure system—2006) joined FASE and began the difficult and arduous task of reviewing documents and mitigating conflicting land claims, some of which dated back to colonial times. Pedro Tapuru worked alongside Girolamo and learned the complex land tenure laws for Brazil. He eventually wrote a manual outlining the process.

Pedro described how innovative FASE had to be to regularize land— creating six legal land-use models. Four of the models—Extractive Reserves, Sustainable Development Reserves, Agroextractive Settlements, and Floodplain Settlements—are based on the first Extractive Reserves established in 1990 by Acre rubber tappers—most famously led by Chico Mendes who was murdered by cattle ranchers in 1988. In Gurupá the models vary principally in terms of the type of resident association created and which government agency has control over the granting of land rights (federal or state). A fifth model, the Quilombo, is based on the recognition of the land rights of remnants of slave refugee populations—a right established by Brazil's 1988 Constitution, Decree 68 (see footnote 27 in Chapter 4). The sixth model is private ownership of land.

In each case, people traditionally associated with the forest extract renewable commercial forest products (rubber, fruits, nuts, resins, fibers, timber) along with some subsistence agriculture, fishing, and hunting in a sustainable manner that does not lead to deforestation (see Allegretti 1990; Barbosa 2000). According to Pedro Tapuru, families of a prospective reserve or settlement must follow four steps: create an association to represent the community, establish legal claim to the land, develop a sustainable resource management plan (*plano do manejo*) approved by IBAMA, and then petition the appropriate federal or state government agency for communal rights to the land. If successful, the land grant is often issued for 10 years—which is then renewable if compliance with environmental regulations is met.

FASE and the rural union worked closely with the local communities to develop the management plans, which set limits to farming, extraction, hunting, and fishing. The process of getting residents to agree on the plans, according to Bira, was very hard work. People of Gurupá, he said, were not used to working cohesively in such large numbers. Bira's job required much patience and negotiation skills to help each community reach a unanimous decision on how they would use their land in sustainable ways. But the benefits of such agreements were of great enough value to the agroextractivists of Gurupá that most communities work diligently to reach consensus on livelihood practices. In many cases the old religious brotherhoods—reinvigorated by the CEB movement of the Church—provided the social foundation to establish trust and cooperation among people (as suggested by Wagley). This foundation helped overcome centuries of community fragmentation created by the divide-and-rule tradition of the patron–client system as well as the necessity of geographic mobility in the extractive economy.

Pedro Tapuru proudly spoke of many successes, such as the first communal forestry sustainable maintenance plan approved in the state of Pará by IBAMA, which occurred in Camutá of the Pucuruí River. The most impressive achievement, though, according to Pedro, was the creation of the Floodplain Settlement plan for interfluvial islands. "It represented the first regularization of land and water on river islands in all of Brazil. I say land and water because much of the islands are inundated not only seasonally by also daily due to the influence of the tides." He continued: "It took over 1000 days of legal processing in Brasília with dozens of trips by FASE personnel to clarify and negotiate terms. But we were successful and now the model is now used throughout the Marajó region of the lower Amazon."

FASE and the rural union also set up a number of pilot projects to improve agroextractivist production. For example, using GPS devises, they trained the rural inhabitants to record and map the location of each commercially valuable tree on their property. Under the terms of sustainable forestry management plans developed for IBAMA, for each tree harvested, another of the same species was planted and plotted. The mapping provided the agroextractivist with a precise record of natural resources and helped regulate the extraction rate because the owner knew when particular trees would be ready for harvest.

Another successful pilot project was the improvement of shrimp production on the *Ilha de Cinzas* (Island of Ashes) in the northeastern fringe of the municipality. The community's main source of revenue came from the sale of shrimp. But the production methods used led to a severe drop in harvest quantity and quality by seasons' end. FASE— now under the directorship of Jorge Pinto—and the rural union first tried raising shrimp in artificial nurseries. They soon discovered the shrimp would cannibalize one another in captivity. The next innovation attempted was the widening of lateral strips in the shrimp trap (called *matapí*) so that small shrimp could escape and continue to grow, while the medium and large shrimp were harvested. This simple solution worked exceptionally well. The quality and size of shrimp sold improved greatly and there was no shortage because the small shrimp had time to grow and were only caught in the later part of the shrimping season.

Without question the most far-reaching pilot program designed by FASE, rural union, and people of Gurupá was the management of açaí trees. Açaí is often cited as a forest commodity whose careful production offers one of the best opportunities for sustainable forestry management, including maintenance of forest cover (Brondízio 2008). Combined with selective harvesting of trees for palm hearts when the palms grow too high for fruit collection, açaí can provide substantial monetary benefits for the local population (Brondízio 2008; Anderson et al. 1991; Murrieta, Dufour, and Siqueira 1999). In Gurupá, FASE and the rural union experimented with various pruning and harvesting techniques until they found ones that provided the maximum sustainable yields for both açaí and palm hearts. Next they worked jointly with the agroextractivists to spread the seeds for the palms to grow in all the places they had existed before the palm heart extraction boom. The process was very successful; and as a result, Gurupá was the only municipality in all of Brazil to increase forest canopy cover during the 2000s.

Good fortune then followed. Açaí's popularity, once restricted to Amazon populations, spread to other parts of Brazil as the technology of freezing the pulp was developed (Brondízio 2008). Outside of Amazonia, açaí is typically mixed with guaraná (high in caffeine) and sugar to produce a type of energy drink. It is also served frozen and greatly sweetened, almost in the form of ice cream. By 2009, açaí in powdered form entered international markets, purportedly as a rich antioxidant health supplement that proponents suggested helps cleanse the body of carcinogenic substances—while others touted its weight loss capabilities. To people in Gurupá, these claims were odd, sometimes laughable. For centuries açaí was known as a staple food that filled the stomach. As Isabel Viana retorted, "eating açaí every day makes you gain weight, not lose it. Eating it leads to sleepiness, not alertness." To Isabel, only the idea of antioxidant cleansing properties seemed plausible. But then she reasoned that people in Gurupá do not have better health or live longer than nonconsumers of açaí, so maybe that was not true as well. Nonetheless, she, as all people in Gurupá, were very pleased when açaí consumption boomed domestically and globally.

Artúlia Lourenço, an agroextractivist from Mojú River, commented that açaí extraction was like a gold mine. She explained that before the açaí boom, people in the interior had to work hard the entire day—extracting timber or palm heart, working in their roças, not to mention hunting and fishing and other chores needed at home. With açaí it is not like that. She continued: "You get up at dawn, but about nine or ten o'clock in the morning you come back with harvested fruit. You wait for your buyer to come by, get your money, then eat lunch and take a nap in your hammock. If you want to continue working the stands, you do so and don't stay home. It's your choice since you already have money to buy things." She sighed and said, "I hope to God this will continue."

The successful struggle to overturn the patron–client system, distribute land to those who work it, and democratize the political system paid off brilliantly with the açaí boom. Most families have found a way to participate in the wealth generated and improve their standard of living. For those not directly benefiting from the boom—such as the urban poor or rural workers on land where açaí does not grow, a series of national programs designed by the Lula administration to alleviate poverty have made a substantial difference in living standards. Retirement pensions for the elderly and the *Bola Família* and *Bola Escolar* (monthly payments given to the poor, low-income families with children in school, and to pregnant women) have provided a substantial safety net. Combined with the slow but steady improvement in the health care system (particularly the rising access to vaccinations for children and reduction in malaria), by 2013 there are no longer masses of children with visibly stunted growth and bellies full of parasites, or groups of children working in the town's streets selling gum, candy, or home-made *salgados* (snacks). The current social class distribution in 2013 also reflects this trend—with only 13.9 percent of households falling into class E (very poor) versus the 70 percent in this category in 1948 (see footnotes 5 and 17 in Chapter 4).

With the new wealth there has been an explosion in consumption of motorcycles and cars in town, despite the limited expanse of roads and overall lack of potential destinations. Cell phone use is widespread and common since 2009, and good quality housing is increasingly available with nice homes being built far from the riverside in contrast to the 1940s. Air conditioners, satellite TV with hundreds of stations, and laptops with Internet access are available to those with enough resources. Processed foods and soft drinks are also readily available, along with the increase in childhood and adult obesity now showing up in the population. People in Gurupá are beginning to get college degrees—with coursework offered during school holiday breaks for those unable to leave the town by professors coming in from Belém. Gurupá even has its first anthropology undergraduate student—whose grandmother was photographed as a child by Wagley in 1948 (see Figure 3.8)—ready to add her research insights to the growing collection of studies of the community.

VII

In the 1953 edition of *Amazon Town*, Charles Wagley concluded the book with these four paragraphs:

> *Any program for the development of the Amazon Valley or for similar underdeveloped areas must envisage and include a wide scope of interrelated problems. Such programs must recognize that in society, health, economics, religion, educational processes, recreation, values, morals, and so forth, are but convenient categories. A society and the culture by which it lives is an integrated system. Change in one sphere evokes changes in the whole system.*
>
> *Improvement of the situation of one group within a society means change for all groups. As the situation of the Amazon ribeirinho is improved, the position of the small-town upper-class (the commercial elite, the bureaucrats, and so on) and the position of the regional aristocrats will be affected. It must be recognized, therefore, in planning technical-assistance programs, that certain groups within a society will not desire change. The status quo is or appears favorable to them, and for want of vision they feel that change challenges their present favorable position. If technical-assistance programs are to have any value for the people of underdeveloped areas, care must be taken not simply to reinforce the status quo. To avoid this danger, the planners of such programs must have a knowledge of the social system of the societies in question and of the functions and the needs of the various groups who together form the*

society. Only in this way will such programs "increase productivity of material and human resources and a wide and equitable distribution of such increased productivity, so as to contribute to higher standards of living for entire populations" (UN 1949:14).

It is inevitable that change will and should come to the Amazon region and to other similar areas. Social anthropologists have often argued "cultural relativity." They have pointed out that progress, good and evil, success and failure, and beauty and ugliness are values relative to the particular culture in which they are found. It is difficult, they say, to judge one way of life as superior or inferior to another. One people, as in India, places a high value on the development of religious and philosophical speculation; another values technology, as in Europe and the United States. This point of view is sound when it teaches us to understand, to respect, and to tolerate other ways of life. Yet when a culture, through lack of technological equipment and for reasons of social organization, fails to provide for the material needs of its people beyond a mere survival level, that society and culture must be judged inferior.

Change is in order in such technologically less complex societies. This does not imply, of course, the obliteration of a way of life or the passing of judgment on a total society. Each culture contains patterns and concepts of tremendous value to the people themselves, which, if lost, would cause irreparable evil to the functions of the society and loss to our world heritage. The traditional folk culture of the Amazon region, built as it is out of generations of experience in that particular environment and derived from three cultural heritages, contains much of great beauty and value that will be necessary in the future and that must be retained. It is to be hoped that a new Amazon culture will be formed combining the productive powers of modern technology and science and the efficiency of modern industry with the many positive values of the present way of life. If the new Amazon culture is achieved, it will be as expressive of the region as that described in this book.

When change came to Gurupá, as described in this chapter, adjustments on many levels were required. Subsistence strategies shifted as economic opportunities widened. Political and class realignments took place as new religious beliefs transformed the population. New patterns of land use occurred as land titling innovations and technological improvements were introduced. As foreseen by Wagley, those in power resisted these changes. Unforeseen, however, was the path taken by the opposition to force out those in power. Religious change through Liberation Theology and the formation of CEBs drove the struggles for the rural union and local political office and eventually led to the ouster of the patrões who were the large landowners and strong merchants. The struggle might not have been as violent as in other parts of the Amazon, but tensions ran high and the potential for danger or harm was ever present.

In 1948 Wagley observed there was a lack of esprit de corps to unite the community, which he understood to be essential for successful development projects. Following the 1980s turmoil and successes of the agroextractivists vis-à-vis the patrões, a very strong esprit de corps emerged. This unity facilitated the work of FASE, which did a remarkable job of regularizing chaotic land titles and initiating sustainable development projects in timber, shrimp, and most important, açaí. The esprit de corps is also evident in the reconciliation that has occurred since the turmoil. The ex-mayor Cecília Palheta, who clashed frequently with the church laity, and Padre Giúlio in the 1980s, can, in 2013, be seen walking side-by-side with the priest as they help plan events for the next Saint Benedict celebration. People talk of José Vicente and all his political misdeeds, but still attest to the respect he showed individuals on at least the personal level. Pedro Tapuru, who was very active in the opposition movement, said that the ex-mayor was never disparaging toward him or his family. Pedro recounted that during the symbolic twist of fortune that led José Vicente to sell his prized round house on the riverfront to FASE in the 2000s, which in turn was given to the rural workers union, there was no remorse or rancor. Even more indicative of the shifts in allegiances was the success of one of José Vicente's sons, Rómulo José Fernandes Barreto Mello, who now lives in Brasília and works in the Environmental Ministry. For a period, Rómulo was the national President of the Chico Mendes Institute, which currently employs Pedro. When Rómulo returns to visit in Gurupá, Pedro said, there is no mention of past conflict as he cheerfully joins up with his childhood friends.

The past has not been forgotten altogether, but small town life in Gurupá requires some accommodation and forgiveness. For example, when a name was chosen for a new plaza built opposite of where the Casa Borralho use to stand, there were grumblings when the name Oscar Santos was proposed. Yet no one stopped the naming process. Edgar Sousa commented one afternoon following a discussion of the union occupation in 1986, "Even the families of the old patrões who opposed the Church and rural union movement now understand that they were wrong."

Wagley maintained that when social change comes, it should never obliterate the existing way of life. Preservation of distinctive cultures is part of our world heritage. People in Gurupá today increasingly understand the value of their culture—due in part to publications such as *Amazon Town* and the steady succession of researchers working in the community. As Pedro Tapuru declared, "We only started giving value to our culture after so many foreigners came to study it." Today the people of Gurupá know that environmentalists are interested in their sustainable development projects, sociologists in their religious and rural union movement, anthropologists in their cultural traditions, and basically the world in their açaí.

But just as Wagley lauded the region's great beauty and value for the future, the struggle continues, now in the form of the challenges posed by the building of the Belo Monte Dam. On completion, the dam will produce an estimated 11,000 megawatts of energy, none of it destined for Gurupá. The destruction of rainforest (approximately 400 square kilometers) and the displacement of at least twenty-thousand people in the vicinity of Altamira is only the beginning as the dam will create long-term socioeconomic, environmental, and public health problems in an extensive area along the Xingú River, reaching the municipality of Gurupá. The initial support for the dam in Gurupá was high, framed with hopes of job creation and generic economic development. However, as people learned from NGOs and the Catholic Church about the impending negative impacts, support has fallen rapidly.

During interviews conducted in 2011 and 2012, people from Gurupá listed the following concerns about the dam's impact: alteration of the Xingú River (decline of water flow) leading to disruption of fluvial transportation between Gurupá and Altamira, decline in fish and shrimp stocks, water pollution leading to drinking water contamination and increases in water-borne diseases, upsurges in dengue fever and malaria, and potential loss of açaí production along the Xingú River as the river recedes. After the dam construction is completed the fears turn to worker outmigration (potentially 80,000 unemployed) spilling into Gurupá and leading to land conflict, crime, and the overwhelming of the already crowded education and health care systems. In addition, data from the World Health Organization's World

Commission on Dams predicts long-lasting effects such as malnutrition from the disruption of food sources and commerce, and psychosocial disorders from elevated levels of stress, social disruption, and substance abuse.

The people of Gurupá worry whether their hard fought victories to reverse centuries of predatory economic patterns, exploitative social relations, poverty, and poor health will be lost as the Xingú River waters recede. Or will the strength of their religious organizations, rural union, political parties, and support from NGOs allow them to mitigate and minimize potential harm and continue creating a better way of life? The hope for a new Amazon culture combining the productive powers of modern technology and science, with the many positive values of the present way of life, as imagined by Charles Wagley in 1948, is today as promising as it is problematic. At the minimum, this book provides a careful description of a rich culture, constructed out of the ashes of Indigenous collapse, amalgamated with African and European traditions and beliefs over the centuries, confronting recurrent and novel problems to arrive in a better present day, with a possible blueprint for an even better future for the community and region.

APPENDIX 1

Pseudonyms and Names of People in Gurupá Identified through Wagley's Photographs and Fieldnotes

Real Life Name	Amazon Town Pseudonym
Abilio Cardoso	Abilio Costa
Alvaro Teixeira	Orlando
Bibi (Benedito) Pará	Bibi Marajó
Dom Clemente	Padre (Chapter 4)
Coronel Filomeno Borralho	Coronel Filomeno Cesar deAndrade
Dica Teixeira	Diquinha
Diná Borralho	Dora
Dico Dias	João Dias
Domingos Veiga	Domingos Alves
Elíos Veiga	Eneas Ramos
Ernesto Meirelles	Ernesto Morais
Feliciana Pará	Veridiana
Francisco Felix	Francisco Firmo
Francisco Nobre de Carvalho	Joaquim Nobre
Jajaba	Oswald Costa
João Coimbra	João Porto
Jorge Palheta	Jorge Povo
José Julio Andrade Ramos	Pereira Silva
Inacinha (Inácia) Barreta Mello Camarão	Branquinha
Manuel Morra Serra	Manuel Serra Feirra
Manuel Paiva	Manuel Pires
Marinho de Abreu Pae	Antonio Noronha
Morena (Olinda) Coimbra	Morena Porto
Nhenduca de Conceição	Juca
Paulo Ferreira de Freitas	Paulo Azevedo
Satiro Ronato de Lima	Rui (Dona Diná's brother-in-law)
Teodosio	Oscar Santos
Tolentino	Teodoso
Verissima	Valentino
Zeca Pará	Catita Dutra
Zeferino Urbano da Fonseca	Zé Marajó
	Barão de Gurupá

APPENDIX 2

Gurupá Researchers and Principal Works

1953	Charles Wagley. *Amazon Town*. New York: MacMillan Co.
1955	Eduardo Galvão. *Santos e Visagens*. São Paulo: Companhia Editôra Nacional.
1957	Charles Wagley. *Uma Comunidade Amazônica*. São Paulo: Brasiliana.
1964	Charles Wagley revisit (1962)— *Amazon Town*. Revisit in 1962 and new preface. New York: Alfred A. Knopf.
1974	Darrel Miller—Amazon Town in 1974. MA Thesis, University of Florida.
1976	Charles Wagley. New Preface and "Ita in 1974: an Epilog" by Darrel Miller. New York: Oxford University Press.
1977	Charles Wagley. Uma Comunidade Amazônica. New Preface and "Ita em 1974: um epilogo," by Darrel Miller. Sao Paulo: Editora Nacional.
1984	Arlene Kelly. Family, Church, and Crown: A Social and Demographic History of the Lower Xingu River Valley and the Municipality of Gurupá. PhD diss., University of Florida.
1986	Penny Magee. Plants, Medicine, and Health Care in Amazônia: A Case study of Itá. MA thesis, University of Florida.
1987	Richard Pace. Economic and Political Changes in the Amazonian Community of Itá. PhD diss., University of Florida.
1990	Charles Wagley. Uma Comunidade Amazônica and "Ita em 1974: um epilogo," by Darrel Miller. Belo Horizonte: Editora Itatiaia.
1991	Paulo H. B. Oliveira. Ribeirinhos e Roçeiros: Subordinação e Resistência Camponesa em Gurupá, Pará. MA thesis, University of São Paulo, Campinas.
1997–2002	*Boletim Projecto FASE Gurupá*. Belém: FASE.
1998	Richard Pace. *The Struggle for Amazon Town: Gurupá Revisited*. Lynne Reinner.
1999	Fabío Poelhekke and Paulo H.B. de Oliveira Jr. Projeto Gurupá: Sustainable Tropical Forest Exploitation through Community Ownership, A Brazilian Initiative. *Development* 42:2:53–56.
2001	Girolamo Domenico Treccani, Violência e Grilagem: Instrumentos de aquisição da propriedade no Pará, Belém: UFPA-ITERPA.
2002	FASE Projecto Gurupá internet site (www.fase.org.br). Accessed 12/2002.

2003   Royer, Jean-Marie. Logiques sociales et extractivisme. Etude
            anthropologique d'une collectivité de la forêt amazonienne, Etat
            du Pará, Brésil. PhD diss., Université Paris III-Sorbonne nouvelle,
            Institut des Hautes Etudes d'Amérique Latine.
2004   Neila Soares da Silva. Like a Mururé: Social Change in a Terra-Firme
            Community on the Amazon Estuary. MA thesis, University of Florida.
2006   Monte Hendrickson. Child Labor in the Brazilian Amazon: An
            Ethnographic Approach. MA thesis, Middle Tennessee State University.
2006   Mônica Barroso. Waves in the Forest. PhD diss., London School of
            Economics.
2006   Girolamo Domenico Treccani. Regularizar a Terra: Um Desafio para
            as Populações Tradicionais de Gurupá. PhD diss., Universidade
            Federal do Pará—NAEA, Belém (PA).
2008   Émina Márcoa Nery dos Santos. A Construção de Espaços Públicos
            na Política Educational em Gurupá. PhD diss., Universidade Federal
            do Pará Núcleo de Altos Estudos Amazônicos—NAEA, Belém, Brazil.
2009   Richard Pace. Television's Interpellation: Heeding, Missing, Ignoring,
            and Resisting the Call for Pan-National Identity in the Brazilian
            Amazon. *American Anthropologist.*
2009   Benedita Alcidema Coelho dos Santos Magalhã. Educação do
            Campo, Poder e Políticas Públicas: A Casa Familiar Rural de
            Gurupá-Pa, Uma Construção Permanente. Master's thesis,
            Programa de Pos-Graduação em Educação: UFPa.
            Richard Pace and Brian Hinote. 2013. *Amazon Town TV: An Audience
            Ethnography in Gurupá, Brazil.*
2013   Richard Pace & Brian Hinote. *Amazon Town TV.* Austin: University
            of Texas Press.

REFERENCES

Adams, Cristina, Rui Murrieta, and Rosely Sanches. 2005. Agricultura e Alimentação em Populações Ribeirinhas das Várzeas dos Amazonas: Novas Perspectivas. *Ambiente & Sociedade* – Vol. VIII n°. 1.

Agassiz, Louis. 1896. *A Journey in Brazil*. Boston: Houghton Mifflin.

Album do Estado do Pará, compiled at the behest of Dr. Augusto Montenegro, governor (1901–1908). Paris, 1910.

Allegretti, Mary. Extractive Reserves: An Alternative for Reconciling Development and Environmental Conservation in Amazonia. In Anthony Anderson (ed). *Alternatives to Deforestation: Steps toward Sustainable Use of the Amazonia Rain Forest*. New York: Columbia University Press. Pp. 252–64.

_____. 1995. Extracting Activities in the Amazon. In Miguel Clüsener-Godt and Ignacy Sach (ed). *Extractivism in the Brazilian Amazon: Perspectives on Regional Development*. MAB Digest 18, Paris: UNESCO. Pp. 157–74.

Amnesty International. 1988. *Brazil: Authorized Violence in Rural Areas*. London.

Anderson, A., P. May and M. Balick. 1991. *The Subsidy from Nature: Palm Forests Peasantry, and Development on an Amazon Frontier*. New York: Columbia University Press.

Arensberg, Conrad. 1954. The Community-Study Method. *American Journal of Sociology*. LX (2): 109–24.

Branford, Sue and Oriel Glock. 1985. *The Last Frontier: Fighting Over Land in the Amazon*. London: Zed Books Ltd.

Barbosa, L. 2000. *The Brazilian Amazon Rainforest: Global Ecopolitics, Development, and Democracy*. New York: University Press of America.

Barham, Bradford and Oliver Coomes. 1994a. Reinterpreting the Amazon Rubber Boom: Investment, the State, and Dutch Disease. *Latin American Research Review*, Vol. 29 (2):73–109.

_____. 1994b. Wild Rubber: Industrial Organisation and the Microeconomics of Extraction During the Amazon Rubber Boom (1860–1920). *Journal of Latin American Studies* 26: 37–72.

Bastide, Roger. 1952. Race Relations in Brazil: São Paulo. Paris: *Courier*, UNESCO, Vol. 5, Nos. 8–9.

_____. 1951. Religion and Church in Brazil. In T. Lynn Smith and Alexander Marchant (eds). *Brazil: Portrait of Half a Continent*. New York: Dryden Press.

Bates, Henry Walter. 1930. *The Naturalist on the River Amazon*. London: J.M. Dent & Sons.

Berryman, Phillip. 1987. *Liberation Theology: Essential Facts about the Revolutionary Movement in Latin America and Beyond*. Philadelphia: Temple University Press.

Betendorf, Padre João Felipe. 1909. Chronica da Missão dos Padres da Companhia de Jesus no Estado do Maranhão. *Revista do Instituto Histórico e Geográfico Brasileiro* (RIHGB) LXXII, Tomo 1.

Blay, Eva. 1981. As Prefeitas: A Participação da Mulher no Brasil. Rio de Janeiro: Avenir Editoral.

Boff, Leonardo and Clodovis Boff. 1986. *Liberation Theology: From Dialogue to Confrontation.* San Francisco: Harper & Row Publishers.

Borromeu, Carlos. 1946. *Contribução a história das paróquias da Amazônia.* Niterói: Escola Industrial Dom Bosco.

Brondízio, Eduardo. 2008. *The Amazonian Caboclo and the Açaí Palm: Forest Farmers in the Global Market.* New York: New York Botanical Garden Press.

Bunker, Stephan. 1985. *Underdeveloping the Amazon: Extraction, Unequal Exchange, and the Failure of the Modern State.* Chicago: University of Illinois Press.

Bruneau, Thomas. 1982. *The Church in Brazil: The Politics of Religion.* Austin: University of Texas Press.

Candido, Antonio. 1951. The Brazilian Family. In T. Lynn Smith and Alexander Marchant (eds). *Brazil: Portrait of Half a Continent.* New York: Dryden Press.

Castro, Josué de. 1946. *Geografia da fome.* Rio de Janeiro: Edições Antares.

Chayanov, Aleksandr Vasil'evich. 1986. *The Theory of the Peasant Economy.* Translated and Edited by Daniel Thorner, Basile Kerblay, and Robert E. F. Smith. Madison: University of Wisconsin Press.

Cleary, David. 1998. Lost Altogether to the Civilised World: Race and the Cabanagem in Northern Brazil, 1750 to 1850. *Society for Comparative Study of Society and History* 40(1):109–35.

_____. 2001. Towards an Environmental History of the Amazon: From Prehistory to the Nineteenth Century. *Latin American Research Review* 36(2):64–96.

Costa Pinto, Luiz de Aguiar. 1952. Race Relations in Brazil: Rio de Janeiro. Paris: *Courier*, UNESCO, Vol. 5, Nos. 8–9.

Cunha, Euclides da. 1944. *Rebellion in the Backlands.* Translated by Samuel Putnam. Chicago University of Chicago Press.

_____. 1941. *Á margem da história.* Pôrto: Empresa Literária e Tipográfica.

Davis, Kingsley. 1947. Future Migration in Latin America. *Milbank Fund Quarterly,* No. 1.

Denevan, William. 2003. The Native Population of Amazonia in 1492 Reconsidered. *Revista da India.* Vol. LXIII, No. 227:175–88.

Denis, Pierre. 1914. *Brazil.* London: Unwin.

Di Paolo, Pasquale. 1990. *Cabanagem: A Revolução Popular da Amazonia.* 3rd ed. Belém: CEJUP.

Dobyns, Henry. 1993. Disease Transfer at Contact. *Annual Review of Anthropology* 22:273–91.

Escobar, Arturo. 1995. *Encountering Development: The Making and Unmaking of the Third World.* Princeton, NJ: Princeton University Press.

Eskenazi, Brenda, Jonathan Chevrier, Lisa Rosas, Henry Anderson, Maria Bornman, Henk Bouwman, Aimin Chen, Barbara A. Cohn, Christiaan de Jager, Diane Henshel, Felicia Leipzig, John Leipzig, Edward Lorenz, Suzanne Snedeker, and Darwin Stapleton. 2009. The Pine River Statement: Human Health Consequences of DDT Use. *Environ Health Perspectives* 117(9): 1359–67.

FASE (Federação de Órgãos para Assistência Social e Educacional). 2002. Brasil: Manejo florestal comunitário na amazônia brasileira. FASE Projeto Gurupá internet site (www.fase.org.br). Accessed 5/2013.

_____. 1997 Marajoí: O Rio do Mururé e do Açaí. Boletim do programa Gurupá 1 (3):2. Belém: FASE.

Ferreira de Castro, José Maria. 1935. *A Selva*. Translated into English, by Charles Duff, as *The Jungle*. New York: Viking Press.

Firth, Raymond. 1951. *Elements of Social Organization*. London: Watts.

_____. 1939. *A Primitive Polynesian Economy*. London: Routledge & Sons.

Follmann, José. 1985. *Igreja, Ideologia, e Classes Sociais*. Petrópolis: Vozes.

Forde, Cyril Daryll. 1948. *Habitat, Economy and Society*. London: Methuen.

Foweraker, Joseph. 1981. *The Struggle for Land: A Political Economy of the Pioneer Frontier in Brazil from 1930 to the Present Day*. New York: Cambridge University Press.

Freyre, Gilberto. 1946. *The Masters and the Slaves*. Translated by Samuel Putnam. New York: Knopf.

Funes, Eurípedes. 1995. Nasci nas Matas, Nunca Tive Senhor. História e Memória dos Mocambos do Baixo Amazonas. PhD Dissertation. São Paulo, FFLCH Universidade de São Paulo.

Galvão, Eduardo. 1955. *Santos e visagens: um estudo da vida religiosa da Itá, Amazonas*. São Paulo: Campanhia Editôria Nacional.

_____. 1952. The Religion of an Amazon Community, unpublished PhD dissertation, Faculty of Political Science, Columbia University.

Gourou, Pierre. 1948. *Les Pays tropicaux*. Paris: Presses universitaires de France.

_____. 1949. L'Amazonie. *Cahiers d'Outre Mer*, Vol. II, No. 5. Pp. 1–13.

Gutiérrez, Gustavo. 1971. *Teología de la liberación: Perspectivas*. Lima: CEP.

Hall, Anthony. 2000. Introduction and Environment and Development in Brazilian Amazonia: From Protectionism to Productive Conservation. In Anthony Hall (ed). *Amazonia at the Crossroads: The Challenge of Sustainable Development*. London: Institute of Latin American Studies. Pp. 1–7, 99–114.

_____. 1997. *Sustaining Amazonia: Grassroots Action for Productive Conservation*. Manchester: Manchester University Press.

Harris, Mark. 2010. *Rebellion on the Amazon: The Cabanagem, Race, and Popular Culture in the North of Brazil, 1798–1840*. Cambridge: Cambridge University Press.

Hecht, Susanna and Alexander Cockburn. 2011. *The Fate of the Forest: Developers, Destroyers and Defenders of the Amazon*. Chicago: University of Chicago Press.

Heckenberger, Michael, Afukaka Kuikuro, Urissapá Tabata Kuikuro, J. Christian Russell, Morgan Schmidt, Carlos Fausto, and Bruna Franchetto. 2003. Amazonia 1492: Pristine Forest or Cultural Parkland. *Science* 301(19):1710–14.

Heckenberger, Michael, James Petersen and Eduardo Neves. 1999. Village Size and Permanence in Amazonia: Two Archaeological Examples from Brazil. *Latin American Antiquity* 10(4):353–76.

Hemming, John. 1978. *Red Gold: The Conquest of the Brazilian Indians*. Cambridge, MA: Harvard University Press.

Hunt, Colin. 2007. *Carbon Sinks and Climate Change: Forests in the Fight Against Global Warming*. Northampton, MA: Edward Elgar.

Hurley, Jorge. 1936. *Traços Cabanos*. Belém: Gráficas do Instituto Lauro Sodré.

IBGE Instituto Brasileiro de Geográfia e Estatística. 2012. *Censo Demgráfico e Censo Econônico*. Rio de Janeiro: IBGE.

———. 2001. *Censo Demográfico e Censo Econômico*. Rio de Janeiro: IBGE.

———. 1984. *Censo Demográfico e Censo Econômico*. Rio de Janeiro: IBGE.

———. 1956. *Censo Demográfico e Censo Econômico de 1950*. Volume X, Tomo 1 e 2. Rio de Janeiro: IBGE.

Instituto do Desenvolvimento Econômico-Social do Pará (IDESP). 1986/87. *1989 Anuário Estatístico do Estado do Pará*. Volume 9, Tomo 1–2. Belém: IDESP.

Instituto Peabiru. 2011. Diagnósico Socioeconômico, Ambiental e Cultural do Arquipélago do Marajó. Programa Viva Marajó. Belém: Institutio Peabiru.

Kelly, Arlene. 1984. Family, Church, and Crown: A Social and Demographic History of the Lower Xingú River Valley and the Municipality of Gurupá, 1623–1889. PhD dissertation, Gainesville: University of Florida.

Kiemen, Mathias. 1954. *The Indian Policy of Portugal in the Amazon Basin, 1614–1693*. Washington, DC: Catholic University Press.

Koster, Henry. 1816. *Travels in Brazil*. 2nd ed. London: Hurst, Rees, Orme & Brown.

Ladislau, Alfredo. 1933. *Terra immatura*. Rio de Janeiro: Civilização brasileira.

Le Cointe, Paul. 1947. *Amazonia brasileira: Arvores e plantas uteis*. São Paulo: Editora Nacional.

Leite, Serafim. 1943 [1938]. *História da Companhia de Jesus no Brasil. Tomo IV. Obras e Assuntos Gerais, Século XVII–XVIII*. Rio de Janeiro: Instituto Nacional do Livro; Lisbon: Livraria Portugália.

Levine, Daniel and Scott Mainwaring. 1989. Religion and Popular Protest in Latin America: Contrasting Experiences. In Susan Eckstein (ed). *Power and Popular Protest: Latin American Social Movements*. Berkeley: University of California Press. Pp. 203–40.

Lima, Deborah. 1999. A Construção Histórica do Termo Caboclo. Sobre Estruturas e Representações Sociais no Meio Rural Amazônico. *Novos Cadernos do Naea*: V. 2, N. 2, Pp. 5–32.

———. 1992. The Social Category Caboclo: History, Social Organization and Outsider's Social Classification of the Rural Population of an Amazonian Region. PhD dissertation, University of Cambridge.

Linton, Ralph. 1936. *The Study of Man*. New York: Appleton Century Crofts, Inc.

Lopes, Robson. 2004. Folias, Irmandades e Festejos:Transformações e Resistência do Catolicismo Popular em Gurupá-PA. Undergraduate Thesis. Belém: Universidade Estadual Vale do Acaraú.

Lorimer, Joyce. 1989. *English and Irish Settlement on the River Amazon 1550–1646*. London: The Hakluyt Society.

Loureiro, Violeta. 1985. *Os Parceiros do Mar*. CNPq/Museu Paraense Emílio Goeldi, Belém.

Magalhães, Benedita. 2009. Educação do Campo, Poder Local e Políticas Públicas: A Casa Familiar Rural de Gurupá-PA, Uma Construção Permanente. PhD disseratation, Universidade Federal do Pará—Graduate Program in Education—Belém.

Magalhães, Pedro de. 1922. *The Histories of Brazil*, Translated by John B. Stetson, Jr. New York: Cortes Society.

McGee, R. Jon and Richard Warms. 2011. *Anthropological Theory: An Introductory History*. New York. McGraw-Hill Companies.

Martins, Cristiane Martins, Denise Schaan and Vera Portal. 2010. Arqueológico do Marajó das Florestas: Fragmentos de um Desafio. In Denise Schaan and Cristiane Martins (eds). *Muito Alem dos Campos:Arqueologia e História na Amazônia Marajoara*. GK Noronha: Belém, PA. Pp. 105–38.

Martins, José de Souza. 1985. *A Militarização da Questão Agrária no Brasil*. Petrópolis: Vozes.

Meggers, Betty. 1971. *Amazonia: Man and Culture in a Counterfeit Paradise*. Chicago: Aldine-Atherton.

Métraux, Alfred. 1927. Les Migrations Historiques des Tupí-Guaraní. *Journal de la Societé des Americanistes de Paris*, Vol. 19, Pp. 1–45.

Meyerhoff, Howard A. 1949. Natural Resources in Most of the World. In Ralph Linton (ed). *Most of the World*. New York: Greenwood Press.

Moog, Vianna. 1936. *O ciclo do Ouro Negro*. Pôrto Alegre: Globo Rs.

Moraes Rego, Orlando. 1977. Feitorias Holandesas da Amazonia. *Revista de Cultura do Pará* XXVI & XXVII.

Morais, Tais and Eumano Silva. 2005. *Operação Araguaia: Os Arquivos Secretos da Guerrilha*. São Paulo: Geração Editorial.

Moran, Emílio. 1993. *Through Amazonian Eyes: The Human Ecology of Amazonian Populations*. Iowa City: University of Iowa Press.

_____. 1982. *Human Adaptability: An Introduction to Ecological Anthropology*. Boulder, CO: Westview Press.

_____. 1981. *Developing the Amazon*. Bloomington: Indiana University Press.

Moreira Neto, C. 1992. Os Principais Grupos Missionários que Atuaram na Amazônia Brasileira Entre 1607 e 1759 (Pp. 63–12), Reformulações da Missão Católica na Amazônia Entre 1750 e 1832 (Pp. 210–61), e Igreja e Cabanagem 1832–1849 (Pp. 262–95). In Eduardo Hoornaert (ed). *História da igreja na Amazônia*. Petrópolis: Vozes.

Murrieta, Rui, Darna L. Dufour and Andrea Siqueira. 1999. Food Consumption and Subsistence in Three Caboclo Populations on Marajó Island, Amazonia, Brazil. *Human Ecology* 27(3):45–62.

Myrdal, Gunnar. 1957. *Rich Lands and Poor*. New York: Harpers.

_____. 1944. *An American Dilemma: The Negro Problem and Modern Democracy*. New York: Harper & Row.

Nash, Roy. 1926. *The Conquest of Brazil*. New York: Harcourt, Brace and Company.

Neto, Mário Santos. 2013. Amazon Town. *Revista PZZ*, March 17, Pp. 15–21.

Neri, Marcelo. 2010. A Nova Classe Média Brasileira: O Lado Brilhante dos Pobres. FGV (http://www.fgv.br/cps/classemedia—accessed 4/2013).

Nugent, Stephan. 1993. *Amazon Caboclo Society: An Essay on Invisibility and Peasant Economy*. Oxford: Berg.

Oliveira, Adélia. 1983. Ocupação Humana. In Eneas Salati, Herbert Otto, Roger Shubart, Wolfgang Junk, Adelia Engrácia de Oliveira (eds). *Amazônia: Desenvolvimento, Integração, Ecologia*. São Paulo: Editora Brasiliense. Pp. 144–327.

Oliveira, Fabiana Luci de. 2012. A Nova Classe Média Brasileira. *Pensamiento Iberoameriano No. 10*. Pp. 105–31.

Oliveira, Paulo. 1991. Ribeirinhos e Roçeiros: Subordinação e Resistência Camponesa em Gurupá, Pará. Master's thesis, University of São Paulo, Campinas, Brazil.

Pace, Richard. 2009. Television's Interpellation: Heeding, Missing, Ignoring, and Resisting the Call for Pan-National Identity in the Brazilian Amazon. *American Anthropologist* 111(4):407–19.

_____. 2006. O Abuso Científico do Termo Caboclo? Dúvidas de Representação e Autoridade. *Boletim do Museu Paraense Emílio Goeldi: Ciências Humanas*. 1 (3):79–92.

_____. 2004. Failed Guardianship or Failed Metaphors in the Brazilian Amazon? Problems with 'Imagined Eco-Communities' and Other Metaphors and Models for the Amazon Peasantries. *Journal of Anthropological Research* 60(2):231–60.

_____. 1998. *The Struggle for Amazon Town: Gurupá Revisited*. Boulder, CO: Lynne Reinner Press.

_____. 1997. The Amazon Caboclo, What's In a Name? *The Luso-Brazilian Review* 34(2):81–89.

_____. 1995. The New Amazons in Amazon Town? A Case Study of Women's Public Roles in Gurupá, Pará. Brazil. *The Journal of Anthropological Research*, Vol. 51, No. 3:263–78.

_____. 1993. First-Time Televiewing in Amazonia: Television Acculturation in Gurupá, Brazil. *Ethnology* 32(2):187–205.

_____. 1992. Social Conflict and Political Activism in the Brazilian Amazon: A Case Study of Gurupá. *American Ethnologist* 9(4):710–32.

_____. 1990. The New Catholic Church in Itá: A Case Study of Liberation Theology, Ecclesiastical Base Communities, and Social Conflict in an Amazonian Community of Brazil. In Looking Through the Kaleidoscope: Essay in Honor of Charles Wagley. *Florida Journal of Anthropology*, Special Publication, Number 6, Pp. 11–17.

Pace, Richard and Brian Hinote. 2013. *Amazon Town TV: An Audience Ethnography in Gurupá, Brazil*. Austin: University of Texas Press.

Petit, Pere. 1996. *A Esperança Equilibrista: A Trajetória do PT no Pará*. Belém: NAEA/Jinkings Editores Associados.

Pierson, Donald. 1942. *Negroes in Brazil*. Chicago: University of Chicago Press.

Pinheiro, L. B. 2001. *Visões da Cabanagem: Uma Revolta Popular e suas Representações na Historiografia*. Manaus: Editora Valer.

Poelhekke, Fabio and Paulo H. B de Oliveria. 1999. Projeto Gurupá: Sustainable Tropical Forest Exploitation through Community Ownership, a Brazilian Initiative. *Development* 42 (2):53–56.

Poschman, Márcio, Marcelo Pereira, Alexandre Barbosa, Ronnie Silva and Ricardo Amorim. 2006. *Atlas da Nova Estratificação Social no Brazil. Vol. 1: Clase Média Desenvolvimento e Crise*. São Paulo: Cortez.

Posey, Darrell. 2000. Biodiversity, Genetic Resources and Indigenous Peoples in Amazonia: (Re)Discovering the Wealth of Traditional Resources of Native Amazonians. In Anthony Hall (ed). *Amazonia at the Crossroads: The Challenge of Sustainable Development*. London: Institute of Latin American Studies. Pp. 188–204.

Posey, Darell and William Balée (eds). 1989. *Resource Management in Amazonia: Indigenous and Folk Strategies*. Advances in Economic Botany 7. Bronx: New York Botanical Garden.

Reis, Artur Cezar Ferreira. 1942. *Sintese da História do Pará*. Belém: [s.n/].

Reis, Artur. 1993. *A Política de Portugal no Vale Amazônico*. Belém: Secult.

Revkin, Andrew. 1990. *The Burning Season: The Murder of Chico Mendes and the Fight for the Amazon Rain Forest*. Washington, DC: Island Press.

Rodrigues, Gomercindo. 2007. *Walking the Forest with Chico Mendes: Struggle for Justice in the Amazon*. Edited and translated by Linda Rabben. Austin: University of Texas Press.

Roosevelt, Anna. 1991. *Moundbuilders of the Amazon: Geophysical Archaeology on Marajo Island, Brazil*. San Diego: Academic Press.

Roosevelt, Anna (ed). 1994. *Amazonian Indians from Prehistory to the Present: Anthropological Perspectives*. Tucson, AZ: University of Arizona Press.

Rostow, Walt. 1960. *Stages of Economic Growth*. Cambridge: Cambridge University Press.

Royer, Jean-Marie. 2003. Logiques Sociales et Extractivisme. Etude Anthropologique d'une Collectivité de la Forêt Amazonienne, Etat du Pará, Brésil. PhD dissertation, Université Paris III-Sorbonne Nouvelle, Institut des Hautes Etudes d'Amérique Latine.

Sahlins, M. 1972. *Stone Age Economics*. Piscataway, New Jersey: Transaction Publishers.

Salles, Vicente. 1988. *O Negro no Pará sob o Regime da Escravidão*. Belém: Secretaria de Estado de Cultura-Secult.

Salem, Helena. 1981. Dos Palácios a Miséria da Períferia. In Antônio Carlos Moura, Helena Salem, Luiz Carlos Antero, Luiz Maklouf, and Sergio Buarque de Gusmão. *A Igreja do Oprimidos*. São Paulo: Editôria Brasil Debates (Brasil/Hoje 3). Pp. 17–64.

Santos, Francenilton, Abel Gama, Alana Fernandes, José Reis and Jocilene Guimarães. 2010. Prevalência de Enteroparasitismo em Crianças de Comunidades Ribeirinhas do Município de Coari, no Médio Solimões. Amazonas, Brasil: *Revisa Pan-Amazonia Saude* 1(4):23–28.

Santos, Roberto. 1980. *História da Amazônia (1800–1920)*. São Paulo: TAO.

Schaan, Denise. 2010. Long-Term Human Induced Impacts on Marajó Island Landscapes, Amazon Estuary. *Diversity* 2:182–206.

Schmink, Marianne and Charles Wood. 1992. *Contested frontiers in Amazonia.* New York: Columbia University Press.

Schwartzman, Stephen, Daniel Nepstad and Adriana Moreira. 2000. Arguing Tropical Forest Conservation: People Versus Parks. Conservation Biology 14(5):1370–74.

Silva, Hilton P. da. 2009. Socio-Ecology of Health and Disease: The Effects of Invisibility on the Caboclo Populations of the Amazon. In Cristina Adams, Rui Murrieta, Walter Neves, and David Harris (eds). *Amazon Peasant Societies in a Changing Environment: Political Ecology, Invisibility and Modernity in the Rainforest.* New York: Springer. Pp. 307–34.

_____. 2002. Aspectos Demográficos e Medico-epidemiológicos, das Comunidades de Caxiuanã, Melgaço, Pará. Em: Lisboa, P.L.B. (organizador), *Caxiuanã: Populações Tradicionais, Meio Físico & Diversidade Biológica.* Belém, Pará: Museu Paraense Emílio Goeldi. Pp. 77–93.

Skidmore, Thomas. 1993. *Television, Politics, and the Transition to Democracy in Latin America.* Washington, DC: Woodrow Wilson Center Press.

_____. 1988. *The Politics of Military Rule in Brazil: 1964–1985.* New York: Oxford University Press.

Steward, Julian (ed). *Handbook of South American Indians.* Washington, DC: Smithsonian Institution, 1946–1950.

Smith, Herbert. 1879. The Amazons and the Coast. New York: C. Scribner's Sons.

Smith, Eric and Mark Wishnie. 2000. Conservation and Subsistence in Small-Scale Societies. *Annual Review of Anthropology* 29:493–524.

Smith, T. Lynn. 1946. *Brazil: People and Institutions.* Baton Rouge: Louisiana State University Press.

Sponsel, Leslie, Robert Bailey and Thomas Headland. 1996. Anthropological Perspectives on the Causes, Consequences, and Solutions of Deforestation. In Leslie Sponsel, Thomas Headland, and Robert Bailey (eds). *Tropical Deforestation: The Human Dimension.* New York: Columbia University Press. Pp 3–52.

Telles, Edward. 2004. *Race in Another America: The Significance of Skin Color in Brazil.* Princeton, NJ: Princeton University Press.

Treccani, Girolamo. 2006. Regularizar a Terra: Um Desafio para as Populações Tradicionais de Gurupá. PhD dissertation, Belém: Universidade Federal do Pará (NAEA).

_____. 2001. Violência e Grilagem: Instrumentos de Aquisição da Propriedade no Pará. Belém: UFPA-ITERPA.

Vergolino-Henry, Anaíza and Arthur Figueredo. 1990. *A Presença Africana na Amazônia Colonial. Uma Notícia Histórica.* Belém: Arquivo Público do Pará.

Viveiros de Castro, Eduardo. 1996. Images of Nature and Society in Amazonian Ethnology. *Annual Review of Anthropology* 25:179–200.

United Nations Children's Fund. 2012. Levels & Trends in Child Mortality. Report 2012. New York; U.N. Children's Fund.

United Nations. 1949. Economic and Social Council Resolution No. 222 (IX), P. 14.

Wagley, Charles. 1988 [1977, 1955]. *Uma Comunidade Amazônica: Estudo do Homem os Trópicos*. Translated by Clotilde da Silva Costa. São Paulo: Editora Universidade de São Paulo.

_____. 1976 [1964, 1953]. *Amazon Town: A Study of Man in the Tropics*. New York: Oxford University Press.

_____. 1968. *The Latin American Tradition. Essays on the Unity and the Diversity of Latin American Culture*. New York: Columbia University Press.

_____. 1959. On the Concept of Social Race in the Americas. 17 in *Actas de XXXIII Congresso Internacional de Americanistas*. San José, Costa Rica. Reprinted in Wagley's *The Latin American Tradition*. New York: Columbia University Press, 1968.

_____. 1952. Race Relations in an Amazon Community. In Charles Wagley (ed). *Race and Class in Rural Brazil*. Paris: UNESCO.

_____. 1946. Review of *The Masters and the Slaves: A Study in the Development of Brazilian Civilization*, Gilberto Freyre and Samuel Putnam. *Political Science Quarterly* Volume 61(4):625–27.

Wagley, Charles (ed). 1974. *Man in the Amazon*. Gainesville: University Presses of Florida.

Wagley, Charles and Eduardo Galvão. 1949. *The Tenetehara Indians of Brazil*. New York: Columbia University Press.

Wallace, Alfred Russel. 1853. *A Narrative of Travels on the Amazon and Rio Negro*. London: Reeve & Co.

Weinstein, Barbara. 1983. *The Amazon Rubber Boom, 1850–1920*. Stanford, CA: Stanford University Press.

Wolf, Eric. 1982. *Europe and the People Without History*. Berkeley: University of California Press.

World Health Organization (WHO). 2012. *World Health Statistics 2012*. Geneva: World Health Organization.

INDEX

....

A Selva (Ferreira de Castro), 97
Aboriginal religious beliefs, assimilated
    by Christianity, 227–228
Acre, 28, 177, rubber tappers,
    278 note 6, 285
African slaves 31, 31 note 13, 34,
    41 note 19, 44 note 22, 45 note 25,
    46 note 27, 133, 133 note 24,
    202 note 9
Agassiz, Louis, 37–38
Agassiz, Mrs. Louis, 37
Agriculture, slash-and-burn 5, 7, 31,
    63, 66–69, 269; sustainability 7
    note 10, 65 note 52, 283 note 7;
    prehistoric evolution of,
    32 note 15; and food imports,
    63 note 48
Amazon climate and seasonal
    variation, 9–10
Amazon diseases and health
    problems, 10–11, 11 notes 14 & 16
Amazon and global climate concerns,
    282–283
Amazon River, 12; by Gurupá, 27
Amazon soils, 12
Amazon underdevelopment, 6–8;
    reasons for, 13
Aviamento, 95–99, 96 note 20

Bacá, 28, 63 note 48, 164,
    239 note 17, 263
Bandeirantes, 45 note 25
Bates, H. W., 38, 39, 134
Belo Monte Dam, 261, 292–293
Benzedeiras (blessers), 249–250
Birthday celebrations, 210–212,
    212–213 note 18
Boi Bumba, 205–209, 209 note 17

Cabanagem Revolt, 46–47 note 28,
    47 note 29
Caboclo, 30 note 12, 108–109,
    109 note 1, 137–139, 143–145,
    145 note 29, 215
Camutá, vila of and timber conflict,
    76 note 9, 278–279, 286
Carmelites in Gurupá, 43,
    43 note 22 & 24
Carnaval, 213, 213 note 19
Carrazedo, 234 note 13, 243 note 23;
    as Mission de Saint Joseph of
    Arapijo, 44 note 24, 46 note 27
Casa Borralho, 22, 49–50, 100,
    107–108, 119–120, 122, 125,
    159–161, 163, 165, 173, 180–181,
    262, 267, 291
Casa Familiar Rural, 261,
    261 note 1, 272
Castelnau, Francis de, 47 note 29
Catholic Church, during colonialism,
    35, 38–39, 227–228; and
    Liberation Theology,
    100 note 22, 274–278; anti-racist
    message in Gurupá, 133 note 25;
    and formation of Quilombos
    in Gurupá, 143 note 28; and
    gender empowerment in
    Gurupá, 167 note 15;
    1940s opposition to religious
    brother hoods, 188, 201, 214;
    1970s support for religious
    brotherhoods, 257; priests and
    Saints Anthony and Benedict
    celebrations, 198–199;
    Catholicism as practiced in
    Gurupá, 219–221; lack of a
    priest, 170, 192, 220;

Catholicism and shamanism,
234; and social justice teaching,
274; opposition to Belo Monte
Dam, 292
Children and childhood, 178–183
Cunha, Euclides da, 97
Community studies, rationale
for, 15–16
Condamine, Charles de la,
44 note 24, 45

DDT (dichlorodiphenyltrichloro
ethane), 4, 11 note 16, 58–59,
58 note 38, 91, 207, 253
Debt-peonage/servitude/slavery, 2, 3,
54 note 37, 90, 94, 96–99,
99 note 21, 100–101, 118, 120,
122, 124, 129–130, 151, 177–178,
262–263, 267, 271
Dutch in Brazil, 40–41, in Gurupá,
40 note 19, 41 note 19,
42 note 21

Economic depression (1950s–1960s)
in Gurupá, 261–264
Empates (human barriers), 277–279
Environmental constraints to
development, 13

Family structure, in Brazil, 148–149;
during colonial times, 149; in
Gurupá, 150–152; *compadresco*
(ritual kin), 153–159, 161 note 13;
compadres (co-parents) of the fire,
155–156; godparents, 156–157;
and social class, 159; adoption,
178, 180–184, 184 note 25; and
economic security, 150, 186
FASE (Federation of Social and
Educational Assistance Entities),
143 note 28, 145 note 31,
257– 258, 261, 261 note 1,
271, 278, 283–287, 291; and
international conference

in Gurupá, 284; and land
regularization, 284–285; and
sustainable management
projects, 285–287; and açaí
production, 287–288
Fishing, 9–10, 34,38, 66, 71, 73–76,
74 note 8, 87, 90, 116–117, 121,
123–124, 157, 164, 179; during
prehistory, 32 note 15; and
panema, 78–81, 83–84; as an
insult, 162; conflict with
commercial fishing, 266, 270,
272–273; sustainable fishing,
283, 285; and Belo Monte
Dam, 292
Franciscans of Piety and Gurupá,
44 note 24
Freyre, Gilberto, 39, 133 note 23,
138, 149, 161

Gender roles in Gurupá, 162–167,
167–168 note 15
Gentleman complex/disdain for
manual labor, 114, 115 note 7
"Green hell" metaphor, 8
Gurupá, as a representative
community, 16; setting, 17–25;
house construction 22–23; as
social center 25–26, 25 note 8,
26–27 note 9; prehistory,
32 note 15; education, 61–63,
63 note 47

High population level model for
pre-historic Amazon,
1 note 1
Hunting, 73, 76, 76 note 9; hunting
and supernatural, 77–81

Indigenous influences in culture,
31–32, 38–40
Indigenous slavery, 34, 37; slaving
raids, 35; 35 note 18; and Just
Wars, 35, 45 note 25

Infant mortality rates, 7 note 8
Itá as pseudonym, 16 note 1
Irish and English in Gurupá,
    41 note 20, 42 note 21

Jesuits, 35–36; in Gurupá, 43,
    43 note 24, 45, 51
Jews, in Gurupá, 50–1, 50 note 33,
    51 notes 34–35, 219
Jocojó, *vila* of, 29, 62, 62 note 45, 70,
    72, 100, 124, 141, 196; river of, 27
June festivals (*festas juninos*), 204–205

Labor, problems of retention, 94–95,
    95 note 19, 215; Chayanov's
    concept of drudgery, 215 note 21
Liberation Theology, 274–276; and
    conflict in Gurupá, 276–277;
    and CEBs, 277–278
Lingua geral (*nheengatu*), 39–40
Livramento (priest's boat), sinking
    of, 281
Lula (President Luiz Inácio Lula da
    Silva) and Gurupá, 281–282

Maria Ribeira, St.Apolonia festival,
    189–196
Manioc, foods produced from, 67;
    cultivation of, 67–72
Marajoí, 261; and palm heart
    extraction, 271
Mariocai, 43 note 23
Marriage, 168–177, 172 note 17,
    176–177 note 21
Media in Gurupá, 1940s, 61,
    61 notes 42 & 44, 123, 289
Medicial plants and folk remedies,
    250–253, 253 note 36
Mendes, Chico, 278 note 6, 285
Missions in Gurupá, 43,
    43–44 note 22, 46, 46 note 27
Military dictatorship (1964–1985),
    264; development plans for
    Amazon, 265–266; development

plans impact in Gurupá,
    266–267; and political conflict
    in Gurupá, 274
Modernization Theories, 2–4;
    ahistorism 4; ethnocentrism 3;
    technology transfer, 14 note 19

Nutrition, 7, 7 note 9

Palm heart boom and conflict,
    270–272
Panema, 78–81, 83, 84 note 15
Patrão, power of, 262, 271
Pombal, Marquis de, 36–37
Post-Modernism, 3
Poverty in Amazon, reasons for,
    2–3, 5–6, 8, 12–14, 104–105
Pregnancy and childbirth, 244,
    246–248, 248 note 29
PT (*Partido dos Trabalhadors/
    Workers Party*) in Gurupá, 281

Quintal (backyards), 21
Quinzena, 28

Racial democracy, concept of, 132
Race, as defined in anthropology,
    134 note 25; as classification
    system in Gurupá, 134–138,
    143 note 28; and beauty and
    marriage, 138–139, 139 note 27;
    folk attributes/stereotypes for
    African descent, 139; folk
    attributes/stereotypes for
    Indigenous descent, 143–145
Rainforest guardian model, 3,
    283 note 7
Religious brotherhoods (*irmandades*
    and *folia*), 188–189, 197–198;
    as key to development, 214
Riberinho, 2, 2 note 2, 4, 30,
    30 note 12, 57, 108, 112, 128,
    215, 226, 279, 289

Rubber, boom and bust, 48, 52–54, 53 note 36; in Gurupá, 48, 48–49 note 32, 50–52, 54–56, 54 note 37; World War II and mini-boom, 56–60; production in Gurupá, 84–90, 85 note 16; plantations (Fordlândia), 91–93; "rules of rubber fields"/ debt-peonage, 97–99, 99 note 21; collapse in Gurupá, 100–104

Saint Anthony, patron saint of Gurupá, 197; religious festival of, 198–200, 203–203 note 12
Saint Benedict, people's saint in Gurupá, 197; *folia* and religious festival of, 198–204, 203–204 note 12; tensions with Church over religious festival, 200 note 6; half-moon (meia lua) fluvial procession, 200; dancing and gumbá, 202, 202 note 9 & 10; as economic incentive, 215; background, 221 note 4; miraculous stories told in Gurupá, 221–225, 224 note 7
Saints, images, 221; and *promessas* (promises)/vows, 222; and ex-votos, 223; punishment for breaking vows, 225, 225 note 8; special attributes, 225
SESP, 2, 57–59, 63, 107–109, 207, 244, 249
Settlement patterns-river-bank neighborhoods, 27–28; villas & hamlets, 29
Science and folk belief, 217–218, 254–255
Shaman (*pajé*), 228–234, 234 note 13; as *sacaca*, 229; and Catholicism, 234
Social class in Gurupá, class structure, 108, 112 note 4, 113 note 5; interclass relations, 110–112; social class characteristics, 112–118, 120–121 note 14, 125–128, 125 note 17, 128 note 19; examples of families in different social classes, 118–125; social class mobility, 129–132, 131 note 20; as barrier to development, 146–147
Socio-environmental and political change in Gurupá, 290–293
Smith, Herbert, 38
Standard model of pre-historic populations, 5, 33 note 16
Supernatural, rainforest spirits, Anhangá, 77, 235–236; Curupira, 77, 236–238, 236–237 note 16; giant snake (*cobra grande*), 238, 238–239 note 17; Matinta Perera, 239; *boto* (dolphin), 239–243, 243 note 23

Terra firme, 12, 67
Timber boom (1970s–1990s), 266–268; and land conflict, 268–270
Town Hall, 25
Trading Posts (barracões), in town, 22; in interior, 25; decline of, 262–263

Union, Rural Worker's, 279–281, occupation of union headquarters, 280

Várzea, 9
Vieira, Padre Antonio, 36, 43 note 24

Wallace, Russell Wallace, 8–9, 39–40
Work patterns, communal labor (*convite*), 69